Contract Law in Greece

Contract Law in Greece

Fourth Edition

Michael Stathopoulos
Antonios G. Karampatzos

This book was originally published as a monograph in the International Encyclopaedia of Laws/Contracts.

Founding Editor: Roger Blanpain
General Editor: Frank Hendrickx
Volume Editor: Jacques Herbots

Wolters Kluwer

Published by:
Kluwer Law International B.V.
PO Box 316
2400 AH Alphen aan den Rijn
The Netherlands
Website: www.wolterskluwerlr.com

Sold and distributed in North, Central and South America by:
Wolters Kluwer Legal & Regulatory U.S.
7201 McKinney Circle
Frederick, MD 21704
United States of America
Email: customer.service@wolterskluwer.com

Sold and distributed in all other countries by:
Quadrant
Rockwood House
Haywards Heath
West Sussex
RH16 3DH
United Kingdom
Email: international-customerservice@wolterskluwer.com

Printed on acid-free paper

ISBN 97890-411-8890-8

e-Book: ISBN 97890-411-8932-5
web-PDF: ISBN 97890-411-8973-8

This title is available on www.kluwerlawonline.com

Printed and Bound by CPI Group (UK) Ltd, Croydon, CR0 4YY.

The Authors

Michael Stathopoulos (born on 4 July 1938 in Athens) is Professor of Civil Law at the Law Faculty of the University of Athens. He studied at the Universities of Athens (1956–1960, where he obtained his Law degree) and Munich (1963–1967, postgraduate studies with a Greek State Scholarship). With his first thesis on 'Die Einziehungsermächtigung' (1967 in German) he obtained his doctorate (Munich); with his second thesis on 'Unjust enrichment' (1972, in Greek), after a second research period in Munich, 1969–1971, as Humboldt-Stiftung Scholar, he was elected as *agrégé* (Athens). In 1975 he was elected Extraordinary Professor in the Law Faculty of the University of Athens (Chair of Civil Law) with a three-year mandate, at the end of which he was elected professor ordinarius. Since then he has taught Civil Law (mainly Contracts and Torts).

In May 1983 he was elected Rector of the University of Athens and he held this office, after two re-elections, till 31 August 1991. He is Doctor *honoris causa* of the Humboldt University, Berlin (1988), of the Demokritos University of Thrace, Greece (2001), and of the Faculty of Musicology of the University of Athens (2007), a faculty founded by him during his rectorship. He is also a member of the Athens Bar Association and has been member of the Legal Council of the National Bank of Greece, and umpire or member of arbitration tribunals (international and domestic). Since September 2005, he has been Professor Emeritus.

His principal books are the (Greek) Law of Obligations (in two volumes) and, with other authors, a Commentary on Greek Civil Code (ten volumes). His papers and articles concern mainly Civil Law issues but also other subjects (e.g., Community Civil Law, General Theory of Law, method of interpretation of legal acts, economic system and Constitution, review of the constitutionality of laws, relations between church and state, human rights, personal data and protection of the personality, modern techniques in financial transactions, etc., in Greek, English, and German).

He has been a member of the Special Supreme Court of Greece, President of the Civil Law Association, President of the Greek Intellectual Property Organisation, a member of several Legislation Committees (e.g., for the Reform of Greek Family Law, of

Higher Education Legislation, etc.). He has been (1984–1989) a member *ad personam* of the Permanent Committee of the European Rectors' Conference (CRE), a member of the Administrative Board of the International Association of Universities (IAU 1990–1995) and Vice-President of the Mediterranean University (Unimed) in Rome. He is also fellow of the 'Wissenschaftskolleg - Institute for Advanced Study', in Berlin. From April 2000 until October 2001, he was Minister of Justice. In October 2011 he was elected Member of the Academy of Athens.

Dr jur. *Antonios G. Karampatzos* (born on 29 September 1977 in Athens) is Professor at the Law School of the National and Kapodistrian University of Athens. Between 2000 and 2004 he obtained his PhD and LLM at the Law School of the University of Tübingen (Germany), under the supervision of Prof. Dr jur. Dres hc Harm Peter Westermann. His PhD-thesis –which was unanimously accepted with '*summa cum laude'*– concerned contracts with protective effects towards third parties and the liability of financial experts for pure economic loss; its title in German read, namely, as follows: '*Vom Vertrag mit Schutzwirkung für Dritte zur deliktischen berufsbezogenen Vertrauenshaftung – Zugleich ein Beitrag zum Ersatz fahrlässig verursachter reiner Vermögensschäden'* (Nomos Verlag, 2005).
After his stay in Germany, he carried out post-doctoral research (post-doc) in London at the Institute of Advanced Legal Studies of University College London, under the supervision of Prof. Dr Sir Basil Markesinis. His post-doc research was presented in his paper under the title '*Supervening Hardship as Subdivision of the General Frustration Rule: A Comparative Analysis with Reference to Anglo-American, German, French and Greek Law'* (*European Review of Private Law 2-2005*, pp. 105–147). In November 2008 he was also certified as an Accredited Mediator of the Chartered Institute of Arbitrators.
Dr jur. Karampatzos has written six books and published a plethora of scientific articles and papers in Greek, German and English, mainly on Private Law issues and more recently on Behavioral Law & Economics. In addition, he has organized and participated in numerous international legal conferences. Last but not least, he has actively participated in the preparation of statutes and regulations, amongst others representing Greece before EU authorities or committees.

Dr jur. Karampatzos is also member of the Athens Bar Association. His professional interests are mainly focused on international arbitration as well as on drafting legal opinions on private law issues.

The Authors

Table of Contents

List of Abbreviations

Abbreviations of Periodicals

AID	*Archeion Idiotikou Dikaiou* (Archive for Private Law)
ArcN	*Archeio Nomologias* (Archive of Court Rulings)
Arm	*Armenopoulos*
ChrID	*Chronika Idiotikou Dikaiou* (Annuals of Private Law)
D	*Dike*
DEE	*Dikaio Epichirisseon kai Eterion* (Law of Enterprises and Companies)
DEN	*Deltio Ergatikis Nomothessias* (Law of Labour Legislation)
Dni	*Dikaiossini* (Justice)
EDPol	*Epitheorisi Dikaiou Polykatoikias*
	Epitheorissi Emborikou Dikaiou (Review of Commercial Law)
EErgD	*Epitheorissi Ergatikou Dikaiou*
EEN	*Efimeris Ellinon Nomikon* (Greek Lawyers' Journal)
EErgD	*Epitheorissi Ergatikou Dikaiou* (Review of Labour Law)
EfAD	*Efarmoges Astikou Dikaiou kai Astikou Dikonomikou Dikaiou* (Theory and Practice of Civil Law and Civil Procedure Law)
	Episkopissi Emborikou Dikaiou (Survey of Commercial Law)
HellD	*Elliniki Dikaiossini* (Greek Justice)
KritE	*Kritiki Epitheorissi Nomikis Theorias kai Praxis* (Critical Review of Theory of Law and Practice)
NDik	*Neon Dikaion* (New Law)
NoB	*Nomiko Vima* (Law Tribune)
NJW	*Neue Juristische Wochenschrift* (German Law Review)
PirN	*Piraiki Nomologia* (Piraeus Case Law)
Them	*Themis*

Other Abbreviations

List of Abbreviations

AP	*Areios Pagos* (Civil Law Supreme Court)
BGB	German Civil Code
C	Constitution
CC	Civil Code
CCPr	Code of Civil Procedure
D	*Digesta*
EmbN	*Emborikos Nomos* (Commercial Law)
EU	European Union
MinD	Ministerial Decision
PrD	Presidential Decree
StE	*Symvoulio Epikratias* (Supreme Administrative Court)

Preface to the Fourth Edition

In the present fourth, widely revised and updated edition the main court decisions and literature from 2014 up till present date have been taken into account. There has also been a considerable enrichment of the content by encompassing some additional doctrines or modern trends of contract law that were not dealt with in the previous editions (e.g., in the field of the interpretation, re-adjustment or termination of contracts, and so forth).

Athens, November 2016
Michael Stathopoulos & Antonios G. Karampatzos

Preface to the Third Edition

In the present third, significantly revised and updated edition – a work basically done by Antonios Karampatzos–, the main court decisions and literature from 2008 to the fall of 2013, as well as the legislative amendments of this period to the subjects related to Greek Contract Law have been taken into account. More recent court decisions without reference to their publication in legal journals may easily be found on the Internet in electronic form. The authors owe many thanks to Ms Christina Katsogiannou, LLM Athens Law School, for her kind assistance during the editing of the present edition.

Athens, November 2013
Michael Stathopoulos & Antonios G. Karampatzos

Preface to the Second Edition

In the present second edition, the main court decisions and literature from 1993 to the spring of 2008, as well as the legislative amendments of this period to the subjects dealt with in this monograph have been taken into account. More recent court decisions without reference to their publication in legal journals may easily be found on the Internet in electronic form.

Athens, July 2008
Michael Stathopoulos

Preface to the First Edition

The exposition of the Greek Law of Contracts in the present monograph is given on the basis of a detailed plan supplied by the editors of this series. For reasons of uniformity with other monographs dealing with the same subject in the legal systems of other countries, this plan has been followed as faithfully as possible, including the reference to the historical and geographical general background.

Mr Geoffrey Cox has taken much trouble over the correctness of the English of the present publication. I would like to thank him for his valuable help. Obviously, the responsibility for the legal terminology in English remains that of the author.

This book was written to a great extent at the University of Münster, during the summer months of 1993. To this University and especially to its 'Altrektor', my colleague Prof. Dr W. Schlüter I also owe many thanks for the excellent working conditions I found there, which greatly facilitated the writing of this book.

Athens, November 1993
Michael Stathopoulos

General Introduction

§1. The General Background of the Country

1. Greece, lying at the south-eastern extremity of Europe, is the southernmost country of the Balkan Peninsula and has at the present time some 11,000,000 inhabitants (latest census of 2011: 10,815,197). It has an area of 131,957 km^2.

The modern Greek state was founded after the Greek Revolution of 1821. Before this Revolution, the Greek people had lived under Ottoman occupation for almost four centuries. Today, after other wars of liberation (the most important being the Balkan Wars of 1912–1913), Greece is divided geographically into: the Peloponnese, Central Greece, Thessaly, Epirus, Macedonia, Thrace, the Islands of the Ionian and Aegean Seas – of which Crete is the largest. (A part of the larger geographical districts of Epirus, of Macedonia and of Thrace belongs to the adjacent states of Albania, Former Yugoslavian Republic of Macedonia, Bulgaria and Turkey). Within its present borders (finalized by international treaties), Greece displays great ethnic (Greek) and religious (Christian Orthodox) homogeneity in its population. Outside Greece, there is a very numerous Greek diaspora throughout the world (with either long-established roots or twentieth-century migrants). The large Greek population of Asia Minor – those who had survived the wars – was moved to Greece after 1922.

2. Culturally, Greece experienced (as it had especially in the last period of the Byzantine state before the Fall of Constantinople to the Turks in 1453, but most of all after independence in the modern period) a meeting – sometimes also a confrontation – of two worlds present in the country: on the one hand, its ancient Greek tradition and in connection with it, modern Western values and the need for rationalism and modernization; and on the other, Eastern Romanticism, religious traditions, and devotion to Byzantium. Modern Greece, though not without difficulty, came to understand that the values of both the former and the latter cultural heritage are reconcilable. On the edge of Europe, but with its European characteristics pronounced, Greece today belongs to the European Union (EU).

3. From 1833 to 1923 and again from 1935 to 1974 Greece was a kingdom. Between 1923 and 1935 and since the referendum of 8 December 1974 (held after the fall of the 1967–1974 dictatorship) it has been and is now a republic. The state is, and always has been since independence, centralized, that is, not federal.

According to the Constitution currently in force (of 1975, amended in 1986, 2001 and 2008), Greece is a 'presidential parliamentary democracy'. The Constitution safeguards the value of man, individual freedoms and rights (the free development of the personality, personal liberty, the right to information, the right of protection of personal data, freedom of conscience, the inviolability of the home, freedom of assembly and association, freedom of expression, particularly that of the Press, individual property, the right to judicial protection before the courts in accordance with the law, etc.), as well as equality before the law, employment, trade union freedom and other social rights. Legislative power is exercised by Parliament and the President of the Republic, executive power by the President of the Republic and the Government, and judicial power by the courts. Members of Parliament are elected by direct, universal, secret ballot by the people every four (at the most) years. The Government must enjoy the confidence of Parliament. The President of the Republic is elected by Parliament by a special majority and procedure. In the case of the judiciary, the Constitution provides for their functional and personal independence. The major political parties, which over the last thirty years have alternated in power, are the conservative-liberal New Democracy Party and the centre-socialdemocrat Panhellenic Socialist Movement (PASOK). After the last elections (2012) and the formation of a coalition government consisted of three parties (New Democracy, PASOK and the smaller Democratic Left – the latter coalition partner has recently resigned from the above formation), the parties also represented in Parliament are the Coalition of the Radical Left (as major opposition), Independent Greeks, Golden Dawn and the Communist Party of Greece.

The economic system is based on the market economy with certain state interventions (of differing extent at different times). Ownership, freedom of contract and the right of inheritance are basically respected. The Greek economy is increasingly orientated towards the European Common Market.

The official, spoken language is Greek. A knowledge of foreign languages is, however, a widespread phenomenon among the Greek people.

§2. The Place of the Greek Legal System in the Legal Families

4. The sources of Greek civil law down to the time of the Revolution were, on the one hand, Roman-Byzantine Law, that is Roman law, as that had developed in Byzantium (the last easily consulted summary was the *'Hexavivlos'* of Constantine Armenopoulos of the fourteenth century) and, on the other, the customary law which had taken shape in various places, while in the case of certain legal relations (e.g., in transactions in real property), Turkish law was applied. In addition, from the beginning of the nineteenth century, French law was prevalent to some extent in commercial relations, particularly on the islands, where shipping was a flourishing commercial activity.

Judicial power in the Greek communities during the years of Turkish occupation was not always exercised by the Turkish *kadi.* The Ottoman administration had, for reasons which do not concern us here, ceded certain privileges to the Greek communities, among them the administration of justice, the organs of which were, on the one hand, the functionaries of the Greek Orthodox Church (particularly in questions of family law and the law of succession) and, on the other, the 'elders' of the communities, who exercised this power to a large extent as arbitrators. Greek litigants, anyway, tended to avoid recourse to the *kadi*, both for reasons of national consciousness and to escape the customary bribery on which his decisions not infrequently depended.[1]

5. With Liberation, it was the more Greek of these sources of civil law which naturally came to the forefront: that is, Byzantine-Roman law and customary law. The former represented the 'learned' and the latter the 'popular' folk tradition. However, the French Commercial Code was translated into Greek and was in force. As to civil law, the legislative act which finally resolved the issue was the decree of 23 February 1835, which stipulated, until such time as a Civil Code (CC) should be drawn up, the parallel force of the laws of the Byzantine emperors, as contained in the *Hexavivlos* of Armenopoulos and of customs (moreover, with a provision that these should take precedence where they had prevailed). The Greek experts in Roman law, professors at the Law School of the University of Athens, which had been set up in the meantime, maintained, by way of interpretation, that the above decree referred one through the *Hexavivlos* of Armenopoulos and the *Basilika* (the *Hexavivlos* was based, at least indirectly, on the *Basilika*, which were to a large extent a translation with commentary into Greek of the legislation of Justinian) to its original sources, that is, the *Corpus Juris Civilis*. Thus modern Greek law was relinked not only with the law of the period of the Fall of Constantinople, but also with the legislation of Justinian, with the very sources of Roman law and those principles which were regarded as the *raison ecrite* of civilized nations and whose contemporary expression was the law of the *Pandects* then in force in Germany.

In this way began the linking of Greek civil law with the teaching of the German Pandectists of the nineteenth century. Since then, Greek law theory and practice has developed under the strong influence of pandectist legal science. Special civil laws which were issued were, however, influenced by France, whilst in the law of succession and, even more so, in family law, the influence of Byzantine laws and Greek customs was dominant. The generation of legislation of a local nature in the area of private law was abundant in the second and third decades of the twentieth century. Many of these laws were of a social character or concerned with employees' rights (law on motor vehicle liability, on accidents at work, on compensation by reason of termination of a labour contract, etc.). At the same time, preparatory work on the drafting of the CC was going ahead. This Code was finally drawn up in the 1930s and came into force on 23 February 1946.

6. In the part of the CC which deals with pecuniary relations, the model was primarily the German Civil Code (BGB), though the national (chiefly Byzantine) legal tradition was not ignored. The critique of the provisions of the BGB was also taken into account to some extent. A typical example of the national legal tradition in this part of civil law is the introduction on a wide scale of general clauses into the CC which are based on the principle of equity. Such general rules had long been a feature of Greek customs. Thus in the CC explicit provision is made for the civil protection of the personality (Article 57 CC), the prohibition of the abuse of a right (Article 281

1. *See* P. Zepos & M. Tourtoglou, in: Handbuch der Quellen und Literatur der neueren europäischen Privatrechtsgeschichte, Vol. III Griechenland, ed. H. Coing, Max Planck Inst., 1988, pp. 473 et seq., 477.

CC), the possibility of dissolution or adjustment of a contract by reason of an unforeseen change in circumstances (Article 388 CC), etc., provisions which are not encountered in the BGB and which have been recognized in Germany subsequently only through court rulings. The CC was also influenced by the Swiss Code of Obligations and (to a somewhat lesser extent) by the French Civil Code. In the part devoted to family law the decisive role was played by Greek traditions and the attitude of the established (Orthodox) church. It is worth noting that in other branches of law (in commercial law, as we have already pointed out, and in public law) the French influence was stronger. In 1983, a major reform of the family law of the CC took place and, *inter alia*, equal rights for the two sexes (in place of the dominant role of the man in the family which had been the rule up to then) and civil as an alternative to religious marriage (which up to then had been the only type of marriage recognized for Orthodox Christian Greeks) were introduced. By way of conclusion, we can say that the *Greek law of contracts*, in particular, belongs to the Romano-Germanic family of law. Today, however, it is also additionally determined by EU law (particularly by Community Directives on consumer protection).

§3. Primacy of Legislation and the Position of the Judiciary

7. The sources of Greek law are *legislation*, that is, the statutes enacted by the State, and *customs*. The latter are today of extremely limited extent. De facto there is a superiority of state law (a quantitative, but also a qualitative superiority, because of its clarity and certainty in comparison with customs). As a third source of law, recognition is accorded to 'the generally accepted rules of international law' (Article 28, §I of the Constitution) and, of course, to those rules of *EU* law which have force in Member States. Generally recognized rules of international law are basically the rules of international customary law (sometimes derived from conventions which have not been ratified, etc.). By way of contrast, international treaties do not constitute a separate source, since these have force in the interior of the country by virtue of their ratification by a law (*see also* paragraph 8 *infra*).

Nor do judicial rulings, that is, the decisions of the courts, qualify as a source of law. The judge is subject to the law (which stems from the above sources). He does not make law. The Constitution distinguishes between the three functions/powers of the state (the legislative, the executive and the judicial, Article 26 of the Constitution), of which only the first, in which the people's representatives take part, legislates. The third is obliged to observe what it decrees (*see also* Article 87 of the Constitution). This does not mean that the task of the judges is not creative. The interpretation of what are often unclear provisions and the concretization of their general, abstract and impersonal stipulations so that they can be applied to the case being heard can be said to 'create' law for the purposes of the specific case under judicial review. Such a decision is binding, however, only as to the specific case (on which judgment is given). The binding nature of this decision ('res judicata') does not mean that the decision gives rise to a rule for the future. The judicial precedent perhaps influences, but it does not bind, precisely because it is not a rule of law. Thus, for example, the next judge who has to give a decision in a similar case is not bound to follow it, even though it may have come from a superior or the Supreme Court. (There is a basic difference here from English law, where case law to a certain degree serves as an actual source of law). What is binding upon the subsequent judge is the statute (or custom) which was applied by his predecessor, provided that he judges it applicable to the new case before the court. He may, however, interpret and render it specific in a different manner, according to his own judicial judgment. If he indeed has a different interpretative view, the subsequent judge not only may, but should follow that and not the view of the earlier decision. The actual influence of court rulings, particularly that of the Supreme Courts, and, even more so, of their consistent practice, is, of course, great. But this influence, which they have, should not be confused with the legal force of a rule of law, which is not a characteristic of a court decision. It is the judge's task to see that the laws are kept. In administering justice, he implements the law, he does not legislate.[2]

8. The administration, that is, the executive power, is also subject to the laws. The *legality of its acts* is subject to the scrutiny of the administrative courts, which can annul them if they are contrary to law. The legislator is subject only to the Constitution. The monitoring of the *constitutionality of laws* (control of their compliance with the Constitution) is carried out by all the courts, but only as to the specific case which is before them. The courts do not deprive the law which they judge to be unconstitutional of its force; they simply do not apply it in the case which they are hearing. There is only one court which can annul a law (with general applicability and beyond the case being heard): the Special Supreme Court (Article 100 of the Constitution). However, the Special Supreme Court has this power only in a few instances, more specifically (Article 100, §1, subparagraph (e) and §4, subparagraph 2 of the Constitution), when contradictory decisions as to the constitutionality of a law have been issued by the Supreme Courts of the three jurisdictions which exist in Greece (the Council of State, that is, the Supreme Administrative Court (StE), the Court of Cassation of Areios Pagos, and the Court of Audit). These Supreme Courts maintain, in every other respect, each in its own jurisdiction, the unity of interpretation and implementation of law in Greece.

As to the relation of Greek law to international law, the following could be noted: international conventions become domestic law only if they are ratified by law (*see* Article 28 §1, C). In a separate category of the international sources of domestic law (as already mentioned in paragraph 7) are the 'generally recognized rules of international law', in accordance with the provision of Article 28 §1 C. Moreover, this provision does not only render these rules a direct source of domestic law; it lends them (as it has lent international conventions from the moment that they are ratified by law) augmented formal force in relation to the ordinary laws (they 'prevail over any contrary provision of the law'). In the hierarchy, that is, they rank after the Constitution and have precedence over common laws.

As to the relation of the EU law with the Greek Constitution, disputes have arisen. It is argued more generally that EU law takes precedence over all the constitutions of the member-countries of the EU. Thus, in particular, the case law of the Court of Justice of the European Union (CJEU/ECJ), which invokes arguments from the point

2. Only if any constant practice of courts creates a sense of a general binding rule (*opinio juris*) in the citizens is a rule of *customary* law generated. But the reason for the legal force of this rule, and therefore the source of production of law, is not the court decision, but the custom.

of view of international law, such as the nature of EU law as common and uniformly mandatory for all the Member States, etc. From the point of view of domestic law, however, objections are frequently raised. But the question of if in the end the national constitution has precedence cannot be examined within the framework of the present study of the Law of Contract.

By way of conclusion, it may be said that the *primacy of legislation* is a characteristic of the Greek legal system. The judges, whose functional and personal independence is provided for by the Constitution, guarantee the observance of the laws and the protection of the citizen from illegalities.

§4. Distinction Between Public Law and Private Law Administrative Contracts

9. In the Greek legal system a distinction is made between private and public law. In spite of the interpenetration of these two broad branches of law, which renders the distinction between them relative, the main criterion for this distinction remains the extent to which in a relation in law one of the parties is a public authority (or an agent thereof) *acting in this capacity.* In this case, we speak of public law relations. Apart from this, we are in the realm of private law.

In the present monograph we shall be dealing with private law contracts. Nowadays in Greece, the expression 'administrative contracts' is used. It is argued that these are in principle subject to special rules and not those of the CC. One thing, however, is certain: that they fall within the jurisdiction of the administrative courts and not of the ordinary courts, as is the case with ordinary (private law) contracts. As to the criteria by which a contract is described as 'administrative', it would seem that, although this has been contested, the view has prevailed, at least in the court rulings,[3] that three criteria must be fulfilled:

- that the contract is concluded by the State or a public law legal person;
- that the contract should be governed by exorbitant clauses and privileges in favour of the public agency, such as to suggest the exercise of public authority; and
- that the satisfaction of some public objective is being pursued.

10. This distinction between contracts sounds somewhat conceptualist and formal to the extent that it is not linked with any production of practical consequences in law from the inclusion of a contract in one or the other category. The chief, and perhaps the only, practical consequence is whether a contract falls within the jurisdiction of either the civil or the administrative courts. It should be noted here that the creation of a double judiciary for contracts by the Greek legislator gives rise to more problems than it solves and is, more generally, of dubious desirability. It is, however, a fact from the point of view of positive law. In every other respect, it must be pointed out, in reference to the above criteria (*see* paragraph 9), that the State or public law legal persons may conclude private law contracts, while private citizens as parties to a

3. See, *inter alia*, the Decisions of Council of State (StE) 3486/1996, 3106/2002, 3774/2003, 3193/2006. *See also* the Decision 4071/1991 of the Athens Administrative Court of Appeal.

contract may pursue more general public aims and satisfy public needs, in which case the contracts are interpreted accordingly. The criterion of the general good, and thus of the public interest, may be crucial or even predominant in any ordinary contract. In the CC, recourse to such criteria is not unknown, particularly in the implementation of its general clauses, for example, as to good faith, *boni mores*, public order, the social and economic purpose of a right, etc. Furthermore, as has been accepted by theory and court rulings, the fundamental concepts and general principles stipulated for contracts in the CC are also applied to administrative contracts, insofar, of course, the law does not provide for otherwise.[4] As to the special legal status which certain contracts may have (exorbitant clauses, etc.), we can make the following distinction: in the case of the terms of a contract, these will be governed by the freedom of contract as this is restricted by law for all contracts. In the case of special provisions of law (which provide or permit the provision of privileges or special protection for one of the parties), it will be a matter of interpretation of these special provisions to find in which contracts or as to which contracting parties they are implemented. Public and private law is made by the same legislator, who may determine in each instance whether he will exercise his authority to intervene in a contractual relation. The above does not preclude, of course, a typology of contracts, on the criterion of whether and to what extent general interests restrict private ones. It questions only the possibility of a sharp and absolute distinction between two separate categories of contract, subject to different rules.

§5. Distinction Between Civil Law and Commercial Law

11. Commercial law constitutes a special branch of law in Greece, regulated by special legislation. It governs the relations in law of businessmen and commercial transactions. In commercial legislation there are special regulations on certain contracts, such as on insurance contracts, on carriage by land, sea and air, on negotiable instruments, on commercial companies, etc. But, supplementarily, the general law of contracts of the CC has force also as to these contractual relations to the extent that the special rules of commercial law do not differ from it. In other words, the general law of contracts governs every contract (between businessmen or between non-businessmen or between businessmen and non-businessmen), while there may be special rules which provide for deviations from general law in the case of certain types of contract, which may be either commercial or civil. Thus, the CC itself provides, apart from the general rules of contracts, for special rules for sale, lease, mandate, partnership, loan, deposit, donation, contract for work, contract for services, etc.

The law on bankruptcy (recently revised by Law 3588/2007) contains special rules which apply only to businessmen and to legal persons which pursue a financial aim, given that bankruptcy is not implemented in the case of non-businessmen.

4. *See* Dagtoglou, General Administrative Law, 6th updated ed. (updated by P.-M. Efstratiou & Th. Papageorgiou), 2012, no. 752–756; Spiliotopoulos, Handbook of Administrative Law, 14th ed., 2011, No. 190. *See also* AP 984/1973, 471/1975; Council of State (StE) 74/1992, 566/1992, 4134/1996, 5362/1996, 2708/2001, 1966/2004, 1093/2005, 1749/2009, Nomos Legal Database.

–12

Introduction to the Law of Contract

§1. Definition of Contract: The Contract as a Source of Obligations

I. Contract in General and Promissory (Obligating) Contract

12. The contract in the Greek Civil Code is a very broad concept. It includes any act in which there is a meeting of two wills with an intention to bind oneself, that is, of producing results in law. It is a matter of indifference whether these results will be the generation of obligations and rights for the contracting parties or the transfer or abolition of rights, etc. In this very broad sense, the contract is provided for in the first of the five books of the CC, that which contains the 'General Principles' of civil law (Articles 1–286). The other four books of the CC deal with the law of obligations (Articles 287–946), property law, or, more precisely, the law of real rights (Articles 947–1345), family law (Articles 1346–1709) and the law of succession (Articles 1710–2035). Thus, in Articles 185–196 of the first book, the CC provides, *inter alia*, that a contract is concluded when the two declarations of will of the contracting parties meet, which is usually when there is an offer for the conclusion of the contract and an acceptance of this. Simultaneous or parallel externalization of the two declarations of will is, of course, possible. It suffices that they should 'meet'. It is also possible for a contract to be concluded by more than two contracting parties, in which case we have a meeting of more than two wills.

More narrow than the above is the concept of the contract as a promissory contract. This is a contract which obligates one or both contracting parties to give or do or not to do something. Its constituents are not the production of any other result in law (such as transfer of rights), but the generation of obligation (*see also* paragraphs 19 et seq. *infra*). It is precisely these contracts which are regulated in the second book of the CC concerning obligations (contractual and non-contractual). These constitute the main body of the contracts being concluded in business transactions and form the principal subject of the present monograph. Such contracts are, for example, sale, lease, donation, contract for services, for work, etc. Their consequence in law is that by these contracts the parties promise and bind themselves to perform an obligation or obligations.

II. The Contract as a Declaration of Will

13. The CC stipulates many basic rules for contracts (both in their broader and narrower meaning – *see* section I *supra*) with reference to a further more general concept, on the model of the BGB: the concept of the *juridical act*[5] (or *legal transaction*, according to another English expression often used for the same concept). This is regulated in its first book (Articles 127 et seq.) and is a declaration of will which produces (willed) results in law (*see* paragraph 14 *infra*). It may be a contract (in the broad sense) or a unilateral act. A unilateral act is an exception in the CC (examples: testament, termination notice, rescission, power of attorney, the announcement of a reward). Contracts remain the rule. According to Article 361 of the CC, for obligation to be generated by a juridical act, a contract is required (and thus a unilateral juridical act is not sufficient) 'provided that the law does not determine otherwise'. Thus the rules provided in general on juridical acts (e.g., legal capacity, defects of will, etc., which will be dealt with below) in the CC find their chief field of application in contracts.

III. Accommodation Agreements: Natural Obligations

14. It is often difficult to distinguish between promissory contracts and relations in which the intention of the parties to produce consequences in law is absent (e.g., benefits which are accorded simply out of kindness, out of generosity, etc.). These latter relations (of a social nature) are usually termed *accommodation agreements* (cf. the English expression 'gentlemen's agreement'). Theoretically the distinction between the two categories of 'agreement' is made by use of a clear-cut criterion: in the first case the agreement is based on the *juridical* will of the parties, that is, on their intention to bind themselves in legal terms. A shared will or even a joint decision of the parties is still not a contract and does not produce results in law (e.g., creation of obligation) if there is no element of *binding oneself.* Those who conclude a contract, in essence and regardless of the words used, do not say simply 'we want this', but 'let this have force' (*ita jus esto*) – *see also* paragraph 108 *infra.* The consequence of this legal commitment is that it produces precisely an obligation in law of the debtor and a corresponding right of the creditor, and, consequently, a relation in law between them. In the second category of agreements there is no intention of legal commitment, nor, consequently, an obligation (in law) or a corresponding right. Nevertheless, in practical terms this distinction is not always easy to handle. The solution will be supplied in each case by the interpretation of the declarations of will on the basis of the proof furnished (*see* paragraphs 75, 107, 175 et seq. *infra*).

15. An accommodation agreement does not always remain inactive in law: the person who has performed such an 'agreement' either *in the knowledge* that he was

5. For the definition of the juridical act *see* para. 69 *infra.*

not legally bound to perform it or *for reasons of special moral duty or of propriety* cannot seek to recover the benefit performed. The knowledge of the payer or the reasons of special moral duty or propriety create for the recipient a legal cause for retaining the benefit.[6]

The above instances could (where they have the vestiges of legal hypostasis mentioned above) be regarded as *natural obligations*. These are forms of 'obligation' in which the creditor cannot compel the debtor to perform his debt, but if the latter has performed it of his own free will, he is not deemed to have performed it without 'just cause'. This cause was existent and so there was not unjust enrichment on the part of the recipient. Thus the recipient is not obliged to return the debt not owed which he has received. Other examples of natural obligations are a prescribed claim or an obligation arising from a game or wager.[7]

IV. The Contract as a Main Source of Obligations: The Concept of Obligation

16. Contracts take on their major practical importance because they constitute a main source of obligations (another important source of obligations is torts, *see 4 infra* – on other sources, *see* 5 *infra*).

Obligation, which has given its name to the second (and longest) book of the CC and which constitutes, as the *Law of Obligations*, a basic – perhaps the most basic – branch of private law (to which belong the law of contracts, the law of torts, the law of restitution, etc., according to the distinctions made by Anglo-Saxon law), is defined, in a definition shaped by jurisprudence since the era of Roman law, as follows in the first Article (287) of the second book of the CC. 'An obligation is a relationship whereby a person is obliged to perform toward another person. An obligation may also consist in forbearance.'

17. The essence of an obligation is that a person (the 'debtor') binds himself to a performance for the benefit of another person (the 'creditor'), who acquires a corresponding claim. The object of the obligation, and therefore of the right of the creditor and of the liability of the debtor, is the performance. By 'performance' we mean any act in a broad sense, that is, positive action or forbearance (thus the CC Article 287, subparagraph 2, in order to avoid any doubt), owed to the creditor.

More specifically, the positive action may be: (a) giving of an object (definite or provisional, for example, for use only) or doing something, for example, executing services for the benefit of the creditor; (b) according to another distinction, a material act (e.g., the execution of a piece of work) or a juridical act (e.g., the transfer of the ownership of an object) or a declaration which is not juridical (e.g., simple notification). The forbearance may be *toleration* (non-impeding) of a positive action of the creditor (which the debtor could prohibit if he did not have the relevant contractual obligation)

6. This is based on Arts 905 § I and 906 CC, respectively.
7. See, respectively, Arts 272, 844 and 845 CC.

or any other form of *abstention* of the debtor from an act which he could otherwise undertake.[8]

The offer of the performance by the debtor requires the co-operation of the creditor, that is, his acceptance of it. If performance is accepted by the creditor, we have fulfilment of it (for effects of non-acceptance, *see* paragraph 287 *infra*). In English terminology, the fulfilment itself of the 'performance' in the above sense is described also as performance, for example, 'the debtor performs the contract'.

In the case of the concept of a performance, a limitation is, nevertheless, required. The behaviour which is owed by the debtor must be *specific*. The general behaviour as a whole of a person towards another person cannot be the object of a performance, but rather a concrete act or forbearance, defined or definable. The debtor's obligation cannot consist only in displaying any overall or general behaviour which is to govern all his dealings with the creditor (e.g., to be honest, to observe fairness, etc. – these are collateral, accessorial duties), but to effect a performance which is defined or definable and, consequently, *limited* in relation to his activities as a whole.

18. Usually the performance is not exhausted by an item of *behaviour* on the part of the debtor (undertaking of an act or an omission), but also means at the same time the *achievement of the result* at which this act or omission aims by virtue of its meaning. This result will be basically the acquisition of some good by the creditor; for example, the performance is fulfilled if the purchaser becomes the owner of the object sold, if the lessee acquires the use of the object leased, if the work which the contractor has undertaken is completed and delivered to the master of the work, etc. In these instances, what is of interest finally is only the result. It is by this that the question of whether the performance has been fulfilled will be judged. How we arrive at it is a matter of indifference. However, in other instances the debtor is obliged to behave in a certain manner, regardless of the result of this behaviour for the creditor and, more generally, of the achievement of any aim. For example, in a labour contract an employee owes only his services as agreed upon and not their result. This explains, for example, why he is entitled to receive his pay regardless of whether the result has been successful or profitable for the employer.

Whether a performance means behaviour only or a result (cf. the distinction made in French theory between *'obligation de moyens'* and *'obligation de résultat'*)[9] will be decided basically by the *nature of the contract* (e.g., sale, labour agreement – see the examples which have been quoted), which also serves as evidence or an indication of what it was that the contracting parties wanted. Finally, however, it is possible for the conclusion to be derived from the *specific will* of the contracting parties, provided that this does not conflict with law, that they intended the performance in a way different from what is usual in the kind of contract which they have. Anyway,

8. Performances of an unusual nature which Greek court rulings have accepted as an object of an obligation: cession of the use of a permit for a bakery (Thessaloniki Court of Appeal 481/1948, EEN 1949, 202), undertaking of revocation of an insult (Patra Court of Appeal 89/1958, NoB 1959, 94), provision of an opportunity for gainful employment (Thessaloniki Court of First Instance 76/1965, Arm 1966, 69), etc.

9. The distinction was introduced into French theory by *Demogue*, Traité des Obligations en général, Vol. V, No. 1237, Vol. VI, No. 599. *See also* on this issue: Wieacker, 'Leistungshandlung und Leistungserfolg', in Festschrift Nipperdey, 1965, I, pp. 783 et seq.

the distinction should not be made schematic. The same event can be regarded either as a result (when we correlate it with previous behaviour which leads to this) or as just behaviour (which may lead to a result beyond itself). Thus the obligation of a surgeon who undertakes to carry out an operation includes the performance of the operation in accordance with the rules of science and of his profession (as a result of whatever preparatory work on his part, a matter which does not concern the patient/creditor), but not, however, the result, positive or negative, of the operation for the health of the patient. The same applies to the obligation of the lawyer who has undertaken to give his opinion in writing (the result of his work in this connection) but not, for example, to achieve a favourable outcome of the litigation for which the creditor requires his expert opinion. The problem whether certain behaviour or a certain result, and which, direct or indirect, etc., is a part of the performance does not finally depend on their classification as behaviour or result, but on the nature of the contract and the specific will of the parties.

V. Distinction Between Rights In Personam and Rights In Rem

19. The obligation creates a personal bond between debtor and creditor. This means that third parties cannot acquire rights or duties from the relationship of obligation. As can be clearly seen from Article 287 of the CC, the creditor has a personal right to require the performance only from the debtor and the latter owes this only to the creditor. The latter could also have a secondary claim to compensation which is generated by the contractual relation if the performance initially owed is not fulfilled or not properly fulfilled. Consequently, the effect of the contractual relation is *relative*, that is, it is developed only between the parties (*inter partes*). With respect to third parties, the obligation is a *'res inter **alios** acta'*. The *relativity* of the obligational relationship is in contrast with the *absolute effect* ('as to all' *erga omnes*) of other rights, such as real rights (Article 973 CC), the right to personality (Article 57 CC), the right of inheritance (Articles 1710, 1871 CC), etc., which everybody is bound to respect.

The movement and enjoyment of goods is served basically by *personal* (*obligational*) *rights* (*rights* in personam) (chiefly the movement of goods) and *real rights* (*rights* in rem) (chiefly the enjoyment of goods). A real right gives *direct* power over the object (Article 973 of the CC). The object is directly subject to the sovereign will of the holder of the right. The directness is also ensured by the absolute effect of the real right, which permits the holder to impose on any third party respect for this power which he holds. As an absolute right, the real right can be, in principle, opposed to everybody. Its holder has the *'power of pursuit'* of the object in whoever's hands that thing is. The holder of a real right also has a *priority*, that is, he is preferred if there is a conflict (e.g., with creditors) concerning the object of his right. On the other hand, in the case of an obligational right, and when the object of the performance is a thing, there is no direct power of the creditor over it, but only power which is directed to the will of the debtor. By the possibility of compulsion of the latter to effect the performance only an indirect power of the creditor over the object is created. There is no direct power on his part either over the person of the debtor, who is a subject and not an object of rights and obligations, or over his performance or, as has already been pointed out, over the object of the performance (the thing). The creditor has no power over the performance by his own will and decision alone. For this, it is necessary for him to activate the will of the debtor. Nor does he have the right to be preferred or to pursue the thing when it is in the hands of third parties.

In accordance with the above, obligating (promissory) contracts which have a thing as their object do not invest the party/creditor with direct power over the contractual thing. This means that we must sub-divide those transactions whose ultimate aim is the definitive transfer of a good to the direct power of another person into two acts. Thus, for example, by the conclusion of an obligating contract for sale only an obligation on the vendor to transfer ownership of the object and to deliver it to the purchaser is generated (Article 513 CC). For the transfer to occur, another act, the real (in rem) juridical act (Article 1033 or 1034 CC) is required. Before this act, the purchaser has only a personal right as against the vendor, not direct power (real right, that is, here, ownership) over the thing. This distinction has been described as 'the backbone of the whole of private law'. Obligation creates liabilities, it does not transfer rights. Thus, 'I sell' means in the literal legal sense only 'I undertake the obligation to transfer the ownership of the object sold'. A new juridical act is subsequently needed – a real contract, if the right to be transferred is a real right – which fulfils the contractual obligation undertaken and brings about the transfer. The first juridical act (promissory) prepares for the second (juridical act of disposition, which, in the case of sale, is an act of transfer) and constitutes its subjacent (underlying) cause. This, however, does not preclude their simultaneous occurrence, as is frequently the case in practice.

This system is derived from Roman law and is followed today by the BGB and those laws which are related to this.

20. It will be seen from the above that the division of contracts into *promissory* and *of disposition* is crucial for transactions. By the former, only an obligation, that is, a liability on the part of one or both of the contracting parties and a corresponding claim on the part of the other party (e.g., sales, loans, leases, etc.), is generated; this is the only juridical consequence. By the latter (disposition contracts), the disposal of a right which one of the parties already has, that is, transfer of, a charge upon, abolition or alteration of this right (e.g., contract for the transfer of the ownership over a thing or of a claim, for the release of a debt, etc. – see, for example, paragraphs 48 et seq., 208 et seq., 236 *infra*), comes about as their (direct) juridical consequence. If disposition contracts have as their object a right in rem, they are called *contracts* in rem (real contracts). Contracts in rem in general are those pertaining to rights in rem and are to be distinguished from contracts pertaining to obligations (*obligational contracts or contracts* in personam), whether the latter create an obligation, as is the case with promissory contracts, or they effect a disposal of a right in personam (*see also* paragraph 22 *infra*).

21. By way of contrast, in France and in England, the generation of a contractual obligation for the delivery of a specific thing, with the purpose of the transfer of ownership, also has as a consequence the effecting of the transfer (cf. *'vendre* c' *est aliéner'*).

The first of the two systems quoted is known as a *system of delivery* (in which delivery – *traditio*, that is, the real act – is also required for the transfer of ownership), while the second is called a *system of consent* (in which for the transfer the agreement of the two parties is sufficient). The latter is certainly closer to the general understanding, that the purchaser has already 'acquired' the object. The first system, on the other hand, in principle, better fulfils the need for publicity of real rights. It should, however, be stressed that the legislator can in the case of both systems arrange the practical consequences (e.g., the transfer of risk) in similar way to a large degree, in spite of having different starting-points.

22. Real rights (rights in rem) are limited in number (Article 973 CC: 'Rights securing over a thing a direct power that can be invoked as against all persons (real rights) are: ownership, easements, pledge, and mortgage.'). That is to say, a *numerus clausus* applies to these. The easements (servitudes) can have varying content. By way of contrast, private will can, in principle, create contractual rights in an unlimited number, freely defining their content. In their case, freedom of contract has force (*see* Article 361 of the CC, according to which for an obligation to be created by a juridical act, a contract is needed – and, therefore, suffices).

As has already been explained, the real contract (real transaction) does not belong among promissory contracts, since its consequence is the constitution or conveyance (transfer), or charge upon or abolition of a real right, and not the constitution of an obligation. The real contract usually follows the promissory contract, and for this reason, although it does not fall within the main subject of the present monograph, more will be said of this below (paragraph 7). Nor is the contract by which a contractual right (right in personam) is *transferred*, a promissory one. Here, the contractual right has already been created by a promissory (obligational) contract and now, by the new (disposition) contract, it is being transferred (*see* paragraphs 209 et seq. *infra*).

§2. Historical Background of the Law of Contract

23. Research into ancient Greek law[10] has shown that liability from a contract was not recognized as a separate responsibility, as something different from delictual liability. In spite of the well-known passage from Aristotle's *Nicomachean Ethics* which distinguishes between 'voluntary and involuntary covenants'[11] and to which modern jurists refer when they distinguish between contracts and torts, it would seem that the law in force in ancient Greece made no such distinction. A promise alone did not give rise to an obligation of performance on the part of the promissor, and, therefore, to any possibility of enforcement to bring about fulfilment on the part of the promisee. Only if the latter suffered loss of property, as in torts, could he be granted the assistance of the courts in the *'dike blabes'* (litigation of injury). The concept of injury is here

10. See, *inter alia,* H.J. Wolff, 'Die Grundlagen des griechischen Vertragsrechts', in *Zur griechischen Rechtsgeschichte,* 1968, p. 483 et seq. and *Die dike blabes in Demosthenes,* p. 100 et seq.; *Velissaropoulou-Karakosta*, Grounds of Responsibility: Generation and Disputation of the Sources of Obligational Engagement (in Greek), Athens 1993, Ch. 3.

11. Aristotle, *Nicomachean Ethics*, 1131a, 2 et seq.:'for of private dealings, some are voluntary, the others involuntary'. Among the former he classifies sale, loan, guarantee, loan for use, deposit and lease; among the latter, theft, adultery, manslaughter, perjury, bodily harm, kidnapping, etc.

the condition for the generation of contractual liability, the key to the law of obligations. Typical of the need for there to be material loss to the creditor is the fact that where responsibility from a contract was recognized, the contract had the character of a contract of *delivery* (*see* paragraph 30 *infra; see also* paragraph 21 *supra*) and not of a consensual one. It presupposed a movement of property from the creditor (the injured party) to the debtor, who undertook the obligation to bring to fruition the purpose of the contract.

It seems that the Greeks, who tended towards general clauses (in contrast with the Romans with their casuistic spirit), had shaped the *dike blabes* (at least in Attic law) into a general rule. If failure to fulfil a performance caused injury, it was precisely for that reason that liability was generated.

24. The Romans, on the other hand, although casuists (or perhaps because of this) gradually developed a separate law of contracts. Initially there was a formal requirement for the conclusion of a contract and, moreover, for certain types of contract only. From types of contracts, development led to categories of contracts. Gaius clearly describes the four-fold division of contracts into contracts concluded by delivery of a thing (*re*), or orally (*verbis*) or in writing (*litteris*) or by consent alone *(solo consensu*).[12] From the categories of contract further development then led to a unified concept of contracts, the essential element being *consensus* in the case of all contracts. This process was assisted by the evolution of *pacta* from *pacta de non petendo* (which did not give rise to a cause of action – *ex pacto actio non nascitur*[13]) to *pacta vestita* (invested with special protection). This development was not completed in Roman law, which always retained *pacta nuda* (*'bare'*, that is, of binding character).

25. The Romans recognized the supreme importance of *consensus* (not only in contracts concluded *solo consensu*), but persisted in casuistry. The Greeks accepted a general rule, which, however, was not based on *consensus*. The combination of the two had to wait until modern times, but the beginnings of this can be seen as early as the Middle Ages. Christian principles (and, indeed, theocratic foundations for the binding nature of contracts) contributed to this. *Novella* 72 of Leo the Wise[14] recognized *pacta nuda* as giving rise to a right of action where the agreement had been concluded in writing and the parties to it 'had inserted by their own hand the holy cross in its text'. The binding nature of contracts was followed in the fourteenth century by the *Hexavivlos* of Armenopoulos, which, as we have seen, was introduced in 1835 as, in essence, the first civil law of the modern Greek state. It was a solution to which a combination of Greek, Roman and Christian ideas led. There were similar influences in the West. The glossators regarded as a sin the neglect of an obligation.

However, the establishment of the general rule of the binding nature of contracts was chiefly the work of the school of *natural law* (seventeenth and eighteenth centuries). Its disciples achieved the full acceptance of the axiom *'pacta sunt servanda'* as a moral imperative (here the ground had been prepared by the teachings on ethics of preceding

12. See, *Inst.*, III, 13,2: *harum aeque quattuor species sunt: aut enim re contrahuntur, aut verbis, aut litteris, aut consensu.*
13. *Paulus, Sententiae, 2.14.1: ex nudo pacto inter cives Romanos actio non nascitur.*
14. See, *inter alia*, Troianos, Die kirchenrechtlichen Novellen Leons VI und ihre Quellen in *Studies in Honour of Nicofaas van der Waf,* p. 233 et seq., Noailles-Dain, *Les Novelles de Leon VI le Sage,* p. 259.

centuries, which were based on Aristotelian metaphysics) and also an imperative of reason. Moreover, the self-binding property of the contract was seen increasingly as a self-evident consequence of the autonomy of the will, on which from that time forward jurists laid emphasis. The contract was sufficient to generate a binding obligation simply because it was a contract.

All these approaches which prevailed in the West also influenced modern Greek legal thought (in the nineteenth century initially through the impact of the principles of the French Revolution and, subsequently, in more specialized ways, through the teaching of the German Pandectists – *see* General Introduction paragraph 5 *supra*). Thus it was that the Romano-Byzantine tradition and Western influence converged on the same course. A practical consideration also undoubtedly contributed to this: the need of the steadily rising, since before the War of Independence, class of mariners and merchants for security in their transactions. It was this need which also demanded the observance of agreed terms.

26. A confirmation of this tradition and of these influences can be seen in the express recognition (Article 361 CC) of the contract as a source of responsibilities and of the freedom of conclusion of contracts (i.e., in the case of persons capable of juridical acts) without further conditions, such as the existence of a counter-performance (quid pro quo) or reward or cause or consideration, stipulated in other systems of law, other than consent. There are, naturally, restrictions as to the content of a contract (which must conform with the law).

The institution of the contract as a general source of obligations which derives from the consensus inherent in the contract has been established in Greece regardless of ideology. It is respected by liberals as a means of advancing private enterprise, by social democrats or socialists (perhaps with a different field of implementation) as a means of serving social needs and ends, and by everyone (including those who do not profess an ideology) as a means of promoting the circulation of goods. Ideological content is taken on by the extension of the restrictions on the freedom of contract, particularly as to the content of the contract.

§3. Classification of Contracts

27. Depending upon the criterion applied, the distinctions which one can make within the concept of promissory contracts are innumerable. Some of the distinctions will be examined at other points in this monograph (e.g., the division into informal and formal contracts and contracts which are dependent or not on their cause – causal or abstract contracts – in the chapters on the formation of the contract and on the conditions of substantive validity, or the category of accessory contracts in Part II on guarantee contract, etc.). Other principal distinctions of contracts will be examined here.

I. Nominate and Innominate Contracts: Compound (Mixed) Contracts

28. In view of the principle of freedom of contract, the contracting parties may give to the promissory contract whatever content they wish, whether or not this is usual in business transactions, as long as it does not conflict with provisions of *jus cogens*. Certain types of contract, because of the great practical importance which they have long had or because of historical tradition, are the subject of special regulation in the CC (in the second half of the section on the law of obligations, Articles 496 et seq.). These are the so-called *nominate contracts*, as opposed to all other possible contracts, the *'innominate' contracts*, which are not regulated in the CC but which may, however, as we have said, be concluded. Particularly in transactions which are of modern origin, new types of contract have been developed, not regulated in the CC (e.g., leasing, franchising, factoring, etc.). In the case of innominate contracts, if there is no rule in a special law outside the CC, the general rules of the law of contracts are implemented, without, naturally, analogous application, on the terms of analogy, for provisions of a related nominate contract being precluded. Moreover, the parties, again by virtue of the freedom of contract, can combine in a single contract the contents of two or more types of contract, chiefly nominate ones. These constitute what are called *compound contracts* (or mixed contracts).

In the case of each type of contract which is regulated by the CC, the special provisions for this type are implemented, but so are the provisions of general contract law. The former usually prevail, as being special, over the general if they conflict with these. The latter are implemented, as a rule, only in a supplementary manner.

29. The compound contract has two characteristics: first, its content consists of elements of more than one different type of contract. Basically, there will be a combination of performances which do not fall within the same kind of contract. Second, it is a consolidated contract and not an accumulation of more than one independent contract between the same contracting parties. The basic problem with compound contracts is which rules will be applied to them. The Greek courts usually start out from the so-called *theory of absorption* and implement the rules of the contract whose type the principal performance has; this 'absorbs' the secondary elements from other contracts. Where, however, it is decided that the different performances which are exchanged are not in a relation of principal to secondary among themselves but are 'of equal importance and of equal force', the courts have arrived at the solution of a parallel, combined implementation of the rules of the different contracts (*theory of conjunction*).[15]

Another theory which is upheld, the *'theory of analogy'*, which would wish it recognized that the judge is able to implement by analogy the rules appropriate to the contract under review, is not necessarily in conflict with the other solutions. The provisions chosen will be implemented directly or by analogy, depending upon the interpretation of the will of the legislator. Beyond the framework of direct application there is still room for an analogous implementation of the same provision, according

15. *See* AP 185/1956, EEN 1956, 727; 743/1971, NoB 1972, 330; Athens Court of Appeal 2224/1970, Arm 1971, 39; 293/1977, NoB 1977, 555; AP 745/2008, NoB 2009, 63; 1024/2010, NoB 2011, 107, etc.

to the rules of analogy, if the interpretation of the will did not yield a solution. The creative work of the judge certainly finds here broad scope for application (*creative theory*). A reduction of the solutions to schematic form would not be proper. In the last analysis, what is crucial is the aim of the juridical act, the state of interests at the time being and the purpose of the provision of law being implemented (directly or by analogy), with the corrective intervention of the principles of good faith and the taking into account of business usage by way of supplementation. Also by way of supplementation – and often, moreover, this proves totally sufficient – the rules of general law of contract can be implemented.

II. Consensual and Delivery Contracts

30. As a rule, obligating contracts are *consensual*, that is, the consent of the parties is alone sufficient for the generation of the obligation (e.g., sale, lease of a thing, contract for services, etc.). Any delivery of a thing or any creation of a real situation provided for by the contract constitutes the performance which the debtor is obliged to fulfil. Thus, for example, the delivery of the thing will mean the fulfilment of the contractual obligation already generated by the mere consent of the parties. The contract was already (before delivery) concluded. The concluding of contracts and the occurrence of their legal result, that is, the generation of obligations, by the consent of the parties alone (*solo consensu*) is a consequence of the autonomy of the private will and of its power to create obligations without there being any need for other terms to have been fulfilled. In *delivery contracts* (concluded *re*),[16] on the other hand, apart from the consent of the parties, delivery of the thing is also required for the result of the juridical act to occur, that is, for the obligation which these contracts create to be generated: for example, a loan in accordance with Article 806 CC, deposit, or loan for use. A promise of a loan (or loan for use, etc.) as a consensual contract is, naturally, valid by virtue of freedom of contract (Article 361 CC), but it gives rise not to the liability of Article 806, that is, to an obligation on the part of the recipient of the loan, but rather to an obligation of the part of the lender to make it. The characteristic of 'delivery' in delivery contracts has the sense that the contractual obligation of restitution of the borrower or depositary (and not other obligations, particularly those of the lender or depositor to deliver the thing to that person) may not be generated prior to delivery (instalment of the loan, etc.). Before this, the contractual obligation of restitution is at the most subject to a suspensive condition (precisely the condition of delivery), which, however, again means that the obligation of restitution has not yet been generated (Article 201 CC). Apart from this particular characteristic, delivery contracts do not cease to be based in the last analysis on the consent of the parties, which here too constitutes the expression of their autonomy.

---

16. These contracts are usually called 'real contracts' also, but it would be better to avoid the use of this term, so that confusion does not arise with real contracts as distinct from obligational contracts (*see* para. 20). Delivery contracts belong with obligational, and more particularly with promissory contracts.

III. Onerous and Gratuitous Contracts: Aleatory Contracts

31. Onerous contracts are promissory contracts in which one of the contracting parties proceeds to effect a performance in return for something else, which can consist in either the counter-performance provided by the other party by virtue of a reciprocal contract (e.g., sale, lease – *see* section IV *infra*) or in some other consideration given by the latter (and outside the framework of a reciprocal contract, for example, a performance on condition of a remuneration – *see* paragraphs 183 et seq. *infra*, an interest-free loan which must be repaid – *see* paragraph 387 *infra*, etc.). For the element of 'onerousness' to exist, it is a matter of indifference whether the consideration is equivalent. *Gratuitous* contracts are those in which the performance of one of the contracting parties takes place without consideration in his favour. The party proceeds to the gratuitous performance out of *liberality*. This is mainly the case when there is a spirit of *generosity*. The main example of a gratuitous contract is the donation. The *practical importance* of the division of contracts into gratuitous and onerous resides in the fact that the former are subjected to special treatment by the legislator, usually less favourable to the recipient of the gratuitous performance, for obvious reasons: the recipient makes no sacrifice for the item of property which he acquires, so that acquisition on his part appears less justified morally than if he had provided something in exchange. For the rule of law, the gratuitous cause of movements of property is a *causa minor*. Thus gratuitous contracts are usually subject to a form, to greater ease of challenge by the creditors and heirs of the donor, and to heavier taxation; the liability of the donor is, as a rule, limited to damage caused intentionally or by gross negligence, and the recipient in certain instances (Article 913 CC) cannot invoke the donation in order to retain his enrichment from it and is obliged to return it if the donor transferred to him an unjust enrichment, etc.

The so-called *aleatory contracts*, in which the performance provided for depends upon the occurrence of an uncertain, contingent event (e.g., the unknown term of life of creditor, the occurrence of an entirely imponderable event, etc.) are not (necessarily) gratuitous. Such contracts are a life annuity (Articles 840 et seq. CC), an insurance contract, etc. (*see also* Articles 844 et seq. CC). Any disproportion between the performances finally exchanged which is likely to arise from the chance event (e.g., decease of the beneficiary immediately after the conclusion of a life assurance) does not mean that this is an instance of liberality. Anyway, the risks which are undertaken by the parties on the conclusion of the contract are included in the calculation of the value of the performances exchanged.

IV. Reciprocal (or Synallagmatic) and Unilaterally Charging Contracts

32. If the contract creates an obligation on one of the contracting parties alone and a corresponding contractual right in favour of the other, it is a *unilaterally charging contract*. Some speak of a 'unilateral' contract, which is a less precise term, since this contract also has two sides, two parties. If the contract creates contractual obligations on both parties with the corresponding contractual rights in favour of the other, it is a *reciprocal* (*or mutual or synallagmatic*) contract. The term 'bilateral' is also used, although the expression 'bilaterally charging or obliging contract' would be more precise. All gratuitous contracts charge unilaterally. Furthermore, all reciprocal contracts are onerous, but the two distinctions are not coterminous, since there are unilaterally charging contracts which are onerous (e.g., loans, at least as to the obligation of restitution).

In reciprocal contracts, each contracting party is at one and the same time a debtor (as to one of the performances) and a creditor (as to the other). That is to say, two performances are owed in opposite directions. One is provided for as a counterbalance to the other. There is, therefore, a proportionality between the two performances. This will be judged basically by the *subjective* ideas of the parties (cf. freedom of contract). One of them by his performance as an item of exchange wishes to acquire the performance of the other. Objectively, it is not necessary that the two performances should be of equal value. Nevertheless, with the increasing number of restrictions on freedom of contract, the subjectivity of this criterion is giving ground. Limits on the extent of the difference between performance and counter-performance are set, for example, by Article 179 CC and as to the subsequent overturning of their balance by Article 388. Thus today we speak of a *limited subjective* equivalence of the performances (*see* paragraphs 150, 290 et seq. *infra*).

In reciprocal contracts, performance and counter-performance are objects of a *single contract* and are *mutually dependent*. This fact manifests itself both *in the generation* of the obligation (e.g., legal incapacity of one of the contracting parties results in nullity for the whole contract; the same applies to the immorality of one of the performances – the initial impossibility of one of the performances has an effect on the other, Articles 380 et seq. CC, etc.), and *in the operation* of the obligation (an obligation in principle of simultaneous performance, Articles 374 et seq. CC – the defendant may refuse performance if there is refusal or delay of performance on the part of the plaintiff, exercising the *exceptio non adimpleti contractus*; effect on supervening impossibility of the one performance on the other, Articles 380 et seq. CC).

V. Adhesion Contracts (Contrats D' Adhésion)

33. In business today, the standardization of certain contracts, particularly by the use of printed terms formulated in advance, is common. Usually the standardization is imposed by one of the contracting parties when, for the concluding of the contract he is addressing himself to the public, from which the other party is drawn. In these instances, the term *adhesion contracts* is used. Characteristic of these contracts is the determination of their content by one of the parties (the stronger, as a rule, a public enterprise, organization, bank or other, often monopolist, enterprise) and the 'adhesion' of the other to the contract, without there being any possibility of changing the content. For the latter there remains, in essence, only freedom of conclusion (or non-conclusion) of the contract, and this is often in practice non-existent (where it is a case of goods supplying basic needs, for example, electric current, telephone, water, etc., which a person cannot do without and so is forced to conclude a contract with the enterprise which supplies them on a monopoly basis). However, what chiefly disappears as far as he is concerned is the freedom of (joint) determination of the content of the contract. Apart from a certain rare and narrow scope for influencing some of the contractual terms, the greater part of these contracts has force as the stronger of the parties has determined them for its public. These are the so-called *general terms of business* (or 'standard business conditions'). Such terms, determined unilaterally by one of the parties become the content of the contract and have binding force for the other only if the latter accepts them. Acceptance, however, may be tacit and be effected by reference to the contents of the offer.

Examples of contracts standardized in business practice are: insurance contracts, contracts for air, rail or sea carriage, contracts for the supply of electric current or telephone connection, bank credits, etc. Basically, contracts for mass transactions in which one of the contracting parties is always the same (the enterprise), while the other parties (the public, the clients) differ in each instance, belong to this category.

The practical advantages of these contracts are that they achieve a saving of time and labour and thus greater speed in transactions, as well as solutions which are consistent, rationalized, studied and from a professional point of view correctly thought-out. Nevertheless, a very serious disadvantage is the inherent danger in making the weaker party an object of exploitation by the stronger through terms which are exceptionally onerous for the latter. Usually there is provision for exclusion clauses in favour of the latter or increased liability clauses affecting the other party (e.g., a clause to the effect that if the client/purchaser withdraws from the contract, he will be obliged, in spite of this, to pay one-fourth or half of the price). The need for the weaker party to be protected from such terms is obvious.

34. General terms of business are subject to *judicial control.* Until the beginning of the 1990s, the judge had at his disposal the general clauses of the CC on good faith, *boni mores*, just judgment, and abuse of rights (Articles 288, 178, 371, 281), which constitute *imperative law* (*jus cogens*). If a term is found to conflict with these provisions, it will be deemed null and void. Today, the Greek legislator (first by Law 1961/1991 and then by Law 2251/1994, which rescinded the previous law, and was then amended mainly by Law 3587/2007 and more recently by Laws 3844, 3853, 3862/2010 and Ministerial Decision (MinD) (joint) Z1-111/2012), in accordance with the initiatives of the Community legislator in the Directive 93/13/EEC, provided, in Article 2 of Law 2251/1994, for significant restrictions which apply to every term which has been formulated in advance for future contracts, as well as to every term of a contract which has not been an object of individual negotiation (this is mainly the case of general terms of business). Thus, it is stipulated that these terms, *inter alia*:

- are not binding upon the consumer if he, on the conclusion of the contract, was unaware of them without his own fault, as when, particularly, the supplier has not indicated their existence to him or has deprived him of the opportunity of taking genuine cognizance of their content;
- must, if they are drawn up in Greece, be formulated in writing in Greek in a clear, specific, and easily understood manner, and be printed in legible lettering in a conspicuous part of the contract form;

- on their interpretation, the need for the protection of consumers must be taken into account. General terms of business which have been formulated unilaterally by the supplier or by a third party on his behalf must, in cases of doubt, be interpreted in favour of the consumer;
- are prohibited and are void if they result in a significant disturbance of the balance of rights and obligations of the parties to the detriment of the consumer.[17]

An indicative list of thirty-two terms which the law regards as per se abusive (i.e., without any need for a check on the criterion of the general clause on the disturbance of the balance of rights and obligations), and consequently void, is provided in Article 2 of Law 2251/1994.

VI. Contracts 'Intuitu Personae'

35. In all promissory contracts there is a bond between the contracting parties, whose personal character, however, with the development of the law of obligations since the era of Roman law, has become loose. Fulfilment *in propria persona* of the obligations is not necessary, transfer of the claim or debt is possible, etc. When, however, the contract is concluded in consideration of the contracting party's person, that is, it is connected with his person (his personality, his qualities, etc. – for example, a labour contract, a contract for work with a specific artist or expert), we speak of a personal contract (*intuitu personae*). In this case, the assignment of the position of the person with whom the obligation is closely connected is not permitted (Article 465 CC), the performance cannot be undertaken by another (Article 317 CC), and so on.

VII. De Facto Contractual Relations

36. The promissory contract constitutes a source for the generation of obligations. Obligations are also produced by law (e.g., torts, unjust enrichment, etc., *see* §§4 and 5 *supra*). Apart from these sources of obligations, a more modern doctrine, first developed by Haupt in Germany,[18] maintains that obligations are also produced by de facto relations, that is, actual facts or situations, such as socially stereotyped conduct, which according to generally accepted understanding create of themselves, without the need of a corresponding juridical will of the parties, an obligation of performance between the two parties. Such obligations are accepted chiefly in two instances:

---

17. These rules can be regarded as a specification of the general principle of good faith. Criteria stemming from this principle, which the AP aptly uses for a check of the general terms of business, are, *inter alia*, the need for protection of the justified expectations of the consumer and the need for transparency of these terms.
18. Haupt, Über faktische Vertragsverhältnisse, 1941. His theory, which had repercussions in Germany (see, *inter alia*, S. Simitis, Die faktischen Vertragsverhältnisse, 1957; Siebert, Faktische Vertragsverhältnisse, 1958; Lambrecht, Die Lehre vom faktischen Vertragsverhältnis, 1994), also had in Greece.

(a) When a performance is being publicly offered (mainly in mass transactions) and is used in fact by one person. Examples are the use of a bus or other means of public transport, parking of a car in a public car park, which, however, is offered by its owner for parking only for a fee, the use of electric current, water, gas, etc., without or before the conclusion of the relevant contract with the companies or with the electricity, water or gas enterprises. The creation of the obligations to effect performance on both sides (and consequently of the obligation to pay the price for this use) cannot depend, in fact, on whether a corresponding will on the part of the person using the publicly offered performance has been expressed. It is argued that the generative cause of the obligation is not the juridical will of the parties, but the *factum* of the use of the performance offered.

(b) In *continuous* (*standing*) *contracts* (e.g., a labour contract, partnership contract, etc.), where these are concluded invalidly (e.g., by reason of legal incapacity) or have been annulled (retroactively, Article 184 CC) *ex post facto* by reason of a defect of will, etc. In these cases, since the contract has been functioning already for a period of time, developing its results, an actual situation has arisen which it is not thought right to reverse. Thus it has been accepted that the contractual relation and the rights of the parties on both sides retain their force, their source being not the will of the parties, since the contract is invalid or has been retroactively annulled, but the actual situation which has taken shape.

37. This opinion on the de facto situation as a distinct source of obligations, for which in such general terms it would be difficult to find a foundation in law, has in its favour the fact that actual situations and, indeed, the labour relation or company relation, etc., cannot be ignored by a legal system and remain without consequences. Nevertheless, this view has unjustifiably taken on major dimensions, to the point where it has been described as 'an atomic bomb for the destruction of legal thinking faithful to the law' (H. Lehmann, Faktische Vertragsverhältnisse, *NJW* 1958, 1 et seq.). It is true that the problems which gave rise to it could have been dealt with to a large degree without it. Thus, the use of a publicly offered performance can today be regarded as acceptance of an offer for the conclusion of a contract, even though the corresponding psychological will of the person who uses it is lacking. The question of whether a person's line of conduct is an expression of will (here acceptance of a proposal for the conclusion of a contract) is a question of interpretation, which will be decided on the basis of objective criteria also, such as the demands of good faith (Article 200 CC – *see also* paragraph 107 *infra*). The juridical act as an expression of the autonomy of private will has today undergone, in accordance with prevailing social and moral ideas, such objectivization that for the interpretation of a person's conduct, his actual will does not serve as an exclusive guide, but to a large degree the possibility of understanding of third parties is involved. This broadening and objectivization of the juridical act permits us to include within its concept instances such as those stated above (paragraph 36, §a) and, consequently, a contract to be accepted here. Any invocation of a contrary psychological will on the part of the person who takes up the public offer, with a view to nullifying the juridical act (here the contract) on the grounds of error, would conflict, as a rule, with good faith, which is an impediment to annulment on the grounds of error (Article 144 CC – *see* paragraph 124 *infra*). Thus there is no need for the creation of a distinct category of source of obligations for these instances. The result, however, would be basically the same, since both foundations lend force in the creation of obligation to actual facts, which are according to current social ideas crucial. It is simply that these facts are in one case included within the (expanded) concept of the juridical act, while in the other they acquire parallel force outside the juridical act, which remains narrowly subjective. The practical difference, and at the same time the advantage, of grounding the obligation in the juridical act is that, on the basis of this latter foundation, active legal capacity of the parties will be required. Only thus will the legally incapacitated be protected from commitments invited by participation in business life, commitments for which the rule of law does not regard him as sufficiently mature (unless a minor acquires only a legal benefit, disposes of money which has been given to him for his own use, etc., in accordance with the distinctions made in Articles 134 et seq. CC – *see* paragraph 96 *infra*).

In the case of defective continuous contracts (paragraph 36 (b) *supra*), a solution can usually be drawn from the legislation in force, interpreted correctly and in a broad sense. Thus it has been accepted that the protective provisions of labour legislation (e.g., on holidays, accidents at work, compensation by reason of termination, etc.) are to be implemented, according to their *ratio*, also when the labour relation rests upon, for example, a void or voidable contract. Even the claim of the employee to his pay is to be recognized. Modern theory bases this solution mainly on the argument that the annulment of the labour contract, as also the invocation of its nullity *after it has begun to function* must have an effect only for the future (*ex nunc*) and not retrospectively. *De lege lata*, this solution could be grounded by teleological contraction of Articles 180 and 184 of the CC (on void and voidable juridical acts), which were certainly introduced with instant juridical acts or contracts chiefly in mind, without the special problems associated with continuous contracts being taken into account. The result, however, is that in the end the actual state of the labour relation develops force between the parties. Similar solutions (*ex nunc* effects of nullity or voidability) have also been accepted in the case of a defective company (or partnership) which has already operated and concluded relations with third parties.

38. The doctrine on de facto contractual relations has contributed significantly to the final imposition of the practical solutions mentioned above through the law of contracts (limitation of the consequences of nullity or voidability and objectivization of the agreement of the two parties on the basis of the prevailing ideas in business as to their, usually stereotyped, conduct). The creation, however, by this teaching of an independent generative cause of obligations has given rise to reservations in view of the vagueness of the criteria, which do not make apparent the *limits* of the range of its implementation, so that security of law can up to a degree be ensured. Anyway, to the degree that it might be held that the *law in force* accepts the generation of obligation when certain, clear actual circumstances or situations are present, this would be a case of obligations directly founded on the law, parallel to torts, unjust enrichment, *negotiorum gestio*, etc., (*see* next paragraphs).

§4. Contracts and Torts

I. Tortious Liability

39. By way of contrast with the casuistic law of *tortious* (*delictual*) liability as in force in ancient Rome or present-day England – and partially in Germany – there is in Greece, as is the case in France (Article 1382 of the CC) and in Switzerland (Article 41 of the Swiss Code of Obligations), a general clause on *tortious* liability. Article 914 of the Greek Civil Code lays down: '*A person who unlawfully and through his fault has caused prejudice to another shall be liable for compensation.*'

This provision, one of the most fundamental in the Greek Civil Code, stipulates one of the broadest *sources of obligations*, the act that is unlawful and faulty, the so-called *civil delict/tort*, which on the fulfilment of the other preconditions of the provision, that is, prejudice (injury, detriment, damage) and causal relation between said act and the prejudice, creates an obligation to *compensate* on the party responsible. Faulty conduct for the purposes of Article 914 CC encompasses, of course, both intentional and negligent conduct.

This general rule of Article 914 CC bases the liability for compensation, apart from the objective precondition of unlawfulness, also on a subjective condition, the fault (*culpa*); it establishes, that is, the *subjective liability* of the tortfeasor. However, there are also instances where the law imposes liability to compensate on the person who has caused the prejudice regardless of his fault or other subjective factors (*objective or strict liability*). As to these cases, no general rule comparable to Article 914 CC is provided for. There are only special provisions, usually in special laws, which impose no fault liability in certain cases.[19] The most usual justification for these cases is that the activity of the person causing the prejudice (e.g., the use of their car, machines, etc.) constitutes a *source of risk* and, usually, a source from which benefits could be drawn for said person (in which case, it seems even more justifiable that the beneficiary should also bear the losses stemming from the same source).

40. More specifically:

In order for a claim under Article 914 CC to succeed, it is necessary for there to be: (a) unlawful and faulty conduct; (b) damage/prejudice; and (c) causation between (a) and (b). The words 'against the law' in Article 914 CC import the concept of unlawful/illegal conduct and mean that the perpetrator must have violated a specific legal provision prohibiting or demanding a certain act or omission, or more often a so-called 'absolute right', i.e., a right that must be respected by everyone and thus develops an erga omnes effect (e.g., a right to ownership, an inheritance law or intellectual property right, or the right to personality). Apart from that, however, it is widely accepted in Greek legal case law and theory that the requirement for unlawful/illegal conduct also is met when the perpetrator violates a duty of care deriving from

19. For instance, the liability of the producer for defective goods (Art. 6, Law 2251/1994); *see* paras 164, 196 *infra*. Other special laws which impose strict liability are Laws ΓϡΝ″/1911, 551/1915, 1178/1981, 1815/1988, 2328/1995, etc.

the principle of good faith under Article 288 CC in conjunction with Article 281 CC which prohibits the abusive exercise of rights.[20]

The violation of a duty of care that each citizen carries towards their fellow citizens entails a *broadening of the notion of unlawful/illegal conduct.*[21] Therefore, the latter tort precondition might be met in case there is a violation of a duty of care, safety and protection of the others and their goods; such a duty is imposed upon any person, within the framework of any social activities of theirs. In other words, said precondition is met when a person does not show the diligence that an average person can and must show with respect to the safety and protection of persons and goods with which their behaviour comes or may come into contact.[22]

More particularly, such unlawful conduct usually stems from: (a) previous dangerous conduct of the perpetrator and their subsequent omission to take precautionary measures against the danger inflicted by said conduct (e.g., a public works contractor leaves open a pothole in road surface, the next day a pedestrian falls into the pothole and breaks his or her leg: unlawful conduct by omission to take relevant precautionary measures, e.g., to fence the pothole), and/or (b) the specific position of the perpetrator as guarantor of certain goods or persons, which places him or her under a duty to act in a certain manner towards their fellow citizens (e.g., a doctor must help a citizen who has been hit on the street by a runaway driver).[23]

According to the decision of *Areios Pagos* (AP) 1802/2013, which is characteristic of long-standing case law on the matter:

For an illegal conduct to be found, the violation of a specific legal provision is not required but, instead, the fact that the conduct runs against the more general spirit of the law or the demands of the legal order suffices. Hence, illegality is also present when there is a violation of the general duty of care and protection within the framework of the transactional and, more generally, social activity of the individuals, that is, a violation of the, socially imposed and deriving from the fundamental legal principle of consistent conduct, duty to take diligence measures in order to avoid causing damages to legally protected goods of third parties. There is negligence, as form of fault under Article 330 CC, when the diligence due in transactions [...] is not shown. [...] On the other hand, the faulty damaging action or omission by means of which a contract is violated may, apart from the contractual claim, also establish a tort claim, when said action or omission would be illegal even if it would be committed without the contractual relationship existing, as running against the general duty imposed by Article 914 CC not to harm other persons at one's own fault,[24] without the fulfilment of any additional precondition being required.[25]

---

20. *See* especially Stathopoulos, Law of Obligations – General Part (4th ed. 2004; in Greek), § 15 esp. no. 39–46.
21. *See* Stathopoulos, Law of Obligations – General Part, § 15 esp. no. 39 et seq.; also AP 2075/2013, Nomos Legal Database; AP 867/2010, Nomos Legal Database; AP 370/2010, Nomos Legal Database.
22. *See* Stathopoulos, Law of Obligations – General Part, § 15 no. 39.
23. *See also* Stathopoulos, Law of Obligations – General Part, § 15 no. 45.
24. Such *dictum* may be seen as reflecting the old Roman law rule '*neminem laedere*', accompanied, however, by the precondition of fault.
25. Legal Database of Athens Bar Association; *see also* AP 1156/2015, Nomos Legal Database.

41. Apart from the general clause of Article 914 CC, of considerable importance is the specific tortious clause of Article 919 CC, which, under the title '*infringement upon good morals*' provides that *'any person who intentionally prejudiced another person, in a manner contrary to good morals, shall compensate the latter'*.[26] This provision pertains to a specific type of tortious conduct. Specifically, Article 919 CC prohibits the immoral and intentional causing of prejudice to another person. It requires grave misconduct on the part of the perpetrator that runs contrary to good morals (*bonos mores*). Regarding the concept of good morals, the prevailing view uses the criterion of '*the generally accepted ideas of a rightly and prudently thinking person at the present time*' – i.e., the notion of *social morality*, as opposed to individual/subjective morality.[27] Within this framework, the prevailing view takes into account 'all conditions and circumstances' accompanying the wrongful conduct.[28]

In order for tortious conduct under Article 919 CC to exist, the perpetrator does not need to know or be conscious of the immoral character of their acts (or omissions); rather, there must only be an objective violation of this standard. In order for a Greek court to determine whether such a violation has occurred, it must have recourse to all relevant circumstances relating to the relevant conduct of the perpetrator and, in particular, to their motives and purpose, to the means and methods used, and so on.[29]

Intent in the form of *dolus eventualis* is sufficient for fault under Article 919 CC (i.e., intent is present when the perpetrator foresees the possibility of their act – or omission – causing damage and nonetheless persists in proceeding with their act or omission accepting the consequences therefrom).[30]

42. Both Articles 914 and 919 CC provide for compensation to the victim of the tort. Under Greek law, when a tort has been committed, the damaged person may seek to be put into the position that he or she would have been *had the damaging event not occurred.*[31] Pursuant to this general rule, a victim of tortious conduct may seek compensation for: (a) actual losses; (b) lost profits; and (c) moral damages, as a result of Article 932 CC, which, under the title '*restitution for moral damage*', provides (*inter alia*) that *'in case of tort, irrespective of the damages to be paid for the economic loss, the court may award, at its own discretion, a fair pecuniary restitution due to moral damage. This holds especially for the person who suffered his or her in their health, honor, or dignity, or who was deprived of his or her liberty...'*.[32] In assessing moral damages pursuant to Article 932 CC, the factors to be taken into account include the degree of fault on the perpetrator's part, the nature of the unlawful conduct, the

26. See, indicatively, *Stathopoulos*, Law of Obligations – General Part, § 15 no. 74 et seq.
27. *See* AP 10/1991 Nomos Legal Database.
28. *See* AP 1346/2000, Nomos Legal Database; AP 1734/2009, Nomos Legal Database.
29. See, indicatively, AP 398/1975 (in Plenary Session), NoB 1975, p. 1164; AP 764/2014, Nomos Legal Database; AP 1942/2013, Nomos Legal Database; AP 1101/2011, NoB 2012, p. 645.
30. *See* , indicatively, AP 2/2008 (in Plenary Session), Nomos Legal Database; AP 2038/2014, Nomos Legal Database.
31. *See* Stathopoulos, Law of Obligations – General Part, § 15 no. 96 and § 8 no. 29 et seq., esp. 31–32.
32. *See* Stathopoulos, Law of Obligations..., § 15 no. 103 et seq.

extent of the damage sustained, the circumstances of its occurrence, the possible concurrent fault of the victim, and the social and economic status of the parties.[33]

II. Comparison with Contractual Liability

43. Tortious liability according to Article 914 CC is primary, since the obligation between the person causing the prejudice and the person prejudiced is created for the first time in the form of this liability (for compensation) when the conditions of the provision are met. Liability for compensation from non-performance of a contractual obligation is, on the other hand, secondary, since it presupposes precisely a pre-existent (primary) obligation between the parties, the obligation to perform the contract, that is, to fulfil the promised (original) performance. This secondary liability for compensation is regulated mainly in Articles 330, 335 et seq., 362 et seq., and 382 et seq. CC.

The distinction between contractual and tortious liability is not as fundamental as used to be believed, nor does it stem from any logical necessity.[34] Often, also, the inclusion of a consequence in law in the contractual or tortious liability, such as of the liability of the producer for defective products in accordance with Community Directive 83/374 and the relevant provisions of adaptation of Greek law (Article 6, Law 2251/1994), should be a matter of indifference to the extent that a recourse to the general law for the filling of any gaps in the special regulation of this liability is not required. This distinction is based chiefly on the fact that in the case of liability within a contract, we must accept a closer bond between debtor and creditor by reason of the binding nature of the contractual obligation which pre-existed and which had been created by the parties' own will – a binding element absent in tortious liability.

De lege lata, there are some differences in the regulation of the two liabilities, the chief of which are the following:

(a) *Burden of proof*: In contractual liability, the fault of the person causing the prejudice (breaking his contractual obligations) is presumed (rebuttable presumption – *see* Articles 336, 342, 363 CC); consequently, he must prove that he was not at fault if he wishes to be discharged. With tortious liability, the burden of proof of all the actual facts which make up the conditions for the claim (i.e., of the fault also) is borne by the injured party, in accordance with the general procedural rule that the burden of proof lies on the plaintiff.

(b) *Non-pecuniary/moral damage* (*non-economic damage*): In the case of contractual liability, satisfaction is given only for prejudice to property (pecuniary damage), not for 'moral damage', for example, injury to reputation, to feelings, etc. (Article 299 CC). On the contrary, as we explained above, in the field of tortious liability moral damage is compensated (and, in the case of causing death, the distress and anxiety of mind of third parties belonging to the victim's family – Article 932

33. *See* indicatively Decision of the Supreme Court no. 864/2014, Nomos Legal Database; Decision of the Supreme Court no. 1630/2013, Nomiko Vima 2014, p. 614; Decision of Larissa Court of Appeals no. 443/2011, Legal Database of Athens Bar Association.

34. *See* Mazeaud-Tunc, Traité théorique et pratique de la responsabilité civile delictuelle et contractuelle, 6th ed., No. 96 et seq., also for the trends towards unifying the two liabilities.

CC). To the degree, however, that the breach of a contractual obligation constitutes independently (independently, that is, of the pre-existing obligation) a tort against the creditor, the application of the provisions on torts (Articles 914 et seq. CC) will be possible, and consequently (if moral damage has been caused) also of Article 932 CC, in which case, of course, the burden of proof, in accordance with the rules on tortious liability, will lie with the injured party. This will be accepted, for example, in case where the breach of contract causes further damage to other goods of the creditor apart from the object of the performance.

Implementation of Article 59 CC (according to which satisfaction for the moral damage is also provided for in the event of an offence against the personality) is also possible if the breach of contract is regarded in the specific instance as having caused offence to the personality of the creditor. However, the breach of a contractual obligation in itself does not fall within Article 59 CC (without the existence of additional circumstances). This, of course, means in practice that the violation of the contract does not necessarily entail moral damage (the other aspect of which is an offence against the moral personality of the creditor). Therefore, for this reason also, there would be no margin for implementation of Article 59 CC. However, in view of the above possibilities, the practical importance of Article 299 CC is perceptibly reduced, and it is located chiefly in the legislative confirmation of the fact that breach of contractual obligations of the debtor does not in itself involve a prejudice to the goods other than those of property of the creditor. Impossibility of performance, default of the debtor, etc. in themselves do not – the legislator has pronounced – injure the creditor morally.

(c) *Vicarious liability* (Articles 334, 922 CC): In contractual liability, fault of the vicarious agent (employee, agent, servant, and other ancillary persons whom the debtor employs in performing his contractual obligations) is more easily transferred to the debtor than to the tortfeasor in tortious liability.[35]

(d) *Degree of fault:* As a rule, the fault principle (liability for each fault – discharge for matters of chance – *see* paragraphs 252 et seq. *infra*) applies in both contractual and tortious liability. Exceptions, mainly in the direction of the mitigation of the liability (e.g., liability only for wilful conduct and gross negligence) are more frequent in the case of contractual liability.

(e) *Prescription of claims:* Under Greek law, the time-limitation of actions is known as 'prescription'. In the case of tortious responsibility, provision is made for a five-year prescription of the claim beginning from the point where the injured party took cognizance of the prejudice and of the identity of the person liable for compensation, which, however, may not be more than twenty years distant from the point at which the act took place (Article 937 CC), while in contractual liability, as a rule (on the exceptions from the twenty-year prescription, *see* paragraphs 329 and 352 *infra*), the general twenty-year prescription of claims has force (Article 249 CC – *see* paragraphs 328 et seq. *infra*).

35. This is accepted by the prevailing view in Greece, by interpretation of the crucial provisions (Arts 334 and 922 CC).

III. Concurrence of the Two Liabilities

44. The non-performance of a contractual obligation must, logically, be regarded as constituting an unlawful act, such as the *tortious act* of Article 914 CC. The consequence would be that Article 914 CC would apply to it. Nevertheless, the non-performance of a pre-existing obligation is governed by special rules (Articles 330, 335 et seq., 362 et seq., 382 et seq. CC). For this reason, according to one view, which receives support mainly in France, these rules prevail as special rules and will exclusively regulate cases of contractual liability. That is to say, they do not concur with the provisions on tortious liability and, consequently, the injured party cannot choose between these or those as best serves his interests (*principe de 'non-cumul'*). But when the act or omission which constitutes the contractual non-performance is simultaneously and in itself unlawful (i.e., it would also have been unlawful if it had been committed without the pre-existing contract), concurrence of the two liabilities, tortious and contractual, is, particularly in Germany and in Greece, accepted (see, indicatively, AP 1802/2013[36] as per paragraph 40 *supra*). For instance, a contractor or employee causes intentionally or negligently damage to the material provided or the goods entrusted to him or her by the principal or the employer; a guardian or tenant of a property causes intentionally or negligently damage to the latter; or an agent usurps the money received by him or her in the course of the execution of the agency duties. In all these cases, the act of the damaging party would be unlawful per se, i.e., even if we hypothetically assume that the contract between him or her and the other party (e.g., work contract, lease, agency, etc.) did not pre-exist. In these cases, the injured party can ground his claim either on the provisions on contractual or those on tortious liability.

Only to the extent that the act of non-performance of the obligation would not have been, without the pre-existing contract, unlawful, should the French view be followed and the implementation of tortious liability precluded, by reason of the special nature of the provisions on contractual liability. For instance, failure to pay a contractual debt only conflicts with the rule of law insofar as the relevant liability was already undertaken by the contract; therefore, only contractual liability is applicable.

To sum up, there are instances where a certain conduct *constitutes, at the same time, a breach of contract as well as a tort*, if said conduct would be tortious independently of the existence of a contractual relationship between the perpetrator and the victim of the tort; in essence, we hypothetically assume here that the contractual relationship does not exist at all and we assess whether the conduct would be tortious in itself, i.e., irrespective of the existence of the contract. If this is the case, there is *a concurrence of contractual and tortious liability*, which means that the damaged party may have recourse not only to the provisions on contractual liability but also to the ones on

36. Legal Database of Athens Bar Association; *see also* AP 1156/2015, Nomos Legal Database.

tortious liability; the latter grants to the damaged party the significant option to additionally request relief for moral damage.[37]

§5. Contracts and Quasi-Contracts: Other Sources of Obligations

45. The well-known four-fold division of the *Institutiones* of Justinian according to which obligations are generated either *ex contractu* or *ex delicto* or *quasi ex contractu* or *quasi ex delicto*[38] is not employed in Greek law. At the present time, it is chiefly the English who, not having a codified civil law, rely on these (at least in the case of the first three categories of sources). In Greece, the contract is recognized as a separate source of obligations. Over and above this, the law stipulates (as the legislator is always at liberty to do) other reasons for the generation of obligations, and therefore other sources, the classification of which is not of any great importance. This is because in their case, whatever is laid down by the provisions which introduce them has force. In all these cases we can speak of 'obligations stemming from law'. Of course, contractual obligations are also ultimately based on the rule of law, which grants them their recognition. However, a characteristic of these is the autonomy of the private will as a moral and constitutionally guaranteed principle, the self-commitment of the individual. All the other instances are precisely without this self-commitment and with their only foundation resting directly on the law: obligations from delictual (tortious) acts (Articles 914 et seq. CC), from unjust enrichment (Articles 904 et seq. CC), from *negotiorum gestio* (Articles 730 et seq. CC), from joint rights relations (Articles 785 et seq. CC), from creditors' defrauding (Articles 939 et seq. CC), from the law on neighbours (Articles 1003 et seq. CC) and other instances which in Roman law were included in obligations *ex delicto* or *quasi ex contractu* or *quasi ex delicto.* Some of these will be dealt with below, in Part II, Chapter 2, simply because they correspond to what in other legal systems is included in the so-called quasi-contracts, a term, as we have said, not currently employed in Greece. Naturally, in certain of the above categories of obligations there are elements of will or action of individuals which set in motion and in implementation the conditions of the law and there are certainly features in common with obligations from contracts, more so in the case of some of these obligations than in others. Moreover, the old contract-tort dichotomy cannot today be perceived so sharply. It is for all these reasons that there is (and this is needed even more today) the single branch of the Law of Obligations, which includes rules having force in principle as to all obligations, regardless of their source. Apart from its rules which regulate in a special manner obligations from contracts or from torts,

37. *See* Stathopoulos, Law of Obligations – General Part, § 15 no. 9 et seq.; AP 653/2008, ChrID 2008, p. 889; AP 1190/2007, Nomos Legal Database; AP 1341/2007, Nomos Legal Database; AP 1709/1999, Nomos Legal Database; AP 25/1998, NoB 1999, p. 390, with comment by Doris; AP 47/1996, Nomos Legal Database; AP 18/1993, Nomos Legal Database; AP 1143/2007, Nomos Legal Database; Athens Court of Appeals 6188/2006, Nomos Legal Database; Athens Court of Appeals 520/2002, Nomos Legal Database; Athens Court of Appeals 7801/1990, Nomos Legal Database.
38. Just. *Inst.*, III, 13, 3.

etc., there are many rules which in an abstraction and generalization speak simply of obligations and have force in every instance (contractual or tortious, etc. obligations). For this reason, the critique of the dichotomy becomes keener, for example, in the Anglo-Saxon countries[39] where no law of obligations has taken shape and there are simply the special branches, such as law of contracts, law of torts, law of restitution, etc. It is typical of the situation that Gilmore expresses the desire to merge in legal education 'the first-year courses in Contracts and Torts into a single course which we could call Contorts'.[40] Those who already have, as in the case of Greece, a law of obligations do not feel this need. We must, of course, realize that there are differences between the different kinds of obligations, but not as great as was once believed.

§6. Contract and Trust

46. The Anglo-Saxon institution of the trust is unknown to Greek law. For the meaning of this institution, we can refer, *inter alia*, to Article 2 of the Hague Trust Convention, which states:

For the purposes of this Convention, the term 'trust' refers to the legal relationships created - inter vivos or on death - by a person, the settlor, when assets have been placed under the control of a trustee for the benefit of a beneficiary or for a specified purpose.

A trust has the following characteristics:

(a) the assets constitute a separate fund and are not a part of the trustee's own estate;
(b) title to the trust assets stands in the name of the trustee or in the name of another person on behalf of the trustee;
(c) the trustee has the power and the duty, in respect of which he is accountable, to manage, employ or dispose of the assets in accordance with the terms of the trust and the special duties imposed upon him by law.
The reservation by the settlor of certain rights and powers, and the fact that the trustee may have rights as a beneficiary, are not necessarily inconsistent with the existence of a trust.

In the Anglo-Saxon countries there have been needs which have led to the development of the trust because other legal possibilities, for example, in the rules of law of continental Europe, were lacking. Thus, the narrow framework of privity in Anglo-Saxon law and non-recognition of contracts in favour of third parties not participating in the contract block the way out which exists in Greek law (*see* Articles 410 et seq. CC – paragraphs 199 et seq. *infra*). It is indeed a fact that up to the end of the twentieth century, English law was attached to the personal character of the contractual *vinculum juris* and to 'privity of contract'. The non-recognition of the institution of contracts in favour of third parties led to the use of more complicated methods, just as to recourse to the institution of trust for the achievement of the same objectives. Finally, after sharp and

39. *See* Gilmore, The Death of Contract, 1974, Atiyah, The Rise and Fall of Freedom of Contract, 1979.
40. Gilmore, *supra* n. 39, at p. 90.

frequent criticism, the 'Contracts (Rights of Third Parties) Act 1999' was voted there; this recognizes, by way of exception and with limitations, genuine contracts in favour of third parties.

The same need arises in connection with the requirement of a consideration as a condition for the validity of a contract in the Anglo-Saxon countries, a requirement which renders gratuitous acts difficult and which does not exist in Greece. If one adds to this, *inter alia*, the fact that the English law of property knows other partial rights but has not developed the Roman institution of usufruct, which allows the co-existence of owner and usufructuary on a movable or immovable thing (*see* Articles 1142 et seq. CC); and if one further adds the fact that the institution of the 'foundation', with a separate fortune, set up in order to serve a specific purpose, which acquires its legal personality by Presidential Decree (PrD) (*see* Articles 108 et seq. CC) has not developed there, it will be appreciated how many needs the institution of the trust meets and how valuable this institution is in the Anglo-Saxon countries.

47. The relevant needs are met by Greek law, *inter alia*:

- by (nominate or innominate or mixed) contracts which have as their object the management of the property of another and which, by virtue of the freedom of contract, can in Greece be concluded without any need for the existence of a consideration;
- by contracts in favour of a third party, in accordance with Articles 410 et seq. CC. As to these contracts, Article 411 lays down that:

The third party may demand the performance directly from the promisor if it appears that such was the intention of the contracting parties or if such conclusion results from the nature and purpose of the contract.

The 'third party' here corresponds to the 'beneficiary' of the English trust:

- by unilateral authorizations granted by one person (corresponding to the 'settlor' in English trusts) to another (corresponding to the 'trustee') by virtue of which the authorized person may undertake material or legal acts which are binding upon the property of the principal. The authorized person may carry out legal acts in accordance with the will of the principal either in the name of the latter (in which case it will be by power of attorney – Article 216 CC) or in his own name. The institution of authorization is recognized in Greek law and is based apart from Article 216 (on the form of the power of attorney) mentioned above – on the more general Articles 236–239 CC (*see also* paragraphs 337 et seq. *infra* on representation);
- by fiduciary transfer of ownership or another right. In spite of contestations which have been caused by the silence of the law, the fiduciary transfer of a right – a revival in a way of the Roman *fiducia* – is today recognized in Greece (though reservations remain as to immovable properties). Its meaning is that full ownership is transferred (only one concept of ownership is recognized by Greek law), but this result goes beyond the purpose actually willed by the parties, which is something less than transfer: e.g., the security of the person acquiring ownership for a claim on his part against the transferor (*fiducia cum creditore*) or the

management without restrictions by the former of items of property thus transferred of the latter (*fiducia cum arnico*). The trust which is inherent in this contract is apparent precisely in the fact that more rights are transferred than is required and that, in accordance with the internal relations between the parties (agreement between them), when the need for which the fiduciary transfer was made has passed, the person who has acquired the right is obliged to transfer it back to the person who granted it to him. Sometimes this restoration of the right is achieved *ipso jure* by the agreement, for the same instance, of a resolutory condition (Article 202 CC);

- by granting of a limited real right on a thing and keeping the ownership of it, so that one person (the grantor) is the owner and the other (the grantee) the holder of this limited right. That is to say, the ownership is encumbered with this real right. If the latter is usufruct, which according to Article 1142 CC gives the usufructuary a right of use and beneficial enjoyment of the thing while its substance is preserved integrally, such ownership with a charge upon it is termed 'nude' ownership (i.e., stripped of its powers). The number of real rights is, of course, limited, as we have said (paragraph 22), but the use of the right of easement provides a variety of possibilities (Articles 1118 et seq., 1142 et seq. – in connection with the most important easement, i.e., usufruct – 1183 et seq. CC);
- by the use of special institutions provided by the law for special needs, such as the institution of the executor of a will appointed by the testator (Articles 2017 et seq. CC), of the liquidator of an inheritance appointed by the court (Articles 1913 et seq. CC), of the liquidator of a legal (juristic) person being dissolved (Articles 72 et seq. CC) or of a partnership (Articles 777 et seq. CC), of the compulsory administration provided for in the law of civil procedure, etc;
- by the setting up of a foundation, in accordance with Article 108 CC, according to which 'a patrimonium which has been attributed to serve a certain purpose' may become, if a certain procedure is observed, a foundation with a legal personality;
- by a combination of the above means.

It is precisely because the above possibilities exist, and they have been listed only indicatively, that the need has not arisen in Greece for the introduction of the trust as a distinct institution. The involvement of the Greek judge with that institution will come about only as a matter of Greek private international law, leading eventually to the application of *foreign* law of trust. It should be noted that Greece has not yet ratified the Hague Trust Convention.

§7. Contract and the Law of Property

I. General

48. To be more precise, this paragraph ought to deal with the concept of the law of real rights, which is not coterminous with the right of property, as seen by the Greek legislator. The third book of the CC (Articles 947–1345) deals with real rights in general. The question of which are real rights and how they differ from personal rights (which stem from obligations) has already been discussed (paragraphs 19 et seq. *supra*). We have also dealt with the real contract and how it differs from the promissory contract, which gives rise to obligation. Here we shall give a fuller account of the terms for the conclusion of the two principal real contracts, that of the transfer of the ownership over an immovable and that for the transfer of the ownership over a movable property. For the constitution of other real rights by a juridical act, *see* Articles 1121 (real easements), 1143 (usufruct), 1211 (pledge), 1266 (mortgage), CC, etc. The general terms for the conclusion of each contract which are examined in Part I of this monograph, concerning offer and acceptance, the intention to create legal relations, the capacity of the parties and the defects of consent, are also applied in the case of real contracts. The contract and, more generally, the juridical act are not the only ways of acquiring ownership or another real right. It is, however, the most important. Of the other ways provided for by law, the most usual in practice is usucapion (acquisition of ownership by long possession) (Articles 1041 et seq., 1121, 1143, etc. CC).

II. Transfer of Ownership over an Immovable

49. The transfer of ownership over an immovable property, in fulfilment of an obligation undertaken (usually by a promissory contract), is effected by contract between the transferor and the transferee (disposition contract, real contract, Article 1033 CC). Apart from the: (a) agreement on transfer, the following are required; (b) that the transferor should be the owner; (c) that the transfer should be made for some just cause; (d) that the agreement should be invested with the form of a notarial deed; (e) that it should be entered in the (public) transcription registers (Article 1192 CC).

A just cause for this real contract usually consists of the promissory contract (sale, Article 513 CC, donation, Article 496 CC, exchange, Article 573 CC, etc.) by which the obligation to transfer was undertaken. The promissory contract is also subject to notarial form, since it leads to the disposition of an immovable (Article 369 CC). In many instances, the two contracts (promissory and real) are concluded at the same time by the same deed. If there is no promissory contract or if this is invalid, the real contract is also invalid. That is to say, the latter is a *causal* contract.

The contract dealt with by Article 1033 CC is also invalid where the transferor is not the owner, regardless of whether the transferee is in good faith (believing the transferor to be the owner) or otherwise. Here the rule that nobody transfers more than the right he himself has (*nemo plus iuris ad alium transferre potest quam ipse habet*) applies; *see also* the general rule of Article 239 CC. Exceptions are made only in special circumstances (e.g., Articles 139, 1203–1204, 1963 CC).

50. Transcription of the transfer means its entry in public registers (transcriptions registers which are kept by a public functionary, the transcriptions registrar, and are available to public inspection). Additionally, subject to transcription are other acts which involve a change in real rights as to an immovable property (Article 1192 CC). The protection of transactions in immovable properties and the need for respect by any third party for the real rights over these presuppose the creation of certain and easily verifiable relations as to these real rights. The first objective is the availability of information to third parties interested as to real rights over immovable property (who from whom, since when, and what real rights or encumbrances he has, with what content, etc.). The second, the basic aim, is the protection of the trust created in the third party as a result of this information, the protection, that is, of the publicity of real relations as to an immovable property. However, the system of transcriptions (which is based on entries by person, the subject of the transactions in immovable properties) is less effective than the land register in force in other countries and based on entries by property (e.g., *'Grundbuch'* in Germany). For this reason, the system of the land register (*ktimatologio*) has been gradually introduced into Greece (*see* Law 2664/1998, as that was amended, *inter alia*, by Laws 3127/2003, 3481/2006, etc.) and nowadays in many municipalities the land registry has been completed and the land register is already in force. As for the majority of areas, however, until the completion of the relevant long-term project and the supersession of the system of transcriptions by the system of the land register, the former remains in force.

On transcription and from the time of transcription, the transfer of the ownership over the immovable property, provided that the other terms are fulfilled, occurs (Articles 1033, 1192, 1198 CC).

III. Transfer of Ownership over a Movable

51. For the transfer of the ownership over a movable, the following are required: (a) an agreement on the transfer (agreement in rem) between the transferor and the transferee; (b) delivery of the possession of the movable to the transferee; (c) ownership on the part of the transferor (Article 1034 CC). The observance of a particular form for the agreement is not required. This means that a private document or a verbal agreement suffices. Nor is the existence or validity of a promissory contract or other legal cause necessary. Usually such a cause will exist (e.g., sale, donation, etc.), but the validity of the transfer agreement does not depend upon this. The latter, that is to say, is a *non-causal* (abstract) contract. The legislator wished this contract to have the abstract character for reasons of the facilitation and security of transactions, which in the case of movables are usually carried out with greater speed. If the cause was absent or was invalid, the ownership over the movable is nevertheless transferred, but the transferee could have as owner, but also as one who has been enriched without just cause, an obligation to refund his unjust enrichment (Article 904 CC). The burden of proving lack of cause is borne by the person demanding restitution of the enrichment.

The delivery of possession of the thing fulfils up to a point the aim of publicity (it corresponds, that is, to transcription in the case of immovables), since it manifests to third parties, at least in most cases, the transfer of the thing.

52. More particularly in the case of movables (and unlike that of immovables), the CC establishes a general exception from the condition that the transferor should have ownership. This exception has force if at the time of the delivery of possession the transferee is in good faith (Article 1036 CC). A person who knows or does not know by his own gross negligence that the transferor was not the owner is not in good faith (Article 1037 CC). This exception does not apply to objects which are stolen or lost, apart from cash or bearer securities or things offered for sale at a public auction or at a trade fair or market, in which cases a person in good faith acquires stolen or lost goods also (Articles 1038–1039 CC). The law, by introducing the bona fide acquisition of ownership over a movable from a person not the owner, wished to facilitate transactions in movables and to protect the security of these transactions and the trust of the public which engages in them. For the person who acquires ownership to be deserving of protection (and for Article 1036 CC to be implemented), the delivery of possession must be, according to the prevailing view, material, that is, the party in good faith at the same time acquires physical power over the movable object.

§8. Good Faith and Fair Dealing: The Related General Clauses

I. The Rule on Good Faith (Article 288 CC)

53. Immediately after the first article on the Law of Obligations of the CC, which defines the concept of obligation (Article 287 CC), the legislator has introduced the provision on the bona fide fulfilment of the performance, that is, Article 288 CC – which resembles §242 of the BGB. The place reserved for this provision reflects its utmost importance. The relation of obligation, after its abstract conceptual definition in Article 287 CC, takes on its social orientation by means of Article 288 CC, which lays down that: *'The debtor is obliged to execute the performance as good faith requires, after consideration also of common usages.'* This general clause is not the only provision which deals with good faith, but can be regarded as the basic rule on the matter. Apart from the duties which the parties have specially provided for, others may arise that will be imposed by good faith during performance. This *broadening* of the obligation has today taken on such dimensions as to constitute one of the most fundamental modern items of progress in the field of the law of obligations and an expression of its social function. By the implementation of the principle of good faith, the obligational relationship is distanced from a purely individualistic spirit. Even if there were no Article 288 CC, the modern interpreter would determine the obligational relationship in accordance with the function which it performs and which would impose restrictions similar to those that are at present drawn from the principle of good faith, as entrenched in Article 288 CC.

Creditor and debtor are usually pursuing opposite interests. But this opposition does not mean that the creditor and the debtor are naturally rivals. In the last analysis, there is some community of purpose as to the best possible fulfilment of the performance. The ethics of obligation permit each to safeguard their own interests, but it does not justify complete ignoring of the other party's interests or a 'war' between them. Moreover, their *collaboration* is required for the smooth development of the relation, so that both are satisfied, the creditor by the receiving of the performance and the debtor by being relieved of her/his obligation. Nor does the CC in the other provisions on the law of obligations describe the two sides as opponents (*see* Articles 287, 374 et seq. CC, etc.: '… the other party'). Basically, however, this spirit is imposed by the provision of Article 288 CC in requiring conduct in good faith from the two parties.

The community of aims extends – in this case without limitations – beyond the internal relations of the two parties. The two subjects of the obligation must not be indifferent to its *general effects*. It is through the performance of an obligation that the movement of goods, the meeting of basic needs, the recovery of losses (e.g., sale, lease of a residence, delictual obligation, etc.) are effectuated. Thus, the obligational relationship is not necessarily an exclusively private affair of the two parties, since it may have repercussions on the general socio-economic life.

Article 288 CC is the basic provision which contains the binding guideline as to the function of every obligation. At the same time, it is available to cover new needs which developments in modern transactions from time to time give rise to, over and above express legislative provisions. A plethora of issues and solutions have found in said provision their legal foundation. The acceptance of collateral duties of the debtor, apart from their principal obligation (see, for example, paragraph 158 *infra*) is the main consequence of the application of Article 288 CC. In extreme cases it can lead even to the adjustment of the principal obligation (*see* paragraph 291 *infra*).[41]

It is interesting to note that § 242 of the BGB, which corresponds to this provision, also covered, up till 2002 (see, however, paragraphs 298–299 *infra*), the scope for which the Greek Civil Code has stipulated two other fundamental provisions (absent in the BGB), that is, the provisions of Articles 281 (on the abusive exercise of a right) and 388 (on unforeseen change in circumstances[42]). And it is no coincidence that said paragraph of the BGB is a provision which is more frequently referenced and discussed. In France, by way of contrast, the corresponding Articles 1134 § 3 and 1135 of the CC have had, particularly in the courts, less influence, in spite of the fact that the latter particularly is very lucidly formulated (French Civil Code Article 1135: *'Contracts oblige not only as to what has been expressed in them, but also in all the consequences which equity, usage and the law give to the obligation in accordance with its nature.'*). In the Swiss Civil Code, the corresponding provision has been embodied in Article 2, precisely in order to stress its importance. In England a similar end is served by the principle of equity. A special expression of this with wide application is the doctrine of estoppel (corresponding to the principle *'non venire contra factum proprium'*), by which a person is 'estopped' in invoking a right or a legal relation in general when such invocation conflicts with a declaration or act on his part and with the conclusions that 'a reasonable man' draws from this. What is also of interest here is the fact that the doctrine of estoppel has been extended to other instances when required by equity (*quasi estoppel*). In Italy, the provision of Article 1175 of the CC imposes on the creditor and the debtor that they should observe correct conduct (*correttezza*).

41. *See* some out of many relevant decisions of the AP: 668/1985, EEN 53, 179 (imposition of collateral duties by virtue of Art. 288 CC); 1191/1983, HellD 1984, 349 (basic equal treatment of employees); 879/1982, NoB 31, 821 (adjustment of performance); 9/1997 (in Plenary Session), NoB 1997, 762; 187/1990, NoB 1991, 913; 1346/1993, HellD 1994, 1597; 1413/1994, EErgD 1996, 227; 902/1995, NoB 1997, 983; 71/1998, NoB 1999, 405; 63/2000, HellD 2000, 758.

42. Today, after the amendment of the German Civil Code in 2002, §313 of the German Code, corresponding to (and broader than) Art. 388 CC, has been introduced.

54. By *good faith* we mean the sincerity and fairness that are required in transactions.[43] The person engaged in transactions must as a decent and honourable man impose limits on the relentless pursuit of their individual interests and not remain indifferent to the lawful goods enjoyed by the other party which are affected or may be affected by the relation of obligation. They must behave, basically, with sincerity and not engage in hypocritical and devious activities and acts which circumvent the interests of the other. Moreover, they must not simply confine themselves to the passive fulfilment of their obligation, but must show willingness and collaboration in the essential achievement of the aim of the obligation. All this, however, will be assessed on the basis of *objective* criteria. In this context, the ideas of due conduct prevailing in society are crucial. Subjective factors (e.g., what the party believes personally as to what constitutes due conduct, if she/he is a person marked by excessive scrupulosity or laxity of conscience, whether or not she/he was aware of how honourable men behave in these transactions, whether her/his intentions were good or bad, etc.) do not matter. The measure, moreover, of the sincerity and fairness required will be sought once again in social reality. Excessive or unrealistic demands for sincerity will not be taken into account.

55. Good faith in the sense described and for the reasons stated is perceived as *objective* and is to be distinguished from *subjective good faith*, which is dealt with in other provisions of the CC. The latter (with which we are not concerned here) means generally the conviction of the party that her/his action is based on the existence of a right on her/his part, that it is lawful, that it harms no one, that the other party also has a right to undertake the contract, etc. The more particular meaning of subjective good faith emerges in each instance from the provisions which refer to it. For instance, a person to whom an alien movable object (i.e., an object that does not belong to the transferor) is transferred is 'in good faith', under Articles 1036 et seq. CC, when she/he believes (provided that this conviction is not due to gross negligence on her/his part) that the transferor is the owner of this thing and consequently has under law the power to transfer it; or a person who has had in her/his possession for a long time an alien object is 'a possessor in good faith' under Articles 1041 et seq. CC, when she/he believes (again, provided that his faith is not due to gross negligence) that she/he is the owner. In this context, good faith (which is one of the preconditions for the acquisition of ownership by the person in good faith in these instances) is basically an 'inner state' of the party in good faith, while objective good faith (Article 288 CC, as also 281, 200, 388, etc.) serves as a criterion of conduct – that is, it refers to objectively honourable conduct on the part of the person engaged in a transaction, regardless of her/his inner states.[44]

---

43. AP (in Plenary Session) 927/1982, NoB 1983, 214; AP 194/1957, NoB 1957, 733; 216/1958, NoB 1958, 355; 1064/1972, NoB 1973, 629; 291/1985, NoB 1986, 71; 1038/1998, HellD 1998, 1590.

44. The German Civil Code makes a terminological distinction between the two concepts (objective good faith: *'Treu und Glauben'*, subjective good faith: *'guter Glaube'*). By way of contrast, the term is common in Roman law (as it is in Greece) (*'bona fides'*; in connection with the objective meaning, there are frequent references to the *bonum et aequum*), as is the case also, today, in French law (*'bonne foi'*, *see* French Civil Code Arts 549–550, on the one hand, and 1134, para. 3, on the other).

56. 'Common usages' (also called 'business/trade usages', a less precise, because narrower, term), to which Article 288 CC also refers, reflect the prevailing practice, that is, the usual manner of acting in legal and business life.[45] Common usages are taken into account only when they do not conflict with morality, that is, when they are in accordance with it or are morally neutral. In essence, they do not constitute a self-contained criterion, but are taken into the consideration for the determination of good faith. Practices that have taken shape and have prevailed in transactions, when they are not in conflict with social morality, do in fact constitute a safe guide as to what bona fide conduct requires. However, where common usages have not taken shape, good faith remains the sole criterion.

It is possible for common usages to be local ones, in which case in the place where they are in force they prevail over any general common usage. It is also possible for *professional* usages to make their appearance in transactions.

The judge is under no obligation to follow a specific common usage if she/he considers that good faith demands something else. The latter has greater force.[46] This is the basic criterion, the measure by which the conduct of the parties will be finally judged.

57. The provision of Article 288 CC is mandatory law (jus cogens). The consequence is that the implementation of good faith in the performance of obligations cannot be precluded generally in advance by a waiver or an agreement by both parties. Such a waiver or agreement would be null and void (*see* Articles 3, 174 CC). Nor may a special regulation that the parties have provided for have force if in the specific instance good faith imposes different conduct. This restriction on the two parties takes on particular practical significance in relation to *general terms of transactions/business*, the contents of which often take shape to the detriment of the weaker party. Control of the content of these terms on the basis of Article 288 CC can lead to the nullity of those terms which an honourable and fair party would not impose on the other party (*see also* paragraphs 33–34 *supra* on general terms of transactions and consumer protection). A waiver in advance of a specific consequence on the part of one of the parties will, however, be valid when it is not the result of her/his submission to the stronger party, but entails that the party that is bound by the waiver assumes the relevant risk in accordance with the purpose of the contract.

It will be obvious that a waiver *ex post facto* of rights based on the bona fide fulfilment of the contractual obligation is possible, as is the case with every acquired alienable right.

Also invalid for the same reasons will be an agreement or waiver that precludes *in advance and in general* any appeal to common usages. On the other hand, a *specific* will of the two parties prevails over a common usage which may have a contrary

45. AP 194/1957, NoB 1957, 733; AP 703/1976, NoB 1977, 52; AP 769/1985, DEN 1986, 558; AP 84/1994, ArcN 1994, 695; AP 678/1996, HellD 1998, 552.

46. On the precedence of good faith over common usages, *see* Stammler, Die Lehre von dem Richtigen Rechte, 2, 1926, p. 221, where it is stressed that the German Civil Code correctly refers us in other provisions to good faith only, omitting business usages (*see also* Arts 207, 376, etc. Greek CC). It is true that any common usages which had taken shape could be taken into account *via* good faith, which, as has been pointed out, draws its demands from social reality.

content, provided that the contrary stipulation of the parties does not conflict with good faith.

58. To sum up, Article 288 CC is a general provision of Greek law that is of paramount importance to determining, among other things, the *ancillary* obligations of parties to a contractual relationship. It aims at ensuring the existence of a minimum level of fairness, reasonableness, and decency in transactions. Being a provision of compulsory law (*jus cogens*) Article 288 CC cannot be waived by the parties.

Good faith under Greek law is a dynamic notion and therefore its exact content and extent is left to be determined by the Greek Courts on the facts of each case. That said, Article 288 CC provides Greek judges with a wide discretionary power. It allows them to intervene in the relation between two parties to a contract by limiting, complementing or weakening the rights or obligations that arise by virtue of parties' contract or the law, either by increasing or reducing the obligations of a party.[47]

In this regard, there are three main ways in which Article 288 CC imposes obligations on contracting parties.

First, Article 288 CC may be used as the basis for incidental, ancillary or additional obligations that were not provided for in the parties' contract. In particular, Article 288 CC may be used to create:

(a) *Secondary obligations that relate to the main obligation*. Examples include obligations to ensure the proper, flawless or safe execution of the main performance, such as to take precautionary measures in order to ensure the proper installation *in situ* of a machine and the safe transportation of a good, etc.
(b) *Protection obligations that go beyond the main obligation*. Examples include the care which an employer owes to his employee to ensure safe working conditions.
(c) *Implied obligations not to hinder or undermine performance of the contract by the other party*.
(d) *Fiduciary obligations*. Examples include the obligation owed by an employee to refrain from any competitive acts against his or her employer.

Second, Article 288 CC can be used to amend or qualify existing obligations, if the full implementation of the contractual obligations would lead to unfairness for one of the contracting parties. For instance, if one party has paid back the greatest part of a debt instalment (e.g., out of an instalment of EUR 1 million he or she only failed to pay EUR 100), then the creditor would not be allowed to accelerate the loan for this reason, even if in principle he or she has the right to do so under the contract or the law. The same may apply in case of a very small delay in performance under the contract.

Article 288 CC also can perform this corrective function in cases where there is a severe supervening change in circumstances (e.g., devaluation of currency, economic crisis, war, legislative change, and so forth) where one party would benefit from the

47. *See*, only indicatively, Stathopoulos, Law of Obligations – General Part (4th ed. 2004; in Greek), § 5 no. 21.

situation, whereas the other party would suffer an extreme damage (in more detail *see* §5 *infra*).[48]

Third, Article 288 CC may, under certain circumstances, be used to abolish an obligation altogether. For example, one party may be granted a right to terminate the contract for serious grounds (e.g., breach of confidence or acts of competition carried out by the counter-party, fundamental change in circumstances, etc., which render the continuation of the contractual relation unconscionable for the party wishing to terminate it), even if such termination is not provided for in the contract (in more detail *see* paragraphs 300 et seq. *infra*).[49]

II. Related Provisions

59. Article 200 CC deals with the interpretation of contracts (and more generally of juridical acts, in accordance with its purpose, *see also* Article 173 CC) and imposes as interpretative criteria good faith and common usage. The interpretation of juridical acts is prior to the implementation of Article 288 CC and has as its purpose the discovery of the decisive meaning in law of the declaration of will, that is, the determination of the parties' autonomous stipulations. The rule of Article 288 CC imposes on the parties heteronomous stipulations in the exercise of their contractual rights and duties. Thus, in contracts, the first thing to be established is their meaning by interpretation and then whatever has been established is supplemented or amended on the basis of Article 288 CC. It will be obvious, then, that Article 288 CC has a more 'social' purpose than Article 200 CC. Moreover, the range of application of the former is broader, since it extends also to non-contractual obligations. However, in contractual obligations the two provisions are complementary. This explains the frequent invocation of the two in common by judicial decisions.

60. Article 281 CC prohibits the abusive exercise of a right (i.e., according to the article's definition, that exercise which is obviously contrary to good faith or morality (*boni mores*) or to the social and economic purpose of the right). This provision is broader than that of Article 288 CC both in that it deals with every right (and, more

48. Karampatzos, Unforeseen Change of Circumstances in a Bilateral Contract, passim, esp. no. 478 et seq.

49. *See* AP 1836/2007, Nomos Legal Database; AP 21/2004 (in Plenary Session), Nomos Legal Database; AP 10/1995 (in Plenary Session), Nomos Legal Database; AP 856/1989, Nomos Legal Database; Stathopoulos, Law of Obligations – General Part, § 5 no. 37, 85, § 21 no. 74, 135; Karampatzos, The Option Right and the Various Ways for its Extinction, DEE 2009 (in Greek), pp. 150 et seq.; *the same*, Unforeseen Change of Circumstances in a Bilateral Contract, no. 47, 122, 654. Cf. also § 314 I of the German Civil Code (BGB).

generally, freedom of action, e.g., freedom of contract[50]) and not only with a special relation between persons, and in that it uses alternatively criteria other than good faith. Nevertheless, the provision of Article 288 CC is broader, on the one hand, insofar as it also governs the conduct of the obligor (debtor), which is the subject with which it chiefly deals, and, on the other, in that it regards as sufficient any conflict with good faith – and not only that which is 'obvious'. Furthermore, on the basis of Article 288 CC, obligations can also be imposed upon the creditor. The two provisions, however, overlap to the extent that they impose a limitation on the exercise of the right of the creditor by virtue of the criterion of good faith.[51]

61. The provision of Article 919 CC prohibits the immoral and wilful causing of prejudice to another. It does not presuppose, as does Article 288 CC, a special relation; instead, it requires more serious misconduct (that contrary to good morals, that is, to morality). For purposes of the concretization of the concept of good morals, the prevailing view uses as criteria 'the ideas according to general acceptance of a right and prudently thinking member of society at the time', that is, *social morality* (and not individual morality, for example, that of the judge who hears the case) and for an assessment of this, it takes into account 'the whole of the conditions and circumstances' which accompany the exceptionable conduct and not isolated criteria, for example, only the motives or the purpose of the tortfeasor.[52] Further concretization and objectivization, as well as the broadening of the concept of good morals can be achieved by the use of the criterion of *public policy*, which also confirms the fact that the general ideas prevalent in society are relevant here, and not the individual ones of the judge. Good faith constitutes a broader criterion, so that conflict with this may occur more easily than conflict with good morals. The latter set the minimal tolerable limits on human conduct. The provision of Article 919 CC provides (as does Article 914 CC) for the obligation of compensation as a consequence in law.

62. The general clause of Article 178 CC ('An act which is contrary to morality shall be null and void') also refers us to good morals, but to impose a consequence other than that of Article 919 CC, that is, the nullity of the immoral juridical act. Article 174 CC also deals with the validity of the juridical act (this declares null a juridical

50. While the prevailing view in Greek theory agrees that Art. 281 CC prohibits not only abuse of a right but also, in accordance with its purpose, the abuse of general freedom of action, the court rulings vacillate. Although the Court of Cassation of Areios Pagos in 1985, altering its previous rulings, agreed (AP 717/1985, NoB 1986, 560), a little later it returned to its initial negative position (but with a strong minority of 14 members), which adopts a narrower interpretation of Art. 281 CC (AP (in Plenary Session) 33/1987, NoB 1988, 324; comments by Ph. Doris). For this negative stance *see also* AP 404/1987 NoB 1988, 907; AP 167/1998 HellD 1998, 856; AP 5/2001 HellD 2001, 671; AP 1547/2007 HellD 2009, 726. On the contrary, *see* AP 1969/1990 HellD 1991, 1499; AP 602/2005, Athens Bar Association Legal Database.
51. In Roman law, as in the law in force in Greece prior to the Civil Code, i.e., before 1946, recognition was given to *exceptio doli generalis,* which the defendant could plead against the plaintiff when the latter exercised his rights in a 'malicious' manner, with an objective meaning, that is, in an abusive way, in bad faith. This *exceptio* is today covered by the broader provisions of Arts 281, 288 and 200 CC.
52. Of the court rulings, *see* AP (in Plenary Session) 821/1977, NoB 1978, 669; AP 398/1975, NoB 1975, 1164; AP 848/1988, HellD 1990, 321; AP 925/1991, NoB 1992, 550; AP 672/1993, HellD 1994, 1271; AP 1023/1993, HellD 1994, 1564; AP 1198/1995, DEE 1995, 982.

act which is inconsistent with a prohibitive provision of law), while, as we have already said, Articles 281 and 288 CC regulate the exercise of rights and obligations. Special instances of the provision of Article 178 CC are regulated by the provision which follows in Article 179 CC (which declares null and void juridical acts which excessively restrict the freedom of the individual and legal transactions which, under special conditions, are usurious and improperly exploitative).

63. The provision of Article 197 CC requires the observance of bona fide conduct at the stage of negotiations for the conclusion of a contract, that is, before the contract has been concluded and, consequently, before the obligation arising from it has been generated, in which case there would be doubts as to whether Article 288 CC were applicable.

64. Finally, the provision of Article 388 CC is simply a special application of Article 288 CC as to the instance of an unforeseen change in circumstances, after the conclusion of a reciprocal contract, which seriously disturbs the balance of the contract. This more particular provision, on the strict conditions which it stipulates, gives to the judge the creative scope to adjust or dissolve the contract. If this did not exist, there would still be the possibility of recourse to the provision of Article 288 CC, which is perhaps less drastic as to the creative initiative of the judge. Such recourse is today possible in instances where one of the conditions stipulated by Article 388 CC is lacking.

§9. Style of Contract Drafting

65. Legislation regulates the law of contracts with some claim to completeness. Even in the case of innominate contracts there are rules from the general part of the law of contracts ready for implementation. Consequently, brief texts of contracts would be as a rule sufficient. Nevertheless, Greek lawyers who draft the texts of contracts and notaries public in practice resort to lengthy texts, frequently reiterating what would anyway have force by virtue of the law.

Moreover, in many instances there are standardized texts (often in printed form) of contracts with blanks to be completed in the particular instance. Such standardized drafts, where they have been formulated by the legal services of major enterprises, banks, for instance, are marked by greater clarity and exactness. However, recently a theoretical elaboration of the problem of the drafting of contracts, both from a technical and a legal point of view has begun, with the shaping of criteria and instructions for future contracting parties in negotiating the text of their contract as it is drafted, on the basis of business needs.[53]

Any lack of clarity can be dealt with by means of interpretation. Moreover, any gaps in contracts are filled by (in this case, supplementary) interpretation. In the case of such gaps in contracts there are also supplementary rules of law. Interpretation and the filling of gaps (together with the relation between supplementary interpretation and supplementary rules) will be dealt with at the appropriate point (paragraphs 170 et seq.).

---

53. *See* Liappis, Drafting of Contracts, 2003.

§10. Sources of the Law of Contracts

66. As we have said, the CC follows the five-fold division, as does the BGB, into General Principles, Law of Obligations, Law of Real Rights, Family Law and Law of Succession. The second of these five parts (which are termed 'books') – Law of Obligations – contained in Articles 287–946, is the main source of the rules of the law of contract. Another important source of these is the basic chapter of the first book (General Principles), contained in Articles 127–200, which regulates in greater abstraction the law of juridical acts (and therefore that of both unilateral acts and contracts). In the three chapters of the General Principles which follow (Articles 201–239) three more particular issues concerning juridical acts, and therefore contracts, are regulated – conditions, representation and approval of a contract by a third party.

In order to give a clearer picture, we quote below all the chapter headings (with, in parentheses, the numbers of the articles which fall within each chapter) of the First (General Principles) and the Second (Law of Obligations) Books of the CC.

Book One, General Principles:

Rules of law in general (1-3), Private international law (4-33), Natural person (34-60), Legal persons (61-126), Juridical acts (127-200), Conditions and terms (201-210), Representation and power of attorney (211-235), Consent and approval (236-239), Time limits (240-246), Prescription and term of extinction (247-280), Exercise of rights, self-redress, self-defence and state of emergency (281-286).

Book Two, Law of Obligations:

Obligation to perform in general (287-334), Impossibility to perform and default of debtor (335-348), Default of creditor (349-360), Contractual obligations in general (361-373), Principles in reciprocal contracts (374-388), Contractual rescission (389-401), Earnest and penalty clause (402-409), Contract in favour of or burdening a third party (410-415), Extinction of obligations (416-454), Assignment (455-470), Assumption of debt (471-479), Joint and several obligation (480-495), Donation (496-512), Sale and exchange (513-573), Lease of thing (574-618), Lease of agricultural land or other fruit-bearing thing (619-640), Lease of land in consideration of a share in the produce (641-647), Contract for service (648-680), Contract for work (681-702), Brokerage (703-708), Announcement of reward (709-712), Mandate (713-729), Management of another person's affairs (730-740), Partnership (741-784), Community of rights/ Joint rights (785-805), Loan (806-809), Loan for use (810-821), Deposit (822-833), Liability of innkeepers (834-839), Life annuity (840-843), Gaming and betting (844-846), Guarantee (847-870), Compromise (871-872), Abstract promise or acknowledgment of debt (873-875), Delegation (to collect payment) (876-887), Bearer bonds (888-900), Exhibition of a thing (901-903), Unjust enrichment (904-913), Torts (914-938), Creditors' defrauding (939-946).

67. Apart from the CC, there are special laws which regulate either special contracts of particular social importance or those which have taken shape recently as a result of the modern form of the economy or special problems, particularly protection of the weaker contracting party. We note below the most important of such laws (of comparatively recent date):

- PrD 34/1995 (codification of provisions of laws on professional leases), as amended mainly by Law 2741/1999.
- Laws 1598/1986, 1703/1987, 1898/1990 and 1953/1991, and 2235/1994 on lease of a residence.
- Law 1652/1986, on the 'time-sharing' contract (*see also* PrD 182/1999).
- Law 1665/1986, as amended, *inter alia*, by Law 3483/2006, on the leasing contract.
- Law 2251/1994, as amended mainly by Law 3587/2007, on consumer protection, which also serves as the adjustment of Greek legislation to Community Directives on defective products liability, on abusive general terms of business, on cancellation of contracts concluded away from business premises, etc.
- Law 2532/1997, whereby the United Nations Convention on Contracts for the International Sale of Goods was ratified.
- Law 2844/2000, on contracts on movables or claims subject to publication and on other contracts for the provision of security.
- Law 3043/2002, on seller's liability for defective goods and lack of agreed qualities (i.e., on conformity with the contract), which also serves as adjustment to the relevant Community Directive and modifies the provisions of CC on sale contract.

68. Laws are officially published in the *Government Gazette*, but are more accessible through collections of legislation, the best known of which are the *'Kodikas Nomikou Vimatos'*, published each year (in issues which appear periodically – usually each month) by the Athens Bar Association and the *'Raptarchis'* collection (named after its founder), which today is under the supervision of the Ministry to the Prime Minister and which sets out legislation by subject-matter in its entirety in the form of a loose-leaf publication. There are, of course, many other private publications of the more important laws. Court rulings are published chiefly in legal periodicals – those of the Court of Cassation of Areios Pagos exhaustively and those of the other courts selectively. The most important of these periodicals are given in the list of abbreviations and the main bibliography in the selected bibliography which follows. Both laws and court rulings can be found on the Internet, particularly on the web pages *http://lawdb.intrasoftnet.com* and www.dsanet.gr. The recent court rulings of Areios Pagos can be found on the web page www. areiospagos.gr.

acceptance, in which case this prevails over any other understanding. Since the offeror can perform the greater act – preclusion of the binding effect of the offer – he can also perform the lesser – setting of a time-limit.

On the elapse of the offer's period of force, it is extinguished. On delayed acceptance, *see* under C. *infra.* Extinction of the offer also occurs if it is rejected by the offeree (Article 187 CC). On the other hand, extinction of the offer is not occasioned, provided, of course, that the contrary cannot be deduced from it, if the offeror or offeree has died or become incapable of concluding any juridical act in the period between offer and acceptance (Article 188 CC). In this case, they are succeeded by their heirs or any necessary declaration of will is undertaken by their legal representative, as the case may be.

A consequence of the binding nature of the offer is that its revocation, taking place within the period when it is binding, is null and void. Any subsequent acceptance brings about – in spite of its 'revocation' – conclusion of the contract. If the offeror insists on the 'revocation', he breaks the contractual obligation stemming from the contract concluded. That is to say, contractual liability arises and he is obliged either to perform the contract or to pay compensation and, indeed, to compensate both for positive damage (*damnum emergens*) and lost profit (*lucrum cessans – see* paragraphs 313 et seq. *infra*). If the contract is not concluded, the offeror may owe compensation for precontractual fault (*see* paragraphs 88 et seq. *infra*).

72. The offer must be distinguished from:

(a) *An invitation to submit an offer – Invitatio ad offerendum:* Here the recipient of the invitation is called upon to submit an offer himself. The person who issues the invitation, who is not bound by it, if the offer of the recipient of his invitation reaches him, may accept it, in which case a contract is concluded, or reject it. In theory, the distinction between an offer and an invitation to make an offer is an easy one to make. The former embodies a declaration of will for the production of results in law. The offeror is bound, at least in the sense of the definitive nature of his declaration, that is, in the sense that he does not need to do anything else for the contract to be concluded. By acceptance alone on the part of the offeree, the contract is concluded. In practice, however, the distinction creates difficulties. In the last resort, the solution, as to whether it is an offer or simply an invitation, will be supplied by the interpretation of the declaration. The placing of goods in a shop window is usually interpreted in Greece as simply an invitation to the public. We must, however, at least see the placing of goods with a price label on the shelves of a *self-service* shop as an offer, so that on their selection by the consumer and presentation at the check-out, a contract is deemed to have been concluded. In the more particular case of auction sales, Article 199 of the CC stipulates that the contract, provided that in the specific instance it is not to be concluded otherwise, is completed on the fall of the hammer. That is, the fall of the hammer constitutes the acceptance of the offer of the highest bidder, while an invitation to an auction sale is an invitation to submit offers.

(b) *A promise to contract:* This is a normal promissory contract, which is only preliminary in the sense that by it the parties undertake the (actionable) obligation to conclude a certain (definitive) contract (*see* Article 166 CC). For example, A and B agree that the former will, the following year, lease his house to the latter by a (new – definitive) contract. The parties are bound as of now, and if either of them fails to conform, that is, refuses to conclude the definitive contract, he will be liable for breach of contract (i.e., of the promise to contract). Unlike a promise to contract, the offer is a declaration of will of one person which awaits the acceptance of the other party for a contract to be concluded. Thus there can be an offer, for example, for the conclusion of a promise to contract.

(c) *The option contract:* This is a contract by which one of the two parties is given the right to bring about by his *unilateral declaration* to the other party the extension of an existing contract or the conclusion of a new contract with a content determined by the two parties as of now. The question of whether this new contractual relation will be generated is the right and option of the one party, who is not bound to exercise it. This is the basic difference between an option contract and a promise to contract, since in the case of the latter, both parties have bound themselves to conclude the definitive contract. Here too, the difference from an offer will be obvious.

C. Acceptance: Conclusion of a Contract

73. Acceptance by the offeree is also a declaration of will which must reach the offeror (Article 189 CC). The time within which acceptance must take place is the period during which the offer is in force (*see* section B. *supra*). Delayed acceptance does not produce results (i.e., the conclusion of a contract), but it may be regarded as a new offer (counter-offer) to the initial offeror. Acceptance with amendments is regarded as declining, with a new offer (Article 191 CC). Acceptance may take place tacitly (if, of course, a specific form is not required for the contract, *see* paragraphs 78 et seq. *infra*) or be concluded from the general conduct of the offeree.

74. The point in time at which the contract is regarded as having been concluded is that at which the acceptance reaches the offeror. By way of exception, the declaration of acceptance suffices, without it being necessary for it to reach the offeror, if this can be concluded from the content of the offer or from common usages or from special circumstances or, in principle, if acceptance is made by means of a notarial document (Articles 192–194 CC).

Articles 195 and 196 regulate the problem of *dissent* (*dissensus*). If the offer and the acceptance do not coincide at all their points (terms) and the parties are aware of this (*patent* dissent), the contract will be deemed not to have been concluded, unless it can be deduced that the parties did not make the contract dependent on the points at which coincidence has not been achieved (e.g., they are non-substantial). If the parties are not aware of the non-coincidence at certain points and regard the contract as being jointly admitted at all points (latent dissent), the contract has force without the points of disagreement, provided that it can be deduced that the contract would have been concluded without the parties deciding upon these points.

II. Intention to Create Legal Relations

75. As has been explained above (paragraphs 14 et seq.), in distinguishing contractual relations from accommodation agreements and natural obligations, a condition for a contract, and, more generally, for any juridical act (even unilateral) is that there should be an intention to create a relation in law, that is, an intention of binding oneself. This, however, will not be judged on purely subjective criteria. Here too, there is an issue of interpretation. The question of whether the conduct of a person will be interpreted as an act of self-binding or an externalization, legally irrelevant, of a wish depends not only on the will of the person but on the other interpretative criteria, chiefly good faith, which takes into account the question of what possibilities of understanding this conduct existed (*see* paragraphs 107, 173 et seq. *infra*). If the absence of an intention to be bound in law was not discernible, interpretation will lead obviously to acceptance of the binding character of the declaration and the declarant will probably be referred to its annulment on the ground of error, if the conditions for this are fulfilled.

III. Consideration

76. As has already been pointed out in the historical background of the law of contract (paragraph 26 *supra*), Greek law regards 'consensus' as being basically sufficient for the conclusion of a contract. The grounds for the force and binding nature of the contract is the mere coincidence of the will of the two parties – *consensus* (*solus consensus obligat*). The meeting of the wills of the parties has in principle this binding force, without there being any need for the agreement to contain a just cause and without its force depending upon any counter-performance (quid pro quo) or consideration or any other justification for the undertaking of the contractual obligations. This is by no means self-evident. At other periods and in other systems of law, grounds for the production of the legal effect of the contract have been or are other factors also or chiefly other factors, such as the conclusion of a certain type of contract (one of the *numerus clausus* of recognized kinds of contract – Roman law) or a just cause of obligations (French law) or the existence of a consideration for the performance (Anglo-Saxon law) or the existence of a content which corresponds to the principles of social life (former socialist laws), etc.

The most characteristic exception to the principle that *solus consensus obligat* is furnished by Anglo-Saxon systems of law. In England, for contracts to have binding force, the coincidence of the wills of the parties is not sufficient. The promise given by one of the parties does not on its own bind him and no contractual claim arises for the other party. For this purpose it is required that, respectively, the promisor acquires a right or has a lawful interest or some economic benefit from the contract or that the other party suffers some prejudice or loss or undertakes some responsibility. What is required, that is to say, is that there should be an economic counterbalance to the contractual performance of the promise for counterbalance which is given by the promisee and constitutes in some way the price by which the promise is bought. This condition, the so-called consideration ('I bind myself because I consider that I shall receive some recompense'), is not a requirement only where the contract is made in solemn form, the form of the sealed document (contracts under seal or deed), which, where observed, is sufficient and is alone the reason for the contract having force. Another exception (binding by the coincidence of the declarations of will alone) may be derived from the principle of equity. By virtue of this, the promisee is provided with a plea (promissory estoppel) against a promisor who has invoked the absence of a consideration if the former believed in the valid undertaking of an obligation and proceeded to any act prejudicial to himself.[55] The chief practical importance, of course, of the doctrine of the consideration lies in donations, which, because of the absence of this condition, must be made in solemn form. However, most continental systems of law also require for donations a certain (even if only different) form.[56] This shows precisely that these laws recognize, in the last analysis, the full force of an informal contractual promise only when this is based on the idea of reciprocity, the expectation of an economic counterbalance, which means that the principle that 'the promise alone is binding' should not be understood in an absolute manner.

77. Apart from this, the doctrine of self-binding by the agreement alone has lost much of its former prestige and force. Freedom of contract, of course, has its foundation and justification in the autonomy and self-commitment of the individual. Nonetheless, a condition for this moral foundation is the existence of circumstances which make possible the exercise of this freedom. This need leads usually to legislative interventions in the contract to protect the interests both of the weaker party (the consumer is an example, but not the only one) and of the wider socio-economic effects of some substantial transactions. Thus many restrictions on the freedom of contract have been introduced by mandatory rules, which usually concern the content of the contract, but which also not infrequently go so far as to impose an obligation to conclude a contract or to prohibit the conclusion of a contract without the permission of the competent authority, etc.[57]

55. On the significance of promissory estoppel, *see* Denning, The Discipline of Law, 1979, 5th Part, p. 195 et seq. Earlier attempts – particularly of Lord Mansfield, late 18th century – to achieve recognition of the moral consideration also were not, or at least not fully, successful.
56. *See* Art. 498 § I of the Greek Civil Code (para. 392 *infra*). Art. 931 of the French Civil Code, §518, I of the German Civil Code, etc.
57. Examples: Law 489/1976 (Art. 2), as amended, requires the owner or possessor of a motor vehicle to conclude (with any insurance company) a contract for the insurance of his civil liability arising from the vehicle in respect of third parties; Law 2643/1998 (Arts 2 and 3), as amended, imposes, on certain terms, on public services, public law legal persons, and public and private enterprises the obligation of a certain percentage of the staff whom they engage being drawn from large families, the handicapped and war wounded, members of the National Resistance, etc.; Law 3959/2011 (Art. 2) prohibits an enterprise with a dominant position in the market from making abusive use of its position: e.g., by unjustified refusal to conclude a contract (*see also* Art. 82 – formerly Art. 86 – of the Treaty of the European Community); an obligation to conclude a contract may stem from the general clauses of Arts 178 and 281 on *boni mores* and abuse of a right in a specific case, e.g., for the avoidance of discrimination, etc.; *see also supra* para. 34 on restrictions for the protection of the consumer. Former prohibitions and restrictions of the Greek monetary legislation in the interests of the protection of the national currency have been to a great extent progressively repealed, in accordance with the rules and principles of the European Union.

In spite of these various restrictions, the binding nature of consensus alone remains the rule. The condition of a consideration does not exist in Greek law.

§2. Formal and Evidential Requirements

I. Formal Requirements

78. The CC establishes *the principle of informality of juridical acts* (*freedom of form*), that is, the rule of there being no requirement of a contractual form (*informal acts – argumentum e contrario* from Article 158 CC, according to which: 'Compliance with form for a juridical act shall only be required when the law so provides.'). This is an extrapolation from the principle that *solus consensus obligat*. A form is provided only for special types of juridical act (*formal or solemn acts*).

Here we need to distinguish between a constitutive form (*ad solemnitatem*) and an evidential form (*ad probationem*). The former (which is meant in Article 158 CC) is required for the juridical act to exist, for it to be constituted. Without it, the juridical act is invalid, that is, it is regarded as not having occurred (Article 180 CC). The latter is not needed for the juridical act to be valid; without its observance, the act is valid, but its proof becomes difficult or perhaps impossible. The document serves precisely as proof of it. In practical terms, that is, the evidential form may be valuable, but only the constitutive form may be a condition for a contract (on the evidential form, *see* II *infra*).

79. A (constitutive) form may be stipulated by law or by private autonomy.

Examples of a form stipulated by law are:

- Article 498, §1: 'A notarial deed shall be required for the constitution of a donation.' Included here is the gratuitous transfer of a right, not the gratuitous cession of its use (only), i.e., a loan for use (Article 810 CC). One reason for the requirement of a form for a donation is the need for caution on the part of the donor and his deterrence from hasty decisions, given that he may not be conscious of the consequences when a simple promise is made. It is for precisely this reason that in the case of the donation of a movable, where the promise of the donor, although informal, has been fulfilled, that is, where the donor has physically delivered the gift (and therefore he has experienced the alienation of the gift in a perceptible manner), the donation becomes valid (Article 498, §2 CC).
- Article 849, subparagraph 1: 'A guarantee shall be null and void if it has not been declared in writing.' Here a private document is sufficient. This also suffices to cover the declaration of the guarantor, but not necessarily the consensus (required for the guarantee contract) of the creditor. Here also, the lack of a written document shall be covered to the extent that the guarantor has paid the debt (Article 849, subparagraph 2 CC).
- Amendments to formal contracts or promises to formal contracts are subject to the form of the main contract (Articles 164, 166 CC). Furthermore, a power of

attorney for the undertaking of a formal juridical act is subject to the form of this juridical act (Article 217, §2 CC).

- According to Article 369, contracts [here are meant promissory contracts and *a fortiori*, real contracts, see, for example, Article 1033, etc.] concerning a right in rem on immovables are required to be concluded in the presence of a notary.

80. Of the forms imposed by law, the simplest is the *private document.* A necessary condition is that it should be signed in his own hand by the person issuing it. (However, according to Article 163 CC, the printing of a signature through a mechanical device shall be equivalent to a handwritten signature if it is affixed on a great number of bearer securities). Today, electronic documents (i.e., data in electronic form serving as a method of authentication of a document) are also accepted. An electronic signature is understood in the sense of Article 2, No. 1 of Community Directive 99/93 (which became domestic law in Greece by PrD 150/2001). The requirement of signature is also met, of course, by a public document. In certain cases, the law, as we have seen, requires a *notarial document.* This is drawn up by a notary public, who is a public officer (also charged with other duties, for example, in the procedure of judicial enforcement), in accordance with the formulae laid down by the code governing notaries public. Thus the notarial deed is a public document. In the case of particular acts, *another public document* is called for (e.g., the renunciation of an inheritance takes place by a declaration made to the registrar of the competent court for the succession – Article 1848 CC).

In all these solemn contracts, the reason for the generation of the legal effect is again the consensus of the parties. Consequently, this is not a case of 'contracts' under seal as in English law (which in essence are unilateral juridical acts, binding a person not because he has consented, but because he has attached his seal to his declaration and delivered it as 'his act and deed'). Such contracts under seal are unknown to Greek law.

81. If a form has been stipulated for the juridical act by the parties themselves, failure to observe it also entails nullity, unless the parties did not will this consequence. It is precisely for this reason that the performance of the juridical act in awareness of the absence of this form remedies such absence (Article 159, §2 CC).

On the other hand, nullity arising from non-observance of the form imposed by law is very difficult to remedy. This legal formality, amongst its other aims, serves the security of transactions. The relevant rule is rigid law (*jus strictum*). Exceptions have been mentioned above (paragraph 75). In extreme cases where this rigidity seems to be unjustifiable, recourse to the provision on abuse of a right (Article 281 CC) is possible. In the past, this was denied by court rulings, in view of the strictness of the provisions on form. Later, however, the Court of Cassation of Areios Pagos changed its rulings: since 1964 it has accepted that the invocation of the nullity of a sale of an immovable because the form was not observed is abusive if the purchaser has for many years made use of the property under the eyes of the vendor who invokes this nullity.[58]

58. See, *inter alia,* AP 528/1964, NoB 1965, 122; AP 652/1974, NoB 1975, 271.

II. Evidential Requirements: Proof – Legal Presumptions

82. The rules of proof are embodied in the Code of Civil Procedure (CCPr), which deals with them at length (Articles 335–465). These rules traditionally belong to the subject-matter of civil procedure. On the other hand, matters of burden of proof belong to a great extent to substantive law and, consequently, also to the law of contract. Here, leaving aside burden of proof, which will be dealt with *infra* (section III), we shall give only a summary sketch of the means of proof, on the one hand, and the weight of these means, on the other.

The CCPr provides for the following as means of proof: the confession, the viewing of the object of litigation (as a direct proof), experts' reports, testimony, the examination of parties, judicial presumptions (*see* paragraph 83 in fine, *infra*) and documentary evidence. In addition, the court may take into account ex officio the general teachings of human experience (e.g., a general knowledge of contemporary life, scientific knowledge accessible to everyone, etc.), events which have occurred and which are known to all, so that there are no reasonable grounds for them to be disputed, as well as facts known to the court from other proceedings held before it.

Articles 901–903 CC also refer to direct proof. These establish, on certain conditions, the obligation of the possessor of a thing or document to show it to a person if such exhibition is necessary for the exercise of claims of that person or if the person in question has another legal interest, for example, in being informed of the content of the document.[59]

83. Proof is often facilitated by *presumptions*, that is, by conclusions about unknown facts, drawn from known, proven facts. If the law entails this conclusion, we speak of *legal presumptions*. Usually, presumptions are *rebuttable*, that is, they may be overturned if proof to the contrary is adduced. The legal rebuttable presumption, then, serves in the last analysis to shift the burden of proof on to the party who seeks to rebut the presumption (*see* section III *infra*). A classic example of a legal rebuttable presumption is the presumption of paternity (Article 1465 CC, following the reform of family law in 1983), according to which a child born during the marriage of its mother or within 300 days from the dissolution or annulment of the marriage (a certain or proven fact) is presumed to have as its father the husband of the mother (a fact which is not certain and, without the presumption, would have to be proven by other means). Anyone who disputes the paternity of the husband (and not the person who invokes it) bears the burden of proving that the husband was not the father, according to the judicial procedure of challenging the paternity provided for in Articles 1467 et seq. CC. An example of a legal rebuttable presumption from the law of contracts: the fault of the debtor in the case of impossibility or delay of performance, which is a condition for certain consequences and particularly for the obligation of compensation, is presumed from the sole fact of the impossibility or delay (*see* particularly Articles 335–336 and 340–342 CC). Thus the creditor, in exercising his rights on breach of contract, does not need to prove the fault of the debtor. The latter, however, may be

---

59. The risk and the expenses of such exhibition are borne by the person who requires it. The possessor of the thing or document may refuse the exhibition, if the expenses are not prepaid and security against possible prejudice is not provided.

acquitted if he proves that he is not at fault for the impossibility or delay. That is, we have here a shifting of the burden of proof of the fault from the creditor to the debtor.

Where counterproof against legal presumptions is not permitted, we speak of *irrebuttable presumptions*, which, however, are rare. In essence, these are not real presumptions, but a way employed by the legislator of expressing his decision on the deduction of a legal effect which is based on a known and proven fact. For example, in Article 1439, §3 of the CC (following the reform), the law adduces from the fact of two years' continuous separation of the spouses an irrebutable presumption of the breakdown of their relations, which constitutes grounds for divorce. This instance may bear a resemblance in its result to legal fictions, where the law accepts that something is a fact when this is not the case (or vice versa), in order to achieve the occurrence of a legal effect.

By way of contrast with legal presumptions, we speak of *factual presumptions* (*inferences*) where it is not the law but the administrator of the law (normally the judge; hence we speak of *judicial presumptions*) who adduces from a known fact or from some indication conclusions as to an unknown fact (requiring proof) and more generally when we employ judgments which assist (usually indirectly) in the discovery of the truth in a dispute.

84. In practice, the two most important means of proof are witnesses and documentary evidence, but the admissibility of witnesses' testimony is only the exception. The rule is that contracts (with which we are concerned here) must be proven in writing. Witnesses are permitted chiefly when the economic value of the contract is very small, when there is a beginning of written proof (Article 394 §la CCPr), that is, when we have a document which, while it does not prove the fact requiring proof, nevertheless lends it probability (e.g., the document has been drawn up with a different purpose and simply mentions in passing the fact to be proven); when written proof has been rendered impossible; and, when, by reason of the nature of the contract or the special circumstances, proof by testimony would appear justified. This last exception is a broad one, since it includes most commercial transactions. Written proof includes public (e.g., notarial) or private documents. The distinction between documents is of basic significance when they are required as a constitutive form of a juridical act (*see* section I *supra*, also on the function of the notary). In the law of proof, this is of importance as to their evaluation by the courts.

85. The evaluation of evidence is not subject to strict rules. In principle, the judge assesses the means of proof freely and decides according to his conviction as to the truth of the allegations. He is bound only in those instances where the law expressly determines the probative force of a means of proof, which it does in the case of documents and confessions. Thus an oral or written confession before the court (and not an extra-judicial admission, which is assessed freely) is considered in principle full proof. The law also grants documents increased probative force as against other means, but it distinguishes between public and private documents. The former, which include chiefly notarial documents, constitute full proof *against all persons* as to facts or declarations which are certified by the document, provided that the public functionary who has issued the document had the competence to make this certification, while private documents provide proof only against the person who signed the private document. Moreover, a counterproof against the former is allowed only by way of exception. The principal way for their probative force to be set aside is for them to be successfully challenged for falsification, which, of course, also applies to private documents. In the case of the latter, however, the litigant invoking them must prove (by any means of proof) their authenticity (i.e., the fact that they originate with the person alleged to have signed them) if his opponent contests this authenticity.

III. Burden of Proof

86. A general rule as to who bears the burden of proof is that stipulated in Article 338 CCPr, according to which each party has to prove those facts which are necessary for the grounds of his claim or counter-claim. In each special legal relationship it will be decided who proves what. The rules which found the legal relationship, and, therefore, the rules of substantive law (usually of the CC), which either render specific the above general rule or introduce deviations, etc., must be taken into account. Normally the plaintiff must prove all the actual facts which give grounds for his affirmative defences. In the account of the conditions for the validity of a contract and of breach of contract in the present monograph, the solutions as to the burden of proof will be specified where necessary. As a general rule in the law of contracts, we can say that the plaintiff bears the burden of proving the conclusion, the content of the contract and its breach by the defendant, while the latter has to prove, for example, its extinction by payment. The defendant also has to prove lack of fault for his breach of contract, in order to be relieved of the obligation of compensation. This is because as to fault, which is in principle required for contractual liability (*see* Chapter 6 *infra*), the law establishes, as we have said, a legal presumption in favour of the creditor to the effect that the breach is due to the fault of the debtor, a presumption which the debtor may overturn by furnishing the above proof. More generally also, the law may establish presumptions when it wishes to facilitate proof in favour of one of the parties, thus shifting the burden of proof on to the other. On the distinctions between presumptions, *see* section II *supra*.

87. As to the distinction between *'obligations de résultat'* and *'obligations de moyens'*, which is maintained in France, chiefly for reasons of the burden of proof, an account has been given above (paragraph 18 *supra*), in which it was explained why, whereas in Greek law such a variety of obligations exists, there is no need for the distinction in question to be made. As to proof, what has been said applies: that is, that the creditor must prove, on the one hand, the existence and the content of the contract – and therefore whether the debtor owed certain forms of conduct or a result or, perhaps, both – and, on the other, the breach of the contract, while the burden of proof of lack of fault lies with the debtor.

§3. Liability and Negotiations

I. Grounds of Precontractual Liability

88. At the stage of negotiation on the conclusion of a contract, the parties do not as yet have any contractual liability. This begins on the conclusion of the contract. This, however, does not mean that the parties do not have to observe certain 'rules' of conduct between themselves and that they do not have any liability if, for example, they tell lies or are negligent, etc. Regardless of the existence of special legislative provision, in most legal systems there is a tendency for certain 'precontractual' liability of the parties to be accepted, but disputes arise as to its foundation. One view finds no legislative support for such liability other than the provisions on torts. According to another opinion, however, the legal treatment of this liability must bear a greater resemblance to contractual liability, since the parties have already been in bargaining contact between themselves for purposes of the conclusion of a contract.

In Greek law such disputations existed before the coming into force of the CC, since this expressly resolved the issue in Articles 197–198 and only where gaps have remained in secondary issues is it still disputed whether an analogy with contractual liability or with delictual liability is more appropriate. Thus Article 197 CC provides that: 'In the course of negotiations for the conclusion of a contract, the parties shall be reciprocally bound to adopt the conduct which is dictated by good faith and common usages', while Article 198, §1 CC lays down that: 'A person who in the course of negotiations for the conclusion of a contract has through his fault caused prejudice to the other party shall be liable for compensation even if the contract has not been concluded.'

The liability, therefore, today is grounded directly in the law. It forms a special kind between contractual and delictual liability.

89. Thus the CC gives rise to a tripartite system of liability which is based on the different degree of 'intensity' of the relations of the two parties between whom the question of liability arises:

(a) The relations which are created by the sole fact that their subjects belong to the same community of law and which impose on all a reciprocal obligation of respect for their goods are looser than in the instances which follow. A consequence in the event of infringement is chiefly the implementation of tortious liability (Articles 914 et seq. CC). The general duty to respect the rights of others is converted into an obligation between two persons from the moment that the right is infringed. At that point, if certain other conditions are fulfilled (Article 914 CC), an obligation arises, consisting in the obligation of compensation.
(b) More intense, as compared with the above, are the relations between those who are already engaged in negotiation for the conclusion of a contract, that is, who are already in bargaining contact. Here (Article 197 CC) we have a case of obligation 'in the making' which justifies special precontractual liability at the stage of negotiation. At this stage, good faith makes more demands upon the

negotiators than it did before their bargaining contact began (i.e., in instance (a)).[60]

(c) Even closer are the relations created by what is now the completed bond of obligation (contractual liability or, more generally, liability from pre-existing obligation). The differentiation of their consequences from those of the second category is also justified. This is apparent chiefly in contracts. In reality it cannot be accepted that the parties have the same weight of liability before and after the crucial point in time of the conclusion of the contract. It is from precisely this point, even by applying generally accepted views and the general understanding, that the legal engagement in the proper sense begins. This explains why the obligations which stem from good faith and their infringement have consequences of differing intensity before and after this point in time.[61]

II. Conditions of Liability: Particularly Bona Fide Conduct

90. Article 197 requires from negotiators conduct which is bona fide (and in accordance with common usage). Again it is good faith which – in accordance with the constant policy of the Greek legislator – provides the yardstick for the conduct of the parties. What is meant here is objective good faith, as to the meaning of which (and of common usages) we may refer to what has been said above (paragraphs 54 et seq.). Naturally, good faith does not demand the conclusion of the contract, since contractual freedom covers the freedom to conclude or not to conclude the contract up to the point when the conclusion is effected (if it is effected) or, when, at least, one party makes a binding offer (*see* paragraphs 69 et seq. *supra*). The interruption of the negotiations in itself, that is, their failure, is in no way contrary to good faith. A basic condition, then, for precontractual liability to be generated is conduct in bad faith. In greater detail, the conditions for this liability are the following:

(a) *Stage of negotiations for the conclusion of a contract*: This stage begins from the moment when the two parties interested in the conclusion of a contract come into bargaining contact for this purpose and it ends with the conclusion of the contract or the suspension or the final failure of negotiations.

(b) *Conduct in bad faith:* This means violation of the principles of objective good faith and common usage. For example, the parties, while they do not have to give all the information in their possession, must not conceal facts or qualities, etc., which they know will be useful for the other party. Such obligations did not exist before negotiations, with, for example, social contact alone. Moreover, the negotiators must take measures for the protection of the goods (health, honour, etc.) of the other party, must respect the use of his time, must be conscientious, etc.

(c) *The fault of the party:* For the generation of the (precontractual) obligation of compensation, Article 198 also requires *the fault of the party* (*culpa in contrahendo*).

---

60. *See* para. 90 (b) *infra, also* para. 91, *in fine* – as to tortious liability or precontractual liability of a minor.

61. *See* para. 90 (under (c)) and particularly paras 92 et seq. *infra.*

Conduct in bad faith is the objective condition. The conduct at fault (i.e., wilful or negligent conduct, whether the negligence is gross or even slight) is the subjective condition (for more on fault, *see* paragraphs 252 et seq. *infra*). The plaintiff (injured party) bears the burden of proof of the bad faith. The same applies to proof of the fault, as is the case, that is, with delictual liability, since the presumption of fault which exists in contractual liability (and which transfers the burden of proof of the fault on to the debtor) is explained by the augmented liability which the legislator wished to shift on to the party who is engaged by the contractual bond – in this case non-existent. It must, however, be accepted that here too the rules of contracts on any reduced liability of the debtor as to the degree of fault have force. For example, a donor is liable only for wilful conduct and gross negligence (Article 499 §1 CC). Similarly, a person negotiating a donation to another will be liable only for wilful conduct and gross negligence also at the stage of negotiations.

(d) *Causing of prejudice to the other negotiator:* The prejudice must be in a causal relationship with the conduct which is due to bad faith and to fault.

91. Failure to conclude a contract is not a condition for precontractual liability. The conditions mentioned can occur whether or not a contract was subsequently concluded or was cancelled, etc.

A precontractual claim is subject, in accordance with the express provision of Article 198, §2 CC, *mutatis mutandis* to prescription of the tortious claim (Article 937 CC), that is, as a rule, to a five-year prescription, from the point where the injured party discovered the prejudice and that this was due to the other party, but in all cases to a twenty-year prescription from the occurrence of the conduct in bad faith.

It must be accepted that a person who does not have the capacity of concluding the contract which is being negotiated (*see* Articles 127 et seq. CC), and who therefore cannot bear contractual liability, for example, a minor, does not have precontractual liability arising from the negotiations on this contract either. His only liability will probably be tortious liability.[62]

III. Consequences: Negative Interest

92. The liability of the negotiator who has acted in bad faith and through his fault consists in an obligation to compensate the other party (Article 198, §I CC). The compensation will not be the *'positive interest' or (non-) performance damages* owed in the case of contractual liability, but the *'negative interest', or damages through relying on conduct of the other party* (e.g., on the validity of his declaration, on the honesty of his conduct, etc.).[63] This distinction requires further clarification.

When the cause in law of the liability is breach of contract, a logical consequence is that, in order to discover the prejudice to the creditor from non-performance (i.e.,

62. While full capacity for having contractual liability is acquired according to the Civil Code (Art. 127) on the completion of the 18th year, full capacity for tortious liability is acquired on completion of the 14th year (Arts 916, 917 CC).

63. *See* AP 969/1977, NoB 1978,895.

the prejudice which is in a causal relationship with non-performance), we must ask what the creditor would have had if the prejudicial event ('non-performance') had not taken place, in other words, what he would have had if a *positive event* (the performance of the contract) had taken place. We must look to the state of affairs which the performance of the contract would have brought about (*status ad quem*). It is for this reason that this compensation has been called *posi*tive interest or non-performance damages. By way of contrast, in the case of precontractual liability, the debtor owing the compensation did not have any obligation to furnish another (initial) performance, since the contract had not yet been concluded.[64] Here the reason in law for liability is the conduct in bad faith and the fault of the party who, betraying the trust shown by the other party, has caused him prejudice. Naturally, a logical consequence of this is that, for the latter's prejudice to be discovered, we shall take into account what he would have had if the prejudicial event had not taken place, that is, if the injuring party had not shown the conduct in bad faith and at fault and, thus, if an event had not occurred (negation of an event). Thus this compensation, whose purpose is to restore the status quo without the contract and negotiations, has been called negative interest or damage through reliance on conduct of the other party.[65] On the other hand, the injured party cannot seek that which he would have had if the contract on which the negotiations took place had been concluded, since the injuring party had no obligation to conclude it.

93. Logically, the interest must also be regarded as negative in the case of delictual liability. This is because the reason in law for the liability is the delictual conduct of the injuring party. Compensation must thus be calculated on the basis of what the injured party would have had if this conduct had been absent and not if an obligation (non-existent in this case) had been performed. Normally, however, the distinction between a positive and negative interest is confined to instances where there is a juridical act, or one is to be undertaken, between the injuring and injured parties, since it is only then that the dilemma arises as to whether the object of the compensation is what the injured party would have had if the contract had been performed (positive interest) or what he would have had if this had not been concluded and no preparatory work (e.g., negotiations) on it had taken place. As has been pointed out, the former may occur only if the contract has been concluded and remains in force, while, if it has not been concluded or has been concluded but is invalid or has been cancelled *ex post facto*, the injured party cannot rely upon a contractual commitment of the injuring party to seek to recover what he would have had from its performance

64. The same holds good (i.e., any compensation owed is negative interest) if the contract has been concluded but is invalid or has been cancelled *ex post facto* with retrospective results and for any reason compensation is owed. Here too there is no obligation to performance and, therefore, no non-performance damages. However, it was instances of precontractual fault (*culpa in contrahendo*) which *Rudolf Ihering* had chiefly in mind when he formulated the theory of negative interest in his work 'Culpa in contrahendo oder Schadenersatz bei nichtigen oder nicht zur Perfektion gelangten Verträgen', published in 1861 in *Jherings Jahrbücher für die Dogmatik des bürgerlichen Rechts,* Vol. 4, pp. I et seq.

65. In Germany, negative interest is sometimes sub-divided into *negatives Vertragsinteresse* (restoration of the status quo prior to the contract) and *Integritätsinteresse* (compensation for legal interests affected which must be protected from encroachments, regardless of the conclusion of any contract).

and, consequently, his compensation will consist of negative interest. In the case of delictual liability, on the other hand, one of the two horns of the dilemma cannot in the nature of things be an issue.

94. It is also possible that if the conduct in bad faith during negotiations had been absent, if, that is, the injuring party had conducted himself in accordance with good faith, he would have concluded such a contract with the injured party and he would now have had the obligation to perform it. In this case, the negative interest also covers non-performance damages. (That is why here we speak of 'quasi positive interest'). The problem which arises is one of causal connection. What is asked is whether in this case such a development can be regarded as being able to be expected. The burden of proof will naturally be borne by the injured party – the creditor. However, such proof will be extremely difficult, since it is difficult to regard something which depends upon the free will of the party (and he remains free to conclude or not conclude the contract) as a causal consequence of a previous act on his part. But even if proof is furnished to the effect that the contract would have been concluded, we must probably accept that good faith requires some reduction in the quasi positive interest which is owed. Lost opportunities always involve an element of uncertainty. We must also accept a similar reduction if the prejudice which the injured party invokes consists in the fact that he, by reason of his negotiations with the injuring party, declined another potentially profitable contract which otherwise he would have concluded, thus gaining the benefits from this.[66]

66. On the problem of the causal relation *see* paras 317 et seq., and on the problem of lost profits paras 313 et seq. *infra.*

Chapter 2. Conditions of Substantive Validity

§1. Capacity of the Parties

95. As to the subjects of contracts, and relations in law in general, the division of the legal capacities of a person into the *capacity of holding rights and duties* (which is a 'passive' capacity) and the *capacity of concluding juridical acts* (which is an 'active' capacity) is fundamental. The former is the capacity of a person to enjoy rights and to have duties. Everyone has this capacity from birth[67] to death (Article 34 CC). For this reason it is equivalent to the identity of the person, the personality. The latter is the capacity of a person to undertake legal transactions *in propria persona*, that is, to play an active part in economic and legal life, binding himself by his own acts. It is only natural that this capacity of concluding juridical acts is held basically only by mature persons who can, in principle, weigh the consequences of their acts. The Greek legislator has preferred, in the interests of the greater security of transactions, the strict system of the exact determination of the age on the completion of which those who up to that point have not held this capacity to conclude juridical acts acquire it. He has not left the issue of the capacity to conclude juridical acts, for example, to the appreciation of the maturity of the person by the judge, as is the case in other systems of law. Exceptions are naturally provided for in both cases (*see* section II *infra*).

In the case of foreigners, the capacity of holding rights and duties and the capacity to conclude juridical acts are governed, according to Greek private international law (Articles 5 and 7 CC), by the law of their nationality. In every other respect, a basic provision of the CC (Article 4) stipulates that foreigners enjoy the same civil rights as Greeks.

Equality before the law also exists today in matters of capacity between the two sexes. Thus, married women may, for example, engage in commercial acts or follow a profession without prior consent of their husbands being required.

I. Incapacity and Limited Capacity to Conclude Juridical Acts

96. Capacity to conclude juridical acts is regulated by the CC in Articles 127 et seq. Anyone who has completed his 18th year is an adult and has the capacity for any juridical act (Article 127 CC). Minors (under the age of 18) either lack capacity completely, that is, they are incapacitated from any juridical act (those under the age of 10) or are of limited legal capacity (those between the ages of 10 and 18). As to these, the law makes the following distinctions: all (those between 10 and 18) may enter into a juridical act from which they acquire simply and only a legal benefit (Article 134 CC). For example, they may conclude a contract of donation as donees, but not a contract by which they acquire obligations in parallel with rights, even if this

67. Even an embryo (*nasciturus*) has the capacity to be a holder of rights, on condition that it is born alive (Art. 36 CC).

is judged to be in economic terms a beneficial contract. To older minors the law gives certain other possibilities, the more important of which are: those who have completed their 14th year may freely dispose of anything which they earn from their individual work or which has been given to them to use or for them to dispose of freely (Article 135 CC), while when they have completed their fifteenth year, they may, with the general consent of the persons in whose care they are, conclude a contract for service as employees (Article 136 CC).

97. Apart from the question of age, mental and psychological, and in some cases, physical health are crucial. Thus, those who have been placed under judicial guardianship (instances of persons who, *inter alia*, by reason of psychological or mental disturbance or physical disability are unable, wholly or in part, to care for their affairs on their own, Articles 1666 et seq. CC) lack totally or partially capacity to conclude juridical acts. Placing of these persons under judicial guardianship is decided by the court on the application of the person him/herself or of his/her spouse or of his/her parents or children, or of the public prosecutor, or ex officio. When the individual is suffering exclusively from a physical handicap, the court decides only on the application of the person himself. Depending upon the circumstances, the court decides whether lack of capacity is total or partial.

98. All the above, that is, minors and those under judicial guardianship, enter into juridical acts as to which, in accordance with the distinctions made above, they are incapacitated through their statutory (legal) representatives (parents, guardians). If the court so decides, it may permit the person placed under judicial guardianship to undertake juridical acts himself, but with the consent of the judicial guardian. Otherwise, the juridical acts are null and void.

A certain flexibility is introduced into this strict system by Article 131 §1 of the CC. If a person suffering from psychological or mental disturbance who has not been placed under judicial guardianship enters into a juridical act, this will be null and void only if it is proven (by the person invoking the nullity) that at the time that the juridical act was entered into, the person concerned was in a state of psychological or mental disturbance which decisively limited the operation of his will. The same applies, more generally, if the person at the time of the juridical act, 'was not conscious of his acts' (e.g., because he was drunk). Such proof is not required, of course, if the person has been placed under judicial guardianship, in which case any act on his part, without the observance of the formalities of the law, is null and void, even if it is proven that at the moment of his entering into the juridical act, the person under judicial guardianship was experiencing a 'lucid interval' (*lucidum intervallum*). Here the security of transactions takes priority. Lifting of the judicial interdiction, if the reasons for this no longer apply, is, of course, possible (again by a court decision).

99. The burden of proof as to capacity to conclude a juridical act is borne, in accordance with the prevailing view, by the party who invokes the lack of capacity and not the one who invokes its existence. This should be accepted at least when we are dealing with an adult, since the instances of lack of capacity in this case are in fact exceptions. They are seen as such by the law, which takes as its starting-point the capacity of adults to conclude juridical acts as the rule. If, however, the age of a person is contested, this person bears the burden of proof.

II. Capacity of Legal Persons

100. Unions of persons or bodies which have not acquired a legal personality do not have the capacity of holding rights and duties or that of concluding juridical acts. Any property which they may 'acquire' belongs to their members. However, from the moment that they acquire legal personality, on the terms of the law (whether they are unions of persons, associations, companies, etc. or the entirety of some property dedicated to the service of a specific end, as in the case of the foundations of Article 108 CC), they have both capacities.[68] The capacity to hold rights and duties of legal persons does not extend, however, according to Article 62 CC, to relations in law which presuppose the characteristics of a natural person (e.g., marriage). The capacity to conclude juridical acts of a legal person is exercised by its 'will', which is basically expressed by the will of its organs, for example, of its administrative board (which may, of course, grant a power of attorney to other persons). Juridical acts entered into *within the bounds of his powers* by the organ administering the legal person are binding, according to Article 70 CC, on the legal person. From this formulation, it can be concluded that the CC has to a certain extent followed the English doctrine of *ultra vires*, since, *e contrario*, it is concluded that juridical acts which lie outside the bounds of the powers of the organ (as those are determined by the constitutive act or the articles of incorporation of the legal person – *see* Article 68 CC) are not binding on the legal person. What, of course, is being dealt with by this provision is not the capacity to conclude juridical acts of the legal person, but the power of representation of its organs. The need to protect the interests of the legal person (i.e., in the last analysis, its members) here prevails over the protection of third parties who enter into transactions in good faith with the legal person and the security of transactions.

101. Thus, in principle, the articles of incorporation of a legal person may limit the representative power of its administrative organs or simply limit the aims of the legal person and, thus – indirectly – the representative power of its organs, and these limitations have force as to third parties entering into transactions with it. More particularly, however, in the case of certain companies (particularly joint-stock companies and limited-liability companies), this regulation has been altered, thanks to the Community legislator. More specifically, by Article 22 PrD 409/1986, Greek legislation on joint-stock companies was adapted to the corresponding Community directives and the relevant provision was supplemented by the stipulation that acts of the board of directors of a joint-stock company 'even if they lie outside the aim of the company bind the company in respect of third parties, unless it is proven that the third party knew that the company's aim was being exceeded or ought to have known this'. The same provision makes it clear that 'the observance of the formalities of publication as to the articles of incorporation and amendments to them does not alone constitute proof'. Similar regulations are contained in PrD 419/1986 on limited-liability companies and Law 959/1979 (as amended by Laws 1892/1990 and 2987/2002) on shipping companies.

This new regulation has brought about a crucial change in the external (i.e., in respect of third parties) powers of the administrative organs of the above companies

68. Furthermore, according to Art. 71 CC, the legal person may have delictual liability from acts or omissions of its organs.

by extending them and constitutes a significant deviation from the general provisions of Articles 68 and 70 CC in the correct direction of strengthening the security of transactions and the protection of third parties who enter into transactions with the legal persons. The limitation of the representative power in respect of third parties of the administrative organs of the legal person in accordance with Articles 68 and 70 CC does indeed create problems not only for the speed but also for the security of transactions. The *ratio* of the limitation (protection of the legal person and its members in respect of its organs) is more appropriate to internal relations – relations of trust – and could be active only in those relations. There are other means of protecting legal persons in respect of their organs. The interests of third parties, that is, the protection of transactions in general, carries more weight.

§2. Defects of Consent

102. The contract is the expression *par excellence* of private autonomy in civil law. The declaration of the will of the consenting parties is the main condition for its conclusion. When, chiefly in the nineteenth century, 'subjective' theories were in the ascendant, the basis of the juridical act was the genuine will of the parties (will theory). If this were absent or suffered from some defect, the juridical act was deemed to be invalid. Later 'objective' theories, however, drawing their arguments from the need to protect the recipient of the declaration of will, attached greater importance to the objective meaning of the declaration and particularly to the question of how the recipient could understand it. According to these theories, the person making the declaration must be bound by the meaning of his declaration, even though he may have meant and wished something else.

103. Neither the autonomy of the will, on the one hand, nor the security of transactions and the confidence principle, on the other, can, however, be entirely sacrificed. Thus, in the end, intermediate and compromise views have prevailed. One such 'in-between' position was adopted by the CC chiefly by limiting the will theory, in line, anyway, with similar developments in other countries of Europe. Its regulation of this matter, which approaches most closely that of the BGB, but with a number of differences (particularly as to the manner in which the consequences take effect – *see* §4, paragraphs 151 et seq. *infra*), permits the parties who enter into a juridical act to invoke the fact that their genuine will was absent or defective only in certain circumstances and on certain conditions. This holds good in the case of a simulated declaration (Articles 138 et seq. CC), substantial error (Articles 140 et seq. CC), fraud (Articles 147 et seq. CC) and duress (Articles 150 et seq.). The Greek Civil Code approaches the leasio of Roman law, on strict objective and subjective terms, as a problem not of will, but of inadmissible content of the juridical act or of an illicit juridical act in general (Article 179 CC – *see* paragraph 150 *infra*).

I. Simulated Declaration

104. The declaration of will is 'simulated' when it was not seriously intended and made only in pretence (Article 138 §1 CC) and the recipient of the declaration, and not only the declarant, was aware of this.[69] Here we are dealing with a declaration, which is made by a party and which intentionally does not correspond to the party's genuine will. If the recipient of the simulated declaration is not aware of the simulation, we have a case of mental reservation (*reservatio mentalis*) on the part of the person making the declaration. Mental reservation could be regarded as a kind of simulation in the broad sense, since here too the person making the declaration does not seriously will what he declares, but the law does not permit the invocation of mental reservation, since it regards the recipient as deserving protection (*see* Article 139 CC). The juridical act will, that is, be valid in spite of the mental reservation.

105. In the case of simulation in the strict sense (i.e., where the recipient of the declaration is also aware that it is simulated) there is no need for protection of the parties and the CC provides for its nullity (Article 138 §1). For example, A transfers to B an immovable property simply in order to escape his creditors and not because he wished to transfer it in reality. If, however, there is latent in a simulated juridical act another which the parties really will, the simulated act is invalid, but that concealed in it will be valid if the parties willed this and if the conditions required for its conclusion are met (Article 138 §2 CC). For example, A sells an immovable property to B when in reality he wishes to make him a gift of it. This he does simply to avoid the higher taxes on a donation. The purchase price is simulated. The sale is null and void, but the donation will be, on the conditions mentioned, valid – and, of course, the tax on a donation will be paid.

106. In one instance a simulated juridical act will be deemed valid: if a third party, that is, persons other than the contracting parties, and providing that these parties were unaware of the simulation, would be prejudiced by nullity (Article 139 CC). Let us suppose that A sells an immovable to B and B (who is aware of the simulation and by reason of this knowledge has not acquired the ownership) subsequently sells and transfers it to C, who is in good faith (i.e., he is unaware of the simulation). For example: in the public transcription registers which C has consulted there is no record of the nullity of A and B's contract – *see* Article 1202 CC on how such a record can be made – nor does C know of the simulation from any other source. In spite of the fact that B was not the owner, C acquires ownership. The simulation cannot be argued against him. The same applies to creditors of B who are unaware of the simulation.

II. Error: Dissent

A. Error as to the Declaration, the Will, the Qualities

107. The CC, in dealing with the problem of error in Articles 140–146, avoids mention of the traditional instances of error derived from Roman law (e.g., *error in*

69. *See* AP 562/1976, ArchN 1977,16; AP 874/1996, HellD 1997, 809; AP 1162/2000, HellD 2001, 1296; AP 483/2005, HellD 2005, 1430; AP 713/2006, ArchN 2007, 202.

substantia, in persona, in corpore, in negotio, error juris, etc.) and confines itself basically to a distinction which it regards as crucial for the consequences: that between error as to the declaration (Articles 140 and 141 CC) and error as to the will (Article 143 CC). (The exact translation of the Greek terms is 'error *in* the declaration' and 'error *in* the will'). It also makes special provision, however, for error as to the qualities (Article 142 CC), on which disputes continue to this day, as in Germany, as to whether this belongs to error as to the declaration or error as to the will, or whether it constitutes a different, self-contained – as against these – third category of error. In all cases, the starting-point is the validity of the juridical act. The person entering into the juridical act, in exercising the right of self-determination, must have in principle the liability for any defective exercise of that right. The CC regards this liability as a necessary supplementation of self-determination. However, the will theory is not overlooked entirely. The possibility remains, on certain conditions, of a person in error achieving the *ex post facto* annulment of the juridical act.

Only if the so-called *will for action* is totally lacking (e.g., acts performed under physical force – *vis absoluta* – or reflex movements or in a state of hypnosis, etc.) is there no legally relevant act and the juridical act is regarded as non-existent. The same is maintained by one view when, although there is the will for action, there is no *will for juridical action*, the will, that is, that the act should have force as a juridical act (of whatever content). For example, a person in full awareness appends his signature to a text in the belief that it is merely a friendly letter (or, generally, not a legal text), but this contains the undertaking of an obligation in law. However, it would be more justifiable to accept the view that the issue of whether an act should be regarded as a juridical act or not, whether, that is, this act will having binding force or not, is a matter of interpretation. If the method of interpretation and the interpretative criteria which have force generally as to the interpretation of juridical acts[70] lead to the conclusion that the act must be considered as having a juridical character and thus a juridical act must be accepted, in all probability it remains possible for its author, who believed that he was not entering into a juridical act, on the terms which will be examined below, to annul the juridical act by reason of error. However, the usual instances of error will concern the *will which concerns*, directly or indirectly, not whether a juridical act has been concluded at all, but *the content of the juridical act.*[71]

1. Error as to the Declaration

108. Error as to the declaration is the name given to that error which is due to a *discrepancy* between the will and the declaration (*see* Article 140 CC: 'the declaration … does not accord … with the will of the declarant'). The discrepancy here is *involuntary*, in contrast with the instance of simulation, where, as we have seen (paragraph 104 *supra*), the will and the declaration are also at variance, but in a way which is *willed.* At this point a clarification is called for: if we accept that the declaration of will is made up of two separate elements, the will as a psychological fact, on the one hand, and the declaration, on the other (as used to be believed), it follows that we should

70. *See* for interpretation, paras 173 et seq. *infra.*

71. The above distinctions of the will into 'will for action', 'will for juridical action' and 'will as to the contents' are taught chiefly in Germany (*Handlungs-, Erklärungs-, Geschäftswillen*).

say that if one of these two constitutive elements is lacking (specifically, the will), there is no declaration of will. In this way they will theory had in former times both influence and persuasiveness. It is, however, closer to the nature of the juridical act to accept that the psychological (e.g., interior) will has no such force;[72] nor does the sole fact that this may be also the 'declared' will. Not every extemalization of the will is a (juridical) 'declaration of will'. What is further required for the declarant is to bind himself, that is, to bring into force what he declares.[73] The declaration of will is not in fact simply declaratory of an inner desire, but a constitutive act which converts the will into self-commitment. In other words, we have a single act, a declaration in which the will is embodied (and, therefore, to some degree, objectified). It is only thus that the will acquires force in the outer world, because that which has force is the declaration of will as a single act in the sense to be concluded, if necessary, by interpretation.

In view of this, the (involuntary) discrepancy between 'declaration and will' in which error as to the declaration consists should be more accurately described as follows: there is a discrepancy between the meaning of the (single) declaration of will, which is concluded by way of interpretation to be legally binding on the parties, and the meaning actually willed by the declarant, which remains outside this. It could be said that the will declared (embodied in the declaration), and, therefore, objectified in this sense, does not coincide with the actual will. What however is crucial, in order to establish whether such a variance – and therefore 'error as to the declaration' – exists, is that the process of interpretation (which, as we have said, will be discussed in the next chapter) should first be finished. The protection *par excellence* of the will is effected through interpretation, in which a basic, but not exclusive or always predominant, criterion is the will of the declarant. It is only if the views of the declarant as to the meaning in force of the declaration of will (i.e., his actual will) have not been considered as decisive by the interpretation and more objective interpretative criteria prevailed, that the issue of error as to the declaration arises.

If, for example, in a lease contract for an apartment it is concluded from some wording, even if unclear, that the apartment has been leased in a repaired condition, that is, that the necessary repairs should have been carried out by the lessor, and the lessor believed that he had leased it as it stood (without repairs), we have a case of error as to the declaration. The same applies if an offer of purchase for a thing states as the price offered (and accepted by the vendor) the figure 15,000 instead of, for example, the correct figure, that is, that actually intended, of 10,500 currency units; or if I buy 'A's car', in the belief that he still has a BMW, while he has replaced this with a Toyota.

A characteristic feature, then, of error as to the declaration is that the party in error thinks that something different has force as having been declared from what is in fact the case. He has understood the declaration in a way different from the meaning which that takes on with interpretation. The fact that there are borderline cases of error as to the declaration will be discussed below (paragraphs 115 et seq. *infra*).

---

72. This has also been accepted by Areios Pagos in its Decision 1057/1974, NoB 1975, 629.
73. *See* the very typical expression of the declaration of will as a 'declaration of force' (particularly well-known in Germany – *'Geltungserklärung'* – since the classic monograph of *Larenz*, Die Methode der Auslegung des Rechtsgeschäfts, 1930.

109. Error as to the declaration may be due to an oversight in its formulation, to lack of clarity in its terms, to defective transmission of the declaration by a messenger of the declarant (*see* Article 146 CC), or it may concern the identity of a person or thing; it may relate to the calculation of sums of money, or to the legal effects of the juridical act, etc. Whatever the reason for or nature of the error as to the declaration, a condition must be fulfilled for this to constitute legally relevant error: that it should be *substantial* error (Article 140 CC). The error is substantial according to the exposition of Article 141 CC, 'when it refers to a point of such importance in regard to the whole of the act that the person in error if he were aware of the true situation, would not have entered into the act'. It is not, then, the type of the error which is of significance but how substantial it is. Of course, the type of the error may help in deciding whether and when the error will be regarded as substantial. For example, error as to the identity of the person of the counterparty will be more easily found to be substantial in the case of contracts being concluded *intuitu personae*, where the person of the contracting party is a dominating factor (e.g., a contract with an artist or an expert, etc.).

110. Again, *error in law* (*error juris*), that is, error as to the conditions or as to the effects provided for in a legislative regulation (or only as to the meaning of a legal term or even as to the meaning of an entire legal institution), may be error as to the declaration and be deemed substantial if it refers to an important point in the contract. For example, someone sells a hotel 'with all its accessories', and, therefore, its movable furnishings (*see* Article 956 CC), believing that in law accessories are only those items which are fitted (*see also* Article 953 CC).[74] Naturally, error in law can be error in the declaration, if the legal effect or legal term, etc. which is misunderstood by the party has become a content of the juridical act and if this effect, term, etc., is one of the possible choices of the parties for the content of their contract. This is because here we are dealing with a discrepancy of the actual will from what has force as a declaration of will. If the consequence in law, the legal term, etc., is not contained in the contract but has force because the law so orders (and not because the parties have chosen it), this will not be a case of the error as to the declaration which we are examining here, but of error as to the will (paragraphs 113 et seq. *infra*, with borderline cases).[75] Other examples of error in law in the declaration: I take on lease (according to the interpretation of my declaration) an object whereas I thought that I had simply borrowed it for use (i.e., gratuitously). I donate a thing while thinking that I have sold it.

111. When the error is substantial, the juridical act is not void but voidable. That is, the person in error shall be entitled to sue for the annulment of the act (Article 140 CC). If he does not do so, or for as long as he does not do so, the juridical act remains valid and develops all its effects. If the person in error wishes to annul it, he must have recourse to the court. Judicial annulment will, however, have retrospective effects. There is, however, some provision for the protection of third parties in good faith who have in the meantime acquired rights. For more on the consequences of voidability and annulment and how these differ from *ab initio* invalidity, *see* §4 *infra*.

74. *See* AP 293/1963, NoB 1963, 1186.
75. On the commonly disputed issue of whether legal error, as well as many categories of error of facts (e.g., error in calculation, as to qualities, etc., – on the latter, *see* paras 118 et seq. *infra*) is error as to the declaration or as to the will, the reply must be given that it may be sometimes the one and sometimes the other, depending upon the case.

112. The question of when error is substantial or not will be decided on the basis of both *objective* and *subjective* criteria. The error is subjectively substantial, according to Article 141 CC, if the person in error would not have entered into the juridical act had he known the true state of affairs. It is to be concluded from the same article, however, that the objective criterion must also be met; that is, the error must relate to an 'important' point of the whole of the juridical act. This will be decided with the help of generally accepted views and, of course, of good faith. An eccentricity, for example, of the declarant does not suffice (*see also* paragraphs 124 et seq., 129 et seq. *infra*).

2. Error as to the Will: Borderline Cases

113. This form of error exists when, although we have a coincidence of will and declaration in the sense explained above, there is a discrepancy between the (actual) will and the reality lying outside the declaration of will; that is, when the actual will has taken shape under the influence of miscalculations or erroneous representations and does not concur with reality. The declarant declares, on the one hand, what he in fact wants (i.e., he transforms it into a declared will), but he willed it for example: because he wrongly thought that the object being purchased would gain in value; because he expected a change in his life which did not occur; because he made his offer as a contractor in ignorance of the latest developments in prices on the market (the 'miscalculation' here did not become a content of the contract), etc. The victim of the error is not in error as to the meaning of his declaration (as is the case with error as to the declaration). The error exists in certain thoughts he had which he did not make a content of the agreement. This is an instance *par excellence* where the term *'defect of the will'* is literally applicable. What is usually wrong here are the reasons which led to the shaping of the will, the motives, its inducements. For this reason the law (Article 143 CC) calls this error 'error on motivation'. (Legal science also uses the term 'error in motive'.) The term is, certainly, somewhat narrow, in order to cover any will which remained outside the content of the declaration (see, for example, example (b) *infra*). The law in the same article adds that this error is not substantial (unless the law determines otherwise, as, for example, on certain conditions, in wills – Article 1784 CC), that is, on the basic criterion set by Article 140 CC, annulment of the juridical act cannot be sought.

Even without the express provision of Article 143 CC, in practice the non-substantial nature of an error as to a point which has not even reached the stage of becoming a content of the declaration of will (an act which is basically controlled by the declarant) would normally be confirmed. It is reasonable to suppose that such an undeclared error which has not come into the sphere of influence of the recipient of the declaration could not be known to the latter. Usually it will be a matter of thoughts which occurred before the finalization of the will and which should be of no concern to the other party. Moreover, it is a *matter of 'seriousness'* (*gravitas*) that one should remain faithful to one's declaration and not invoke *ex post facto* undeclared inducements. This was undoubtedly an additional reason for the regulation of Article 143 CC.

Other examples:

(a) I buy an immovable property because I wrongly believed that somewhere near there an underground station is to be built. I did not wish to make this a term of the contract. Thus I willed the purchase. There was, however, a miscalculation. The inducements proven inaccurate (error of facts).
(b) I wished to insert a term in the contract but I omitted to do so. Although I know that the term has not been included, I sign the contract in order not to delay its performance (also error of facts).
(c) I am in error as to a regulation of law which lies beyond the content of the juridical act (error of law). For example, I think that the counterparty is also liable for chance events, while according to the general rule (Article 330 CC, from which, let us suppose, there is no exception here), he is only liable for fault; or I sell something without knowing that I have the strict (objective) liability of the vendor for material defects, in accordance with Articles 534 et seq. CC.
(d) I am in error as to a legal term not included in the contract (this is the difference from error in law in paragraph 110 *supra*, example of the accessories). For example, I know that I am liable in law for negligence, but I understand this as gross negligence.

114. In view of the difference in their consequences, the distinction between error as to the declaration and error as to the will takes on crucial importance. The former may be annulled if it is substantial. The latter, with certain exceptions, is not substantial and therefore cannot be annulled. The borderlines, however, between these two categories of error are not clearly defined. This is chiefly because it is often not certain whether the point as to which the declarant is in error belongs or does not belong to the declaration of will, in the meaning with which this has force. Only if this is the case is there a variance between 'will and declaration' and the question of whether this error is substantial can then be examined. Otherwise it is a case of (non-substantial) error as to the will.

115. Borderline and dubious cases easily arise where, for example, the inducements are mentioned in the declaration not as a condition or as an obligation of the other party; in cases of more general error in law at the stage of the shaping of the will which, however, indirectly affects the content of the juridical act; in cases of reiteration of a regulation of law (which would in any case have force) in the contract, etc. Frequently, the evaluation of the specific instance is bound up with issues of interpretation and proof, where the criteria are fluid, thus demonstrating that a solution can be found through the use of substantial criteria, that is, of how substantial (objectively and subjectively) the specific borderline case of error is, rather than through the notional inclusion in categories of error. Imponderable psychological criteria for acceptance (more or less conscious) of a thought as being inherent, even if indirectly, in the contract would seem to convert error as to the will into error as to the declaration.

116. The criterion of the substantiality of the error is for the regulation of Article 143 CC ('error on motivation'), as it is for the whole of the law of error, crucial. This, anyway, also stems from the principle of good faith, to which also the provisions on error expressly refer (*see* paragraphs 124 et seq. *infra*). It should be noted, moreover, that the evidence of a lack of seriousness and consistency which is perhaps present in the attempt to extricate oneself from the contract on the grounds of possible undeclared errors (*see* paragraph 113 *supra*) does not exist if, for example, the person in error took care to include in the contract reiterations (albeit superfluous) of legislative regulations as to which there was error. Thus an absolute schematization of the distinction between error as to the declaration and error as to the will would not be teleologically justifiable. Article 143 recognizes (as a regular legal situation) rather than stipulates the non-substantial nature of error as to the will. It contains an instruction rather than an order.

117. The real reason for the fact that error as to the will is not legally relevant does not lie in the concept of this kind of error, but in the fact that as a rule the substantial criteria which justify annulment are not met (*see* the summary of these in paragraphs 131 et seq. *infra*). When, exceptionally, they are met, particularly when the error finds some expression outside the inner world of the party in error and acquires importance for the contract, the rule of Article 143 CC does not have, in accordance with its aim, scope for implementation. Its teleological contraction is called for. This rule is binding to the extent that the purpose of the provision is served. Apart, probably, from the borderline cases which we have looked at and the express exceptions made by the law (e.g., Article 1784 CC on wills), a broad exception to the rule of Article 143 CC, which confirms its relativity, is contained in the regulation of error as to the qualities of a person or thing (Article 142 CC *see* section 3 *infra*) and in the case of common error (*see* section B *infra*). Finally, an additional exception exists where error as to the will is due to fraud, which is recognized as a special ground for the annulment of the juridical act (*see* under section III A *infra*).

3. Error as to Qualities: As to Identity

118. A special provision is contained in the CC on error as to the qualities of a person or thing. Article 142 CC lays down that:

An error as to the qualities of a person or a thing shall be considered a substantial error if such qualities are, according to the agreement of the parties or on the basis of good faith and common usages, of such importance in regard to the whole of the act that the person in error if he were aware of the true situation would not have entered into the act.

Qualities of a person are, for example, his health, age, occupation, abilities, experience, professional knowledge, criminal record, creditworthiness, etc. Qualities of a thing are, for example, its material of manufacture, the year of manufacture, the genuineness, chemical composition, quality, usefulness and, in general, the possibilities and conditions of use, etc. It has been said that the economic value of a thing is not a quality. This is not entirely accurate. It is simply the case that error as to the value of the thing as a rule will not be substantial on the criteria of the law. Error as to qualities is not sufficient for annulment: substantial error as to qualities is required.

119. Error as to qualities is to be distinguished from error as to identity. In the case of the latter, the party in error had in mind a different person or thing and not with the same but with other qualities. Nevertheless, the distinction, in theory clear enough, sometimes loses its clarity in practice. When the different qualities are so crucial that they distort the physiognomy of the person or the substance of the thing, there is deemed to be another person or another thing, and, therefore, error as to identity.

120. Whether error as to qualities should be included under error as to the declaration or error as to the will is disputed, while the view is also argued that this is a third, different, category of error. On the other hand, it is usually maintained that error as to identity is error as to the declaration. In fact both these types of error can be either error as to the declaration or error as to the will, a matter which will be decided on the criteria which have been explained above (paragraphs 108 et seq., 113 et seq.; *see also* paragraph 110.

121. Examples:

(a) *Error as to the identity of a person or a thing:* An art dealer sells A a work of art, thinking that A is the well-known collector of that name, whereas A is merely a namesake. In the agreement, A is mentioned by name as the purchaser, that is, his identity becomes part of the content of the agreement. The agreement has force, on its interpretation, as to this A (the namesake of the famous A), while the vendor thought that he was making the sale to a different person (the other A). There is, that is to say, a variance between declaration and will (error as to the declaration). If, on the other hand, by way of exception, the identity of the purchaser had not become a content of the agreement, that is, the vendor finally accepted the sale to the person who presented himself, regardless of his identity, but came to this decision because he thought that the other was the well-known collector (without, however, wishing to make his identity a content of the agreement), this would be a case of error as to the will (in the inducements lying outside the content of the agreement). The latter will be the case in traders' transactions with an unknown consumer public. The same holds good as to the example of error as to the identity of a thing quoted above (paragraph 108 *in fin.* – purchase of a Toyota instead of a BMW). This is an instance of error as to the declaration, unless the identity (and therefore the make) of the car was a matter of indifference to the purchaser and did not become a content of the contract. In this last case, the purchaser, in spite of his error, in the last analysis wanted the car of the vendor, whatever it was. It is this, anyway, which explains why his error is non-substantial.

(b) *Error as to qualities:* This will normally be error as to the will. I buy an object, wrongly believing that it is of good quality; or I make a loan to someone, wrongly believing that he is creditworthy. I made neither the quality of the object nor the creditworthiness of the counterparty a content of the contract. Therefore this is error as to the will. More rarely, error as to qualities may, however, be error as to the declaration: a goldsmith who makes gold and gilt trays in a certain pattern offers to sell A a gilt tray for EUR 1,000. In the offer (which A accepted) by oversight he wrote that he was selling A a 'gold' tray (and not gilt, as he wished to do). Here we have a variance between will and declaration (in force as interpreted), that is, error (as to qualities) in the declaration. Naturally, the price of the gold tray would be much higher. The same would be accepted if the client wished to buy gold jewellery, but there were unclear points in his negotiations with the jeweller and – even by interpretation – it is concluded that he ordered gilt jewellery. More generally, if in the agreement, the technical qualities of the object are correctly described but the non-specialist counterparty does not understand them and assumes from certain terms that other (better) qualities are involved, there will be error as to the declaration.

122. Article 142 CC, since it makes no distinction, means any error as to qualities, whether this is error as to the will, which is more usually the case, or error as to the declaration. It makes the question of whether this error justifies the annulment of the juridical act dependent not upon its inclusion in one category or another, but on whether it is substantial or not, which will be decided by virtue of criteria of substance, which it states. These criteria give the more general spirit of the criteria of Article 141 CC with more specification as to the *objective criterion*, which is to be explained by the fact that we may have error here which is on a point that lies outside the content of the juridical act, perhaps only in the interior will of the person in error, and therefore the error may be lacking here in 'objectivization'. While Article 141 CC requires simply an important point for the whole juridical act (which, however, will be a point in the content of the act), Article 142 CC speaks of qualities of importance for the whole juridical act 'according to the agreement[76] of the parties or on the basis of good faith and common usages'. This last addition of particulars which indicate some extemalization of the will and objectivization of the error and the possibility of its perception by the outside world seeks to supply to some extent the lack of objectivization which we have here. As to the subjective criterion which must also be present, the same applies as in Article 141 CC (*see* paragraph 112 *supra*). Where the error as to qualities is error as to the declaration, the same solution would also be reached on the basis of Articles 140–141 CC, with more particular confirmation, however, in Article 142 CC. But this article retains chiefly practical importance when the error as to qualities is (and this, as we have said, will be the rule) error as to the will. A fortiori, Article 142 CC will be applied where there is error as to the identity (or error as to qualities so crucial as to touch upon identity itself) of a person or thing, which is in the specific case only error as to the will.

123. Article 142 CC also provides express legislative confirmation of the fact which has already been noted (paragraph 117 *supra*) that where error as to the will goes beyond the inner world of the person in error, where it acquires more general importance for the contract, it can be deemed to be substantial. Its notional classification is no obstacle. Article 142 CC proves that the distinction between error as to the declaration and error as to the will, which is conceptually faultless and as a rule useful in practical terms, does not give a faithful account, from a teleological point of view, of the crucial distinction made by the law between a substantial and therefore voidable and a non-substantial and therefore non-voidable juridical act. 'Substantiality' is simply a less conceptual criterion and closer to the deeper *ratio* of the law.

76. 'Agreement' of the parties does not mean here that the quality necessarily became a content of the contract. A shared opinion of the parties (or acceptance on their part and, therefore, finally, their consent) that the quality is of importance is sufficient.

4. Preclusion of Annulment: Compensation

124. According to Article 144, annulment of the juridical act by reason of error is precluded, even if such a possibility would arise from the preceding provisions, in two instances:

(1) If the recipient of the erroneous declaration of will accepts it as it is meant by the person in error. This instance is equivalent to that of coincidence of the wills of the two parties in spite of defective description, as to which the rule *'falsa demonstratio non nocet'* applies (*see* paragraphs 175, 178 *infra*).
(2) If annulment is contrary to good faith. Here too the principle of (objective) good faith serves, as in other instances, as a corrective factor to solutions derived from other, stricter, provisions. Preclusion of annulment by virtue of good faith can be accepted, for instance, if the person in error has shown negligence without which he would have avoided the error or if, in general, his error may be regarded as not pardonable; or if annulment would be an excessive burden and injustice for the other party, who has not been negligent, has already incurred expenses for the use of the performance which he has received, etc.; or if the contract is a continuous one (partnership, contract for services, etc.) and its fulfilment has already functioned for a certain period so that for it to be overturned by the retrospective (*ab initio*) effects (*ex tunc*) of annulment would conflict with the security of transactions.[77]

125. In exceptional cases we could accept a reverse influence of good faith: for it to render voidable a juridical act which by the other criteria would not be voidable. Good faith can operate in this way particularly as an additional, reinforcing argument in cases on the borderline between error as to the declaration and error as to the will.[78]

126. Where the person in error achieves the annulment of the juridical act and security of transactions accordingly yields to the will theory, Article 145 CC provides a counterweight for the conscientious counterparty of the victim of the error: it gives him the right, but only if he was inculpably in ignorance of the error, to *seek compensation* from the party in error. The compensation is *negative interest* (e.g., expenses which the counterparty has incurred for the conclusion of the contract), which, however, may not exceed the positive interest.[79]

B. Common Error: Dissent

127. If both contracting parties share in the same error, nothing changes if this common (joint, mutual) error, had it been unilateral, would have been substantial and would have rendered the juridical act voidable. This will be the case here, the only difference being that either of the parties may seek annulment (it will be obvious that

77. In this case, the termination of the continuous contract, that is, its cancellation only as to the future (*ex nunc*) remains possible. *See also* para. 37 *supra*.
78. *See also* the reference to good faith in Art. 142 CC (and paras 112, 122 *supra*). On good faith more generally, *see* paras 53 et seq. *supra;* on borderline cases *see* para. 115 *supra*.
79. On the distinction between positive and negative interest, *see* paras 92 et seq. *supra*.

if it is a case of common error *as to the declaration*, the actual will of the parties may have force through the principle of *falsa demonstratio non nocet* (*see* paragraphs 175, 178 *infra*), in which case it is no longer a matter of error). If, however, this error, had it been unilateral, would have been non-substantial (e.g., non-substantial error as to the will), perhaps the fact that it is shared is of significance, since it constitutes some sort of 'objectivization' of the error, which, as we have seen, is one of the criteria for the substantiality of the error. It is in fact accepted in the case of joint error that annulment is possible if one further condition is fulfilled: that the error should refer to a fundamental point of the juridical act, to a point, that is, on which the parties have chiefly based the conclusion of the juridical act (basis of the transaction).[80] This basis has not entered into the content of the contract, for example, as a condition for the fulfilment of the contractual obligations (since in that case there would be no problem), but cannot be regarded also as non-substantial and of no legal relevance. Although here too an argument could be sought from the spirit of the provisions on error, the general clause on good faith of Article 288 CC is regarded as the legislative foundation of the substantiality of common error as to the fundamental elements of the transaction. This is also reinforced by the spirit of the more particular provision of Article 388 CC which provides for the dissolution or adjustment of a reciprocal contract on the condition of the collapse of the underlying basis of the transaction. This provision does not have direct application to error, since it presupposes the collapse of the basis 'ex post facto' (and only in the case of reciprocal *contracts*).[81]

In this instance of common error we have another exception to the rule of the non-substantiality of error as to the will (Article 143 CC). Anyway, usually here either a legal interest is lacking on the part of the counterparty to oppose annulment or it would be in bad faith on his part to deny the substantial nature of the error. An example: the prices in a contract for the regular supply of goods have been determined before a war or an economic crisis which has unexpectedly broken out and which has completely overturned them. The parties had erroneously based the clause on the prices on relative economic stability.

For a special case of common error justifying annulment, *see* paragraph 394 on compromise *infra*.

128. There is also a type of joint error when the parties believe that their two declarations of will have coincided and that therefore their contract has been concluded, whereas the two declarations of will do not coincide at all their points (latent dissent). Here we do not judge the formation of the will of one of the parties and its coincidence with his declaration, as hitherto, but we compare the declaration of will of one of the parties (which, let us suppose, does not suffer from error as to the will or as to the declaration) with the declaration of will of the other (which, let us suppose, also does not suffer from such a defect). We find that there is a lack of that coincidence in the two declarations of will which is necessary for the contract to be concluded. The error

80. Cf., the German theory on *'subjektive Geschäftsgrundlage'* (*inter alia, see* Larenz, Schuldrecht, Allg. T. 14. Aufl. 1987, §21, II). The corresponding theories in France on *'cause de l'engagement'* (*see, inter alia, Carbonnier*, Droit Civil, Tome 4, Les Obligations, 22ème éd., 2000, No. 41, under I c 2) and the English theory on the 'root' of the contract (see, *inter alia, Anson's Law of Contract*, 28th ed. 2002 (J. Beatson), Ch. 8, pp. 311 et seq.) do not greatly differ.
81. On this provision, *see* paras 290 et seq. *infra*.

here consists in the fact that the parties think that there was coincidence. Normally, the consequence is that the contract was not concluded, not because there was a defect in the will of one of the parties, but because *consensus* is lacking. If, however, the terms as to which there was no coincidence are not substantial, in the sense that the parties would have concluded the contract even without them, the contract has force as to the rest of it where there was coincidence (thus Article 196 CC – *see* paragraph 74 *supra*, where also the patent – and therefore without error of the parties – *dissensus* and its consequences are discussed).

C. *Conclusions: The Material Criteria of the Law on Error*

129. In the Greek law on error, we can say by way of conclusion that the will theory as a rule yields place, as, anyway, is the case in most European legal systems. In any case, any annulment of the juridical act is preceded by the interpretation of the declaration. During the process of interpretation, as we shall *see* (paragraphs 173 et seq. *infra*), both the subjective views of the declarant and the possibility of understanding of the recipient are taken into consideration. The findings of interpretation give the meaning of the juridical act which (now objectivized) will have force. Any different actual (psychological) will on the part of the declarant, to the extent that it did not find expression in the objectivized meaning of the juridical act in question, will not have force. Error can lead to annulment of the juridical act by court decision only if this is sought by the person in error, but for this end, the existence of the error is not on its own sufficient. Special reasons are required, which render annulment difficult.

130. The distinction between legally relevant error (which justifies annulment) and legally irrelevant error (which does not) is not made casuistically, for example, on the basis of the various familiar case groups of error of Roman law (*error in substantia, in persona*, etc.). These can only have importance as a typology of instances of error which can sometimes lead to annulment and sometimes not (see, for example, paragraph 109 *supra*). The differentiation, crucial in law, between voidable and non-voidable erroneous juridical acts is undertaken by the CC by including, basically, in the former category error as to the declaration and in the latter error as to the will. The conception of this distinction, known to legal systems under German influence, had (apart from its psychological value) a well-grounded starting-point (*see* paragraph 113 *supra*) and contributes to the transcending of a confusing casuistic approach and to the strengthening of the security of law, in spite of the fact that this distinction in interpretation is in danger of being reduced to conceptualistic rigidity. This is because, from the point of view of its legal relevance, the distinction is not always confirmed *de lege lata*, nor does it always lead with certainty to teleologically just results. There are forms of error as to the declaration which are non-substantial from a legal point of view, just as there are many forms of error as to the will which can in the specific case be of preponderant significance. The CC itself is forced to make express provision for exceptions.

The above conceptual distinction made by the CC is useful as a guide, but requires its teleological control on the basis of the inherent material criteria, which in some cases are expressly stated in the CC and in others are derived from the intent of the rules and exceptions of the law of error, which lie behind it. Usually, these material criteria are undervalued in the interpretation of the relevant provisions, since they are overshadowed by the putting forward of the above conceptual distinction. It is, however, these criteria, which must be brought back to the surface and given their due importance. They are the criteria which, basically, supply the final solution. These may be systematized into the following three.

131. First, it is crucial for the will of the person in error to be regarded as to the point of his error as *subjectively* (for the person himself) substantial and deserving of protection. This criterion will not be met:

(a) if the person in error would have entered into the juridical act even if he had known the true situation (*see* Articles 141, 142 CC);
(b) if the person in error could by taking care have avoided the error (unpardonable error). In this respect the quality of this person as professional, consumer, etc. could be crucial. The degree of his negligence which would be relevant here can only be determined *in concreto*. The more painful is the sacrifice of the victim of the error required for keeping the contract in force, the higher will be the degree of negligence which will be required for the preclusion of annulment;
(c) if the other party accepts the declaration of will as the person in error means it (Article 144 no. 1 CC).

132. Also crucial, *second*, is the *sharing, to some degree, of the other party* in the error of the declarant. Such participation in the error is present:

(a) in common error;
(b) in cases where the other party was not in error himself, but knew of or could or should have known of the error of the other (whereby the quality of the other party as professional or as consumer could be crucial). The error here is not an 'inner', personal matter for the person in error (cf. willed mental reservation, paragraph 104 *supra*) and does not remain exclusively in his sphere of influence (as especially in the case of error in motive), but enters into the outside world and more particularly into the sphere of influence of the other party and concerns him too. Thus there is here an objectivization;
(c) most importantly, in cases of *active* participation of the other party, when, that is, he has caused the error by his conduct, for example, by inaccurate declarations on his part.[82] This holds good all the more if the inaccurate declarations were not made without fault (e.g., through negligence), but with malice. But then, they constitute fraud, in which case there is a special reason for annulment (*see* section III A *infra*).

82. The English institution of misrepresentation [*see Anson's Law of Contract*, 28th ed. (J. Beatson), Ch. 6] belongs here. This means precisely the causing of error by inaccurate declarations as to facts which have not, however, reached the point of becoming a term of the contract but which have influenced the victim of the error as to the conclusion of the contract and which give him the right to rescind the contract. What is of interest here is innocent or negligent misrepresentation and not fraudulent misrepresentation, which is equivalent to fraud.

This criterion corresponds to the whole attitude of the legislator towards the will theory. For the will to have some kind of legal relevance it must as a rule be made manifest (cf. Article 143 CC) and acquire an existence for the outside world – and especially for those whom it concerns. Otherwise it remains the rule that everyone shoulders the risk for his own mistakes.[83]

133. The error must, *third*, also be *objectively* substantial, in accordance, that is, with (objective) good faith and common usages (Article 142 CC, and, indirectly, Article 141 CC). It is not sufficient that the person in error himself considers the error substantial – he may be excessively pedantic, eccentric, superstitious, etc., and may attach great importance to insignificant points, which, however, he did not take care to make terms of the contract. This is shown by the requirement that the unknown facts should be of a fundamental character in common error; and by the requirement that the quality as to which there is error should be important for the specific contract (e.g., the creditworthiness of the borrower in credit contracts, the state of the physical health in a life assurance contract or in a contract for physical, manual services, a previous record of mismanagement for management contracts, previous bankruptcy for a partnership contract, etc.). The application of this criterion permits a weighing of interests so that it can be decided, on the basis of equity also, when the error is of great importance for the particular contract. The aim and the meaning of the contract are crucial. In the case of a donor, for example, generally accepted views will more easily pardon an error (and thus will more easily accept its substantiality) than in that of the party in a reciprocal contract.

134. The three criteria above are not peculiar to the Greek legislator. They are to be found in other European legal systems, precisely because they are *material criteria*, independent of terminology, the manner in which law is generated, and established institutions.[84] Under current Greek law, criteria (a) and (c) must be met cumulatively (*see* particularly Articles 141 and 142 CC). Error which is subjectively substantial without being objectively so or *vice versa* is not sufficient for the annulment of the juridical act. Criterion (b) will usually be crucial and will be imposed by virtue also of good faith, that is, through criterion (c). It cannot, however, be elevated into a necessary condition for annulment. If the subjectively substantial error was also objectively substantial, in accordance with good faith, but not diagnosed or diagnosable

83. As to this criterion, we do not have, as in the case of (a) and (c), an *express* reference in the Civil Code. As to instance b, moreover, the non-necessity of knowledge or culpable ignorance of the recipient of the declaration may be concluded *e contrario* from the provision of Art. 145 § 2. The criterion, however, even if not as necessary (*see* para. 134 *infra*) corresponds to the notions of good faith and common usages (to which the law refers us) and to the purpose of the relevant provisions. The treatment of error in motive by the legislator is also an indication of the legal relevance of some kind of objectivization of the error.

84. Cf. the significance of a mutual error as to a fact *at the root* of the contract or as *a fundamental* error, of instances of error which is, actually or inferentially, *known to the other party,* or causing *undue hardship in the circumstances of the case* or induced by misrepresentation, the intervention of the *equitable* remedy, etc. of English law; the significance of *motifs déterminants* or *principals,* of *qualités substantielles,* of *cause de l'engagement* of French law; of *'verständiger Würdigung'* and *'Verkehrswesentlichkeit'* of the German Civil Code (§119) and of the German doctrine on *Geschäftsgrundlage,* which is grounded in the principle of good faith, or on the *Vertragswesentlichkeit* of qualities, etc.

(a state of affairs not impossible but somewhat rare, since usually the objective substantiality is diagnosed in the course of transactions, and therefore by the other contracting party), annulment will be possible. This, as we have said, can be seen from the formulation of Articles 141 and 142 CC. That is to say, criteria (a) and (c) are conditions for annulment, whereas criterion (b) is in principle a crucial criterion.

III. Other Defects of the Will

A. Fraud

135. Fraud is the second defect of the will which gives grounds for the annulment of a juridical act. By way of contrast with the difficulties involved in determining the borderline between voidable and non-voidable juridical acts which error gives rise to, in the case of fraud matters are simpler: any fraud is a ground for the annulment of the juridical act by the victim of the fraud, provided that the fraud has been practised by the other party. If a third party committed the fraud, annulment can only be sought if the other party was aware or should have been aware of the fraud[85] (Article 147 CC). Fraud is regarded as being any item of conduct which takes place with the purpose of the creation or reinforcement of an erroneous impression either by representation of falsehoods as true facts or by the concealment or passing over in silence or incomplete communication of true facts[86] as to which, naturally, there exists an obligation of communication (in accordance with the agreement or with law or with good morals or good faith and common usages).

136. The question of whether the error of the person defrauded is substantial or not does not signify. If, however, in the case of non-substantial error caused by fraud, the other party accepts the declaration of will as the person defrauded wished it, the court is at liberty not to annul the juridical act (Article 148 CC).

Annulment is effected by recourse to the court (*see* §4 *infra*, also on the consequences of annulment). In parallel with annulment (or even without annulment, if he prefers), the person defrauded may seek compensation for a tort (*see* Articles 149 and 914 CC) – since fraud is in any case a tort.

B. Duress

137. The last (third) defect of the will which gives grounds for the annulment of the juridical act stipulated in the CC is duress ('threat' according to Articles 150–153 CC). Duress exists when someone is forced by psychological pressure ('indirect'

---

85. If from the declaration of will of the person defrauded by X the counterparty does not acquire a direct right, but someone else (contract in favour of a third party – Art. 411 CC – *see* paras 199 et seq. *infra*), it suffices that this other person knew or ought to have known of the fraud of X. For example, A and B conclude a contract in favour of C. But A has been inveigled into this contract by the fraud of X, which was known to C but not to B. The knowledge of C is sufficient for A to seek annulment, since it is C who directly acquires a right from the contract.

86. So AP 249/1976, NoB 1976, 785; AP 709/1999, HellD 2000, 357; AP 26/2000, NoB 2001, 30; AP 898/2000, ChrID 2001, 223.

violence – *vis compulsiva* – the threat of some harm) to enter into a juridical act. If the violence is 'direct' (physical – *vis absoluta*), there is no question of a declaration of will. This is non-existent and, consequently, any annulment would be superfluous (*see* paragraph 107 *supra*). Serious problems of drawing borderlines do not arise here either. For the person threatened to be able to seek the annulment of the juridical act, the threat (under the influence of which he was forced to proceed to the declaration of will) must simply have been made unlawfully or contrary to morality. Thus, if I threaten someone that I will take him to court (perhaps to the criminal courts for embezzlement) if he does not return to me an object which I have lent him for use, since the term of the loan for use has expired, this threat does not conflict with the law or with good morals. It is permissible. If, however, the threat is irrelevant to the declaration of will to which I want to force the person threatened, it may be contrary to morality, a matter which in the end will be decided *in concreto* on the basis of the specific circumstances.

Duress gives grounds for annulment even if it is exercised by a third party. In this case, however, the counterparty of the person threatened, provided that he is in good faith, may, depending on the circumstances, seek compensation from the person threatened, if he has achieved annulment, consisting of negative interest (e.g., expenses for the conclusion of the contract).[87]

138. There are, of course, instances of (subjectively or objectively) insignificant threats, which do not justify legal relevance. The CC, in a provision which has not caused particular difficulties in implementation, regards as being legally relevant (and justifying annulment) only a threat which in the specific circumstances 'causes fear in a reasonable man and exposes to grave and imminent danger the life, health, freedom, honour or property of the person threatened or of persons very closely connected with him' (Article 151 CC). Here too the person threatened may seek (solely or in parallel with annulment – *see* §4 *infra*) compensation from the person who made the threat in accordance with the provisions on torts.

§3. Other Conditions of Validity

I. Existing and Licit Cause

A. The Cause in Contracts: Freedom of Contract

139. To begin with, two basic regulations of Greek law should be recalled: first, the distinction between promissory and disposition contracts, where the just cause (*justa causa*) of the latter is as a rule the former (*see* paragraphs 19 et seq., 48 et seq., *supra*), and, second, the sufficiency of consent for the generation of the effects of promissory contracts (*solus consensus obligat*), that is, the validity of these contracts without the law requiring (as does, for example, French law, No. 1108 Code Civil) the existence of a cause or (as in English law) the existence of a consideration (*see* paragraphs 23 et seq., 26, 76 *supra*). The principle of *pacta sunt servanda* is established

87. On the concept of negative interest, *see* paras 92 et seq. *supra* .

as a rule in Greek law. This can be seen chiefly from Article 361 CC, which indirectly establishes freedom of contract, without requiring other factors for the generation of the obligation by the consent of the parties (*cf.* §311 (1) German CC).

Nevertheless, the difference from other legal systems is not as great as it seems at first sight. A promise is normally not given without any reason which justifies the action of the promissor. The promissory contract is indeed regarded by those who accept the principle *solus consensus obligat* as itself containing its cause. And its cause (i.e., the reason for which the immediate juridical effect is being brought about, which here is the undertaking of the obligation by the promissor) is as a rule *either* the acquisition by the promisor of the claim for a counter-performance or the receipt by him of some other benefit in law (*credendi* or *acquirendi causa* = a cause of acquiring a claim: reciprocal, and, more generally, onerous contracts), *or* the intention of liberality towards the promisee (unilaterally charging and, more particularly, gratuitous contracts, even if for selfish motives, donandi causa). What are often thought of as special causes, such as the securing of a claim (e.g., guarantee, promise of the transfer of rights for the securing of a claim, etc.), the achievement of mutual concessions of the parties (compromise, Article 871 CC), etc. in the last analysis can be reduced to one or other category of causes (acquisition of a quid pro quo – liberality). In the Greek law the cause does not constitute a formal element but the substantive justification of the promise. It should not be understood today as a strictly technical concept, but as an economic or social or moral reason for the promise. It may be asked, however, what are the consequences if such a cause – justification – is completely lacking (or it cannot be seen to exist) in promissory contracts. Are there, that is to say, abstract promissory contracts, contracts whose validity is not affected by any absence or invalidity of the reason for which they have been concluded?

B. Non-causal (Abstract) Promissory Contracts

140. Any prudent person in principle enters only into promises with a cause (e.g., A promises B EUR 10,000 as a loan, or as a price for the object which he has bought, or as a donation, or as remuneration for work, etc.). It is not, however, out of the question that he should render the promise independent of any cause (even if such a cause exists, as would be the case in normal instances). For example, A promises B EUR 10,000 intentionally avoiding any reference to the reason for the promise. The question which arises is whether this promise, abstract and isolated from any (onerous or gratuitous) direction of the will, should be recognized as valid by law, just as onerous and gratuitous promissory contracts are.

The fact that Article 361 CC, as we have seen, contents itself in principle for the generation of the obligation with the coincidence of the wills of the two parties (creditor and debtor) suggests that the law accepts as valid an abstract promise of debt. This is confirmed particularly by Article 873, subparagraph 1. According to this provision, a contract by which 'a promise is given or a debt is acknowledged in such a manner as to give rise to an obligation irrespective of the cause of the debt' is regarded as *valid*, provided that the declaration on the promise or acknowledgement is made *in writing*.

Written form is not required when the debt of a balance of 'a current account which has been closed' is acknowledged (Article 874 CC). If, however, the promise or the acknowledgment concerns a cause for which the law requires a special form (e.g., a notarial document, as in the case of a promise by reason of donation, Article 498, paragraph 1 CC), this must also be observed in the case of the abstract promise or acknowledgement, otherwise it will be null and void (Article 875 CC).

141. De lege ferenda, the recognition of the validity of the abstract promissory contract has, of course, the advantage that it obviates what is often difficult proof as to the cause of contracts and helps to speed up transactions. Nonetheless, this recognition is dangerous. Abstract contracts may involve illegal or socially, morally or economically inadmissible performances. For example, A blackmails B into acknowledging that he owes him some (non-existent) debt; A acknowledges as a result of error some non-existent debt on his part to B; A promises usurious interest as an alleged abstract debt, etc. The legislative provision for written undertaking of such promises, so that the debtor will enter into them at least after some reflection, does not perhaps always prove sufficient. It is for this reason that it is widely argued that it would be more adequate in principle for contracts which have a cause and contain the justification for the binding of the debtor alone to be recognized as valid and for the creditor in cases where the contract does not state a cause to bear the burden of proof that this exists (even if outside the contract) and that it is lawful. Exceptions could be accepted in special cases, particularly in trade, by the acknowledgement of special abstract titles (such as promissory notes, bills of exchange, etc.).

However, the law does not leave the debtor of an abstract promissory contract who has been validly bound, but without there being a just cause for his debt, entirely without protection. If the debtor himself proves the absence of a just cause, although the validity of his debt is not cancelled, he can claim what he has paid without cause by means of the provisions on unjust enrichment (Articles 904 et seq. CC). If he has not paid this and is sued by the creditor for payment, he may, again by proving the lack of just cause, rebut him by the plea of unjust enrichment. What we have finally, then, is the shifting of the burden of proof that the just cause is lacking from the creditor (who retains a valid abstract contract) to the debtor (in favour of whom the claim for the recovery of the unjust enrichment arises). If such proof is impossible, the creditor is entitled to collect, while the debtor is not entitled to recover.

C. Licit Cause

142. The licit nature of the cause is not separately examined in Greek law. It is an aspect of the licit character of the contract in general, which is decided not only by the particular contractual content, but by all the factors which are involved in the conclusion of the contract, such as the cause or the effects or the object (i.e., the performance or the object of the performance, for example, the thing owed) of the contract or the circumstances in which the contract is concluded. The matter is examined as a whole. Conflict with good morals in particular, even if this concerns one point in the whole juridical act, is regarded as reflecting upon the whole juridical act (*see* Article 208 CC on the illegal or immoral conditions of a juridical act which render null and void the whole act. On the issue, *see* section IV *infra*).

II. Determined or Determinable, Possible and Licit Object

143. The object of the obligation is the performance which is owed. The performance must be determined or, at least, determinable. By the time of fulfilment, the latter must have become determined.

If the performance is undetermined and its determination has been entrusted 'to one of the contracting parties or to a third party, it is in case of doubt considered that the determination must be made in accordance with fair judgment. If the determination was not based on fair judgment or has been delayed, it shall be made by the court' (Article 371 CC). There is also a type of lack of determination in *obligations in kind* (non-specific or generic obligations, that is, defined by reference to their *genus*) and in *alternative obligations* (where among two or more performances, one is due), as to which the CC has special provisions (Articles 289 et seq., 305 et seq.), where, *inter alia*, in case of doubt, the right of specification of the obligation in kind or of option in the case of alternative obligations is given to the debtor (*see also* paragraphs 266 and 349 *infra*).

On the question of whether the performance must be possible, *see* section III *infra*, while as to the licit nature of the performance, what has been said above (paragraph 139) applies.

III. Initial Impossibility

144. For the validity of the obligation undertaken, it is not necessary that the performance should be possible. Even if the impossibility of the performance exists *ab initio* and is 'objective' (i.e., would be impossible for anybody), the validity of the juridical act is not affected. On this point the CC was innovative, in comparison with the law previously in force or with foreign laws, and did not adopt the rule of Roman law that *'impossibilium nulla est obligatio'*. In the interests of clarity and unity, it introduced a uniform system for every instance of impossibility of performance (initial or supervening, subjective or objective): the obligation is valid and the debtor, if he is at fault for the impossibility, will owe compensation. (For more on this, *see* paragraphs 264 et seq. *infra*). If, however, the impossibility is due to legal reasons, for example, if there is a conflict with a prohibitory provision of law, it will depend finally on this special provision what the consequences are. The rule is, if nothing else emerges from the provision, that we have nullity of the contract (Article 174 CC). If, however, the prohibition specially concerns only the object of the contract (e.g., 'things outside the ambit of transactions' – *res extra commercium*), there will be, according to Article 365 CC, impossibility of performance and not nullity of the contract.[88]

145. By things outside the ambit of transactions are meant those which are common to all (e.g., fresh air, sea), those in common use (e.g., roads, squares, rivers, lakes, etc.) and those intended for the serving of state, municipal, community or religious purposes (Articles 966 et seq. CC). Private rights to objects in common use (which as a rule belong to municipalities, communes or the state) are permitted by

88. The value of this latter distinction is disputed. On the consequences of an infringement of a prohibitory provision of law, *see also* para. 152 *infra*.

concession of the public authority, provided that by those rights common use is served or not impeded.

IV. Illegality and Public Policy

146. The juridical act (its cause, object, content, effects, the conditions under which it was effected) must not be contrary to a prohibitory provision of law (Article 174 CC) or contrary to morality (Article 178 CC).

Prohibitory provisions of law may be understood in two senses, one broad and one narrow. The broad sense includes any provision of mandatory law (*jus cogens*) in the sense of Article 3 CC (which uses the term 'public policy') (any provision, that is to say, which cannot be displaced or amended by private will – e.g., by a contract). The narrow sense (also public policy in the narrow sense) includes only provisions which contain the fundamental legal, moral, social and economic values and views of a law community and which usually disapprove the content of the juridical act or the conditions under which this is effected (e.g., provisions on usury, excessive penalty clauses, oppressive exemption clauses, etc.). More technical matters (procedures, form, etc.) are regulated by *jus cogens*, which, however, is not public policy in the narrow sense. Article 174 CC provides as a consequence, if nothing else is to be concluded from the prohibitory provision of law, for the nullity of the juridical act in conflict with it. It is disputed whether this consequence is stipulated by Article 174 CC as to prohibitory provisions in the broad or the narrow sense, but this dispute has no particular practical significance, on the one hand, because the special prohibitory provision (in the broad or the narrow sense) may provide, as to the consequences, for a deviation from the regulation of Article 174 CC, and, on the other, because also in the case of prohibitions which do not belong within the narrow sense, the relevant provisions as a rule stipulate nullity as a sanction for the infringement of the prohibition.[89]

147. The freedom of contract that basically governs the Greek law of obligations includes not only, as a rule, the freedom to conclude or not to conclude the contract, but also the freedom to determine the content of the contract. This means that the rules of the law of obligation constitute basically non-mandatory law (*jus dispositivum*). However, a large number of them are mandatory law and are usually introduced by special laws (labour laws, market police provisions, protection for consumers, protection for those renting professional or residential premises, monetary restrictions –which are gradually being reduced in view of European Monetary Union-, legislation on unfair competition, etc.). *See also supra* paragraph 77.

148. The general clause of Article 178 CC is broader in scope. It provides for nullity for any juridical act which is contrary to good morals (*contra bonos mores*). 'Good morals' are the prevailing morality of society. However, because of the indeterminate nature of their content, particularly from the point of view of the extent of their acceptance among members of society, problems arise as to their precise meaning. It would be closer to the *ratio* of the provision to accept that by the term 'good morals', the law basically means rules (dictates, prohibitions, etc.) of the morality of society which are *generally accepted* (with possible exceptions in the case of extreme

89. Another possible consequence is the obligation of compensation (*see* § 4, I *infra*).

standpoints), and not accepted simply by that view which prevails as one among many. It means, that is, the fundamentally undisputed moral concepts of society and not those which divide it or those as to which differing views are strongly and widely maintained. This is justified by the fact that in cases where the rules of law refer us to good morals, usually these good morals have a restrictive effect on the freedom of action of the individual. Restrictions on freedom must at least be generally accepted.

149. Null and void juridical acts do not give rise to obligations or rights (for more on nullity, *see* in the next paragraph). If, in spite of this, a performance is fulfilled, it may be claimed back as unjust enrichment of the recipient (Articles 904 et seq.). More particularly, however, in the case of a performance which has been fulfilled for an immoral cause (Article 907 CC) by way of exception, annulment is precluded 'if the immoral cause also involves the giver'. *A fortiori*, it should be accepted that the preclusion has force when the immoral cause involves only the giver. 'Immoral cause' is a formulation used by the law to express the conflict of the cause with good morals. The *ratio* of the preclusion of the claim lies in the decision of the legislator to deny the protection of the law to persons who share in the immorality; apart from this, it is regarded as more generally inadmissible for someone to invoke his own immorality (*'nemo auditur propriam turpitudinem allegans'*). This sanction against the giver who is responsible for the immorality is reasonable, although in some, albeit exceptional, cases it would appear inequitable. What is not reasonable, on the other hand, is the retention of the enrichment by the recipient (a result to which preclusion of the claim leads) when he, although he may not have had a share in the immorality, nevertheless has not supplied a quid pro quo for his enrichment (which is not based upon the valid will of the giver either, by reason of the immorality of the performance), or, *a fortiori*, when the recipient is himself involved in the immorality. The Roman principle that *'in pari turpitudine melior est causa possidentis'* ('where the immorality is equal, the cause of the possessor is stronger'), which is what lies behind the favour shown here by the legislator towards the recipient, is not sufficient justification for the regulation, since it can lead to real unjustified enrichment of the recipient or to unequal treatment of giver and recipient who may be equally immoral; it can lead, that is, in the end to the same inequality and injustice as the broader principle of *'beati possidentes'* ('possession is nine points of the law') often does. For this reason it has been argued[90] that it would be more correct *de lege ferenda* for the recipient not to gain the benefit of the enrichment, but that this should be confiscated, for example, in favour of the state or for some public benefit purpose, probably at the discretion of the court.

150. A special type of juridical acts which are contrary to good morals are those which are covered, also with nullity as a sanction, in Article 179 CC. This provision stipulates two particular acts as being contrary to morality and, consequently, null and void: the juridical act 'whereby the freedom of a person is hampered excessively'; and the juridical act 'whereby a party through exploitation of need, mental levity or inexperience of the other party, stipulates or receives for his own benefit or the benefit of a third party, in consideration of a performance, pecuniary advantages which in the circumstances are obviously disproportionate to the performance'. Typical examples of the first instance are the 'agreements in restraint of trade' or contracts which bring about restriction of the personal freedom of the contracting party. The second of the

90. See, for instance, Litzeropoulos, EEN 1947, pp. 117 et seq., 157 et seq.

two instances in this article refers to the usurious and, more generally, improperly exploitative juridical acts (e.g., 'catching bargain'). In this regulation we can see what remains of the *leasio enormis* or the *justum pretium* of natural law. These institutions, which sought to make the content of contracts as objectively just as possible, have been rejected by the CC as being contrary to the freedom of contract. The sole restriction in cases of 'obvious disproportion' between performance and counter-performance is the prohibition of Article 179 CC, which, however, greatly narrows its field of implementation by the strict conditions which it lays down (including subjective ones, such as the exploitation which presupposes intention to exploit the need, mental levity or inexperience of the other party).[91] In extreme cases, further protection of the economically weaker party can be sought in the general clauses of the CC (particularly Articles 178, 281, 288 CC), which, in giving expression to the idea of equity, can contribute to the more general contemporary trend for the contract not to be regarded merely as a formal coincidence of two declarations of will but also as a means of private autonomy for the pursuit of legal interests in a licit manner (*see also* paragraphs 53–64 *supra*).

§4. The Consequences of a Defect of Consent or of a Lack of Substantive Validity

I. Nullity: Voidability and Annulment – Damages

151. A basic distinction of Greek law as to the consequences of the infringement of a rule of law is that between *nullity* and *voidability* of the juridical act by which such an infringement is effected. In the case of a null and void juridical act, we have *ipso jure* non-occurrence of the effects of the juridical act. According to Article 180 CC, which gives the meaning of nullity, 'An act which is null is deemed not to have taken place'. Therefore, the effect willed by the juridical act is deemed not to have taken place *ab initio.* Any contestation between the parties as to whether or not there were grounds for nullity can, of course, be resolved by the courts. The court's decision, however, if it accepts that there were grounds for nullity and therefore that the juridical act was null and void, is simply 'declaratory', that is, it will ascertain the pre-existing legal situation that no effect of the juridical act had occurred (*declaratory judgment*); it will not itself overturn the contract. Even without the court's decision being issued, where there are grounds for nullity, no effects willed by the juridical act have occurred. In the case of voidability, on the other hand, all the effects of the juridical act occur, as if the act were valid, and these effects will remain if no one has recourse to the courts. However, the *ex post facto* reversal of the effects of the juridical act is possible if the case is taken to court and the court accepts the grounds of voidability and annuls the act. In this case a judgment modifying the legal status (and not simply a declaratory one) is issued and this itself gives rise to a new state of affairs in law, the annulment of the act, that is, the reversal of the effects willed by the parties. A voidable act which

91. On protection by means of Art. 388 CC in the event of *ex post facto* collapse of the contractual balance, *see* paras 290 et seq. *infra* .

is annulled is then equivalent with one null and void *ab initio* (Article 184 CC). This means that the law gives the annulment a retroactive effect and, moreover, an effect 'in rem'. Thus, for example, ownership transferred by the annulled contract reverts *ipso jure* to the transferor (cf. paragraph 284 *infra*). By requiring an annulment by the court, the law here sacrifices the simplicity and speed of the effect of a legal defect (the ground of voidability) in the interests of the security of transactions. The court's judgment guarantees a strict test of whether or not there is a defect in the juridical act.

152. However, in both instances, whether *ab initio* or *ex post facto*, the juridical act is assailed in a direct manner. The sanction is full, the rule is 'perfect' (*lex perfecta*, in the terminology of Roman law). On some occasions, although there is a sanction, it is 'less full', the rule has reduced imperative or prohibitory force and it is somewhat 'less than perfect' (*lex minus quam perfecta*). Thus, an act contrary to the prohibitory rule remains valid, but the offender owes compensation or is subject to other sanctions (such as penalties, etc.). Examples: there are certain things which the law does not wish to be the object of transactions (those *'extra commercium'* Article 966 CC – *see* paragraphs 144 et seq. *supra*). If, however, someone promises some such thing to another person (e.g., in common use, Article 967 CC), the relevant (promissory) contract will not be null and void. Simply, the promisor will as a rule owe compensation because of impossibility of performance (Articles 361, 362 CC – on impossibility of performance and the significance of the validity of the contract for the determination of damages, *see* paragraphs 264 et seq. *infra*).

On other occasions, infringement of the prohibition entails both nullity (or annulment *ex post facto*) and other sanctions (e.g., an obligation of compensation), in which case the rule is considered 'more than perfect' (*lex plus quam perfecta*). For example, it is prohibited for fraud to be employed in order to induce someone to enter into a juridical act (conclusion of a contract, etc.). If, however, this occurs, that is, someone is induced by fraud to enter into a juridical act, both consequences may occur cumulatively: the juridical act may be annulled (Article 147 CC) and compensation will as a rule be owed by the person who committed the fraud (Article 149 CC, subparagraph 1).

II. Instances of Nullity: Distinctions

153. When a prohibitory provision of law or morality is infringed by a juridical act, the act is null and void (Articles 174 and 178 CC). Only in those juridical acts prohibited by law (Article 174 CC) will, by way of exception, the provision which is infringed be able to stipulate a consequence other than nullity, e.g., compensation (*see* paragraph 152 *supra*). Otherwise, the consequence is always nullity when good morals are infringed by the juridical act.

Nullity may be divided into *absolute* and *relative*. Absolute nullity may be invoked not only by the contracting parties, but by any third party who has a legal interest. Absolute nullity is also taken into account ex officio by the court where it emerges from the facts of the dispute before it. This is always the case where the grounds for nullity are stipulated in the public interest. A classic case is conflict with good morals (Article 178 CC). When the provision infringed serves a private interest, only those private citizens who have the interest can invoke the nullity (relative nullity), since it is only these that the provision infringed wished to protect. This may be concluded indirectly from the *ratio* of the provision or be expressly laid down in it. For example, Article 764 §I CC, referring to the contract of partnership, stipulates as a general rule: 'An agreement whereby one of the partners has been excluded from the profits or exonerated from losses shall be null. Such nullity may only be invoked by the partner concerned'.[92] *See also* Article 175 CC: 'The disposal of a thing shall be null if such disposal was prohibited by the law. If the nullity was laid down for the benefit of certain persons, the nullity may only be invoked by such persons'.

154. The question of who may invoke nullity differs from that of *against whom* it is advanced. The rule here is that nullity has an absolute effect (= *against all*). An issue arises if third parties who are in good faith are protected, that is, those who are unaware of the nullity. The answer here is in principle negative. Nullity applies to everyone, whether in good faith or not, otherwise the purpose of the provision infringed would be largely defeated. There are, however, exceptions. We have already seen one of these in the case of simulation: the nullity of the simulated juridical act does not have force against third parties in good faith (Article 139 CC, paragraph 106 *supra*). The broadest known exception applies to a real transaction, that is, the transfer of ownership of a movable to a person in good faith (Article 1036, paragraph 1 – *see* paragraph 52 *supra*).

In the event of the nullity of a part only of the juridical act, the CC has accepted the Roman rule that the valid part is not drawn into the nullity (*utile per inutile non vitiatur*), unless it is deduced that it would not have been entered into without the part which is null (Article 181 CC). To conclude, attention should be drawn to the provision of Article 182 CC, according to which a null and void juridical act may be converted into another, valid, act (conversion) if the latter is contained in the invalid act and provided that it can be deduced that the parties would have willed it had they known of the nullity.

III. Instances of Voidability

155. A juridical act is voidable (but not void) in three instances according to the CC: those of error, fraud and duress (§2 II and III above – by way of contrast, in the case of simulation, we have a null and void juridical act). Here the defect is less obvious and the CC wished the certainty of the judicial control for the reversal of the juridical act. Annulment may be sought *from the court* only by the person in error, defrauded or threatened and their heirs within two years from the point when the state of error, fraud or duress ceased and, at all events, within twenty years (Articles 154 et seq. CC). By judicial annulment the juridical act is reversed, as we have said, retroactively and with effects in rem (Article 184 CC). Provision is made, however, as we have seen, especially in the case of movable objects, for the protection of a third party in good faith who may in the meantime have acquired ownership (Article 1036 CC). In the case of immovables also third parties in good faith are protected if they

92. *See* para. 384, *infra* .

have acquired the immovable before the noting at the public transcription registry of the decision on annulment (Articles 1203–1204 CC).

Chapter 3. The Contents of the Contract

§1. The Different Clauses

I. The Terms of the Contract and Their Effect

156. All the terms which have been formulated in a contract or those which are concluded to exist by means of interpretation are, in principle, equally binding upon the parties. Without prejudice to the fact that, by way of exception, the parties may have wished something else (see, for example, sections III, IV and §3 *infra*), each term of the contract obliges the parties (or one party if it applies only to him) to observe it and, correspondingly, confers the right on the counterparty to *claim the performance.* If it is not performed, it may give rise (usually when there is also fault as to the non-performance) to an obligation of *compensation* and the corresponding claim for the other party, or it may give him the right (again usually in the case of culpable non-performance and in reciprocal contracts) to *rescind* the contract, being relieved of the obligation of counter-performance. The exercise of these three rights (for fulfilment of the original performance, compensation and rescission) is not dependent on the nature of the contractual terms. The distinction made in English law between conditions (the breach of which entitles the innocent party either to discharge himself from his contractual obligations or to claim damages) and warranties (the breach of which does not entitle to discharge but only to damage claims) is not in this sense known to Greek law.

The institution of conditions exists, of course, in Greek law (§3 *infra*), but has another meaning (though not without some affinity with the English term). The condition which becomes a term of the contract means an uncertain and future event on which the effects of the contract (and more generally of the juridical act) depend. A condition, consequently, is a term which does not generate an obligation (the party concerned is not obliged to fulfil the condition), nor, therefore, rights to compensation or rescission by reason of its infringement, but it hinders, as far as it is pending, the production of the contractual effects.[93]

II. Implied Terms: Supplementary Terms

157. Apart from the express terms of the contract, implied terms may be accepted through interpretation (*see* paragraph 155). If it is proven that the parties willed them, they will have the same consequences in law as any contractual term. These terms also have the will of the parties as the source of their force. However, other terms may also be supplementarily accepted which are imposed on the parties, chiefly in order

93. In the text, suspensive conditions are meant. On the opposite effects of resolutive conditions, *see* § 3 *infra.*

to fill gaps in the contract. A basic source of these is Article 288 CC, according to which: 'A debtor is obliged to effect the performance as good faith requires, after consideration also of common usages' (*see* paragraphs 53 et seq. *supra*, with the corresponding provisions of foreign systems of law).

158. The question of what is imposed by *good faith* on the parties for the filling of gaps in the contract (e.g., as to the manner, place, time of the performance, etc.), or, probably, also for some deviation from contractual provisions, will be decided in the specific case. However, we could mention here by way of indication the following *collateral obligations* of the parties, which, although they have not been expressly undertaken or are not stipulated by special provisions of law, are regarded as mandates of the principle of good faith:

(a) *Duties* to secure performance, so that the end pursued by the contract is fulfilled. Thus, as the case may be, the debtor may be obliged, for example:

- to take preparatory measures which may be necessary for the fulfilment of the performance;
- to safeguard the object of the performance;
- to ensure its safe packaging and transport or dispatch;
- to ensure that it retains its value;
- to insure it;
- to supply the creditor with information on the performance owed; more particularly in the case of machinery, for example, an electrical appliance, to deliver the handbook with instructions for use, operation, maintenance, etc. for it, written, moreover, in intelligible language;
- to deliver plans of the machinery which will assist a technician in the event of repair;
- to supply spare parts when the debtor is the exclusive supplier, for example, of machinery, and when the spare parts are essential for the continuation of its operation;
- to remove any obstacles to fulfilment.
- Moreover, the creditor must not hinder the debtor in effecting the performance or make it more difficult, but must provide the debtor with 'every assistance for the fulfilment of the performance'.[94]

(b) *Duties of protection* of the other party in relation to goods, which over and above the object of the performance may by its fulfilment be imperilled. Thus normally a duty to inform the other party of any irregular development of the obligation, to warn him of dangers which may arise during the fulfilment of the performance and generally an obligation to take safety measures so that the performance does not prejudice the life, health, property and other goods of the other party will

94. *See* AP 179/1956, NoB 1956, 707, as well as AP 350/1971, NoB 1971,984.

usually arise.[95] For example, the vendor of a machine must give information to the purchaser on the risks arising from the way in which it is used and on its correct operation (cf. (a) above, where the same obligation has as its aim the protection of the object of the performance itself); a technician who undertakes a repair on another's premises must not do damage to the adjacent furnishings and areas; the creditor must give notice to the debtor that a payment has not been made if he discovers that the latter wrongly thought that he had made it; the creditor must not fail to act or omit actions with the result that the liability of the debtor is increased, etc.

(c) *Trust duties* towards the other party. These duties more usually arise, in accordance with the purpose of the obligation, in continuous contracts, as in a partnership contract, a contract for service, etc. Basically, they rest upon both parties (thus: not only on the employee, but also on the employer). These include, for example, the duty to avoid competitive acts, of not betraying the trust of the other party, of supporting him against third parties; the duty to render account (where it is a case of the administration of the affairs of others), etc.

159. Often, gaps in contracts are filled by special provisions of law which are provided (as rules of non-mandatory law) for this purpose, or by the so-called supplementary interpretation of the contract. On the relation between the different means of filling the gaps in a contract or clarifying its obscurities, *see* §2 *infra.*

III. Exoneration Clauses

160. By virtue of freedom of contract, the parties may agree on the limitation of the liability or the complete relief from it of one or both of them for various violations of the contract (e.g., inexecution, delay, defective execution of the contract). This is, however, only the rule, since these clauses providing for relief or restriction (*exoneration* or *exemption* clauses) must not conflict with provisions of mandatory law.

161. The most basic prohibition of these clauses is contained in Article 332, §1 CC, which lays down: 'Any agreement excluding or limiting beforehand liability resulting from wilful conduct or gross negligence is null.' That is to say, limitation of or relief from the liability may be validly agreed upon only for slight negligence and not for *gross negligence or for wilful conduct.* It would, anyway, be of dubious morality for a party to a transaction to be relieved for his deliberate or gravely anti-social acts. Moreover, such exemption would not be desirable from the practical point of view, since it would mean the removal of a serious reason for the deterrence of such acts. These agreements usually would be imposed (or those which are valid are imposed) by the stronger on the weaker party. This occurs chiefly in accession contracts with general terms of business (*see* paragraphs 33 et seq. *supra*).

95. Today, by virtue of Arts 5 and 6 of Law 2251/1994 'on consumer protection', as amended mainly by Law 3587/2007, provision is made for such obligations for suppliers in favour of the consumer (obligation to market only safe products, particularly in matters of the composition, functioning, packaging, maintenance, instructions for use, etc., of the products).

An agreement, as we have noted, is void when it provides not only for complete exemption, but also for the limitation of liability for wilful conduct or gross negligence, whether the limitation is quantitative (e.g., A agrees to be liable for his intentional acts only up to the sum of EUR 10, 000) or of another nature (e.g., chronological, as when exemption from liability has been agreed upon for certain periods of the performance only).

An exoneration clause is void when it is made before the causing of the prejudice (Article 332, §1 CC: '... beforehand ...'). This regulation is understandable, since only then is there a risk that the weaker party will be the object of exploitation. After the occurrence of the prejudice (and since the claim for damages is generated by this), an agreement on exemption or limitation will mean the waiver by the creditor of his pecuniary (and alienable) right to compensation. Such a waiver of a party, which does not involve risks for himself, is valid (*see also* Article 454 CC).

162. By way of exception, relief from or limitation of liability in advance for *slight negligence* also is null in the following instances:

(a) If the creditor is 'in the service' of the debtor (Article 332, §2, which is a mandatory provision), that is, when the injured party (creditor) is in a relationship of dependence on the injuring party (debtor). This will be the case chiefly in contracts for dependent services, and consequently when the injuring party is the employer of the injured. In these cases, the legislator has deemed the creditor to be much more than normally exposed to unreasonable behaviour and exploitation on the part of the counterparty, who could easily impose exoneration clauses at the expense of the former.

(b) If liability arises from the functioning of an undertaking (enterprise) for which a prior concession has been granted by the authorities (again, Article 332, §2). That is to say, the injuring party (debtor) must be an enterprise for the running of which a concession of the authority has been required. The concept of a concession is narrower than that of a simple permit from the authority, for example, for the practice of a profession. It presupposes activities which by their nature, since they relate to vital subsistence needs of citizens, that is, to the supply of public benefit services, belong in principle to a public authority (state, municipalities, communes, public law legal persons), but are ceded to another, public or private, agency. This prohibition has force *a fortiori* in the case of public authorities which have not conceded these activities but carry them out themselves.

(c) Apart from the special provisions of law on consumer protection, which in many cases stipulate a prohibition of exoneration clauses (*see infra* paragraph 164), Article 332, §2 CC, following its amendment by Law 3043/2002, provides as to every contract, with or without a consumer, that the exoneration clause for slight negligence is void also if 'it is contained in a term of the contract which was not an object of individual negotiation'. Clauses as to which there has been no individual negotiation are chiefly general terms of business, but also individualized clauses in a contract as to which no negotiation has taken place, but where, for example, the consumer (or other contracting party) has accepted them as he is unable to influence their content and has acceded to their wording by the stronger counterparty (at least on this particular matter). The exoneration of the latter from liability for slight negligence was not a product of the free will of the weaker party, and, consequently, the legislator has judged that this party must be protected, by being released from the clause which is 'imposed' upon him in this way.

(d) A last exception provided for in Article 332, §2 CC (this too was added by Law 3043/2002) is that in accordance with which the exoneration clause for slight negligence is void also if 'by the clause the debtor is released from liability for an offence against goods which stem from the personality and particularly life, health, freedom, or honour'. The special moral value of non-property goods does not justify any neglect of their protection, even if the victim accepts it.

163. According to the new regulation of Article 334 §2 CC (which was introduced by Law 3043/2002 and is, naturally, *jus cogens*), clauses exonerating the debtor from liability for fault of his vicarious agents (auxiliary and other persons whom the debtor employs in performing his contractual obligations) are permitted (as the provision lays down by its reference to Article 332 CC) only in cases where they are also permitted as to the fault of the debtor himself. That is to say, these clauses are prohibited for *intentional* (*wilful*) *conduct* or gross negligence of vicarious agents (Article 332 §1) and for slight negligence, when the exceptions cited in Article 332 §2 apply. Exoneration clauses are permitted only in the other instances of slight negligence of the vicarious agent. In this way the easy escape-routes of exoneration of debtors, and particularly of enterprises, which usually perform their obligations not in person, but by the use of associates, assistants, employees, etc. (vicarious agents), are cut off. Any fault on the part of the debtor is not as a rule that of the debtor himself, but of one of his vicarious agents, and without assimilation to the regulation of Article 332 CC (as to the debtor's own fault), there would be (apart from special exceptions) no obstacle to the conclusion of exoneration clauses.

It goes without saying that the debtor will be exonerated if the action of his vicarious agents is not among the contractual obligations which he himself (the debtor) has undertaken towards the creditor or is not among the typical risks as to the specific performance.

164. For the protection of the consumer, Law 2251/1994, as amended, is stricter towards exoneration clauses. It provides as to the *liability of the producer for defective goods* (liability which it renders strict – regardless, that is, of the fault of the producer) for nullity of 'any agreement limiting, or releasing the producer from, his liability' (Article 6 §12), and therefore for slight negligence and for chance (fortuitous) events (apart from instances of exoneration which the law itself provides for, Article 6 §8).[96] The same applies (by virtue of Article 8 §6 of the same law) to agreements limiting, or releasing a *provider of services* from, his liability (which, according to the law, requires fault, though this is rebuttably presumed, Article 8 §§1 and 4). In addition, the provision of Article 5 §6 (former §5)of the same law (as replaced by Article 3 of Law 3043/2002) stipulates nullity for any advance waiver by the consumer of the protection afforded to him by the new (following Law 3043/2002) provisions of the CC on the liability of the vendor from defects of the thing or lack of agreed qualities.

When, in particular, it is a case of General Terms of Business, their nullity is provided for (Article 2, §7 of Law 2251/1994), *inter alia*, if 'they restrict the liability

96. Directive of the EC Council of 25 Jul. 1985 (85/374/EC).

of the supplier for hidden defects of the thing', 'excessively preclude or limit the liability of the supplier', and 'entail a waiver by the consumer of his rights in the event of non-performance or of performance not duly fulfilled of the supplier, even if the supplier is at fault' (i.e., a fault of any degree, and so slight negligence).

IV. Penalty Clauses: Earnest

165. In order to strengthen the position of the creditor, the CC provides for two clauses, related to one another, which the parties may agree: the earnest (*'arrha'*) and the penalty clause (Articles 402–409 CC).

An *earnest* is an accessory contract by which one of the parties *gives* the other an object (also called the earnest), usually a sum of money, with the meaning that if he does not fulfil his performance, this object will remain in the hands of the recipient, that is, the giver will irretrievably lose it. If the recipient of the earnest does not fulfil his counter-performance, he will return it doubled (Articles 402, 403 CC). For example, purchaser A gives to vendor B, before payment of the price, EUR 5,000 as an earnest.

A *penalty clause* is an accessory contract whereby one of the parties *promises* the other that if he does not fulfil or does not properly fulfil the performance owed (Article 404 CC), he will give him an object, usually a sum of money. Example:

(a) Contractor A promises to the master of the work B that for each day of delay in the delivery of the work undertaken he will pay him a penalty of EUR 100.
(b) A, the vendor of an engine, promises to purchaser B that if he does not deliver the engine to him, he will pay him a penalty of EUR 10,000.

A. Shared Characteristics of and Differences Between Earnest and Penalty Clause

166. These are accessory agreements – agreements which presuppose another, principal, obligational relationship between the parties, which they are intended to reinforce. Without this, accessory agreements do not have force.

Thus, Article 408 CC stipulates that if the principal obligation, as to which the penalty clause is agreed, is void, the penalty clause is also void, regardless of whether the parties knew of the nullity. The same is true where the principal obligation is voidable and is annulled, in which case it becomes *ex post facto* the equivalent of void (Article 184 CC).

Nullity affects the obligation, that is, the promissory contract. For this reason, in the case of an earnest, which is already given on its conclusion (= delivery contract), the disposition contract, provided that it is abstract, will be valid, but in the absence of a valid underlying obligation, that is, in the absence of a just cause, what has been given will be claimed back by virtue of the provisions on unjust enrichment.

Naturally, the conclusion of an agreement on a 'penalty clause', that is, the undertaking of an obligation to pay a penalty is possible without the existence of the principal obligation. Such an agreement can be valid by virtue of the freedom of contract (Article 361 CC), but this is not a case of a (genuine) penalty clause, which has only an accessory character, and the provisions of the CC on a penalty clause will not in principle be implemented. If the parties have called it a penalty clause, it will be *a non-genuine penalty clause, not the clause of Article 404 CC.*

Example of a non-genuine penalty clause: A attempts to persuade B not to perform a certain act, which A considers prejudicial (perhaps prejudicial also to B, whom, let us suppose, A is protecting). B promises to give A EUR 100 (as a 'penalty' against B) if he performs the act. Here B is not undertaking an obligation (which would be the principal obligation) not to perform the act, but is directly undertaking the obligation to pay the EUR 100 on the condition that he performs the act.

It would be possible to think up a similar instance of a non-genuine earnest, but such cases are not met with in practice.

167. The *aim* both of the earnest and of the penalty clause is the same: *The strengthening of the position of the creditor*, who could suffer prejudice from possible unreliability of the debtor and needs to ensure covering of such a prejudice. If the debtor wishes to avoid the payment of an earnest or penalty, he must take care to be reliable in his obligations.

Freedom of contract, however, allows the parties to alter the purpose of the earnest or penalty clause, for example, to give the agreement the meaning of a '*forfeit money' contract.* In this case, recognition is simply given to the debtor's right to 'repent of' the conclusion of the contract and to withdraw from it, in which case, however, he will suffer the 'sanction' of the loss of the earnest or the payment of the penalty.

Moreover, the agreement on an earnest or a penalty clause may also serve (in parallel with the above, perhaps first and foremost) *purposes of proof.* For example, the creditor collects the penalty against the prejudice which he has suffered as a result of the unreliability of the debtor without it being necessary to prove that he has suffered prejudice. This is because he receives it as a penalty, by virtue of the penalty clause, and not as compensation (on the relation between penalty and compensation, *see* more in paragraph 170 *infra*).

168. The principal differences between an earnest and a penalty clause are the following:

(a) The contracting party *gives* the earnest to the counterparty, while he *promises* the penalty. In the one case we have giving and in the other a promise.
(b) The earnest functions *bilaterally*, that is, at the expense of both contracting parties.

If the giver of the earnest is (culpably) unreliable, he loses it – that is, the earnest remains irretrievably in the hands of the recipient. If the recipient is (culpably) unreliable, he returns the earnest doubled. The penalty clause, by way of contrast, functions *unilaterally*, that is, only at the expense of the party who promises the penalty and not to the detriment of his counterparty. If the promisor is (culpably) unreliable (as to the fulfilment of his duties from the principal obligation), he is obliged to pay the penalty. It will be obvious that two penalty clauses may be stipulated in a contract, one at the expense of one of the parties and the other at the expense of the other.[97]

97. *See* Athens Court of Appeals 7637/1975 NoB 1976, 634.

B. Forfeiture of the Earnest or Penalty

169. The earnest is *forfeit*, that is, is irretrievably lost for the giver or the obligation arises on the part of the recipient to refund it doubled, from the moment when the giver or the recipient, respectively, fail to perform their contractual obligations *through their fault* (i.e., intentionally or by negligence) and regardless of the existence of prejudice (Article 403, subparagraph I CC). In cases of innocent non-performance the earnest is not forfeit. If forfeiture is cancelled, the earnest which has been given will be regarded as a prepayment of the performance of the giver, who will owe only the balance of this.

The penalty is also forfeit, that is, becomes due from the creditor if and when the debtor fails *by his fault* to perform his obligations, regardless of whether the creditor has in fact suffered a prejudice (culpable impossibility of performance through fault of the debtor, default, fulfilment not duly performed by fault, Article 405 CC).

The regulation is one of non-mandatory law. Consequently, the parties may stipulate more or fewer conditions for forfeiture, within the limitations, naturally, of Articles 174, 178 etc. CC (*see* paragraphs 148 et seq. *supra*).

C. Relation Between Earnest and Penalty Clause and a Claim for Performance or Claim for Compensation

170. As to the penalty clause, the law makes the following distinctions:

(a) If the penalty has been agreed for the instance of non-fulfilment of the performance, the creditor cannot seek cumulatively both the fulfilment of the performance and the penalty, but either the one or the other, alternatively (Article 406, paragraph I). In this case, the penalty is agreed as the counterweight to the performance and takes over its place (and its total value) if that proves impossible. Consequently, the level of the penalty agreed accords with this.

(b) If, on the other hand, the penalty has been agreed for the instance of fulfilment not being duly performed or of default of the debtor, this is a penalty whose purpose is to make good the inadequacy of the performance and not to serve as a counterweight to the whole of its value. Consequently, the performance and the penalty are owed cumulatively (Article 407, subparagraph I – *see* Article 343 CC, compensation is owed together with the performance in arrears). The level of the penalty is here correspondingly lower.

If, in both the above instances, the creditor seeks the penalty, it is not necessary that he should prove that he has suffered a prejudice. Thus the penalty functions also as compensation, with the advantage, of the creditor, of his being relieved of the burden of the relevant proof. If, however, the creditor proves that he has suffered prejudice to an extent greater than the level of the penalty, he may seek the excess sum (over and above the level of the penalty) as compensation (Articles 406, paragraph 2, 407, subparagraph 2). The penalty, that is, is included in the level of the compensation.

Example: The penalty which has been agreed upon is of the level of EUR 1,000. The creditor suffers a prejudice of EUR 1,500, but he only proves a prejudice of a value of EUR 800. He will receive only the penalty (EUR 1,000). If he had proven the whole of the prejudice, he would have received the penalty plus EUR 500 compensation.

The situation is similar as to the relation between an earnest and claims for the performance or for compensation (*see* Article 403, subparagraph 2 CC, which regulates only one issue – in every other respect, the provisions on penalty clauses will be implemented *mutatis mutandis*).

A different agreement of the parties is possible.[98]

D. Excessive Penalty or Earnest

171. According to Article 409 CC, if the penalty which has been agreed is disproportionately high, the court, on the petition of the debtor, may reduce it to the 'due measure'. This provision, intended to protect the debtor thus burdened (usually the weaker contracting party, on whom the creditor can impose onerous terms) is *jus cogens*. That is to say, an agreement on a waiver of this right is not valid (thus expressly Article 409, subparagraph 2 CC).

In view of its purpose, this provision must also be implemented accordingly in the case of excessive earnest.

V. Arbitration Clauses

172. The parties may provide in their contract for an *arbitration clause* if they wish to submit any disputes which they may have arising from the contract to arbitration. A condition is that they should have the power of the free disposal of the object of the dispute. For example, matrimonial disputes (divorce, relations between the spouses, etc.) cannot be submitted to arbitration. The law (Article 867 CCPr) also prohibits the submission of labour disputes to arbitration. The arbitration clause must be agreed, in principle, in writing. Basically, it is governed by the rules of the law of contract, to the extent that these are not modified by the CCPr, which devotes one of its chapters (Articles 867–903) to the institution of arbitration, an institution which by tradition belongs to the subject-matter of civil procedure. *Compromise* (Articles 871–872 CC), on the other hand, is a civil law contract, by which the parties resolve their disputes by reciprocal concessions. On this contract, *see* Part II *infra* (paragraph 394).

§2. Interpretation of the Contract

I. The Regulation of the Civil Code: Purpose of Interpretation

173. The CC contains two general provisions on the interpretation of juridical acts, namely Articles 173 and 200 CC. The former lays down that: '*When interpreting*

98. See, for instance, AP 762/2000 HellD 2001, 153; Piraeus Court of Appeals 108/2005 PirN 2005, 194 (the provisions on penalty clause are jus dispositivum).

a declaration of will, the true intention shall be sought without adherence to the words', and the latter: *'Contracts shall be interpreted according to the requirements of good faith, after consideration also of common usages.'* Both provisions are of German origin (cf. paragraphs 133, 157 German CC).

Even though Article 173 CC refers to a 'declaration of will' and Article 200 CC refers to 'contracts', both these fundamental interpretative rules are engaged whenever a juridical act or declaration of will is being interpreted, regardless of its specific form or content. Moreover, these provisions are hierarchically equivalent, and they both govern the interpretation of *contracts*. Article 173 CC concerns the *subjective* element in the contractual interpretation process. In relation to a unilateral declaration of will (e.g., a testament), a Greek judge's objective in applying Article 173 CC is to ascertain what the declarant's true, subjective intention was, regardless of the exact words that he or she may have used in the declaration of will. Article 200 CC concerns the *objective* element in the explanatory interpretation process. It is concerned with how the contractual commitment is to be understood through the lens of good faith and trade usages. Under Greek law, the principle of good faith requires that *the interests of both contracting parties be taken into account,*[99] particularly the interests of the party (if any) whose interests the particular term in question was intended to protect. It enables a Greek judge to determine as legally binding a meaning that does not necessarily coincide with the selfish unilateral interest of either declarant, but instead represents a fair balance of the two opposing interests. For instance, in decision no. 274/2008 of *Areios Pagos*, the Court stated that:

the second [Article 200 CC] exalts the objective element, i.e., the viewpoint of the transactions and requires that such declaration be interpreted as required by good faith, for the determination of which (and only for that purpose) trade usages have to be taken into account. Good faith is the conduct that is required in transactions under the judgment of a prudent man and is approached objectively, while trade usages are the customary manners and conduct during transactions. In order to form the pertinent judgment the court of the merits shall take into account – with different weight each time – the parties' interests and in particular the interests of the party that the clause under consideration was intended to protect, the purpose of the contract, the usages and other local or temporal circumstances under which the parties' pertinent declarations of will took place as well as the nature of the contract. Thus, each declaration of will shall be understood in the sense that trade fairness requires and under the rules of which such declaration of will would have been comprehended also by a third party.[100]

To say that Article 200 CC involves an *objective* exercise is not, however, to say that the purpose of a Greek judge interpreting a contract in accordance with Article 200 CC is to identify the meaning that a hypothetical reasonable man or average prudent transacting party would have understood the words to have. To the contrary, the parties' contractual commitment should always be interpreted by reference to what the two particular contracting parties intended.

174. In general, the interpretation (construction) has as its purpose the discovery of the meaning of the declaration of will which will be decisive and have force. The

99. *See* Papanikolaou, Methodology of Private Law and Interpretation of Juridical Acts, no. 492–493.

100. Nomos Legal Database.

rulings of the courts have accepted that only unclear declarations of will are subject to interpretation.[101] In practical terms, indeed, the principal efforts of interpretation are devoted to unclear declarations. Nevertheless, a clear declaration is also conceived and has force with a certain meaning, the determination of which (in this case easy) constitutes precisely interpretation. The legal relevance of this issue is that the proper application of the rules of interpretation is subject to judicial control (*see* paragraph 182 *infra*). The decision as to whether a declaration is clear or not falls also within the judicial control of the Court of Cassation of Areios Pagos.

Greek courts take a broad approach to the question whether vagueness or ambiguity exists. As a matter of practice, if a Greek court is faced with *contractual* language that could be interpreted in more than one way, or with a factual background that puts into doubt the meaning of the allegedly 'clear/plain' wording of a contract, the court will proceed to interpret the contract pursuant to Articles 173 and 200 CC (i.e., it will conduct, in the first place, an 'explanatory' interpretation of the agreement).

Indeed, the prevailing view amongst Greek legal scholars is that (a) there is hardly any declaration of will or juridical act that is so clear and unambiguous as to escape the need of interpretation, and (b) the suggestion that a declaration of will is clear and unambiguous itself logically presupposes an initial interpretative effort.[102]

In light of the above, under Greek law, the need for interpreting a *contract* arises whenever contractual language is understood to be vague or ambiguous, as well as when a contract contains a 'gap/lacuna', that is, does not address an issue that the parties would have addressed had they considered the issue in good faith at the time they concluded the contract. Within this framework, the Greek judge has always recourse to the *intention of the contracting parties*, which he or she seeks to ascertain, and the principle of good faith, whose requirements the judge must observe in order to reach a fair interpretative result for both parties involved.

Moreover, the primary question that must be answered when reviewing a contract under Greek law is not whether the *wording* of a contract is clear or unambiguous, but rather whether the *meaning* of the declaration of will is clear and unambiguous, when taking into account all surrounding circumstances. While the wording of a contract is an important factor to consider, it is not determinative, and Greek courts instead must strive to determine what the parties really agreed to. Therefore, even the most 'clear' wording can end up being subjected to interpretation when other circumstances – e.g., common sense, customs, precontractual discussions, and post-contractual conduct – indicate that it does not necessarily reflect the true understanding of the parties. *More specifically:*

---

101. *See inter alia,* AP (in Plenary Session) 590/1968, NoB 1969, 277; AP 1002/1973, NoB 1974, 612; AP 1176/1976, NoB 1977, 709; AP 911/1980, NoB 1981, 291; AP 747/1986, NoB 1987, 738.
102. *See* Stathopoulos, in: Georgiadis & Stathopoulos' Commentary to CC, General Principles of Civil Law – vol. I^B (2016), Art. 173/200 no. 51 et seq. and Papanikolaou, Methodology of Private Law and Interpretation of Juridical Acts, no. 456.

II. Method and Criteria of Interpretation

175. As to the *method* of interpretation of contracts, it should first be borne in mind that the interests of the contracting parties have priority. It is required – and it suffices – that these persons should come to an understanding and that they are reciprocally responsible (a responsibility which constitutes a necessary supplementation of self-determination), each for the intelligibility of his declaration.

Thus, we can distinguish between the following instances:

(a) *Coincidence of the apprehension of both parties:* if both the declarant and the recipient apprehend the declaration of will in the same way, this meaning of it understood in common is that which has force, even if a third party (even the average reasonable man) would ascribe another meaning to it. This explains the force of the rule according to which (if the parties have reached a common understanding) any *false description* is irrelevant (*falsa demonstratio non nocet*). For example, if a contract provides that X will supply 100 litres of *milk* to Y, but it can be demonstrated that both parties subjectively intended that X should supply 100 litres of *soda* to Y, then the contract is for soda, despite what was written. In practical terms, this is a matter of *proof* of the coincidence of the apprehension of the two parties. Proof, however, does not displace interpretation, as is sometimes said. When coincidence has been proven, interpretation consists in the judgment that the meaning as to which there is coincidence is the legally relevant one.

(b) *Divergence of the apprehension of the parties:* if the declarant and the recipient of the declaration have not apprehended the declaration of will in the same way, the meaning which can be attributed to both the parties (but only to these), on the basis, on the one hand, of what they could have apprehended and, on the other, of their responsibility to one another as to the use and understanding of the language or any other symbols by which meaning is conveyed is decisive. This entails that that meaning will have force which the declarant might expect to be intelligible to the recipient or, otherwise, that which the latter ought and was able to apprehend.[103] These two as a rule coincide. Generally accepted views on business transactions will, of course, serve as a valuable guide, but in the last analysis the specific circumstances and capabilities of the parties are crucial. In the case of declarations of will which are addressed to a wide circle of persons (e.g., articles of incorporation of partnerships or associations, companies, contracts for modern mass transactions with the use of general terms of business, etc.), the interests and, therefore, the possible apprehension of all these persons must, of course, be taken into account.

(c) If, in the case of divergence of apprehension, the meaning attributed to each of the parties is, by way of exception, different, that is, that which the declarant might expect to be intelligible to the recipient does not coincide with that which the latter ought to have apprehended, the relevant term of the declaration will be regarded as capable of more than one meaning or unclear and, consequently, void.

103. In the wording of AP (Decision 269/1972, NoB 1972, 1024): 'the meaning with which the declaration should, according to the rules of responsibility in transactions, be understood by the interested party'.

This instance differs from that of dissent, which exists if the meaning of the declaration of one of the parties, as may be concluded by interpretation, does not coincide with the meaning of the other, as that too may be concluded by interpretation (*see* paragraphs 73, 128 *supra*).

176. The *criteria* which must be applied in the above mentioned interpretative context in case of divergence of the parties' apprehension are, with differing weight in each case, the interests of the parties (particularly of that one of them whom the term being interpreted may have been intended to protect), the aim of the juridical act, usages (e.g., linguistic), the environment and other local, chronological, etc. circumstances of the declaration, the negotiations, the nature of the juridical act (e.g., in the case of a donation, the opinion of the donor will carry greater weight). What is to be taken into account first and foremost is the true will/intention of the declarant (Article 173 CC), good faith and common usages (Article 200 CC). However, the weight attaching to each criterion, particularly in the event of conflict between them, cannot be determined in advance by general rules, but will be judged in each instance *in concreto*. Thus, factors from outside the texts of the declaration will also be taken into account.

The fact that the interpretation of an item of conduct in the question of whether it is a juridical act or not will be carried out on the basis of the same method and the same criteria has already been pointed out – paragraph 107 *supra*.

Especially in relation to the interpretation of *contracts*, a Greek judge's task when interpreting a *contract* in accordance with Article 200 CC is to arrive at the meaning that best suits the individual circumstances of the specific contracting parties, taking into account everything that they (and particularly the recipient of the declaration) knew or ought to have known. The elements of potential relevance to this analysis include (among other things):[104]

(a) the whole structure, content and specific nature of the contract in question;
(b) the nature and purpose of the transaction sought by the parties;
(c) the interests of the parties, particularly the interests of the party (if any) whose interests the particular term was intended to protect;
(d) the typical interests of parties to this type of contract;
(e) the parties' precontractual negotiations;
(f) the general surrounding circumstances before and after the signing of the contract;
(g) national or international business or trade usages, that is, the customary manners of conduct during transactions (i.e., customs that dominate, through frequent repetition, in a specific business sector or area);
(h) what is common practice;
(i) the usual contractual conduct of large undertakings when entering into contracts with complex subject-matters;
(j) other circumstances relating to the time and location at which the parties made their contract; and
(k) the post-contractual conduct of the parties.

104. In detail Stathopoulos, in: Georgiadis & Stathopoulos' Commentary to CC, General Principles of Civil Law – vol. I^{B} (2016), Art. 173/200 no. 100 et seq.

177. In concluding, as regards the interpretation of *contracts*, the starting-point of every interpretative process must be the true intention of the parties to the specific contract under scrutiny, regardless of the exact words, labels, expressions or notions used by the parties (Article 173 CC). Thereafter, the judge shall consider all facts important for interpretation purposes either before or after the execution of the contract; these include precontractual negotiations and post-contractual conduct, and so on.

In fact, the subjective test can be determinative of an issue of interpretation because, if it can be shown that both parties to the contract subjectively understood the contract to have the same meaning, effect shall be given to that meaning, even if it does not coincide with the typical meaning of the words which they actually used.

If the issue of interpretation cannot be resolved by reference to common subjective understanding, it must be resolved pursuant to Article 200 CC, which sets out an objective test. The judge's task is *not* to identify the meaning which a hypothetical reasonable man, or an average prudent transacting party, would have understood the words to have; it is to determine what the two particular contracting parties actually intended the words to mean. The judge may find that a party has a contractual obligation either because this is explicitly agreed in the text or because such an agreement can be inferred from the text upon its interpretation. If the judge considers that there is any ambiguity in relation to the interpretation of a particular term of the contract, he or she shall proceed to interpret it by reference to the aforementioned various interpretative criteria.

178. The above also applies in principle to the interpretation of *formal* juridical acts. Added to these, however, is an investigation of the purpose of the provision imposing the particular form. If the form was imposed – basically – on the interests of the parties (e.g., the form for a donation, Article 498 §1 CC, for a guarantee, Article 849 CC, etc.), no deviation from the above can be justified. The formal declaration of will has force with the meaning which the declarant and the recipient ascribed or ought to have ascribed to it. If, however, a basic reason for the imposition of the form was also the protection of third parties (e.g., in the case of contracts relating to real rights on immovables which must be transcribed and hence have publicity in the interests of third parties), the apprehension of these persons, who have an interest in a form of wording intelligible to them, must also be taken into account. Thus the rule *falsa demonstratio non nocet* does not apply, unless it is a case of a *lapsus calami* obvious to all. What is crucial here is a more general criterion: the objective meaning in the eyes of third parties. Consequently, any false description of an immovable in a notarial act subject to transcription cannot have force as the parties otherwise intended it.[105]

The taking into account of *items in texts outside the formal declaration of will* is possible.[106] (The case is different with a bill of exchange, where the document is something more than a form: the right is incorporated into it). It is not required that these items, which can also be proven by the testimony of witnesses, should also be covered by the form; they serve only for the discovery of the crucial meaning of the declaration (subject to a specific form) itself.

105. *See* AP 627/1961, NoB 1962, 366.
106. *See* AP 182/1976, NoB 1976, 711; AP 1390/1999, HellD 2000, 702.

III. Filling of Gaps in a Juridical Act: Supplementary Contractual Interpretation under Greek Law

179. If even after interpretation as per above, the juridical act or contract contains *gaps*, these will be filled by means of *supplementary interpretation*. More specifically:

Under Greek law, a court can supplement a contract with terms that the contract otherwise does not contain by means of *supplementary* (or *completive*[107]) interpretation. Greek courts engage in supplementary interpretation when a situation has arisen that the parties to a contract have not made provision for in their contract – while they would have done so, i.e., they would have agreed to a certain contractual regulation of the issue, had they considered the issue in good faith at the time they concluded their contract – and the court acts to fill in the gap/lacuna in the parties' agreement.

Supplementary interpretation under Greek law occurs in accordance with Article 200 CC, usually in conjunction with Article 288 CC. However, the invocation of Article 288 CC for the supplementary interpretation is not necessary. Supplementary interpretation constitutes neither interpretation of an *autonomous* private regulation (as in case of interpretation of the declaration of will in accordance with the above), nor a *heteronomous* assessment imposed on the parties by law. It is, of course, interpretation (i.e., deduction of the crucial meaning), but not of a declaration of any will, but of a private regulation as a whole. It lies in some way between interpretation of an autonomous regulation and regulation imposed by law. However, the frequent invocation by court rulings of the two provisions together (Articles 200 and 288 CC) is to be explained by the fact that usually the same solution is imposed according to both.

When engaging in supplementary interpretation, a Greek judge seeks to identify what *the contracting parties (and not any third party or the judge)* would have stipulated in accordance with good faith and trade usages if they had dealt with the issue at the time they concluded their contract. The object is to find a solution – always for the specific parties – that is in line with the scope and the 'economy' of the entire agreement.[108] To accomplish this, the court will take into account numerous factors, including the economic or asset positions of the parties, the manner in which they have dealt with similar issues (if applicable), and the like.

The overriding concept when engaging in supplementary interpretation is to take into account *the interests of both contracting parties* in the spirit of good faith.

180. *Supplementary* interpretation under Greek law may allow for the *implication of terms* (*see* paragraphs 157 et seq. *supra*) that are able to give effect to the parties' agreement and that preserve or restore the contractual balance, thus reconciling and satisfying both parties' interests.

Indeed, the implication of terms by means of supplementary interpretation is permissible, and required, where, in the absence of a provision concerning a matter, the contract cannot be implemented in a manner that corresponds to the intention of the parties and the purpose of the contract. When a Greek judge engages in supplementary interpretation, he or she is attempting to identify the hypothetical intention of the

107. Markesinis, Unberath & Johnston, The German Law of Contract (2nd ed. 2006), pp. 139 et seq.

108. *See also* Stathopoulos, in: Georgiadis/Stathopoulos' Commentary to CC, General Principles of Civil Law – vol. I^{B} (2016), Art. 173/200 no. 184 et seq., 204 et seq., passim; Papanikolaou, Methodology of Private Law and Interpretation of Juridical Acts, no. 520 et seq.

parties, rather than their actual intention; the judge seeks to identify what the *particular contracting parties* would have stipulated in accordance with good faith and trade usages if they had dealt with the issue at the time they concluded their contract, having regard to the purpose of their contract.

Greek case law supporting the inclusion of new contractual terms, by means of a supplementary interpretation pursuant to Article 200 CC (sometimes also in conjunction with Article 288 CC), may be found, for instance, in the following decisions:[109]

- AP 1450/1995 (EEN 1997, 272): Lease agreement, whereby the rent was uniformly set for both the premises and its equipment, without being therein determined which part of the price referred to the premises and which to the equipment (flat rent); the court determined itself the appropriate rent ratio (85% for the premises and 15% for the equipment).
- First Instance Court of Athens 1268/2010 (Nomos Legal Database): Housing loan agreement, whereby the floating interest rate clause – according to which the bank was able to unilaterally increase or decrease the interest rate in view of certain indices – was deemed to be invalid; the court ruled that '*fair criteria*' should be set for the re-adjustment of the interest rate with the main one to be the ECB's interest rate – that is, the interest rate of said loan agreement should follow the fluctuation of the ECB's interest rate.

Furthermore, the Greek Courts' adherence to the supplementary interpretation of a contract is often emphatically reiterated as obiter dictum – in cases where the court interferes, in a *corrective* way, with the content of a lease agreement in order to adjust the rent to a supervening change in circumstances, by virtue of the general clause of Article 288 CC (in more detail *see* §5 *infra*).[110] In addition, the instrument of supplementary interpretation of a contract is also used in the Greek case law pertaining to the gaps of constitutions of 'horizontal ownership' (storey-building titles) and building regulations.[111]

In German law – which sometimes has a considerable impact upon Greek law, since the Greek Civil Code is based to a large extent on the BGB and as a result it is quite frequent for Greek legal scholars to cite German counterparts as well as decisions of the German Supreme (Civil) Court (*Bundesgerichtshof*) – the German Supreme Court has applied the methodological instrument of supplementary interpretation of a contract, for instance, in order to establish a claim for the assignment of *rights to*

---

109. *See also* Stathopoulos, in: Georgiadis & Stathopoulos' Commentary to CC, General Principles of Civil Law – vol. I^B (2016), Art. 173/200 no. 184 et seq., 204 et seq., passim, esp. fn. 309, 312 and 339.

110. *See* indicatively AP (in Plenary Session) 9/1997, Nomos Legal Database; in more detail Karampatzos, Unforeseen Change of Circumstances in a Bilateral Contract (2006; in Greek), passim, esp. no. 478 et seq., 491 et seq. and *the same*, Financial Crisis and Re-adjustment of Contractual Performances – Especially in View of the Recent Case Law of Instance Courts on Commercial Lease, ChrID 2013 (in Greek), pp. 92 et seq. Some scholars also regard this case as a case of supplementary interpretation; *see* Papadimitropoulos, The Supplementary Interpretation of Juridical Acts (2009; in Greek), no. 45 et seq., 568 et seq.

111. *See* , indicatively, AP 1588/1999, Nomos Legal Database and *Papadimitropoulos*, *supra* n. 49.

recourse against the first seller in a sales chain, insofar as in the sales contract between the next seller and the final purchaser the parties have agreed to a liability exclusion (waiver) in favour of the seller.[112]

In general, Greek and German Courts interfere with the contract more often than their English counterparts – in whose case law very rarely can a term be implied.[113] Greek courts are more readily prepared to imply terms into a contract via supplementary interpretation, so as to give a contract 'business efficacy.'[114] In essence, Greek Courts act similarly to the German ones, namely they:

> imply a term more easily where they think fit than their English counterparts [...]. The interpretation of the contract, by applying § 157 BGB [or, respectively, Articles 200, 288 CC], extends beyond the bare text of the agreement. It includes also the context of the contracting process, peripheral circumstances, and an analysis of the parties' interests. This is why in German [as well as in Greek] law interpretation can be a powerful tool for the implication of terms.[115]

181. Frequently, the legislator provides *supplementary rules* to deal with instances where there is a gap in a contract, as well as elucidatory (*interpretative*) *rules* to clear up its obscurities. It is disputed whether these rules take precedence over supplementary interpretation. In theory, it is possible for the legislator, between the introduction of provisions of mandatory law and the leaving of complete freedom to the private will, to give to a dispositive rule of law a position of precedence, for example, immediately after the declaration of will which is express only, or after any (express or implied) declaration of will, or even after supplementary interpretation adjusted to the specific contract. The degree to which a rule of law prevails *vis-à-vis* other regulations is a matter for the legislator who introduces it. That is to say, the answer will be given in each case by the interpretation of the special provision of non-mandatory law (more than by any terminological distinction into special or general interpretative rules or

---

112. Examples may be found in Wolf & Neuner, Allgemeiner Teil des Bürgerlichen Rechts (10th ed. 2012; in German), § 35 no. 58–59 and 67, *Ellenberger*, in: Palandt Kommentar zum BGB (Commentary to German CC, 72th ed. 2013; in German), § 157 no. 6, Markesinis, Unberath & Johnston, The German Law of Contract, pp. 139 et seq. Furthermore, the entire institution of *contracts with protective effects towards third (non-contracting) parties* is based upon a supplementary interpretation of the relevant contracts, according to which, for instance, (i) the landlord of a leased property may be held contractually liable towards relatives of the tenant for damages suffered by them within the leased property, or (ii) many experts (civil engineers, architects, auditors, legal or financial advisors, etc.) may be held (once more, contractually) liable towards third parties for the reports they have drafted for their clients, which have been shown to third parties who in their turn, relying upon the experts' opinion and credibility, made substantial investment decisions, e.g., to finance a project or to purchase a real estate property; *see* in detail Karampatzos, Vom Vertrag mit Schutzwirkung für Dritte zur deliktischen berufsbezogenen Vertrauenshaftung (2005; in German); also Wolf & Neuner, *supra* ; Markesinis, Unberath & Johnston, *supra* , pp. 204 et seq.
113. *See* , indicatively, *Monde Petroleum SA v. Westernzagros Limited* [2016] EWHC 1472 (Comm), whereby the High Court once again considered the circumstances in which a duty of good faith could be implied into a contract, rejecting an argument that a party's contractual right to terminate a consultancy contract had to be exercised in good faith.
114. *See* Markesinis, Unberath & Johnston, *supra* , p. 141.
115. Markesinis, Unberath & Johnston, *supra* , pp. 138–139.

supplementary rules, as is often said). However, it will normally emerge from the non-mandatory supplementary rule that this rule yields to the autonomous juridical regulation, that is, to the express or implied declaration of will as this is determined by interpretation, but takes precedence (much more so when it is a case of an elucidatory and not merely supplementary provision) over supplementary interpretation, which is not an autonomous regulation. If, however, the specific juridical act (e.g., sui generis sale) diverges significantly from the type of the contract regulated which the legislator had in mind and in view of which he provided the dispositive rule, supplementary interpretation adjusted to the special conditions of the juridical act will take precedence. In practical terms, the solutions will usually coincide, because both supplementary provisions and supplementary interpretation would lead to similar solutions.

IV. Procedural Issues

182. The person who invokes a meaning of the declaration of will must *prove* the actual facts which are relevant, particularly any coincidence of apprehension of the parties, as well as the establishment of a common usage, etc. In every other respect, the question is a *legal* one and cannot be the subject of proof;[116] it is also to be taken into account ex officio by the judge (thus particularly the deduction by the interpreter of the crucial meaning).

Apart from the factual issues, as to which, naturally, there is no control of the Court of Cassation of *Areios Pagos*, the rules on the basis of which the crucial meaning of the declaration of will is discovered are to some extent rules of logic, but also rules of law. Their implementation is consequently subject to the control of *Areios Pagos*. This also applies to Articles 173, 200 CC, which contain legislative orders and not merely (non-obligatory) instructions.[117]

§3. Conditional Contracts

I. Concept, Distinctions

183. A condition is a term which is added to a juridical act and which makes the effect of the act dependent upon a future and uncertain event. Often the future and uncertain event itself is termed the 'condition'.

Basic for the nature of the dependence involved is the division of conditions into *suspensive* and *resolutive*. If the effects of the juridical act are suspended by the condition until such time as the condition is fulfilled, that is, until the occurrence of the future and uncertain event, we have a suspensive condition (Article 201 CC). For example: I promise to sell A an immovable at a certain price if A makes a gift of his personal historical archive to the University. The condition does not constitute an

116. *See* AP 176/1973, NoB 1973, 920; AP 960/1996, HellD 1997, 831.
117. This control by the *Areios Pagos* is confirmed by the Code of Civil Procedure (Arts 559 no. 1, 560 no. 1, 561 §I).

obligation on A, but its fulfilment gives rise to my own obligation; or I will buy an immovable if I receive the loan which I have asked for from a bank. If, on the other hand, the effects of the juridical act occur immediately on the conclusion of the act, but the condition provides for their reversal on the occurrence of the future and uncertain event, that is, the ceasing of the effect of the juridical act and an *ipso jure* return to the *status quo ante*, we have resolutive condition (Article 202 CC). For example: I transfer to my creditor A the ownership of a movable object on condition that when my debt to A is paid, ownership will *ipso jure* revert to me;[118] or I sell an immovable to A, who wants it for tourist development, on the resolutive condition that the development projects should have started (or should be finished) within one year.

Any juridical act, whether obligational or real, can be conditional. Only in exceptional circumstances, for reasons of public interest, security of transactions, the protection of third parties, etc. does the law prohibit conditions in certain types of juridical acts; for example, the contracting of marriage, adoption (which are, *inter alia*, also juridical acts) are not susceptible to conditions (Articles 1350, 1548 CC). The same applies to the exercise of the option right in the case of alternative obligations or to the declaration of offsetting of claims, etc. (Articles 306, 444 CC).

184. If the event in which the effect of the juridical act depends is not uncertain or not future (e.g., it has already occurred, but the contracting parties are not aware of this), this will be a *non-genuine condition.* For example: I lease my house in Athens to civil servant A, on condition that he is transferred by the service to Athens. The service has already taken the decision on his transfer. Here there is no objective uncertainty. The effect of the juridical act has already occurred. Only if the parties wanted their *knowledge* of the transfer to be the future event do we have a genuine condition and the effects of the juridical act will occur with this knowledge. *Conditions of law* (*conditiones juris*), in which the event is a prerequisite in law for the effect of the juridical act, are among non-genuine conditions. Here the addition of this condition is superfluous, since the relevant dependence on it is stipulated by law. For example: I make a gift of something to company A 'if that still legally exists and has not been dissolved'.

So-called *potestative conditions*, in which whether the future and uncertain event will occur or not is dependent on the will of one or other of the parties, are among those which are valid. The CC does not prohibit them.[119] It will be questionable, however, where the fulfilment of the condition depends on the *absolute power* of the conditional obligor ('*si voluerim*' condition) whether there was in fact an intention of concluding the juridical act as of now (e.g., I sell you something if I judge that the sale is of interest to me personally).

185. Conditions which are *unlawful* or *contrary to morality* or *unintelligible* or *contradictory* render the juridical act void. The same applies to a suspensive condition

118. This is a case of the 'fiduciary' transfer of the ownership (*fiducia*) which is made to secure a claim of the transferee. It is regarded as valid (*see* para. 47 *supra*) and is preferred in practice to a pledge, because it renders possible the non-delivery of possession to the transferee (through a '*constitutum possessorium*', Art. 977 CC) so that the transferor can continue to have this, which is prohibited in the case of a pledger (Art. 1213 CC).

119. By way of contrast, Art. 1174 of the French CC lays down that: 'any obligation is null if it is contracted under a condition which is potestative on the part of the person obliged'.

the *fulfilment of which is impossible.* On the other hand, an impossible condition set as resolutive has no effect (Article 208 CC). There is a special provision for conditions in the law of succession (which are added to wills). For example, unintelligible conditions in wills are regarded as not having been written, that is, they do not affect the validity of the will. The condition of celibacy (e.g., of an heir or legatee) is also deemed not to have been written, though the condition of widowhood of a spouse who is the beneficiary of the will is valid (Articles 1794 et seq. CC), etc.

II. The Effect of a Condition

186. As long as the suspensive condition is *pending*, that is, the future and uncertain event has not occurred, none of the willed effects of the juridical act is generated (e.g., generation of a contractual right and of the corresponding obligation by the contract, transfer of ownership, etc.). However, the contract (or the unilateral juridical act) has been concluded and the parties cannot unilaterally disengage themselves from its binding force. This means that there is the so-called right of expectation of the conditional beneficiary who is protected by the law. For example, the beneficiary may seek the judicial recognition of this state of affairs in law (Articles 69, paragraph 1, e and 70 CCPr), seek injunctions, etc., if, for example, as a result of the misconduct of the obligor there is a risk of the fulfilment of the condition (which, let us suppose, has not been made dependent on the will of the obligor) being frustrated; may seek compensation from the other party, when the condition is fulfilled, if the latter during the course of the uncertainty culpably frustrated or prejudiced the conditional right (Article 204 CC), etc. If, moreover, the other party has impeded, in a manner contrary to good faith, the fulfilment of the condition, this will by a *legal fiction* be deemed to have been fulfilled (Article 207 CC, which also provides for the opposite instance, that is, fictitious non-fulfilment of the condition if the party benefiting from this has brought about its fulfilment in a manner contrary to good faith). Another strong form of protection of the conditional beneficiary is the regulation of Article 206 CC, on which, *see* paragraph 188 *infra*.

The above finds application *mutatis mutandis* also in the case of a resolutive condition (non-reversal of the effects of the juridical act as long as the resolutive condition is pending – protection of the party benefiting from a possible fulfilment of the resolutive condition, etc).

187. If the suspensive condition is *fulfilled*, the (suspended) effects of the juridical act (e.g., generation of obligation, transfer of ownership, etc.) occur *ipso jure* without any new act by the parties being required. If a resolutive condition is fulfilled, the reversal of the effects which have occurred takes place also *ipso jure* (Articles 201 and 202 CC).

The fulfilment of the condition has *not* in *principle retroactive effects*. The occurrence or reversal of the effects of the juridical act (e.g., transfer of ownership to the beneficiary on suspensive condition, return of the ownership to the person who transferred it on resolutive condition, etc.) begins with the occurrence of the uncertain event (*ex nunc*). The interim owner may keep the fruits, etc. The parties may agree on the retroactive force of the fulfilment of the condition, but this will have effect only in personam and not in rem (e.g., retroactive obligation of the furnishing of fruits, non-retroactive transfer of ownership – Article 203 CC).

188. When there is *disposition* of the object of the conditional contract for as long as the condition is pending, Article 206 CC stipulates that if the condition is fulfilled and if the disposition which has taken place frustrates or prejudices the conditional right, such disposition will be regarded as *ipso jure* void. Thus, if A transfers on suspensive condition an object to B and while the condition is pending (as long, that is, as A is the owner) A transfers it to C, this transfer to C, if the condition in favour of B is fulfilled, is void. B acquires the ownership *ipso jure* on the fulfilment of the condition. If while the condition is pending, A simply leases the same thing to C, this lease is not void. This is because this is a promissory contract and not a disposition contract. Anyway, the simple lease right of C is no obstacle to the acquisition of the ownership of the object by B. The possession and use of the object is another matter: as a rule (principle of relativity), B will not be bound by others' promissory contract on the lease and will be able to claim possession of the object also (*see* Articles 1094 et seq., but also the broad exception of Articles 614 et seq. CC paragraph 194 *infra*).

The regulation of Article 206 CC also applies to resolutive conditions. For example, A transfers an object on resolutive condition to B, and B, while the condition is pending and he is the owner, transfers it to C. When the condition is fulfilled, the ownership reverts to A, because the transfer to C is void.

As to the acquisition of ownership of *movable objects*, the CC (Article 1036 CC) provides for the protection of third parties in good faith. That is to say, the transferee acquires the ownership of the movable object if he did not know, without there being gross negligence on his part (Article 1037 CC), that the person transferring it was not the owner (*see* paragraph 52 *supra*). If the bona fide third party acquired the movable from the conditional obligor (in our examples, let us suppose that C was in good faith), it is disputed whether the spirit of Article 1036 CC or that of Article 206 CC prevails. It is teleologically preferable to accept that Article 1036 CC, which has the broader purpose of protecting transactions and those who act in good faith from unknown vices and even more so from the 'vice' in the case of Article 206 CC, prevails (C is owner, not A or B).[120] (In Article 1036 CC, ownership on the part of the transferor is completely lacking, while in Article 206 CC, there is ownership and only power of disposition is lacking). It corresponds to the broad aim of Article 1036 CC for us to accept that this article introduces an exception from the provisions which prohibit the disposition of a movable object either because the disposer does not have the ownership (Articles 239, 1034) or because he does not have power of disposition (e.g., Article 206 CC).

189. A condition, if there is no set term for it, may be fulfilled at any time. If fulfilment has been *frustrated* (e.g., it has become impossible or a time-limit has been agreed for fulfilment and the time-limit has passed without fulfilment), that is, if it has become certain that the event will not happen, the parties are released from the condition. If the condition was suspensive, the (suspended) effects of the juridical act are never generated, while, if it was resolutive, these remain in a final manner.

120. *See* Athens Court of Appeals 2748/1982 NoB 1983, 511 (with comment by Ap.Georgiadis).

III. Terms (Time Clauses)

190. If the event on which the effects of the juridical act have been made dependent is, on the one hand, future, but, on the other, it is certain that it will occur, the CC speaks not of a condition, but of a 'term', i.e., a time clause (dies). For example, I sell and transfer an apartment today, agreeing that the effects of the (promissory and disposition) contract will occur in three months' time (suspensive time clause); or I sell and transfer it with immediate effect, which, however, I determine shall cease in three month's time (when the ownership will revert to me) – resolutive time clause. Here the fulfilment of the time clause is certain. There is simply a chronological difference between the occurrence of the effects and the conclusion of the juridical act. In the case of a time clause, the provisions as to conditions are, according to Article 210 CC, implemented mutatis mutandis.

Chapter 4. Privity of Contract: The Parties of the Contractual Obligation

§1. The Contracting and Third Parties

I. The Principle and the Exceptions

A. The Relativity of Obligations: Plurality of Parties

191. As we have seen in examining the concept of obligation, one of its basic characteristics is *relativity*, that is to say the fact that its effect develops only between creditor and debtor, as it does not create rights or obligations for third parties (paragraph 19 *supra*). In English terminology, what corresponds to the principle of relativity is the 'doctrine of privity'. By way of contrast, rights in rem have force as against all (*erga omnes*), that is, they have absolute effect.

The preclusion of the absolute effect of rights in personam is reasonable. Their relativity is a consequence of the freedom of individuals to formulate between themselves, within the bounds permitted by public policy, whatever relations, with whatever content, they wish. Third parties cannot be, nor do they always have an interest in being, privy to these relations and their content. As a rule, the need for rights in personam to be publicized does not arise in transactions. Moreover, it would be an excessive burden for third parties to have imposed upon them the obligation to inform themselves of whether and what obligations exist between other individuals. Consequently, public policy cannot demand of them to conduct themselves in such a way as to ensure the right of the creditor. It could be said, further, that such a demand would constitute an excessive commitment in principle for the person who happened to know of the existence and content of rights in personam which did not concern him. A similar line of thought explains the fact that third parties cannot derive rights from the obligational relation. The debtor has undertaken the obligation to the creditor. If it were incumbent upon him to take into account any third party who might have an interest (known to the debtor or otherwise) in the specific obligation, the limits of his obligation would be lost.

This has particular application, basically, to obligations which stem from a contract. Here private autonomy requires that one should undertake contractual commitments or acquire corresponding rights, basically, only by his own will and not by an act of others. For the third parties, the contract of others is *res inter alios acta*. The problem of the relativity of obligations presents itself in practical terms chiefly as a problem of relative effect of contracts. However, the rule of privity has force for all obligations, including those which stem from the law. In the case of the latter it is, of course, always possible for the legislator to determine in each instance (by the provision which establishes the obligation) who is the creditor and who is the debtor, on criteria which he considers crucial for the creation of the obligation and which at the same time constitute the explanation of why the relation has force only between these two persons. From these criteria, two specific persons will usually, but not always, emerge as creditor and debtor. Thus in obligation from tort (Article 914 CC), the creditor is, for example, the owner of the thing which has been destroyed and the debtor the person who is at fault for its destruction. According to the provision of Article 904 CC, the obligor for the restitution of the enrichment is the person enriched ('who has become richer') and the individual who fulfils this description can change, for example, in the event of gratuitous transfer of the enrichment (Article 913 CC).

Naturally, the case of *plurality of parties* to an obligation (i.e., plurality of creditors or plurality of debtors or both) does not constitute an exception to relativity. Such plurality may arise either because a number of persons, more than two, conclude a contract or because an obligation *ex lege* is created simultaneously for many persons (see, for example, Articles 926–927 CC for a delict committed by many). The CC regulates these instances by non-mandatory rules in Articles 480 et seq. CC. In the event of doubt, the obligation is divisible, that is, it is divided (as against the creditor) among the debtors or (as against the debtor) among the creditors, and, again in the event of doubt, in equal shares. If, on the other hand, it can be concluded (from the contract or *ex lege* – for example, Article 926 CC) that each of the many debtors has an obligation as against the creditor to effect the whole performance, but the creditor is entitled to demand the performance only once from whichever debtor he chooses, or if each of the many creditors (if he precedes the others) is entitled to demand the whole performance from the debtor, but the debtor is obliged to perform only once, the obligation is termed *joint and several.* If nothing different emerges from the relations between the joint and several debtors or the joint and several creditors, their liability is stipulated to be in their internal relations in equal shares. This liability manifests itself in the recourse right of the debtor who has fulfilled the obligation against the other debtors or in the similar right of the creditors who have not collected against the creditor who has. The parties may, by virtue of freedom of contract, determine the relations between them in a variety of different ways.

192. Nevertheless, a strict implementation of the privity of obligations would not answer to the *spirit* and *needs* of our times. The idea that each of us should concern himself only with his own affairs and not with those of others, inflexibly applied, can lead to an individualism which is indifferent to (whatever) rights of third parties. Furthermore, the advanced division of labour in modern societies increases the need for certain third party effects of obligational relations. Often, the expectations and interests of third parties from an obligation of others are deserving of protection. Today, the relations which, although they are created by contracts, cannot be regarded as an affair exclusively of the contracting parties are constantly on the increase.

By way of indication only, the following instances could be quoted:

Transactions that aim at channelling a consumer product from its source (the producer) to the consumer. Usually, a whole 'chain' of contracts (conclusion of a new contract each time that the product changes hands) takes shape, with the result of an absence of any direct contractual bond between producer and consumer.

Trilateral or multilateral relations for dependent services in which, for example, the employee in the last analysis provides his services not only to his employer but to another person or persons (cf. the gradation: master of the work - general contractor - subcontractor - employee). Contracts which provide for performance to the employer of team work by more than one employee with an effect on the relations between them, etc.

Financing by banks (or other sources of financing) of the economic activity of clients (e.g., loans for the supply of goods, for the construction of projects, etc.). In this way, contracts are facilitated by a supplier of financing who is not himself a party to these.

Contracts for the transport of things which also constitute the object of another contract (e.g., a sale contract) or contracts for the transport of a group of persons who are not contracting parties.

Conclusion of contracts by one person for (in the interest of) another (indirect representation). Bank deposits in favour of third parties. Insurance contracts in favour of third parties, etc.

In these and other similar cases, the fact that there is a need, deserving protection, on the part of third parties to be able to rely on the contract of others and to expect its normal fulfilment or that the contracting parties (particularly the creditor) have a justifiable interest in demanding respect for their contract by third parties – or possibly both – is easy to see.

It is, therefore, understandable that legislation today lays down as a basis, for the reasons which have been given, the principle of the privity of contracts, but accepts, in response, up to a point, to the needs of society, exceptions from that principle (particularly from the relative effect of contracts).

B. Exceptions: Subcontracting and Other Cases

193. We give below, by way of indication, some of the instances of *exception from the principle of the privity of contracts which are recognized by law*:

In a number of cases, where there are two contracts with three subjects (contract of A with B, and B with C), so that finally trilateral relations are created, the Civil Code allows a direct claim between the persons who are not parties to the same contract (between A and C). This is the case, for example, when the lease of a thing (Article 574 CC) is combined with sub-leasing by the lessee; or a contract for work (Article 681 CC) with the engagement by the contractor of employees for its completion; or a mandate (Article 713 CC) with the entrusting of the matter by the mandatary to his substitute; or a loan for use (Article 810 CC) with ceding of the use of the thing by the user (borrower) to a third party; or deposit (Article 822 CC) with the depositing of the thing by the depositary with a third party. In these trilateral relations only the intermediary has a contractual bond with the other two. Between the latter there is no contract. In spite of this, the Civil Code, recognising that the second contract is based on the first and that to detach one from the other and to make them independent of one another is not socially and economically justifiable, puts aside relativity and permits (apart from claims against the counterparty) the lessor to seek the thing leased direct from the lessee (Article 599 § 2, cf. also Article 604 § 2 CC); the employee to claim salary against the master of the work (Article 702 CC); the mandator to take action directly against the mandatary's substitute (Article 716 § 3 CC); the lender or depositor to seek the restitution of the thing by the person to whom the user or depositary has given it (Articles 819, 825 §2). It creates, that is to say, a direct obligation between the two persons who do not have a bond between them by contract (without, of course, abolishing the existing obligation between the contracting parties).

In this way the familiar and more general problem of subcontracting is solved. The subcontract presupposes a main contract. One of the parties to the main contract either cannot propria persona fulfil his contractual duties or a part of those and entrusts them by another contract, the subcontract, to another (e.g., subcontract for work, submandate, subagency, etc.) or extends his contractual advantage by a new contract, the subcontract, to third parties (e.g., sub-lease, sub-bailment, etc.). The subcontract is an independent contract, permitted by virtue of freedom of contract. The rules of contracts are applied to this as they are to the main contract, and both are governed in principle by the doctrine of privity. By reason, however, of the interdependence of the interests of three persons, the Civil Code, as we have seen in its provisions immediately above, which, basically, concern precisely subcontracts, breaks the principle of privity of contracts and in certain cases provides for a direct suit between the two persons who are not linked by the bond of the same contract. An application of these provisions by analogy to other trilateral relations is possible, as far as the conditions of analogy are in the specific case fulfilled.

194. A basic exception to privity of contracts is introduced by a provision of great importance – that of Article 614 CC. Its purpose is the protection of *lessees of immovables*, who have only a contract right against the lessor. This provision lays down that a person who acquires the ownership of an immovable from the lessor is subrogated on certain terms (provided that the lease is proven by a document of certain date and it has not been determined otherwise in the lease agreement) to the rights and obligations of the lease and, consequently, is obliged to respect the right of the lessee stemming from it.

Of even greater importance is the instance of a *genuine contract in favour of a third party* (Articles 411 et seq.), which will be dealt with under II *infra*. (Additionally, *transfer* of a claim and of an obligation, which from a certain point of view relaxes the personal character of the obligation, will be discussed in §2).

195. Frequently, the extension of the effect of an obligation (usually arising from a contract) to third parties is to be explained by the fact that there are additional features of a delictual nature present. This is the case where an 'attack' on the relation of obligation by the third party has so strong an anti-social character that the legislator creates a new relation of obligation (arising from a delict) or provides for other consequences at the expense of the 'attacker'. Of importance on this point is Article 919 CC.

According to this provision, he who causes prejudice to another 'intentionally' and 'in a manner contrary to morality' is obliged to compensate him. These terms may also apply in the case of an 'attack' on a contractual right by a third party. Examples:

- Two successive sales of the same thing, in which the second of the purchasers has concluded the contract under inadmissible circumstances and with the intention of prejudicing the first.

- Immoral recruitment of the employees of another or stealing of his clients; or an employer, in order to take revenge on his competitor A, incites the latter's staff to terminate their contract for services with him and conclude a new contract with himself.
- A destroys in a malicious manner the object which B had sold to C, so that the latter shall be deprived of its use.

It not infrequently happens that there is collusion of the third party with the debtor to the detriment of the creditor. The latter has in principle rights only against his debtor, since his right is relative. Third parties have no obligation, as we have already said, to respect the contractual rights of others and, consequently, the act as an 'offence' against such a right is not unlawful. In spite of that, in accordance with Article 919 CC, if two conditions are fulfilled, that is, immoral conduct and intention on the part of the third party,[121] a new obligation is created by the law between the offendor and the creditor, by virtue of which the former is liable for damages.[122]

196. The relaxation of the strictness of the doctrine of privity finds confirmation in certain EC Directives, which, in keeping with the more general spirit of the Community as to the overall protection of the consumer, put aside this doctrine in the issues which they deal with. Apart from the Directive on the *liability of a producer* of defective goods (*see* paragraph 164 *supra*), which provides for liability of the producer for prejudice arising from a defect in one of his products, even if the injured party (e.g., final consumer) had no direct relation by contract with the producer, it is worth mentioning two other EC Directives and the corresponding Greek acts of adjustment:

(a) In the Community regulation on *consumer credit agreements*[123] (Article 15, §2), the following instance is provided for in the case of credit contracts: if the recipient of the credit uses the credit in order to acquire goods or services with which he is not finally provided or provided in a manner which is contrary to the contract, and the supplier of the goods or services is linked by contract with the credit institution, by virtue of which consumers are provided with credit for the acquisition of goods or services from the supplier in question, the recipient of the credit (consumer) is entitled to take action subsidiarily (if, that is, he does not receive satisfaction from the supplier) against the credit institution. The breaking of the principle of privity is obvious, since the credit institution is a third party in respect of the supply contract as to which the breach of contractual obligations has taken place. This, however, is justified, since the credit institution, in view of what are

121. Eventual intent (*dolus eventualis*) also suffices.
122. Thus also para. 826 of the German Civil Code. The same practical solution has been reached in France, where intentional breaching of the right of another, including a right in personam, is regarded as legal ground for compensation, by way of exception from the principle of privity (see, *inter alia*, Carbonnier, *Droit Civil IV*, 22ème éd., 2000, No 122 I b).
123. Directive 2008/43/EC of the European Parliament and of the Council of 23 Apr. 2008 on credit agreements for consumers and repealing Council Directive 87/102/EC, as amended by Commission Directive 2011/90/EU; corresponding Greek Act of Adjustment: MinD (joint) Z1-699/2010 (Government Gazette B'' 917/23.6.2010), as amended by MinD (joint) Z1-111/2012 (Government Gazette B'' 627/7.3.2012).

here interlinked trilateral interests, cannot regard as a matter alien to itself the supply of the goods or services and 'wash its hands' on whatever development takes place in these supplies, from which it derives benefits.

(b) In the Community regulation on the *maintenance of the rights of employees in the event of transfers of enterprises*[124] (Article 3) it is stipulated, *inter alia*, that by the contract transferring the enterprise between the transferor and the transferee 'also transferred to the transferee are the rights and duties which the transferor has from a contract for services or a labour relation', that is, as against a person who is a third party (the employee) as far as the contract transferring the enterprise is concerned. The employee acquires a new employer, without his consent being required. This, of course, is with a view to his protection (for the maintenance of his rights). However, according to the general regulation of the CC, his consent would have been required. (*See* paragraph 208 *infra* on the necessity for a trilateral agreement, since it is a case here not only of the assignment of a claim, but also of the assumption of a debt, that is, of the transfer of the whole contract for services). By the depersonalization of the relation (since the enterprise is a self-contained transferable economic unit) the consent of the third party (the employee) for the effect of the contract – alien to him – on himself is not required.[125]

197. The recognition in Greek law of the institution of *direct representation* (Articles 211 et seq. CC) brings about, in effect, a similar loosening of the personal bond and the relativity of the obligation on the conclusion of the juridical act. *In formal terms*, of course, the direct representative, on the one hand, himself enters into the juridical act, but in the name of the person represented, who alone (and not the representative) becomes the subject of the consequences (rights and obligations) of the juridical act. It is considered that the party represented is the contracting party and not a third party to the contract. *In reality*, however, he acquires rights and duties (including obligational ones) from the act of another, his representative. As a rule, of course, this power on the part of the representative is created by the person represented himself by granting of a power of attorney (Article 216 CC). By way of exception, the representative has this power *ex lege* (legal or statutory representative, such as the parents, guardians of minors, etc.). For more on representation, *see* paragraphs 337 et seq. *infra.*

198. The list of exceptions from relativity given here cannot be exhaustive. We shall simply note two further related institutions where provision is made for the possibility of intervention of third parties in the contract of others: on the one hand, the institution of oblique action (Article 72 CCPr), which means the exercise of the rights (also the rights in personam) of a person by his creditor (apart from those rights

124. Directive of the Council of 14 Feb. 1977 (77/187/EC), as amended by the Directive of 29 Jun. 1998 (98/50/EC); corresponding Greek Act of Adjustment: PrD 178/2002 (Government Gazette A' 162/12.7.2002). *See* Art. 4 of the Pr.D.

125. Thus already the Court of the European Communities in the 'Besi Mill' case (*Berg, Busschers v. Besselsen*, 144 and 145/1987, 5.5.1988, Journal of the Court, 1988, 2577, 2581 et seq.).

which are closely bound up with the individual person of the debtor).[126] For example, A, who is the creditor of B, exercises the claim which B has against C by seeking from C (if need be, before the courts) payment to B (who thus will become more financially creditworthy, so that A can be more easily satisfied from the property of B); on the other, the institution of creditors' defrauding (Articles 939 et seq. CC), which will be dealt with in §3.

II. Contracts in Favour of or Burdening a Third Party

A. Contract in Favour of a Third Party

1. General: The Position in Law of the Third Party

199. The performance of the debtor, as we have said, may consist in any act or omission. Therefore, the performance may consist in some payment by him to a third party. The claim against the debtor is that of the creditor and not of the third party. That is, it will be the creditor who will seek from the debtor (compelling him, if need be, by judicial means) payment to the third party, and not the third party, who is not linked by any bond of obligation with the debtor. All this can be seen from the general provisions (and particularly from the breadth of the concept of performance) and special mention is not required. A deviation from the above is the instance in which the third party to whom the debtor has undertaken to effect the performance acquires a *direct* contractual right (claim) against the debtor to seek the performance himself also. This instance is an exception from privity of contracts and for this reason required special regulation by the law.

In the first instance (performance to a third party can be required only by the creditor) we have a *non-genuine contract in favour* (*or for the benefit*) *of a third party* (Article 410 CC, which provides for something which is self-evident, so that a contrast can be made with Articles 411 et seq. CC); in the second (performance can be claimed by the third party, who himself thus becomes creditor, as well as by the creditor) we have a *genuine contract in favour of a third party*, which is provided for, and thus permitted, by the CC (Articles 411–414).

200. In the event of *doubt*, the contract in favour of a third party is not genuine. This can be seen from Article 411 CC, which stipulates that for the third party to have a direct right against the debtor (i.e., for the contract in favour of a third party to be genuine), it must be possible to conclude this from the will of the parties (e.g., the parties have agreed that the third party should have a direct right) or from the nature and aim of the contract (e.g., the aim of the juridical act may be fulfilled only by a

126. The exception is of a procedural nature. A creditor who exercises the rights of his debtor does not have his own right (of substantive law) against the debtor of the latter. He exercises the alien right, if need be, through the court. The consequence is that he will seek payment not to himself, but to his debtor (and creditor of the defendant). This is unlike the cases quoted *supra*, para. 193, where, for example, the lessor will seek from the third party (sub-lessee) restitution of the leased thing directly to himself, etc.

recognition of a direct right of the third party). If such a conclusion cannot be drawn, the contract in favour of a third party is not genuine.

In such a contract, the two contracting parties are termed the *promisor* (the person who undertakes to fulfil the performance to the third party) and the *promisee* (the counterparty of the promisor), while the *third party* is referred to as such. The first promises to the second to fulfil the performance to the third. Examples:

(a) With bank A, B deposits a sum of money in favour of C (he opens an account in favour of C). Thus, A promises to B to make payment to C.
(b) Carrier A undertakes by his contract with B to transport to C the object which B has sold to C. Thus, A promises to B to fulfil a performance to C.
(c) Doctor A agrees with B to operate on C, the son, in his minority, of B. Thus, A promises to B to fulfil a performance to C.
(d) Insurance company A concludes an insurance contract with B (the insured) by which it promises that, when B dies, it will pay a sum of money to C, B's spouse.
(e) A concludes a contract for a donation of EUR 10,000 to B, on condition that he pays the EUR 10,000 to C, creditor of B.

201. It should be noted that the promisee concludes the contract in favour of a third party in his own name and not in the name of the third party, that is, *not as his direct representative.* If the latter is the case, the counterparty of the promisor would be the 'third party', as to whose person alone (and not that of the representative) contractual rights and obligations would arise. We would have not a contract in favour of a third party, but a contract which develops its effect only between the two contracting parties, of whom, however, one acts through his (direct) representative (*see also* paragraph 197 *supra*, as well as paragraphs 332 et seq., 337 et seq.).

In genuine contracts in favour of a third party, the third party acquires a contractual right, although he is not a party to the contract. He must, that is, have *legal capacity* of holding rights and duties (Article 34 CC) but it is not required that he should also have the *capacity to conclude juridical acts* (Article 127 CC), since he is not *in propria persona* concluding a juridical act.[127] Anyway, he is acquiring only rights, not obligations. If at the time of the conclusion of the contract in favour of a third party the third party does not as yet exist, it may emerge from interpretation of the contract that the parties have concluded it with the suspensive condition that the (as yet non-existent) third party should exist, for example, should be born or should acquire a legal personality. In this case the contract gains effect and the third party acquires the right as soon as the condition is satisfied, for example, when the third party is born (Article 201 CC). If the child is an embryo, Article 36 CC has force.[128]

The third party, however, who has acquired a right without being asked also has a right to decline it by a declaration on his part to the promisor, in which case it will be reckoned that he never acquired the right (Article 413 CC). The declaration, that is to say, has retroactive force.

202. As a consequence of the freedom of contract, by a contrary act of the parties (*actus contrarius*) the obligation may be extinguished. The parties, that is, may cancel

127. On these capacities, *see* para. 95 *supra.*
128. *See* para. 95 *supra* .

their contract and the rights which stemmed from it. This also holds good for non-genuine contracts in favour of a third party, where rights and obligations are acquired only by the contracting parties, not the third party. In the case of genuine contracts of this kind, however, Article 412 CC introduces a reasonable exception: the promisee cannot absolve the promisor of his obligation (*see* Article 454 CC), that is to say, the two contracting parties cannot agree on the revocation of the right of the third party from the moment that the third party has declared to the promisor that he will exercise his right. Before this declaration is made, the revocation of the right of the third party by the contracting parties is valid. No special form is required for the declaration of the third party, hence it may be tacit, that is, indirectly presumed.

2. The Relations Between the Three Parties

203. The promisor and the promisee are linked by the contract in favour of a third party. This contract contains the cause for which the former fulfils a performance to the third. The performance is fulfilled to the third party because the promisor is 'covered' by his contractual relation with the promisee, which is thus termed a *cover relation.* The cover relation may be an onerous juridical act (usually a reciprocal contract) or a gratuitous one: the promisor fulfils a performance to the third party since he has received or will receive a quid pro quo from the promisee or because he wishes to engage in some act of liberality towards the promisee (*see* examples in paragraph 200 *supra*). This contract between the promisor and the promisee regulates their relations.

204. The cause for which the third party, although extraneous, is entitled to collect from the promisor lies in the relation of *the third party with the promisee.* The relations will usually be a contract (onerous or gratuitous) by virtue of which the promisee owed a debt to the third party. The latter, that is, had a claim, a 'value' against the promisee. For this reason, their relation is termed a *value relation* (*see* examples in paragraph 200 *supra*). If there were no other obligation of the promisee towards the third party, the value relation will be a relation of liberality of the former to the latter.

205. The promisor and the third party, on the other hand, are not usually linked by a direct contractual relation. The direct right of the third party against the promisor is derived from the contract in favour of a third party (which covers the promisor) and is to be explained by the value relation. If the contract in favour of a third party has some defect, for example, if it is void, the promisor has the right to oppose this to the third party when the third party requires fulfilment from him. This is reasonable, given that the promisor is bound only to the extent to which a binding obligation arises from the contract in favour of a third party. Anyway, this is expressly stipulated in Article 414 CC. *E contrario* from this provision and from the purpose of the contract in favour of a third party it can be seen that the promisor cannot derive rights and oppose relevant exceptions to the third party from the value relation. Even if this is void, for example, the third party has a direct right against the promisor, who has been bound by the contract in favour of a third party alone to fulfil the performance to the third party. The value relation does not concern the promisor, who, for that reason, cannot invoke it.

If the promisor has fulfilled the performance to the third party in spite of the existence of a defective cover relation or value relation, what has been paid will be claimed back by virtue of the provisions on unjust enrichment (*see* paragraph 408 *infra*).

3. Anomalous Development of the Contract in Favour of a Third Party

206. If the contract in favour of a third party develops in an anomalous manner (e.g., impossibility of performance, default, etc.) certain difficulties arise from the fact that as against the promisor there are as creditors not only the promisee but also the third party. If the promisee does not fulfil his contractual obligations, the promisor has the rights, for example, of compensation, rescission, etc. (*see* Articles 382, 383 etc. CC). If, however, the promisor does not fulfil his obligations from the contract in favour of a third party, the right to compensation (together with the primary claim for fulfilment) will be that of the injured party, that is, of the third party. It is, however, disputed whether the third party will be able in this case to exercise the right of rescission and thus completely reverse the contract of others.

B. Contracts Burdening a Third Party

207. We would have a contract burdening a third party if from a contract between two persons, a third person, not a contracting party, acquired a contractual obligation. For example: A agrees with B that C will fulfil a performance to B. Such a contract is not valid, in the sense that it does not bind the third party. We cannot be burdened with obligations by the contracts of others and without our consent. It is a different question whether this contract is valid between the two contracting parties (principle of the relativity of promissory contracts). This can be accepted (principle of the freedom of contract) in the sense that the party promising that the third party will furnish a performance simply undertakes the obligation to try and persuade the third party to do so, without being liable if he does not succeed in this; or in the sense that if the third party does not fulfil the performance of his own free will, the promisor will compensate the promisee (a kind of 'guarantee' contract). In both these two forms, the contract develops effects only between the parties and does not bind the third party. In the event of doubt, the second of the above two types of contract will be accepted (Article 415 CC).

§2. Transfer of Contractual Rights or Debts

208. In earlier times, obligation was personal. It had force only between the creditor and the debtor. In order to change either of these two persons, it was necessary to agree on the extinction of the old obligation and for a new obligation to be established by agreement between its new subjects. This could be effected by a single agreement between its new subjects. This could also be effected by a single agreement, the *novation* (novatio – *see* Article 436 CC). Today, contractual rights and debts are negotiable, that is, transferable, without their identity being lost (which is a matter of importance for, for example, the maintenance of any securities which may exist). Perhaps the circulation of the above claims is not as easy a matter as that of commercial securities (particularly those to bearer or to order, which are transferred by simple delivery or by endorsement, respectively, in accordance with the needs of commerce). Nevertheless, simple claims, as well as debts may by agreement be transferred to another person in accordance with the CC (Articles 455 et seq. on the *'assignment of a claim'* and Articles 471 et seq. on *'assumption of debt'*). Negotiability is, then, today also a feature of the bond of obligation. If, moreover, the assignment of claims from a contract (section I *infra*) is combined with the assumption of the debts from the same contract (section II *infra*), we can have a contractual *transfer of the whole contract* (a matter not specially regulated in the CC). For this will be required the meeting of the conditions for assignment and of those for assumption of a debt. Finally, a trilateral contract (between the two old subjects of the contract and the new party entering into it) will be needed.

I. Assignment of a Claim

A. General: Conditions

209. The obligational right, the claim, may be transferred by its holder, the creditor, to another. Such a transfer is made by a contract of *the creditor with the third party* to whom the claim is transferred, in which the debtor does not need to participate (with his consent) (Article 455 CC). The transfer of the claim by contract, that is, the *assignment*, brings about a change of the person of the creditor. The transferor (*assignor*) ceases to be the creditor and the new creditor is now the *assignee.* Assignment is regulated in Articles 455–470 CC.

210. The conditions for valid assignment are:

(1) A contract between the assignor and the assignee (Article 455 CC). The assignor must be the creditor. Transfer of a claim by a third party and not the holder of the right (creditor) is not valid, even if the assignee was in good faith, that is, regarded the assignor as the creditor (Article 239 CC, which gives exceptions, for example, in the case of approval by the creditor. However, a general exception in favour of a transferee in good faith, as is the case with movable things – *see* paragraph 52 *supra* – does not exist for claims). Assignment is a *disposition contract*, since its immediate legal effect is not the undertaking of some contractual obligation (e. g., an obligation to transfer) by the assignor, but the loss of his claim, the disposition of it (transfer) to the assignee. In addition, assignment is an *abstract* contract. Its cause is as a rule a promissory contract, between the assignor and the assignee, by which the former undertakes the obligation to transfer the claim to the latter. This contract, which may precede or be concluded at the same time as the assignment, may be, for instance, a sale or donation. Thus sale of the claim (= a promissory juridical act, Article 513 CC) must be distinguished from assignment of the claim (= a juridical act of disposition, Article 455 CC), in the same way as the sale of a thing (Article 513 CC) is distinct from the transfer of

its ownership (Articles 1033, 1034 CC).[129] The abstract nature of assignment means that its effects (i.e., the transfer of the claim to the assignee) occur even if the cause were absent or void or had been annulled.[130] The assignee, however, may be liable in accordance with the provisions on unjust enrichment if he acquired the claim without just cause. Liability will consist in an obligation to restitute the unjust enrichment, that is, to re-transfer the claim to the assignor or, if the assignee has already collected from the debtor, in an obligation to restitute what he has collected.

In the last analysis, the cause of the assignment is onerous or gratuitous. For example: A, who has a claim for EUR 10,000 against B, assigns it to C for a price of EUR 8,000, that is, by reason of sale. A (vendor and assignor) will collect immediately EUR 8,000 from the purchaser – assignee C, who acquires the, let us suppose, non-due, claim for EUR 10,000 against the debtor, B. Or the assignor donates his claim to the assignee.

A *fiduciary* assignment of claim (to secure the assignee for a claim on his part against the assignor – *see* paragraph 47 *supra*) is also possible. Frequently, assignment also takes place solely so that the assignee can collect the claim. In the contract type, in common use today, of *'factoring'*, the factor is the assignee of claims of his clients: he undertakes by this factoring contract with his client, within the framework, usually, of broader, long-term business with him, the collection of the latter's claims, which are assigned to him for this purpose. [Law 1905/1990 (as amended by Laws 2232/1994, 2367/1995 and 3601/2007), which governs this contractual relationship, stipulates, *inter alia*, who may practice the activities of a factor, and under what control]. In the factoring contract, the factor may be given, instead of assignment, only an '*authorisation for collection*'. On this latter institution, which can have wider application, *see* paragraph 231 *infra*.

(2) *Notification to the debtor of the assignment* (Article 460 CC). The assignment contract is without further formality valid between the parties, but for the assignee to acquire the claim *against the debtor and third parties*, there must be *notification* of the assignment to the debtor. He must, that is, be given notice by the assignor or the assignee of the assignment, so that the debtor knows who his creditor is. Such notification is a quasi-juridical act, which means that its legal effects occur because they are stipulated by law, and not because they were willed (if they were) by the notifier. Before notification occurs, the debtor may and is obliged to make payment to the assignor and such payment releases him (Article 461 CC); after notification, he is relieved only if he makes payment to the assignee. If, in spite of this, he makes payment (after the notification) to the assignor, he will be obliged also to make payment to the assignee and will simply have a claim to recover what has been paid to the assignor by virtue of the provisions on unjust enrichment.

Thus, if creditor A assigns his claim against B first to C and then, by another assignment contract, to D (two successive assignments of the same claim) and D gives notice first to B, B validly makes the payment (and is relieved of his

---

129. *See* paras 19–20 *supra*.
130. *See also* paras 52 and 140 et seq.

obligation) to D. C must refer himself to any possible rights against A (*see* paragraph 212 *infra*).

211. Assignability of the claim. As a rule, it is permissible for any claim to be assigned. There are, however, three exceptions, where the claim is *unassignable:*

(a) When the claim is not subject to attachment (Article 464 CC).
(b) When the claim, by reason of the nature of the performance, is closely bound up with the person of the creditor (Article 465 CC), for example, a claim for the performance of a certain task where the personal factor is predominant (such as provision of confidential services).
(c) When the creditor and debtor have agreed on its unassignability (Article 466 CC).[131]

B. *Effects of Assignment*

212. As we have said, on the conclusion of the assignment contract and notification to the debtor, transfer effects occur, that is, succession in the person of the creditor, not extinction of the claim. Securities (guarantees, pledges, mortgages, etc.) which secured the claim continue in force in favour of the assignee, that is, they are transferred *ipso jure* to him (Article 458 CC). The assignment refers to an individual obligation and not, for example, to the whole of a contractual relation.

The relations which are created between the three parties are as follows:

(1) *Assignor – debtor relation:* Up to notification, the assignor continues to have all his rights against the debtor, who is obliged to make payment to him only and is released by this payment (Articles 460–461 CC). After notification, the debtor in making payment to the assignor is not released and must, as we have said, make payment again to the assignee, as he is now his creditor.
(2) *Assignee – debtor relation*: On the significance of the notification, *see* paragraph 210 *supra*. After notification, the assignee has the same rights against the debtor which the assignor had and the debtor has the same pleas which he had before notification against the assignor (Articles 462, 463, §1 CC). The debtor had pleas against the assignor arising from his relation with him, that is, from the contract from which (as a rule) the claim stemmed. The debtor can, consequently, oppose pleas from the assignor – debtor relation existing before notification (e.g., plea of nullity of their contract) and not arising after notification (e.g., release from debt between assignor and debtor, concluded after notification – *see also*, Article 463, §2 CC on plea of offsetting).
It may be asked if the debtor can oppose pleas against the assignee from the assignor – assignee relation. Here we must make a distinction: if the assignment contract between the assignor and the assignee (disposition contract) is itself void or is annulled, this means that the results of the transfer have not occurred or have been reversed (Articles 180, 184 CC), that the claim has not been transferred,

131. *See also* the exception in subpara. 2 of Art. 466 CC (if the assignee relied on a document which did not contain a term as to non-assignability).

that the 'assignee' has not acquired the claim. The debtor may, therefore, oppose him with the fact that he does not owe him anything. If, however, the defect lies in the promissory contract between assignor and assignee (which constitutes the cause of the assignment), the debtor cannot invoke it and oppose it against the assignee. This emerges from the abstract nature of assignment. The transfer is valid and, therefore, the assignee has acquired a claim against the debtor (who is now obliged to make payment to him), even if its cause was defective. The absence of cause may at the most entail, as we have said, implementation of the provisions on unjust enrichment in the assignor – assignee relations.

(3) *Assignor – assignee relation*: The basic problem in the assignor assignee relations is whether the former is liable as against the latter, a. if the claim assigned was non-existent (e.g., the contract from which it stemmed was void); b. if, although the claim was existent, the debtor is insolvent. In the first instance, the assignee does not acquire a claim; in the second, he acquires a claim which is, however, economically dubious.

The question is, then, whether the assignor is liable to the assignee for the existence (*veritas*) of the claim and whether he is liable for the quality (*bonitas*) of it. The answer depends upon whether the cause of the claim was onerous or gratuitous. In the first instance (onerous cause), the assignor is liable only for the existence of the claim, not for the solvency of the debtor (Article 467, §1); in the second (gratuitous cause), he is not liable either for its existence or for the solvency of the debtor (Article 467, §2). This regulation is one of non-mandatory law. Greater (or less) liability may be determined by an agreement of the parties.[132]

If the claim was non-existent and the assignor was liable for this (Article 467, §1), liability will consist in the general liability which the debtor has in the event of impossibility of performance (paragraphs 264 et seq. *infra*), since the undertaking of an obligation to assign a non-existent claim is the equivalent of undertaking an obligation for an impossible performance.

213. The provisions on assignment (Articles 455–469 CC) are also implemented *mutatis mutandis* in the case of the transfer of other – non-obligatory – rights as to which the law does not provide any special manner of transfer (Article 470 CC).

II. Assumption of Debt: Liberation Promise

A. *Cumulative, Privative Assumption of Debt*

1. General: Conditions

214. Succession in an obligatory relation may also occur on the side of the debtor. A new debtor may take the place of the old by assuming the debt from that

132. If this is assignment arising *ex lege* (*cessio legis*, e.g., Arts 319, 488 etc. CC), the original creditor is not liable for the existence of the claim or for the solvency of the debtor (Art. 469 CC).

point on. This change in the person of the debtor is termed *assumption of debt.* We can distinguish two kinds of assumption of debt:

Privative and cumulative. In the case of the former (Article 471 CC), the old debtor is released and the obligation is from then on that of the new debtor (= 'assumer').

In that of the latter, although the new debtor undertakes the obligation, the original debtor is not released (Article 477 CC), so that the creditor now has two debtors to himself, each according to the purpose of the cumulative assumption of debt (if it is not determined differently by the agreement) for the whole of the debt. Consequently, cumulative assumption of debt gives rise to joint and several obligation (*see* paragraph 191 *supra*).

Assumption of debt, both privative and cumulative, is effected by *a contract between the creditor and the new debtor who assumes the debt* (Articles 471, 477 CC), without there being any need for the involvement of the original debtor. Whether the assumption is a privative or a cumulative one is a matter of interpretation of the contract. What will be examined is what the parties wanted. In case of doubt, cumulative assumption will be accepted (Article 477 CC).

2. Effects

215. There are two consequences of privative assumption of debt in accordance with the above: on the one hand, the original debtor is released and, on the other, the new debtor assumes the debt. As to the first consequence, privative assumption of debt is a *disposition contract* and as to the second, a *promissory* one. Thus privative assumption of debt has a double character. By way of contrast, cumulative assumption has as its sole consequence the (additional) assumption of the debt by the new debtor as well. Namely, it is only a promissory contract.

In the case of privative assumption of debt, any securities in favour of the creditor (guarantees – pledges, mortgages) are not maintained *ipso jure* as in the case of assignment (Article 458 CC), but only if the guarantor or the owner of the pledge or mortgaged immovable consents (Article 475, paragraph 1, subparagraph 2). This difference is to be explained by the fact that the person who provides the security takes into account the person of the (original) debtor and his creditworthiness and solvency. For this reason, the change in the person of the debtor is not immaterial for those who provide security as is the change in the person of the creditor.

216. In the relations of the assumer with the creditor, the former has the same duties and the same pleas as the first debtor (Articles 472, 473, paragraph 1; the same applies in the case of cumulative assumption of debt). Consequently, the assumer may oppose pleas against the creditor from the original debtor – creditor relation, for example, that the contract between these two persons from which the debt stems was void or has been annulled (Article 473, paragraph 1). If, however, the original debtor had a counter-claim against the creditor, the assumer cannot oppose it in offsetting against the creditor (Articles 473, paragraph 2, 440).

217. The cause of the assumption of debt lies in the relations between the original and the new debtor. For example: A assumes the debt of B to C because he owed B (let us suppose, from a sale contract) a sum of money (the price of the thing which he bought from B). A assumes the debt of B to C from liberality to B (donation of A to

B), or because he undertook by contract an order to complete this affair of B (mandate contract, Article 713 CC). If there were no contract between A and B, it may be a question of management of another's affairs, with the assumer A as manager and B as principal (Article 730 CC). However, whatever are the relations between the original and the new debtor, the latter cannot invoke them and draw pleas from any defect (e.g., nullity) in these against the creditor (Article 474 CC). Accordingly, then, the assumption of debt is abstract. From these (internal) relations between the original and the new debtor it will be decided whether the latter, having paid the debt to the creditor, has a right of recourse against the original debtor (in the case of donation, no; in that of sale, yes; *see also* Articles 722, 736 et seq. CC).

If the assumption contract itself has a defect (e.g., it is void), the new debtor (a contracting party to this contract) may invoke this against his counterparty, the creditor. That is to say, the assumer has pleas from his relation with the creditor.

218. The autonomy of the original debtor is somewhat affected by the privative assumption of debt, since he, without being asked, is released (cf. *also* Article 317 CC). This is accepted in principle by the law, since this consequence favours the original debtor.

If, however, the justification of the privative assumption of debt cannot be seen from its cause (the relations between the original and the new debtor), if, that is, the new debtor has assumed the debt without other reason, this will be the equivalent of a 'donation' on his part to the original debtor, which, to be valid, requires a contract (Article 496 CC), that is, consent of the original debtor also. If he does not consent, there is no donation contract, that is, there is no valid cause for the assumption of debt. The latter, of course, will be valid and will produce its effects, as being abstract, but, if the absence of cause is proven, a liability for unjust enrichment will be created between the original and the new debtor. That is to say, it will be deemed that the original debtor has been validly released from his debt, that is, he has been enriched in this way, but that this enrichment is unjust (without just cause) and is refundable to the new debtor, who is the party impoverished (by the assumption or payment of the debt). The refund will be effected by the restitution by the original to the new debtor of any sum (or other object) which he has given to the creditor (if need be, by public deposit, Article 427 CC), or, if the new debtor has not yet made payment to the creditor, in any way which results in the new debtor being released and the original debtor shouldering the debt anew (e.g., Articles 317, 471, etc. CC).

B. Liberation Promise

219. If the agreement on assumption of the debt of the original debtor by a third party (the new debtor) is made between these two persons (original and new debtor), without the involvement of the creditor, this is called a *liberation promise* (*or contract*). This contract is valid by virtue of freedom of contract and develops effects only between the two contracting parties (principle of privity of contracts). That is to say, the person who promises the original debtor that he will pay the latter's debt to the creditor has, by virtue of this promissory contract, the obligation *as against the original debtor* to fulfil his obligation and make payment to the creditor. However, only the original debtor, and not the creditor, has the right to demand the fulfilment of the obligation of the promisor (Article 478 CC). Naturally, the original debtor is not released from his debt to the creditor (except, only, through any payment by the third party, that is, the promisor, Article 317 CC – paragraph 233 *infra*).

Consequently, the liberation promise is in principle a *non-genuine contract in favour of a third party.*[133] As we have already said, however, rendering a contract in favour of a third party *genuine* depends upon the will of the parties (here the original debtor and the third party-promisor). In this instance, a third party acquiring a direct right against the promisor will be the creditor. For example: A promises B (by his contract with B) that he will pay B's debt to C. The parties (A and B) wish this contract to be a genuine contract in favour of C. C acquires a direct right against A. This is already clear from Article 411 CC. It is this possibility (conclusion of a genuine contract in favour of a third party) which is meant by Article 478 CC with its reservation 'in case of doubt'. If the reverse cannot clearly be established, the liberation promise will be a non-genuine contract in favour of a third party.

§3. Actio Pauliana (Creditors' Defrauding)

220. Third parties who acquire items of property of the debtor have no liability as against the creditor, even if the reduction in the estate of the former is to the detriment of the latter. Third parties, by reason of privity of contracts, are not obliged to take into account the right of the creditor, which for them is *res inter alios acta.* When, however, certain special conditions, which are, basically, of the nature of *creditor's defrauding* are fulfilled, the third party who has acquired an item of property of the debtor is liable to the creditor. The relevant regulation ('Paulian action', as descended from the *actio Pauliana* of Roman law) is provided for in Articles 939–946 CC. In such extraordinary cases, the law considers that the third party is breaching the contractual right of another. The liability of the person who does this does not consist in an obligation to compensate,[134] but in the 'contest' of the alienation of the item of property of the debtor to the third party. The creditor has an interest in contest in the event of the insolvency of the debtor. It should be noted that the state of bankruptcy, in which an insolvent debtor is declared to be for the satisfaction of his creditors is implemented only in the case of traders.

I. Conditions of Creditors' Defrauding

221. The conditions for the contest of fraudulent alienation by the debtor are the following (Article 939 CC):

(a) *Alienation* (valid) of an item of his own property by the debtor, that is, transfer or encumbrance or alteration or abolition of his right over it, not simply undertaking of obligations (*see* paragraph 20 *supra*), either by onerous or by gratuitous acts.

133. *See* paras 199 et seq. *supra*.

134. Unless the conditions of Art. 919 CC are also fulfilled in the person doing this (*see* para. 195 *supra*).

The payment of a debt which has fallen due is not regarded as alienation (Article 940, paragraph 2, subparagraph 1).

(b) The alienation must have occurred *with an intention of prejudicing the creditors.*[135] Eventual intent (*dolus eventualis*) is sufficient, but not gross negligence.

(c) The alienation must cause *insolvency* of the debtor, that is, insufficiency of his estate remaining after the alienation to satisfy the creditors. (The existence of a *causal relation* between the *alienation* and the *insolvency* is required).

(d) The third party to whom alienation is made must be aware that the debtor is carrying out the alienation to prejudice the creditors (Article 941, paragraph 1), unless alienation occurs as the result of a gratuitous cause, in which case knowledge on the part of the third party is not required (Articles 941, paragraph 1 and 942 CC). The law, moreover, provides (Article 941, paragraph 2 CC) that in the event of onerous alienation, the knowledge of the third party is presumed[136] (for a period of one year from the alienation to the lodging of the action) if at the time of alienation, the third party is the spouse of the debtor or a close relative (in the degrees specified by the law).

II. Effects

222. If the above conditions are fulfilled, the creditors have the right within five years from the alienation to contest it (Articles 939, 946 CC). The effects of this contest, if this right is exercised, are limited to the parties of the action. The ownership (if this right has been alienated) does not come back *ipso jure* into the estate of the debtor as to all the consequences of ownership. The third party to whom alienation has been made has simply 'an obligation to restore the *status quo ante*' (Article 943 CC). The many theoretical questionings and theories as to the legal nature of this consequence, which gain force from the obscurity of the law (particularly as to whether the exercise of the contest means an obligation for the third party to transfer the right back to the debtor, or partial annulment of the alienation with automatic return of ownership to the debtor, but only in favour of the creditor and to the extent which is required for him to be satisfied, or non-reversion of ownership, but an obligation on the part of the third party to tolerate enforced execution on the right by the creditor, etc.[137]) cannot be entered into here. It suffices to stress that the contest operates only in favour of the creditors who have challenged the alienation.[138]

---

135. According to the opinion stated in theory, even those who became creditors after the alienation have the right to contest it (*see* para. 222 *infra*), if the prejudice of them too was intended by the debtor.

136. This is a legal rebuttable assumption (*see* para. 83 *supra*).

137. It is argued that, according to the provisions of Arts 936 §3, 953 §2c, 992 §1, subpara. 2 CCPr, as amended by Law 2298/1995, the contest of the alienation has a direct effect, so that the creditor who has challenged the alienation has the right to enforced execution upon the alienated right, without the involvement of the third party.

138. For an extensive analysis of the consequences *see* the monograph of *Avgoustianakis*, The Contest of Fraudulent Alienation, 1991.

If the third party (beneficiary) has further transferred the right alienated, his successor in title has a similar liability as against the creditors if he was aware of the intent of the debtor when he acquired the right from the third party. Here too knowledge is not required in the case of a gratuitous cause or is presumed in the case of the successor being a relative of the debtor (*see* paragraph 221, (d) *supra*).

In the event of alienation for a gratuitous cause, the beneficiary has a liability, as we have said, whether he was in good faith or not. If, however, he was in good faith, he is liable only in accordance with the provisions on unjust enrichment (Articles 904 et seq. CC).

Chapter 5. Performance and Termination of the Contract

223. Obligation, it is often said, is born in order to die. The debtor must at some point fulfil his performance (or complete its fulfilment). This is the natural extinction of the obligation, which is termed by the CC (Article 416 CC) 'payment' (regardless of whether or not the performance is monetary). As long as the fulfilment of the contractual (more precisely, the original obligational) performance itself is possible, the creditor has a claim to seek this specific performance, if need be through judicial compulsion (*see also* the next Chapter 6, §1). Over and above the payment there are other natural – that is, ultimately attributable to the will of the parties – ways of the obligation being extinguished, as by the agreement of both parties. These issues of the 'physiology' of the obligation are examined in the present chapter. In order to give a complete picture of the extinction of the obligation, ways in which it can be extinguished regardless of the will of both the parties will be examined in §3.

The problems of a particular practical importance of the anomalous development of the obligation, such as non-performance, defective performance, frustration, etc. ('pathology' of the obligation) and its consequences, particularly rescission and the claim for compensation (which in the Anglo-Saxon world are described as 'remedies') are examined in the next chapter, which will close with the institution of the time-limitation (prescription) of actions.

§1. Normal Performance and Termination of the Contract

I. Place, Time of the Performance: Partial Performance

A. Place of Performance

224. The performance may be fulfilled either at the place of residence of the debtor or the place of residence of the creditor. It is also possible that the performance must be sent by the debtor to the creditor, in which case, the place of performance is, as a rule, the residence of the debtor, since by the dispatch of the performance from the residence of the debtor, the performance is deemed to have been already fulfilled.

The question of the place of performance is provided for by Articles 320–322 CC, which are rules of non-mandatory law. That is, the place may be determined in principle by the parties (i.e., by agreement). If the parties have not made provision for it, the place of performance may be concluded by implication from their contract, from its purpose, from the circumstances, good faith or common usages, etc. (e.g., the extraction of a tooth which a dentist has undertaken will take place at his surgery). If the place of performance cannot be concluded by these means, the place provided for by the CC (Articles 320–322 CC) has force. That is to say: In the case of debts of a non-monetary nature, the place of performance is the place of residence of the debtor (or his professional premises if the obligation is derived from the exercise of the profession of the debtor). On the other hand, in the case of monetary debts, the place of performance is the residence of the creditor.[139]

The significance of the place of the performance lies chiefly in the fact that for the performance to be proper and for it to develop normally, it must be effected in the right place. Otherwise (if the debtor fulfils the performance, but not in the proper place), there is improper performance or non-performance and the relevant consequences follow, while the creditor is not in default if he does not accept the improper offer of the performance. Moreover, the place of performance may have importance in private international law (for the determination of the law to be implemented) and in procedure (for the determination of the competent court).

B. *Time of Performance*

225. The time at which the performance must be fulfilled (and the creditor is entitled to demand it), the time, that is, at which the debt becomes due may also (as in the case of the place of performance) be provided for by an agreement of the parties, or, if there is no such provision, be concluded from the purpose or nature of the contract or the circumstances, etc. If it cannot be concluded by these means either, the performance is to be fulfilled 'forthwith' (Article 323 CC), that is, immediately (after the generation of the obligation), without delay, culpable or otherwise.

If the time of performance is specified, the creditor is not entitled to seek fulfilment before it. The debtor, however, is entitled to early fulfilment, but with the limitation that as a rule he cannot subtract the *discount interest*, that is, the interest which the creditor earns from early collection (the interest which corresponds to the period from early fulfilment to the time when the debt would become due). The right of the debtor to early fulfilment exists 'in case of doubt', that is, if nothing else can be concluded from the obligational relation. A different case may arise, for example, when we have a loan at interest, since the creditor has a lawful interest in collecting the interest up to the stipulated time of fulfilment.

The fulfilment of the performance at the proper time is of great importance. *Inter alia*, delay in fulfilment normally entails (if certain other conditions are also fulfilled) default of the debtor and the relevant liability on his part (*see* next Chapter, §3 II).

C. *Partial Performance*

226. If the performance is divisible (e.g., a sum of money), may the debtor fulfil it in instalments? Article 316 CC replies to this in the negative. The debtor is obliged to furnish the *whole* performance at the due time. If he furnishes only a part, the creditor may decline to accept it without being in default. The debtor, on the other hand, will be in default as to the whole of the performance.

The prohibition of partial fulfilment by Article 316 CC is non-mandatory law. The parties may make a different agreement. Moreover, the law in certain cases permits partial performance regardless of agreement (e.g., in the case of debts from promissory notes, bills to order or bank cheques). Finally, good faith (Article 288 CC) may call

139. An exception is provided for by Art. 322 CC in the case of a change of the creditor's address which causes serious difficulties for the debtor.

for a relaxation of the prohibition of Article 316 CC when its implementation would be very severe and hard for the debtor. For example, if the debtor offers 99% of the debt, it would be contrary to good faith for the creditor to reject it. The latter does not, of course, lose his claim for performance, even in arrears, of the remaining 1%.

II. Suspensive Pleas of Non-performance

227. The debtor, on certain conditions of non-performance by the other party, is entitled to suspend his own performance. In these cases, the law grants him purely defensive rights (pleas), which have temporary effect, leading only to the suspension of the performance and not the negation (rejection) of the right of the creditor. These provisional remedies, stipulated in the CC, are the 'right of retention' (Articles 325–329 CC) and the 'plea of unperformed contract' (*exceptio non adimpleti contractus* – Articles 374–378 CC).

A. Right or Plea of Retention (Lien)

228. The debtor is entitled to refuse the payment of his debt to the creditor if this falls due (i.e., the time of fulfilment arrives), where the creditor has some (other) debt to the debtor and does not pay it. In this case, the debtor exercises the right (or the plea) of retention (*jus retentionis*), that is, withholding of the performance which he owes.

Conditions for the exercise of the right of retention (Article 325 CC):

(1) *Reciprocity* of two claims. That is, there must be two claims in an opposite direction. The creditor of the one must be the debtor of the other. In other words, the debtor who exercises the right of retention must be (himself and not a third party) creditor of a claim against his creditor.
(2) The debtor who exercises the right of retention must have a *due* counter-claim against the other.
(3) The two reciprocal claims must be *related* to one another. For example, they must be derived from two contracts connected with each other or from the same contractual or, even social relation (e.g., dealings between colleagues which stem from their shared profession). Relatedness is also present in the instance of Article 326 CC: e.g., A owes a thing to B, but is entitled to seek from B the expenses which he has incurred for the maintenance of it.

A *consequence* of the exercise of the right of retention is only the *suspension* of performance until the time that the creditor pays his own debt (Article 325 CC). The judge, if the case comes to court, will find against the defendant debtor (who advances the plea of retention) 'on condition of simultaneous performance' also of the obligation of the creditor (Article 329 CC).

B. Plea 'of Unperformed Contract' (Non Adimpleti Contractus)

229. In the case of reciprocal contracts, the rule that the parties are obliged to fulfil simultaneously their two performances holds good. This can be concluded *e contrario* from Article 374 CC. The rule is one of non-mandatory law. The parties, that is, may agree that one of the two is obliged to effect prior fulfilment of his performance.

Where the rule of simultaneous fulfilment of the two performances of a reciprocal contract has force, that is, if prepayment on the part of one of the parties has not been stipulated, each contracting party, if a defendant before the court or if called upon extra-judicially by the other party to fulfil his performance, is entitled to oppose the plea of *non adimpleti contractus* (Article 374 CC). A consequence of the advancing of this plea is not that the party who puts it forward is released, but that he will be obliged to fulfil performance (or be found against by the court), on condition, however, of simultaneous fulfilment of the counter-performance of the other contracting party (Articles 374, 378 CC).

This plea resembles that of retention. The basic difference between them is that the former is provided where the two reciprocal claims in opposite directions stem from a reciprocal contract, while the latter is for cases where the two claims are simply related.

In the former case, the link (and the interdependence) between the two claims is closer; for that reason, the plea of unperformed contract cannot be rebutted by the provision of security to the debtor (pledge, mortgage, guarantee) on behalf of the creditor: Article 375 CC. The case is different with the plea of retention as to a pledge and mortgage (Article 328 CC).

If it has been agreed that one of the contracting parties should effect prior performance, he may refuse such prepayment until such time as the other party provides security in the event of the latter's insolvency which was unknown to the former without his being at fault (Article 377 CC).

III. Monetary Obligations

230. In Greece, the system of the mandatory circulation of the drachma used to prevail; this was supplemented by the following two basic prohibitions. First, by the prohibition in principle of the free purchase and sale of 'foreign exchange and foreign banknotes', which could, initially, only be carried out by the Bank of Greece and, on certain terms, by the lawfully authorized banks or public organizations. Violation of the prohibition entailed nullity of the undertaking of an obligation to buy or sell foreign exchange. Second, by the prohibition in principle of safety monetary clauses (such as gold clauses, foreign currency clauses, etc.), with some exceptions.

Before the replacement of the drachma by the euro, under the influence chiefly of the mandates of Community law, the foreign exchange restrictions were already being progressively reduced. A purpose of the EU was the free movement of capital, in accordance with the relevant principle laid down by the Treaty founding it.

A turning-point for the Greek monetary system was Greece's accession to the EMU in June 2000, and the introduction of the euro. The euro has circulated in Greece since 1 January 2002 (as a common currency of the Member States which belong to the EMU). The conversion rate of drachmas into euro was set at 340.75 drachmas to a euro (Article 1 of Regulation 4478/2000). Thus today euro alone has the 'character of lawful money' in the Member States which belong to the EMU, and therefore in Greece (Article 10 of Regulation 974/1998).

The EMU and the introduction of the euro were an important step in the process of European unification, since monetary management, and in part economic management also, for the Member States belonging to the EMU, passed from national to Community organs (such as the European Central Bank), that is, finally, to joint management by the Member States controlling the Community organs.

With Greece's accession to the EMU and the introduction of the euro, the existence today of prohibitions of safety monetary clauses is no longer meaningful. Countries which belong to the EMU have a common European currency (the protection of which falls to the European Central Bank) and are governed by a common monetary regime. Furthermore, outside the EMU also the euro is a competitive currency as against the dollar, the Swiss franc, the yen, etc. It was, then, reasonable that the law which replaced drachma with the euro (Law 2842/2000) should have provided (Article 5) the abolition of the provisions which prohibited safety clauses, with the retention of the competences of the Bank of Greece in establishing the terms of purchase and sale of gold, gold coins, and foreign exchange by other persons (credit institutions, foreign exchange agencies).

Thus the conclusion of safety clauses is now free, not only in international but also in domestic transactions, without restrictions. The parties can undertake obligations (and also discharge them) in a currency other than the euro. Any future prohibition or restriction of the conclusion of a safety clause by the Greek legislator would be likely to be meaningful only as to a price index clause, to the extent that the reason justifying it (e.g., protection of the consumer) differs from the reason of protection of the common European currency.

The question of whether the debtor can pay a money debt with cheque book money is a subject of dispute. The prevailing view is that, in principle, he cannot do this without the consent of the creditor, unless in the specific case good faith demands the acceptance of cheque book money. On the interest, see on the loan agreement (paragraphs 386–387 *infra*).

In extreme cases of a major devaluation of the currency, Article 388 or 288 CC could be implemented (*see* paragraphs 290 et seq. *infra*).

IV. Termination by Payment

A. Concept and Legal Nature of Payment: Payment to Third Parties

231. The CC (Article 416 CC) means by payment the fulfilment of the performance, that is, the satisfaction of the creditor in accordance with the aim of the obligation. This is the most 'natural' means of extinguishing the obligation.

Payment cannot as a rule, as will be obvious, be made to *a third party*, that is, to a person other than the creditor. It must be made to the creditor. This is laid down by Article 417 CC, which, however, also provides for exceptions, where payment to third parties which brings about effects of extinction, that is, releases the debtor, is permitted. These exceptions are:

(a) When payment to the third party has been permitted by the creditor himself. For example: A *authorizes* C to collect a claim which A has against B. The person authorized (C) either has the power to act as direct representative of A, in which case he acts in his name (*see also* Article 211 CC, paragraph 197 *supra* and paragraphs 337 et seq. *infra*) and the authorization is termed a power of attorney, or to act in his own name, in which case, again, extinction in accordance with Article 417 §1 occurs. The question of whether the former or latter occurs depends upon the will of the party who gives his authorization (the creditor). The authorization is a unilateral juridical act. The *approval ex post facto* by the creditor of collection by the third party has the same effects (Article 417 §2 CC).
The person authorized to collect the claim *in his own name* can be given more powers than those of a simple collecting agency: he can be empowered, according to the will of the authorizing creditor, to enforce payment against the debtor. In this case, which is, in legal systems distinguishing between acting in one's own name and acting in another's, distinct from the power of attorney (and also differs from assignment, since the creditor grants only the collection power – in principle, at any time revocable – he does not assign the claim), we speak of '*authorisation for collection*'. The basic questions arising in this connection, that is, whether recourse to this institution satisfies business needs and legitimate interests, and whether it is legally permissible, should be answered in the affirmative. This does not mean that non-recognition of the '*authorisation for collection*' in parallel with several other legal possibilities of collection would strike a serious blow to the interests of the parties and would give rise to grave injustices. Undoubtedly, however, the institution provides the parties with one more possibility for the satisfaction of legitimate interests in a variety of specific situations. And no rules of mandatory law can be found to prohibit this expression of private autonomy. The debtor can have the necessary protection since we have to recognize to him here too pleas which he would have against the assignee or against the representative of the creditor, so that in the end he is not treated unfavourably at all.[140]

140. In Germany, where this institution (*'Einziehungsermächtigung'*) in former times was highly controversial, the prevailing opinion today has come to recognize it, giving an affirmative answer more usually to the former, but often also to the latter of the two questions arising in this connection. See, representatively, Larenz, Schuldrecht, I, 14th ed., 1987, para. 34 V (c), with further references there. A variant opinion, which retains reservations as to the permissibility of the institution (of a rather conceptualist nature), invokes for its final recognition judicial or customary law. But even if an *opinio juris* has taken shape today, this is due, in the present author's view, to the fact that there were not compelling reasons from the law in force against the private autonomy which has established itself here. Anyway, this variant opinion often admits (in spite of its negative starting-point) that the situation can be settled in such a way that the debtor does not incur any unfavourable treatment.

(b) When payment to the third party has been permitted by the court or the law.[141]
(c) When the creditor benefits from payment to the third party; when, that is, the third party is a creditor of the creditor and the latter's debt is extinguished by this payment.

In all other cases, payment to a third party does not release the debtor, who can claim back what has been paid from the third party in accordance with the provisions on unjust enrichment (if the relevant conditions are fulfilled).

Payment must be that which is appropriate: namely, that which is actually owed is supplied. If the creditor has accepted without reservation[142] the performance offered, it is presumed that the payment was the appropriate one. This presumption is rebuttable. Proof for the presumption to be overturned (i.e., to the effect that payment was not the appropriate one) must be provided by the creditor (Article 418 CC).

232. A question arises as to the *legal nature* of the payment – more specifically, as to whether payment is a juridical act (and, moreover, a contract between debtor and creditor) or not. This question is also of practical importance. This is because if it is a juridical act, the conditions for its valid conclusion, such as defectless will, capacity to conclude a juridical act, etc., must be fulfilled. If, for example, the person making payment does not have the capacity to perform a juridical act, extinction does not occur, that is, he is not released (see, however, Article 134 CC on persons who have completed their tenth year: release from debt, as a sole effect of the juridical act, constitutes a legal benefit and, therefore, it suffices for the person thus released to have completed his tenth year). The prevailing – and well-founded – view accepts that basically payment in itself is simply a material act (e.g., a painter paints a house in accordance with his obligation; he is released whether he possessed the *animus solvendi* or not; whether he had the capacity to perform a juridical act or not; whether the creditor had the will to accept performance or not). Payment, then, does not necessarily have the character of a juridical act. Sometimes, however, the effect of the performance can only be achieved by a juridical act. For example, a vendor is obliged to transfer ownership over the thing sold to the purchaser (Article 513 CC). The transfer of ownership occurs by means of a contract (Articles 1033, 1034 CC). Consequently, for

141. By the court: We could quote such an instance from the law of enforced execution. In the procedure for attachment of claims, which is followed on the basis of a court decision for the satisfaction of a claim (e.g., A, who has a claim which has fallen due against B, certified by a final court decision, proceeds to attachment of the claim of B against C in the hands of C), the creditor may finally collect up to the level of his claim from the third party against whom an attachment has been levied (in the example, C): Art. 988 of the Code of Civil Procedure.
By law: E.g., Art. 1179, §2 CC (collection of a non-monetary claim from its usufructuary, in which case, usufruct of a claim is transformed into usufruct of a thing) or Art. 1254 CC (collection of a claim by its pledgee creditor).

142. Reservation as to the appropriateness of the payment is not an obstacle to the extinction of the obligation, but it impedes the interpretation that acceptance of the performance involved, for example, a waiver of the rights of the creditor as to any defects in the performance (see, for example, Arts 534 et seq., 540 on the rights of the purchaser in the case of an object sold being defective and the abolished Art. 545 CC; as for the latter *see* Karampatzos, The Abolition of Arts 545 and 546 sent. b–c of Greek Civil Code: An Unfortunate Legislative Initiative, EfAD 2010 (in Greek), pp. 880 et seq.).

the fulfilment of the performance (payment), a juridical act (the contract of Article 1033 or 1034 CC) is required.

B. Payment by Third Parties

233. The debtor fulfils the performance; but as a rule *any third party willing to do* so *may fulfil the performance* (Article 317 CC), with the release of the debtor as a consequence. Whether the third party who made the payment to the creditor may seek to recover what has been paid from the debtor who has been released from his debt is another question. This issue will be decided by the internal relations between the third party and the debtor, for example, by the contract which may link them or the relation of unjust enrichment which will arise between them. The third party will have no such right if he made the payment out of liberality to the debtor, that is, by a gratuitous disposition (donation) to him.

There are *two exceptions* to the above rule in the case of which a third party cannot pay the debt of another (and if he does, the debtor is not released and any creditor who declines this is not in default):[143]

(1) If the creditor has an interest in the debtor paying the debt in person, Article 317 CC (personal debts). For example: artist A has undertaken to paint the portrait of B, or lawyer A has undertaken the case of B – here B entrusts to (artist or lawyer) A, and not to a third party, the performance, which is closely bound up with the person of the debtor. It will be obvious that money debts cannot fall within this exception – they are not personal.
(2) If both creditor and debtor agree on the rejection of performance by the third party (Article 318 CC). On the other hand, if even one of the two wishes performance by the third party (and providing the instance does not fall within the first exception above or the exception to the second exception below), the rule of the permissibility of performance by a third party holds good. That is to say, in the event of such disagreement, the person who is in favour of such performance is considered to have a prevailing interest.

234. An exception to the second exception above is provided for in the instance of Article 319 CC (right of a third party to make an *offer with subrogation*).

According to this article, if proceedings for an enforced sale have been instituted against a debtor, any person who thereby runs the risk of forfeiting a right in rem on or possession of the thing sold off shall be entitled to satisfy the creditor by means of payment, a deposit with a public authority, or offsetting. To the extent that the creditor has been satisfied, the party who provided satisfaction shall be subrogated to the creditor's rights. The subrogation of the third party who made payment to the claim of the creditor occurs *ipso jure.*[144] Example: B leases his house to C. A, creditor of B,

143. If it is not a question of an exception and the creditor rejects the payment by the third party, the creditor is in default and must bear the relevant consequences (*see* next chapter, §4 and Athens Court of Appeals 3791/1954, NoB 1954, 1199).
144. Subrogation, that is, is equivalent to assignment *ex lege* (*cessio legis* – *see* para. 212, *supra* n. 101 in the previous chapter).

proceeds to attachment of it and threatens enforced sale by auction. C, who is a third party as to B's debt to A, may, nevertheless, pay B's debt to A (even if the two of them, that is, A and B, disagree on this – see second exception above), in order not to lose the leased premises because of the auction which is being threatened. If he makes payment, he now has the rights which A had against B.

§2. Discharge by Agreement

235. Obligation is extinguished in a natural way either when the debtor pays his debt (paragraphs 228 et seq.), thus satisfying the creditor, in accordance with the purpose of the obligation (and the *will* of the parties, if it is a case of an obligation from a contract or a unilateral juridical act) or when extinction occurs in accordance with the *subsequent will of the parties*. These 'regular' instances of extinction will be examined in the present paragraph. It will be obvious that one voluntary method of extinction of the obligation is any such method provided for from the beginning in the contract itself. For example: fulfilment of the resolutory condition or time clause stipulated (*see* paragraphs 183 et seq. *supra*, Article 184 CC) or expiry of the term of duration of the obligation (which is equivalent to a resolutory time clause), or contractual provision for a right of rescission, etc.

I. Actus Contrarius: Release of Debt

236. By virtue of freedom of contract (Article 361 CC), the contracting parties may by a later contrary agreement on their part (*actus contrarius*) amend or completely abolish their own contract.

They can, however, provide for something similar as to an individual claim from the contract. If they wish to cancel it, this will be a case of release of debt, which is provided for in Article 454 CC. Release of debt is an *agreement* between creditor and debtor to the effect that the latter is released from his debt (Article 454 CC). A unilateral waiver on the part of the creditor does not release the debtor. Release of debt is a *disposition* and *abstract* agreement. The former means that by this agreement, disposition, and specifically extinction of the contractual right, occurs as a direct effect of the juridical act of the agreement.[145] The latter means that the force of the disposition agreement on the release of debt does not depend on the existence or the validity of its cause, that is, the relevant promissory agreement (which may be a donation of the creditor to the debtor or some other promissory agreement between them). If the cause was lacking or defective, the release of debt remains valid – extinction, that is, occurs – but the debtor is released from his debt without justification (without just cause) and is obliged to refund his enrichment in accordance with the provisions on unjust enrichment (Articles 904 et seq. CC), that is, he is obliged to reconstitute his debt.

145. Extinction will not be accepted if the law prohibits expressly or by implication waiver of the claim. Thus, for example, as to the claims of the employee from a labour relation (*see* AP 978/1975, NoB 1976, 279).

II. Other Performance in Lieu of Payment: Promise in Lieu of Payment – Novation

237. Other performance in lieu of payment occurs when the debtor effects a performance to the creditor other than that which is owed. Other performance in lieu of payment is permissible and brings about extinction of the obligation if the creditor (without being under any obligation to do so) consents and accepts the other performance (Article 419 CC; *granting instead of payment, datio in solutum*).[146]

Promise in lieu of performance is the promise which the debtor gives to the creditor to the effect that he will fulfil a performance other than that originally owed (Article 421 CC). This is a contract between creditor and debtor which brings about extinction of the old obligation and its replacement by the debtor's new contractual obligation. It differs from other performance in lieu of payment in that here an *obligation* is *undertaken* for a new performance – a new performance is not *given.* With other performance in lieu of payment we have only extinction of the obligation, while with promise in lieu of performance we have extinction of the old and the generation of a new obligation.

Examples: A owes B a car. Instead of this, he pays him (with B's consent), in fulfilment of his debt, EUR 20,000 (= other performance in lieu of payment).

A owes B a car. Instead of this, he undertakes the obligation (by contract with B) to pay B EUR 20,000 (= promise in lieu of performance).

There is a difference between promise in lieu of performance (*in solutum*) and promise for the sake of payment (*pro solvendo*). In the latter case, a promise is given by the debtor as to a new performance (by contract with the creditor), but without extinction of the old obligation. The creditor, if the debtor does not fulfil his new obligation (fulfilment by which extinction of the original obligation also comes about), may demand the original performance (in which case the debtor will also be released from the new obligation). In this way, we have greater protection of the creditor. In the event of doubt, extinction does not occur, that is, the contract will be deemed to be a promise for the sake of payment. Promise in lieu of payment, that is, the intention of the parties that the old obligation should be extinguished, must emerge clearly (Article 421 CC).

238. Promise in lieu of performance is a form of *novation* (Articles 436 et seq. CC).

Novation is a contract between creditor and debtor by which the old obligation is abolished and a new obligation created between the two parties (in which case we have a promise of a new performance, that is, in essence, a promise in lieu of payment) or a new obligation is created with a new creditor or a new debtor. In the latter case, the new creditor or debtor must participate in the contract, while the consent of the old debtor is not necessary (Articles 455, 471 CC).

The change in the person of the creditor (assignment of claim) or of the debtor (assumption of debt) is the subject of special regulation (Articles 455 et seq., 471 et seq. – *see* paragraphs 209 et seq., 214 et seq. *supra*). Thus novation is an otiose institution, since all the instances which it covers fall within the three other institutions

146. If the performance effected is defective, the debtor is liable as vendor in the case of defects in the thing sold (Art. 420 CC).

which have been discussed (promise in lieu of payment, assignment of a claim, assumption of debt). Anyway, the regulation of novation in the CC (a relic of Roman law, in which, initially, a relation of obligation could not be transferred to another person) coincides with the regulations of the other institutions. For example, in case of doubt, an intention of novation and consequently of extinction of the obligation will not be accepted. It must be possible to clearly deduce this intention (Article 438 CC). Today, when assignment and assumption of debt are basic institutions of the law of obligations, novation would have had its own *raison d'être* if there were no special provision for promise in lieu of payment, in which case it would have covered the area which this does.

There is, however, a special regulation on the issue of the maintenance or otherwise of the securities in the event of novation (Article 439 CC). This requires, if they are to be maintained, consent of the guarantor or of the owner of the mortgaged or pledged thing. In the case of assignment of a claim or assumption of debt, the corresponding special provisions of Articles 458 and 475 CC *prevail* (*see* paragraphs 212, 215 *supra*).

§3. Irregular Termination

I. General: The Cases of Frustration, Impossibility and Breach of Contract

239. In contrast with the instances of extinction examined above, where extinction is finally based on the common will of the parties, there are grounds of extinction not based on agreement: at least one party does not consent to the extinction. A variety of ways in which such an 'irregular' extinction of an obligation (which is caused by the unilateral will of one of the contracting parties, for example, offsetting or by something lying beyond the will, for example, impossibility of performance) can take place is provided for by the law. Most of these are a consequence of anomalous development of the bond of obligation, which gives the contracting party various remedies, among them the right of release from the contract. Thus, the instances of frustration, impossibility and breach of contract, with their consequences of whatever kind, cannot be detached from the more general problem of non-performance of contractual obligations, which is examined as a whole in the next chapter, on remedies. These are remedies with which the contracting parties are provided when something goes wrong with the contract. These are, basically, a claim for fulfilment of the performance per se, the claim for compensation and various kinds of termination of the contract (such as rescission by reason of non-performance through fault of the debtor, exoneration by reason of innocent impossibility of performance, dissolution of the contract by reason of an unforeseen change of circumstances, etc.) and thus release of the contracting party.

Here we shall examine certain methods which are to a large degree independent of the problem of non-performance (including a case of frustration of the obligation's purpose). It should be noted that in specific contracts the CC provides for special ways of termination, for example, in the case of donations, *revocation* on certain grounds (such as ingratitude – Articles 505 et seq. CC); in that of sale, *rescission* by reason of defects in the thing sold (Articles 540 et seq. CC); in that of the lease of a thing or of a contract for services or a contract for work, or of a mandate or a partnership, *termination notice* for a grave cause or for another stipulated cause (Articles 585, 587, 594, 608, 609, 669, 670, 672 et seq., 700, 725, 766 et seq., 770 et seq., etc.),[147]etc.

II. Deposit with a Public Body

240. Extinction of the obligation occurs if the debtor makes a *deposit with a public body* (with the Deposits and Loans Fund – that is, a service empowered to receive such deposits) of the thing owed. The deposit with a public body is equivalent to the payment of the debt (Article 431 CC).

The debtor has the right to make a deposit with a public body only if certain reasons exist. These are *the case of the creditor's default* (Article 427 CC) and *insecurity of the debtor* arising for reasons connected with the person of the creditor (e.g., the creditor has been absent for a long period or has gone bankrupt and there is no trustee, etc.) or from reasonable uncertainty as to the person of the creditor (e.g., the creditor has died and it is not known who his actual heirs are) – Article 434, § I CC.

A further condition for a deposit is that the things owed should be *capable of deposit.* Such things are, for example, money, securities (e.g., promissory notes, bills, cheques, shares, etc.), movable 'valuables' (e.g., jewellery, precious stones, etc.). If, however, the thing owed is a movable, but not capable of deposit, the debtor may proceed to public auction of it (after notification to the creditor or with the court's permission) and then make a deposit with a public body of the sum realized (Article 428 CC). If the thing owed is an immovable, instead of such deposit, provision is made for the appointment by the court of a sequestrator, which also brings about the extinction of the obligation (Articles 359, 360 CC).

241. The legal effects of deposit with a public body are, apart from the extinction of the obligation (Article 431 CC), the generation of a contractual right on the part of the creditor to require directly from the Deposits and Loans Fund the object deposited with them (Article 432, subparagraph I). Deposit with a public body is a private deposit contract between the debtor and the Deposits and Loans Fund (Article 822 CC; normally it will be a case of irregular deposit – Article 830 CC – *see* paragraph 390 *infra*). The contract has the added characteristic that it is invested by the law (regardless of the will of the parties) with the status of a genuine contract in favour of a third party, since the depositary (the Deposits and Loans Fund) has the obligation to make payment not to the depositor, but to a third party (as to the deposit contract), that is, the creditor. If the latter owed a counter-performance to his debtor (depositor), that is, if it was a case of a reciprocal contract, the debtor may, by a declaration made at the time of the deposit 'make the claim of the creditor to the thing deposited dependent on the furnishing of the counter-performance' (Article 432, subparagraph 2). If the creditor makes a declaration to the Deposits and Loans Fund to the effect that he does not accept the

147. This notice reverses the contract for the future (*ex nunc*); the effects up to the present remain. Rescission, on the other hand, operates retroactively (*ex tunc*). *See* next chapter, §3, IV.

deposit, its effects of extinction remain in favour of the debtor and the thing which has been deposited remains with the Fund; however, a right arises for the debtor to withdraw it. If the debtor exercises this right and withdraws the thing, the effects of the deposit are reversed retroactively, that is, the obligation which had been extinguished revives (Article 433 CC).

III. Set-Off

A. *Types of Set-Off*

242. Set-off presupposes two reciprocal claims between two parties – reciprocal in the sense that each has a direction opposite to that of the other (claim and counter-claim – the debtor of the one is the creditor of the other, for example, A owes EUR 10,000 to B and B owes 8,000, from another cause, to A). Set-off means the extinction of the two reciprocal claims, normally (unless there is an agreement to the contrary) to the degree to which they overlap.

We can distinguish two types of set-off: *contractual* (or *voluntary*) and *unilateral* (or *involuntary*). The former is agreed upon by both the contracting parties by virtue of the freedom of contract (Article 361 CC). No special regulation exists for it in the law, nor was there any need for its regulation, since the parties are free to determine the fate and, consequently, the extinction of their obligations by their common consent. It follows that contractual set-off is possible whether the conditions for unilateral set-off are met or not.[148] In practice, it is the equivalent of two reciprocal release of debt contracts, which, however, brings about reciprocal satisfaction of the claims.

Viewed in terms of system, contractual set-off is a 'regular' extinction of the obligation, in the sense that it is based on the will of the parties (*see* paragraph 235 *supra*).

B. *Unilateral Set-Off*

1. Conditions

243. The law provides special regulation only in the case of unilateral set-off (Articles 440–452 CC) which is compulsorily imposed by one party on the other. The conditions for unilateral set-off are:

(a) *Reciprocity of claims* (Article 440 CC). That is, the debtor of the one claim must be the creditor of the other.[149] Exceptions from the condition of reciprocity are provided for in Articles 447, 448 CC (in the case of a guarantee, assignment), etc.

---

148. *See* AP 780/1958, NoB 1959, 414; AP 313/1999, HellD 1999, 1366; AP 337/2001, ChrID 2001, 420; AP 1254/2003, ChID 2004, 126.

149. It will be obvious that the claims must be valid. If one or both of the two claims are void or annulled or extinguished, set-off is prevented. If it is declared, its effects do not occur. Thus the valid claim remains intact.

(b) *Claims must be of the same kind* (Article 440 CC). That is, the objects of the performances of the two claims must be of the same kind, for example, both parties owe money or both parties owe fuel oil (of the same kind), and so on.
(c) *Claims must be due* (Article 440 CC). In accordance, however, with the aim of the provision, it is sufficient for one of the claims – that of the person who declares the set-off – to have fallen due. That is, while the person who declares the set-off must have a claim which is due, it is not required that he should also have a debt (that to be offset against his claim) due.
(d) *Set-off must be permitted* (Articles 450, 451 CC). (Unilateral) set-off, that is, must not be prohibited by law. It is prohibited in the exceptional instances of Articles 450 (cases of delict intentionally committed or of waiver of set-off), 451 (case of unseizable claims) CC.

2. Exercise: Effects

244. The extinction of reciprocal claims by set-off *does not come about ipso jure*, simply by the fulfilment of the four conditions above. For the occurrence of the effects of extinction, it is required that set-off should be exercised by one of the parties by a *declaration* to the other (Article 441, subparagraph I CC). Each creditor, that is, of one of the two reciprocal, similar claims, provided that his own claim is due, has the *constitutive right* to bring about extinction by his declaration – a declaration of set-off. This declaration is a unilateral juridical act (to be addressed to the other party).[150] Its effect is the extinction of the two claims 'as from the time that they co-existed' (Article 441, subparagraph 2) and to the extent that they overlap (Article 440 CC). Thus, in the example above (paragraph 239) of the two claims of EUR 8,000 and EUR 10,000 the claim of EUR 8,000 will be extinguished completely, while that of EUR 10,000 will be extinguished up to the level of EUR 8,000 and the remaining EUR 2,000 will be owed.

3. Related Concepts

245. Set-off should be distinguished from the right of retention (Articles 325 et seq. CC – paragraph 228 *supra*) and the plea *non adimpleti contractus* (Articles 374 et seq. CC – paragraph 229 *supra*). All these remedies presuppose reciprocity of claims, the last within the context of a reciprocal contract. Set-off, however, brings about extinction of the claims, while the other two remedies give rise only to postponement of fulfilment. In addition, set-off must be distinguished from co-calculation (compensation) of loss and profit: see in this connection the next chapter, paragraphs 313 et seq.

150. Apart from extra-judicial set-off, there is also the judicial set-off – that exercised before the court against a pending claim. Moreover, if the counter-claim is proven forthwith, it may be exercised for offsetting at every stage of the litigation, even at that of execution (Art. 442 CC). A valid declaration of set-off at a hearing presupposes a clear exposition of the grounds of the counter-claim, otherwise the plea of offsetting will be dismissed on the grounds of indefiniteness (AP 7/1976, NoB 1976, 537; AP 789/1975, NoB 1976, 155).

IV. Merger

246. According to Article 453, subparagraph 1 CC 'An obligation shall be extinguished by merger when the capacities of creditor and debtor have been united in the same person.'

Example: A owes B EUR 10,000. B dies and A is his heir. A, who had the debt, now acquires the claim as successor in title to B. That is, A now owes the EUR 10,000 to himself. This means a merger of the capacities of creditor and debtor in the same person and entails extinction of the obligation. The same would be the case if A died and B inherited from him (including his debts).

If the above coincidence of the two capacities in the same person later ceases to exist (e.g., the heir in our example – having inherited *ipso jure* – disclaims the inheritance and the next in succession is invited to inherit), the obligation which had been extinguished revives (Article 453, subparagraph 2 CC).

V. Frustration or Achievement of the Purpose of the Obligation by Other Means

247. This reason for extinction of obligations is not expressly provided for by Greek civil law, but it emerges from the purpose of the obligation. *If the creditor no longer has an interest in the fulfilment of the obligation*, there is no longer any point in keeping it in force. Thus the obligation will be deemed to have been extinguished if its purpose *has been frustrated* irretrievably (its achievement is impossible, because, for example, the patient whom the doctor has undertaken to treat has died), or if *it has been achieved*, not by fulfilment by the debtor, but in some other way (e.g., the wall which A has undertaken to demolish was derelict and has fallen down of its own accord). *See further infra* under paragraphs 290 et seq.

Chapter 6. Remedies in Case of Non-performance

§1. General Provisions: Claim for Performance

248. As a bond in law, obligation is characterized by the element of *commitment, engagement* (the debtor is engaged as against the creditor) and that of *enforceability* (if the debtor does not conform of his own free will with his obligation, he can be compelled to conform, that is, he can be sued by the debtor and be subjected to the procedure of enforced judicial execution). These features correspond on the side of the creditor with his right against the debtor and with his power to realize his right, that is, to lodge an action and, possibly, to proceed to enforced execution in order to obtain satisfaction.

The (enforceable) obligation means a binding of the *will* of the debtor, with effects, basically, upon his property, not the binding of his person as in Roman law. Enforcement will not be directed against the person of the debtor (e.g., by his arrest or imprisonment), but by intervention in his property.[151] The 'attachability' of his estate constitutes, in the last analysis, the *liability* of the debtor.

The liability of the debtor takes on practical importance in cases of his non-voluntary conformity to his obligation. Then it may manifest itself *in two ways:* either, first, by constraint upon the debtor to conform with the obligation which he has undertaken, that is, the fulfilment of the original performance itself; or, second, by the ability of the creditor to obtain satisfaction by other means (equally coercive for the debtor) when the conformity of the debtor with his primary obligation is no longer possible.

In the first instance, we have compulsory specific performance achieved by the means of enforcement provided for in the CCPr, following a court decision (e.g., removal of the thing owed by a court bailiff, eviction from the immovable, provision for a fine in the event of failure to carry out the act owed or of the carrying out of the act to be omitted – indirect execution – a court decision ordering a declaration of will

151. Nevertheless, intervention against the person of the debtor (a relic of earlier attitudes) for the satisfaction of the creditor was (until recently) provided for in Arts 1047 et seq., CCPr in cases of imprisonment as a means of enforced execution for the collection of civil claims against traders. This institution, much disputed and of dubious constitutionality, is contrary to the UN International Covenant on Civil and Political Rights (ratified by Greece by Law 2462/1997) and was abolished by Art. 62 of Law 3994/2011. According to Art. 11 of the Covenant, 'no one shall be imprisoned merely on the ground of inability to fulfil a contractual obligation'. See, for the application of this Article of the Covenant before the aforementioned abolition, AP 253-254/2000, HellD 2000, 1000; AP 1597/2000, HellD 2001, 1304; AP 60/2001, NoB 2002, 116; AP 971/2001, DEE 2001, 1104; AP 1635/2001, HellD 2002, 729; AP (in Plenary Session) 23/2005, NoB 2005, 1090 (with comment by *Doris*); AP 1422/2008, NoB 2009, 424.

when the conclusion of a juridical act is owed,[152] seizure of property for the satisfaction of pecuniary claims, etc. – *see* Articles 941 et seq. CCPr). In the second instance, we have conversion of the original obligation into a (secondary) obligation to compensate, as a rule in cash terms and also enforceable.

249. The meaning of the above is that the first and fundamental protection of the creditor in the Greek law of contracts is the recognition to him of the *claim for performance* of the debtor's obligation in the form (non-monetary or monetary) in which it has been undertaken. The law makes it possible for the creditor to enforce the initial performance itself. On this basic issue Greek law resembles most continental European systems of law and differs from the Anglo-Saxon systems, in which the sanction for non-performance consists mainly in the payment of compensation or in the discharge from the contract, with provision only by way of exception, as a supplementary remedy (which, moreover, remains at the discretion of the court), for specific performance, that is, the possibility of the court directing the defendant to perform the contract which he has made and in accordance with its terms.[153]

250. More particularly in the case of obligations which have *an obligation of forbearance from an act* as their object, the protection in law of the creditor and the liability of the debtor are in principle also complete. Certain difficulties arise only in their realization. As has already been noted, liability manifests itself either in the form of constraint to fulfil the performance, to which the creditor's claim for performance corresponds, or in the form of liability for compensation for non-fulfilment, which means a corresponding claim on the part of the creditor. In the case of the latter, there is no difficulty. Failure of the debtor to conform, that is, the carrying out of the act to be omitted, has as its consequence his liability to compensation on the terms of the law. The difficulty is in connection with the first form of liability. The question arises *whether the creditor has a claim for performance*, whether he can constrain the debtor to observe his obligation of omission (*claim for omission*). Obviously, execution of any court decision directing forbearance of the debtor from the relevant conduct can be carried out only *indirectly*, that is by psychological constraint (*threat of a fine*, etc.), which is also in the case of certain positive acts the only manner of execution. The problem takes a different form if the debtor has already infringed his obligation or if, on the contrary, he continues to conform with it, in which case it is a matter of a *preventive claim for omission*. In the latter case, the question of whether infringement is threatened is of importance.

251. In light of the above, a distinction should be made between three instances: *Instance a.:* There has not yet been any infringement of the obligation of omission, nor is any threatened (the situation is one of conformity). *Instance b.:* The obligation

152. Thus, if A owes to B to transfer to him (e.g., by reason of sale, donation, etc.) the ownership of a thing and refuses to conform, the adverse decision of the court on this ('order for a declaration of will', Art. 949 CCPr) is equivalent to his declaration of will (which 'is deemed to have been made'). The plaintiff, if a contract is required (as in the above example), has only to declare unilaterally acceptance of this declaration (deduced in this way) of the defendant who has lost the case. On this acceptance, the contract is concluded (and, in our example, the ownership of the thing is transferred). The fulfilment of the performance has been achieved.

153. See, for preference, *Anson's Law of Contract*, 28th ed. (By J. Beatson), Part V, Ch. 18 II, pp. 632 et seq.

of omission has been infringed. *Instance c.:* The debtor continues to conform, but infringement is threatened:

(a) In the first instance, there is no failure of the performance, and, consequently, no violation of the right of the creditor such as to justify any legal interest and, consequently, a claim on his part for (judicial) constraint against the debtor that he should conform. As long as the debtor is conscientious, only an action for a declaratory judgment is possible, if there is a legal interest in this (Article 70 CCPr).

(b) In the second instance, liability for compensation for the prejudice caused by the infringement naturally arises. This will be the only manifestation of liability if the violation of the right of the creditor is of its nature momentary and cannot be repeated. For example, A, although he had undertaken towards B the obligation not to make known to third parties a piece of information of an economic nature, has nevertheless published it in the Press. In such cases, constraint to conform is no longer possible. When, however, there is a risk that a momentary violation will be repeated (e.g., A, who has undertaken the obligation not to make noise during certain morning working hours each day, one day infringes this obligation), or when the violation is a standing one (e.g., although A has undertaken the obligation not to use his premises as a place of entertainment, he opens and runs such a place on them), there are grounds also for a claim for performance. Thus the creditor may demand either that there should be no repetition of the momentary infringement or that the standing infringement which continues should cease and, probably, that it should not be repeated. The relevant possibility of constraint to perform (by indirect enforced execution) stems from the existence of a relation of obligation (Article 287 CC), which entails a commitment to perform for as long as performance is still possible. Additional foundation is not needed.[154] Of course, in the event of the infringement being momentary, but able to be repeated, it might seem that in the period of time between two infringements there is a situation of conformity on the part of the debtor which should be an obstacle to the claim for performance. However, such an understanding would lead to a conceptualist solution. When infringement of the obligation can be effected by repeated positive acts, the carrying out of one of these demonstrates by action the unreliability of the debtor, who, consequently, must be treated as not complying with his obligations.

154. On the other hand, the grounding in law of a claim for omission when no obligation of omission has been undertaken is difficult. Thus there is a problem as to whether, for example, after a *tort* which has resulted in harm to a person's legal interest (Art. 914 CC), the injured party can require of the injuring party the omission of a repetition of the harm. The theoretical difficulty is that the lawful interest of each person that he should not be harmed by third parties cannot automatically be transformed into a right which generates a claim of a preventive nature, while, on the other hand, there is general provision for a claim of a suppressive character for compensation after the harm has been done (Art. 914 CC). This much-disputed issue is not within the ambit of the law of contracts. However, it should be mentioned here that in special cases the law provides for a claim for omission, e.g., when the right of personality (Art. 57 CC) or of ownership (Art. 1108 CC) is prejudiced.

(c) In the third instance, the problem is more difficult and has led to divergence of opinion. According to the above, a claim for performance should not be accepted, since there is still a situation of conformity on the part of the debtor. But more particularly when the danger of violation is not an abstract one but is expected to occur with a certainty or high degree of probability which can be established from specific facts, the prevailing view, at least in Greek theory, tends to the recognition of the claim. Indeed, if there are serious indications that the debtor will not perform his obligation (e.g., steps have been taken preparatory to the infringement), it would be teleologically unjustifiable for the debtor to continue to enjoy the treatment which is accorded to those who are conscientious in their duties. In the last analysis, prevention is preferable to suppression and more in keeping with the purpose and essence of law.[155]

However, the issue is not of major practical importance, since (if a regular action to obtain omission is not recognized) when there is an imminent risk of violation of any right, contractual or otherwise, the holder of the right may, in accordance with the CCPr (and by summary proceedings, Articles 682 et seq. – *see* particularly Articles 682, 692, 731, 732 CCPr) seek an injunction for the protection of his right. The court may order any measure which it judges appropriate, even 'the omission of a specific act' (Article 731 CCPr). The execution of the decision will be by means of indirect (psychological) constraint (Articles 700, 947 CCPr).

On *suspensive remedies*, and on the possibility of *offsetting*, *see* paragraphs 227 et seq., 242 et seq. *supra.*

§2. The Significance of *Fault* in Cases of Non-performance

I. The Fault Principle

252. In the matter of the liability of the debtor, his fault is of crucial significance. The importance which it has for the law of remedies calls for its examination now and for us to distinguish this from cases where it is absent (instances of chance events). Apart from the action for performance which we examined in the preceding paragraph and which is inherent in the obligational claim and independent, naturally, of fault, the other main remedies in the case of non-performance (compensation, rescission) as a rule presuppose fault.

By 'fault', the law means the psychological bond which exists between a person and an action on his part or its result which justifies the imputation of blame to him. In other words, conduct which is at fault on the part of a person is that which permits him to be censured *personally* for his act, for this person to be deemed psychologically

155. The opinion in favour of the possibility of judicial protection when harm to the interests of a person has not yet occurred, but when there is a specific threat to it has prevailed at an international level. Cf. the German institution of '*vorheugende Unterlassungsklage*', the French '*mesures preventives*' (sanctioned, if necessary, by an '*astreinte*', and the English institution, based on equity, of a '*quia timet injunction*'.

responsible for it. In common parlance too, the expression that a person 'was at fault' over something (and not merely the cause of it) is a form of censure on him. There are two degrees of fault, depending upon its gravity: *intent* (*wilful conduct*, *dolus*) (the more serious instance) and *negligence*. Basically, the former is present when the culprit willed or accepted[156] the (unlawful) result (wilful – deliberate acts). The latter is present when such will on the part of the culprit is lacking, but he has not devoted the care which he could and ought to have given to the averting of the (unlawful) result, when, that is, his will 'was inert'. Thus both wilful conduct and negligence are forms of fault – indeed the only ones. Fault can exist only in one of these two forms.

253. Failure to perform the contractual obligation in itself has an *objective* character and, alone, does not justify personal censure of the debtor. It is imputed to him only objectively. For example, the thing owed is destroyed by a third party. With fault for failure to perform the contractual obligation, this subjective condition for liability is added, as a rule, that is, it is also required for the right of compensation, rescission, etc. to be exercised (fault principle – Article 330 CC – subjective liability). Cases of liability without fault (objective (strict) liability) constitute the exception. See, for example, paragraphs 163, 164 *supra* in connection with the strict liability of the debtor for the fault of another or that of the producer of defective products; or paragraph 272 (b) *infra* in connection with the debtor in default and fortuitous events.

In the case of innocent non-performance (without fault being present), the claim for performance will continue to exist (if, of course, performance is possible). Liability will not exist in any other respect. Other consequences will be examined below.

II. Imputability

254. For there to be personal, subjective imputation of blame to the debtor, another element, equally subjective, apart from the fault, is needed: *imputability* (*accountability for one's actions*, *culpability*), which, moreover, *precedes the fault*. Before we examine whether someone is at fault for an unlawful act on his part and consequently is deserving of blame and its imputation, we must look into the question of whether he had the mental capacity to be in general responsible, that is, the mental maturity and health such that disapprobation by law is permissible. This general capacity, which anyone who is mentally mature and healthy (*compos mentis*) possesses, that is, as a rule, any adult (and which is naturally not required in the case of strict liability), consists basically in the fact that this person is capable of perceiving whether his act is right or wrong. Since the rule is that this capacity exists, that is, that a person is of sound mind, the law regulates the negative side of the question, that is, it defines when there is a mental disorder and, more generally, when imputability does not exist. If the stipulated reasons for non-imputability are not present, the rule holds good, that is, it will be deemed that the capacity is present and we shall proceed to the investigation of fault.

156. If the culprit foresees the unlawful result (i.e., here the debtor foresees the breach of his obligation) as a likely (not necessary) consequence of his conduct and, in spite of this, accepts it, we speak of *eventual wilful conduct* (*dolus eventualis*).

The CC (Article 331 CC, in conjunction with Articles 915 et seq. CC) stipulates the following reasons for non-imputability in the case of liability from a pre-existing obligation: where a person (a) has not completed his 14th year;[157] (b) is not conscious of his acts; (c) is in a state of psychological or mental disturbance which decisively limited the operation of his judgment and will.

III. Negligence in Particular: Its Relation to Unlawfulness

255. More particularly in the case of negligence, we must draw attention to the fact that its meaning today has been to a large degree *objectivized* (in a way comparable to the corresponding evolution in Germany), so that the differences from English law, which, in dealing with breach of contract, does not concern itself at all with whether the breach is culpable or otherwise (so that it is regarded as basically establishing strict liability of the debtor), have been much reduced. More specifically the question arises as to what is the measure by which it will be judged whether the conduct of the culprit was negligent or careful and, more particularly, who will constitute the model for deciding, for example, that it was possible for the unlawful result to be foreseen. Are we to take into account the powers of foresight of the culprit, of an objective observer or of some other third party? According to subjective views, the measure consists of the conduct of which the culprit himself was capable. The question of what he himself was in a position to understand and do is regarded as crucial. Thus, what is taken into account are his individual characteristics, for example, any physical or mental defects (though not to the degree of non-imputability), his possible lack of experience, etc. If the culprit deviates from this conduct, if he did not act with the care with which he himself could have done, he will be deemed to have been negligent. Otherwise, he will be judged not to have been negligent, even if other people (the majority) would have shown greater care. It was in this sense, in fact, that the prevailing opinion formerly understood negligence: a personal criterion responds more to the need of personal censure against the culprit, a need interwoven with the concept of fault. The subjective criterion is crucial for the concept of negligence in criminal law (where, of course, the consequences are more serious for the negligent person).

256. At the present time, however, a more *objective* criterion prevails in civil law.[158] The capabilities of the average prudent and conscientious man will be regarded as crucial. The deviation of the conduct of the culprit from those capabilities constitutes negligence, even if he himself was not able to behave in any other way. Thus the debtor in civil law is liable for any personal defect which he may have. In this case, discharge of the negligent party would only be possible if – in extreme cases – the defect reaches the point of robbing him of his imputability. On the other hand, if the culprit because of his exceptional abilities is capable of acting with greater care and attention, he will not be regarded as negligent if this greater attention does not correspond to the

157. A person who has not completed his 14th year (but has completed his 10th), as well as a deaf mute, has a liability provided that he is able to distinguish between right and wrong (Art. 917 CC in conjunction with Art. 331 CC).

158. *See* AP 603/1972, NoB 1972, 1443; AP 1274/1977, EEN 1978, 323; AP 1427/1979, NoB 1980, 1036; AP 634/1988, HellD 1989, 964.

capabilities of the average prudent man. In the law in force, this more objective approach to negligence can be seen in the stipulation of Article 330, subparagraph 2 CC, where we find the definition that there is negligence when the generally required care (in business and legal practice) was not exercised.

Nevertheless, extreme objectivization would not answer to the spirit of the law. The average representative of the occupation, the environment, the age, the place of residence, etc. of the negligent party should be taken into account. That is, what is of importance is a typical representative of the *circles in which he moves.* Local variations, particularly, should not be steam-rollered. The care required in a major city is one thing and that required in a village another. The care required will also differ particularly from occupation to occupation[159] and perhaps from age to age (e.g., adolescents).

257. As a consequence of the above objectivization of negligence, confusion has arisen as to whether negligence belongs with the objective or subjective conditions for liability. The problem arises particularly because today it has been widely accepted that the objectively unlawful character of an act (in the law of contracts: the failure, independent of fault, to perform a contractual obligation) also exists when the culprit has infringed the obligation generally required of every member of society to exercise the care which a reasonable man is capable of taking, regardless of whether his conduct constitutes a violation of a specific rule of law. That is to say, negligence is prohibited as a way of behaving, that is, there is an objective disapprobation of the negligent act (and therefore it is deemed to be unlawful). The law, however, considers the same act, seen as conduct of a certain person, sufficient to censure that person. Here, that is, this conduct is treated as a form of fault. The fact that the person concerned should have foreseen and avoided the violation which has occurred means that his conduct is unlawful. The fact that he was able to foresee and avoid the violation (according to the criteria of the average prudent man) means that his conduct justifies personal censure, that he is at fault. Here 'should' and 'am able' coincide. Thus, affirmation of fault, in this sense, will mean affirmation of contrariety to the law, and vice versa. The same act (negligent conduct, contrary to the care generally required) also constitutes the unlawful conduct and the conduct at fault. The same term, negligence, is used here for both. But this does not alter the fact that, according to Greek law, which is based on the fault principle, two conditions – an objective and a subjective one – must be met. It is simply that they are fulfilled by the same act.

It is a matter of the law in force to stipulate that an act should have the character of being both unlawful and at fault for the affirmation of the liability. Other systems of law, such as the English, treat negligence solely as an unlawful manner of conduct and attach no importance to whether it constitutes a form of fault. Thus negligence, according to this law, constitutes no more than one of the torts and exists when the duty of a person to exercise that care which a prudent and reasonable man would

159. AP Decision 1274/1977, EEN 1978, 323 accepts as crucial the care shown 'within the circle and the occupation of the party at fault'. From then on, consistent court rulings have spoken of the care which must be shown in accordance with good faith by the party at fault 'within the circle of his competence' or 'of his occupation' or 'of his social activity'. See, *inter alia,* AP 666/1986, HellD 1987, 835; AP 103/1989, D 1990, 396; AP 250/1992, NoB 1992, 1062; AP 90/1993, EEN 1994, 85; AP 1586/1998, EEN 2000, 241; AP 447/2000, NoB 2001, 836; AP 2193/2007 EEmbD 2008, 598.

exercise is infringed, with the result that prejudice is caused to another person, and which gives rise, in principle, to the liability of the culprit.

IV. Types of Negligence: Chance Events – Force Majeure

258. The CC distinguishes between 'gross' and 'slight' negligence. The distinction has special practical significance. In exceptional cases the law provides for liability only for gross negligence (and, of course, for wilful conduct (*dolus*), which is a graver form of fault) and not for slight, for example in instances of gratuitous transactions (in which case, liability is reduced only for the donor, Article 499 CC, and for the lender for use, Article 811 CC, and not for the recipient).[160]

259. When the failure to perform the contractual obligation is not due to fault, there will not, as a rule, be liability. Such failure will then be due to *chance* (*fortuitous*) *events*. These (in their broad sense) are sub-divided into *chance events in the strict sense* and events *of* force majeure (*vis major*).

A chance event in the broad sense can most accurately be defined in a negative way, to include anything which is not wilful conduct or negligence of the person responsible. Where negligence ends, chance events begin. Thus, to their content belong events which have not been foreseen and could not be foreseen or avoided by the average prudent man. Naturally, the chance event for the party responsible may be due to the fault of another person. Fault or chance events are to be understood in relation to some person, to whom they are attributed.

The rule is, as we have said, that there is no liability of the 'culprit' for chance events. By way of exception, however, his liability may be extended to include all or some such fortuitous events. This extension is either effected by contract or is directly provided for by law.

260. The category of chance events for which the term force majeure is used includes basically the extreme cases of those events which cannot be averted by human powers, or, at least, of which it is more difficult to avert than other chance events, that is, those in the strict sense, which are closer to negligence. The distinction between chance events in the strict sense and force majeure is of practical importance when the law relieves a debtor only in the event of force majeure, making him liable for fault and chance events in the strict sense (e.g., liability of the owner of a motor car, of an employer for the pay of his employees, etc.). The delimitation of cases of force

160. In some cases the Civil Code distinguishes between slight negligence which is abstract and that which is specific (*culpa levis in abstracto, culpa levis in concreto*); while in the former the average prudent person belonging to his circle is taken as the model and measure with which the specific conduct of the person at fault is compared, in the latter the measure of judgment is provided by the individual conscientious conduct of the person himself, the '*diligence exercised in his own affairs*' (*diligentia quam in suis*) (*see* Art. 333 CC), i.e., the care which the person concerned normally shows in his own business. The rule is for the former to be required. When the law wishes to be more lenient, it requires 'only' diligence exercised in his own affairs (e.g., liability of a depositary, Art. 823 CC). This individual criterion does not function to the detriment of the debtor. Thus, in cases where he is particularly conscientious in his own affairs, the care shown by the average person will be sufficient.

majeure (and, consequently, the definition of the area remaining between these and negligence, that is, that covered by chance events in the strict sense) is difficult. Two different theories, the objective and the subjective, are taught on this subject.

The *objective* (or *absolute*) theory[161] recognizes a narrower range *of* force majeure. In regarding as crucial for their meaning that these events should be *by their very nature* impossible to avert, it looks for them only in events which are 'external' to the debtor. Thus by events of force majeure are meant those which objectively lie outside the field of the economic activity of the debtor and which, consequently, cannot be averted by him. For example: for the debtor A, who is a businessman, war, earthquake, revolution, a strike by employees of another business (e.g., that of A's supplier) and other similar occurrences which happen to A's business 'from without' constitute force majeure. By way of contrast, those which occur in his business, even if they are unavoidable (e.g., a strike of the employees of A's own business) are not regarded as *constituting* force majeure.

The *subjective* (or *relative*) theory, which is the prevailing one in Greece,[162] results in a widening of the range of events of force majeure to include 'internal' occurrences. That is to say, it does not require for these the factor of their origination 'from without', but regards as crucial only the fact that these events could not be foreseen and averted *even by measures of extreme care and prudence on the part of* the perpetrator. This view is, then, more lenient towards the debtor, when force majeure constitutes grounds for his discharge and since those grounds are finally made broader. In many instances, however, the weaker of the contracting parties, and thus the one in need of greater protection, is the other party (e.g., employee), for whom this theory turns out to be harsher.

In EU law there is a tendency towards the shaping by court decisions of the concept of force majeure. Thus the ECJ has held that occurrences of force majeure are events which are 'unusual, regardless of the will of the entrepreneur and whose consequences could not be avoided, even though every possible diligence has been shown, except by disproportionate sacrifices'.[163] In requiring basically the inevitability of the event with whatever diligence on the part of the debtor, this definition comes close to the subjective theory of *vis major*, although the condition that the events should be independent of the will of the debtor and the addition in certain decisions of the

---

161. First formulated by the German jurist *Exner* in *Grünhuts Zeitschrift,* 10, 497.
162. This theory was developed chiefly by *Goldschmidt*, Zeitschrift für Handelsrecht, Vol. 3, pp. 58 et seq., 331 et seq., and Vol. 16, pp. 324 et seq. See, in favour of this, AP 462/1970, NoB 1970, 1305; AP 698/1973, NoB 1974,186; AP 267/1976, NoB 1976, 790; AP 1850/1987, NoB 1988, 1646; AP 1592/1988, EEN 1989, 754; AP 16/1995, NoB 1996, 192; AP 266/1995, HellD 1996, 671. There are, however, tendencies, particularly in theory, to favour the objective theory.
163. *See* ECJ of 17.12.1970, C-11/70 (consideration 23); ECJ of 30.5.1984, C-224/83, coll. 1984, 2349 (consideration 13); ECJ of 13.10.1993, C-124/92, coll. 1993 I, 5061 (consideration 11); ECJ of 17.10.2002, C-208/01 (consideration 19). In one case (decision of 30.1.1974, C-158/73, Kampffmeyer, consideration 10), the ECJ speaks of the showing of every diligence which one can equitably expect of an average trader.

need for these events to lie outside the field of influence of the debtor[164] are moving in the direction of the objective theory, without, however, reaching the point of clearly requiring an external origin.

V. Procedural Issues

261. Burden of proof: In the case of liability from a pre-existing obligation, usually from a contract (Article 330 CC), the creditor – injured party must prove the infringement of the obligation of the debtor, but not the latter's fault, which is presumed to exist. Consequently, the debtor bears the burden of proving, in order to be discharged, that he was not at fault (*See* paragraph 82 *supra*). On the other hand, in a case of delictual liability (*see* particularly Article 914 CC), the creditor, that is, the injured party, must, *inter alia*, also prove the fault of the debtor – the injuring party. The burden of proof of the existence of an exemption agreement is borne by the party who invokes it.

262. Control of the Court of Cassation of Areios Pagos: Fault and its gradations (wilful conduct, gross, slight, specific or abstract, negligence – *see also* paragraph 258 *supra*), ordinary chance events and force majeure are legal concepts. Consequently, the question of whether the actual events which have been established lie within one of these categories, for example, constitute gross or slight negligence, etc., is reviewed by the *Areios Pagos.*[165] On the other hand, the establishment of the actual events which constitute, or not, force majeure, gross or slight negligence, etc. is not subject to the control of the *Areios Pagos.*[166]

§3. Breach of Contract

263. The CC makes no provision for a single instance of non-performance, but for special categories of non-compliance of the debtor: impossibility of performance, on the one hand, and default (the debtor being in arrears through his own fault), on the other. All other instances fall within a third category, that of improper performance. The CC provides regulations separately for the consequences of the above anomalies, first in general and then for reciprocal contracts.

Criticism has been levelled at the Greek Civil Code because it has regulated (as did the BGB until its revision in 2002) only the instances of impossibility of performance and default of the debtor and has left without regulation other instances where, although one of these two forms of anomaly is not present, performance is not brought, for other reasons, to its normal fulfilment. It was theory (initiated by Staub in Germany) which

164. *See* ECJ of 30.1.1974, C-158/73, Kampffmeyer (consideration 9); ECJ of 28.5.1974, C-3/74, coll. 1974, 589 (consideration 8); ECJ of 22.1.1986, C-266/84, coll. 1986, 149 (consideration 27); ECJ of 5.2.1987, C-145/85, coll. 1987, 565 (consideration 11); ECJ of 11.7.2002, C-210/00 (consideration 79).

165. *See* AP 1274/1977, EEN 1978, 323; AP 1346/1989, HellD 1992, 304; AP 727/1995, NoB 1997, 768; AP 262/1996, EEmbD 1996, 486.

166. *See* AP 598/1971, NoB 1972, 52; AP 1346/1989, HellD 1992, 304.

basically placed the cases not provided for by a general regulation in the category of 'improper performance'. It would have been, of course, better, according to this line of criticism, for the CC to have set as a basis for regulation a more general concept which would at least have covered all cases of anomaly on the side of the debtor (thus, for example, the Anglo-Saxon and French legal systems). Such a concept is non-performance (wholly or in part). In this way there would not have been gaps which had to be filled by analogy of law, as is the case today. At the same time, the legislator would have succeeded in producing a unified and simpler regulation, which is within the bounds of possibility, because in all cases of non-performance the same rules, basically, have force – such as the fault principle, the retention of the force and binding nature of the obligation in spite of the existence of an anomaly and, consequently, the duty, on terms, of payment of the positive (but not the negative) interest, the rule that the fault of the debtor is presumed, etc. The particularities of individual categories of non-performance could then have been dealt with separately.

Many consider an advantage of the regulation particularly of impossibility of performance in the Greek Civil Code the complete abandonment of the Roman rule *impossibilium nulla est obligatio* (which has still partial force, for example, in the French or BGBs), that is, the acceptance of the validity and binding nature of the obligational relation in any instance of impossibility of performance, which renders superfluous – at least from the point of view of the consequences which follow – the distinction between the various forms of impossibility and permits a uniform regulation of them. Thus, under the Greek Civil Code, the obligation (or, more accurately, the contract from which the obligation stems) has force even in a case of initial, objective impossibility of performance, where also, if there is fault on the part of the debtor, the positive interest is owed.

I. Impossibility of Performance

A. In the Case of All Obligations

264. When the debtor is irreversibly not in a position to fulfil the performance which he owes, we speak of impossibility of performance. The law regulates its consequences separately for initial impossibility (Articles 362 et seq. CC) and for supervening impossibility (Articles 335 et seq. CC). In both cases the regulation is basically similar, in spite of the division by the legislator of the subject-matter regulated into two chapters. A special regulation is contained in the CC, as we have said, for impossibility of performance in the case of reciprocal contracts (Articles 380 et seq. CC).

When there is impossibility of performance, *we must distinguish between cases where this arises from fault of the debtor or not.*

The consequences are different. Thus:

If the impossibility was due to fault: the debtor is not released, but owes compensation to the creditor in place of the original performance, which can no longer be fulfilled (Articles 335, 362, in conjunction with 330 CC). The compensation is the positive interest or performance interest (see paragraphs 92 et seq. supra). This is because the contract from which the obligation stems remains valid after the impossibility. Thus the creditor will be able to seek as compensation what he would have had if the (valid) obligation had been performed, e.g., the value of the performance, any lucrum cessans from its non-fulfilment, etc.

If the impossibility was not due to fault of the debtor:[167] The debtor is released from the original obligation, as well as from the obligation of compensation (Articles 336, 363, in conjunction with 330 CC). He has, however, two collateral obligations:

(a) He must *inform* the creditor of the impossibility as soon as he is informed of it himself (Articles 336, subparagraph 2, 363, subparagraph 2), otherwise he owes him compensation for prejudice resulting from failure to inform him.

(b) He owes the creditor any *substitute (surrogatum)* (Articles 338, 363, subparagraph 3). A 'substitute' or 'surrogate' is 'everything which has devolved' upon the debtor as a result of the impossibility of performance. This is a benefit to the debtor which is in a causal relation with the impossibility of performance and constitutes a value which takes the place, wholly or in part, of the impossible performance.
Examples of surrogates: The insurance compensation which the debtor has collected as a result of the destruction of the thing which he owed; the price which he has realised from the sale to a third party of the thing which he owed (this sale and transfer to the third party causing the impossibility); what material remains of the thing which has been destroyed, etc.

265. Another basic rule governing impossibility of performance is that *the fault of the debtor for the impossibility* is *presumed.* The creditor does not need to prove it. However, the presumption is rebuttable. It is overturned, that is, if the debtor himself proves that he was not at fault (see the wording of Article 336 CC; the same can also be concluded from Article 363 CC).

It should be noted that we speak here of impossibility due to fault or otherwise, in the interests of brevity and having in mind the regular instance of the fault principle. More precisely, Article 336 CC (like other provisions which distinguish in contractual liability between non-performance due to fault and otherwise, for example, Articles 342, 380 et seq., etc. CC) makes no reference to an event *not due to fault*, but to an event for which the debtor *has no liability.* This is, however, according to the rule of Article 330, subparagraph I, an event which is not due to wilful conduct or negligence, that is, not due to fault. The broader formulation of Article 336 CC has as its purpose also to cover those exceptions where the debtor is also liable for chance events (in which case, a chance event is here equal to fault) or where the debtor is not liable, for example, for slight negligence (in which case, slight negligence is equal to a chance event).

266. Impossibility of performance exists, basically, if the object of the performance is specified. If the obligation is still determined in kind ('generic', that is, defined by

167. AP(Decision 105/1961, NoB 9, 970) has, for instance. accepted that the loss of the performance by an act of a third party if he is not an assistant in the fulfilment or legal representative of the debtor (Arts 330, 334 CC) is a chance event and not one due to fault. *See also* AP 93/1967, NoB 1967, 791; AP 1812/1990, EEN 1991, 747.

reference to 'genus'), for example, a motor car of type X is owed, without it being particularized yet which specific car of type X must be delivered (*see also* paragraph 143 *supra*), we do not yet have a specific obligation and, therefore, if one of the more general class of things is destroyed while it is in the hands of the debtor, this is not a case of impossibility of performance. This is because the debtor can provide another thing from the same class. His original obligation continues to exist. He bears the risk of the loss in his own property. Only if all the genus is destroyed, which would be a rare event, can there be impossibility of performance – or, perhaps, in extreme cases of economic impossibility (*see* (c) *infra*). This applies a fortiori in the case of money debts.

Included within the concept of impossibility of performance are:

(a) *Natural (or material) impossibility.* For example, the natural existence of the thing owed is destroyed.
(b) *Legal impossibility*, which exists when the fulfilment of the performance is prevented on legal grounds. For example: the vendor of a thing is not the owner of it (or after the sale loses the ownership, for example, by sale and transfer to a third party) and consequently, although he validly undertakes the obligation to transfer the ownership (Article 513 CC), he cannot perform it (Articles 1033, 1034 CC). There is also legal impossibility when the debtor and the creditor have validly concluded the contract, but for a performance which is prohibited by law, for example, for a 'thing outside the ambit of transactions' (*res extra commercium*) (Article 365 CC – *see also* paragraph 144 *supra*). If there is fault on the part of the debtor (see, for example, Articles 362–363 CC), he will owe a positive interest. The situation is different when the contract itself is void (Article 174 CC), in which case the rules of impossibility of performance, which presuppose the valid undertaking of an obligation, are not applied. In this case, at the most, negative interest will be owed, if there are legal grounds for liability.
(c) *Economic impossibility.* Economic *difficulties* in the fulfilment of the performance do not constitute impossibility. For impossibility to be accepted (by a broadening of the concept, in accordance with the purpose of Articles 335 et seq., 362 et seq. CC), the expenditure which the debtor is called upon to incur in order to fulfil the performance must go beyond the *maximum sacrifice* which can be demanded of him (*see also* Article 288 CC). For example: the object which I owed fell to the bottom of the sea (at a great depth). Whilst materially it continues to exist, I must incur vast expense – out of all proportion to its value – to raise it to the surface. There is some dispute as to this broadening of impossibility of performance.[168] The problems in this connection could also be dealt with up to a point by possible implementation of Article 388 CC (§5 *infra*).

168. The courts, in particular, are reluctant to accept impossibility of performance in cases of excessively great economic difficulty of the debtor which goes beyond the bounds of his endurance. See, however, Decision AP 93/1967, NoB 1967, 791, which accepted impossibility of performance 'when it is something which is theoretically possible, but which can be achieved by expenditure which is excessively great and by disproportionate economic sacrifices and risks in general in no logical relationship with the result pursued'. *See also* AP 595/1999, HellD 2000, 34.

(d) *Moral impossibility.* Here too, for impossibility to be accepted, the maximum sacrifice on the part of the debtor must be exceeded (*see also* Article 288 CC). For example: an actor who has the obligation to appear in a performance on a certain day suffers a tragic loss on that day, such as the death of his child.

267. The above regulation holds good uniformly for every kind of impossibility of performance. Thus the distinctions made below are of systematic rather than practical importance, since the consequences are basically the same:

- *Initial impossibility* (e.g., I promise a thing which has already been destroyed) *supervening impossibility* (e.g., I promise a thing which after my promise – and before performance – is destroyed). (*See* Articles 335 CC et seq. (supervening impossibility), Articles 362 et seq. CC (initial impossibility)).
- *Objective impossibility* (the performance is impossible for all, for example, by reason of the destruction of the thing owed) – *subjective impossibility* (the performance is impossible only for its debtor, for example, he does not have the thing owed in his ownership or possession and cannot fulfil the performance, while a third person, as owner and possessor, could). Subjective impossibility is sufficient for the implementation of Articles 335 et seq., 362 et seq. CC. See the wording of Articles 335, 362 CC: 'for reasons either of a general nature or relating to the debtor'.
- *Total impossibility* (e.g., the entire quantity owed is destroyed) – *partial impossibility* (e.g., a part of the performance owed is destroyed). *See* Article 335 CC: 'wholly or in part'. If the impossibility is partial (initial or supervening), the rules of impossibility of performance (discharge by reason of lack of fault, owing of a positive interest in the event of fault, etc.) will be implemented only as to the impossible part; the possible part will continue to be owed. A deviation from this is provided for by Article 337 CC (*see also* Article 362, subparagraph 2): if the creditor does not have an interest in partial performance, he is entitled (within a reasonable time-limit from the time of the offer or the invitation of the debtor) to decline it and to regard the impossibility as total. This means that the creditor will be able to seek compensation for the entire performance and not merely for the impossible part of it, provided, of course, that impossibility was due to fault (since only then does the rejection of the possible part have practical significance for the creditor). For example: A owes B a 24-volume encyclopaedia which is available on the market only as a single work and not in its individual volumes. If, owing to the fault of A, half of the volumes are destroyed, B declines the other half so as to receive as compensation the total value of the work and to be able to purchase it elsewhere.

268. By impossibility is meant *irretrievable* impossibility, not *temporary.*[169] The latter means simply delay in fulfilment.

However, in the two following instances, temporary impossibility will be, by way of exception, equivalent to irretrievable and the consequences of impossibility of performance will occur:

169. *See* AP 369/1973, NoB 1973, 1196; AP 435/1990, EEN 1991, 68.

(a) In the case of *fixed-date* contracts. For example, A orders foodstuffs for a reception which he is giving in the evening of a specific day. On the evening in question the foodstuffs are not yet ready. Although the impediment is temporary, there is impossibility of performance.
(b) Where this is demanded by good faith (Article 288 CC). For example, temporary impossibility is extended for a long and indefinite period, so that it is not possible for us to expect the creditor to wait any longer.

B. Particularly in the Case of Reciprocal Contracts

269. The issue becomes more complicated when the obligation in which the anomaly makes its appearance stems from a reciprocal contract, when, that is, apart from the performance, as to which there is an anomaly, the creditor owes a counter-performance. The above rules continue in principle to apply as to the individual obligation which is not, or not properly, performed. The new question which arises, however, is whether this anomaly will also have an effect on the fate of the counter-performance, as to which per se there is no problem. For example: A sells B a thing for EUR 10,000. The thing is destroyed before performance. A, according to what we have seen up to now, owes compensation or is released, depending on whether or not there is fault on his part. But will B continue to owe the EUR 10,000?

The problem of impossibility in reciprocal contracts, with emphasis on the fate of the counter-performance, is regulated in Articles 380 et seq. All the varieties of impossibility are here approached in a unified manner. The CC distinguishes between three instances, depending on whether anyone is at fault for the impossibility, and who:

(1) If impossibility of performance is *not due to fault* (whether a fault of its debtor or of its creditor), in accordance with what we have said up to now, the debtor of the impossible performance is released. This also has force here, but Article 380 CC adds that the creditor of the impossible performance is also released from the duty to fulfil the counter-performance, although the latter is not itself impossible (rule of common release, Article 380, subparagraph 1, which adds that if the counter-performance has already been fulfilled, its recovery is sought by means of the provisions as to unjust enrichment – Articles 904 et seq. CC). For example: A sells B a motor car for EUR 10,000. The car is destroyed as a result of a chance event. Both A and B are released from their obligations. If B had prepaid the EUR 10,000, he seeks its recovery by virtue of Articles 904 et seq. CC.
By this regulation, although *the risk to the performance*, which becomes impossible without anyone being at fault, is borne by the creditor of the impossible performance (since the debtor is released, Articles 336, 363 CC), *the total risk* arising from the same event (which is given the unfortunate name of risk to the counter-performance) is borne in reciprocal contracts by the debtor of the impossible performance, who loses both the performance which he owed and his claim for the counter-performance.
There is an exception (Article 380, subparagraph 2): The creditor of the impossible performance (in our example above, B) is not released from the obligation of

counter-performance if he seeks the surrogate from the debtor of the impossible performance (Article 338 CC, for example, in the above example, the insurance compensation which A will possibly collect as a result of the destruction of the car). If the value of the surrogate is only a part of the value of the impossible performance, it is just and in accordance with the purpose of Article 380, subparagraph 2 (although this cannot be seen from the letter of the provision) that there should be a corresponding reduction in the counter-performance which is owed.

(2) If the impossibility of performance is *due to the fault of the creditor* of this performance, the debtor of the impossible performance, according to the general rule, is released as not being at fault, but its creditor continues to owe the counter-performance. Thus, in the example (I) above, if B takes the car to give it a trial run – before final delivery – and writes it off as a result of his negligence, he continues to owe the price, while A is released.

However, from the counter-performance which continues to be owed, the benefits which the debtor has derived from the impossibility or which he has intentionally omitted to derive are subtracted (Article 381, paragraph 1, subparagraph 2). For example, A has marketed the parts of the car which remain after its destruction or has by his wilful conduct failed to market them.

Article 381, paragraph 2 makes equivalent, as to the consequences, the fault of the creditor of the impossible performance and his default (on *creditor's default, see* §4 *supra*). For example, A, as vendor, offers the car which has been sold to B; the latter refuses to take delivery of it; he is then in creditor's default and during the course of the default, the car is destroyed without the debtor being at fault. A is released while B owes the price. According to one view, the 'without his fault' of Article 381, paragraph 2 is interpreted as 'without wilful conduct or gross negligence', since, according to Article 355, the debtor, for as long as his creditor is in default, is liable only for wilful conduct and gross negligence. Consequently, according to this view, B will owe the price, while A will be released, even if the car was destroyed through slight negligence on the part of A. This solution, however, can result in injustices, since creditor's default does not presuppose his fault. That is, the party at fault (for slight negligence) – A – will be released, while B, who is not at fault, will owe his performance. For that reason, the view according to which Article 381, paragraph 2 takes precedence over Article 355 CC, the view, that is, that the continuation of the liability of the creditor – B – for the counter-performance to A holds good only if A was without fault (and consequently not even slightly negligent) for the impossibility of his performance should be considered closer to the *ratio* of Article 381 CC. This article in fact deals with the special problem of the fate of the counter-performance, a problem alien to Article 355 CC, which regulates only the fate of the performance. However that may be, the regulation of Article 381, paragraph 2 is somewhat harsh for the creditor in default, since, as we have said, his default may be due to a chance event. The consequences of Articles 355 et seq. CC are not as painful for the creditor (in essence, he undertakes only the obligation of Article 358 CC) and their imposition on the creditor who is not at fault is justified, but those of Article 381, paragraph 2 CC (imposition of the obligation of counter-performance in spite of the loss of the claim for the performance) are harsher. For this reason, the teleological restriction of Article 381, paragraph 2 CC is preferable: the provision will not be implemented (and the creditor will be released from the obligation of counter-performance, Article 380 CC) if his default is due to force majeure. This is of importance in borderline cases (*see* §4, III *infra*). If the default of the creditor was caused by force majeure, he will be released from the obligation of counter-performance. He will owe only the expenses of the ineffectual offer, etc. (Article 358 CC – *see* paragraph 287 *infra*).

(3) If the impossibility of performance is *due to the fault of the debtor* of this performance, according to the general provisions (Articles 335 et seq., 362 et seq. CC), the debtor would owe compensation and the creditor (having received full satisfaction for the impossible performance) would continue to owe the counter-performance. This also has force in principle in accordance with Article 382 CC, which, however, adds two rights for the creditor of the impossible performance. Thus, in total, the creditor has three rights, which can be exercised *alternatively, not cumulatively*:

(a) *To invoke the rights of Article 380 CC*, as if the impossibility were not due to fault (paragraph 269 *supra*). This is mainly of practical importance, not so much for the creditor to be released from the obligation of counter-performance (since he can achieve this, for example, by the right of rescission – (c) below), as for him to be able to seek any surrogate which there may be (Article 380, subparagraph 2 CC).

(b) *To seek compensation* (positive interest) for the *damnum emergens* and the *lucrum cessans* which he has suffered as a result of the impossibility of the performance. This right, as we have said, also emerges from the general provisions. Here the method of calculating the damages is sui generis. In this connection, three views have been put forward:

(1) *Exchange theory.* The compensation will include all the value of the impossible performance and any extra *damnum emergens* or *lucrum cessans* of the creditor, who, however, will be obliged to fulfil his counter-performance. That is to say, there will be in the end an exchange of the two performances (of the one, in the form of compensation). For example: A promises to give a machine of a value of EUR 1,000 to B against 100 bottles of wine of a value of EUR 800 (exchange contract, Article 573 CC). The machine is destroyed by the fault of A. B seeks by way of compensation the value of the machine (EUR 1,000 – let us suppose that he has suffered no other loss) and delivers the wine.

(2) *Difference theory.* The compensation will be calculated in correlation with the value of the counter-performance. The latter will be deducted from the prejudice to the creditor by reason of the impossibility of performance and the difference will be the net prejudice. This will be the level of the damages. At the same time, the creditor is relieved of the obligation of counter-performance, since this has been included in the calculation of the prejudice to him. Thus, in the above example (ii), B will seek compensation

of EUR 200 (1,000–800) and will be released from the obligation as to the wine.

(3) *Intermediate theory.* The creditor may choose the compensation freely either in accordance with the exchange theory or in accordance with the difference theory. This latter theory is the one which prevails.

(d) *To rescind the contract.* The consequences of rescission are the release of both contracting parties from their obligations and seeking of the recovery of what may have been performed by means of the provisions on unjust enrichment. At the same time, the creditor of the impossible performance may seek reasonable (reduced) compensation from the court (Article 387 CC – *see also* paragraph 311 *infra*). He would be able to seek full compensation only if he exercised the right of (b) above. Rescission, which we shall discuss in greater detail under section IV *infra*, entails extinction of the contractual obligations. Thus the legislator has judged that the creditor of the impossible performance can no longer invoke the contract (since he himself has reversed it by rescission), that is, that he cannot seek positive interest. This logically sound position frequently does not serve the practical need for greater protection of the creditor who is not at fault for the anomalous development of the obligation. It was within the power of the legislator to provide, if he had so wished, for these two rights cumulatively (rescission and positive interest), as other legislations (e.g., the French Civil Code) do. In the end, the CC has preferred an intermediate solution. It insists, in principle, that these two rights shall be mutually exclusive (as does the BGB), but it gives the rescinding party the right of reduced compensation.

270. The system which has taken shape as a result of the above regulations appears rather complicated, with its divisions and subdivisions of cases and the provision in each instance of different remedies for the creditor. In practical terms, there are *two* possibilities for the creditor: Either, (a) he keeps in force that part of the contract whose performance is possible, that is, his own obligation as to the counter-performance, and seeks compensation for the non-fulfilment of the impossible performance; the compensation could include the surrogate (this is the reason why the obligation as to the surrogate takes on special practical importance when compensation is not owed, that is, in the case of impossibility of performance not due to fault, Article 338 CC). It is this solution, in essence, wholly or in part, that Article 380, subparagraph 2 and compensation in accordance with the exchange theory arrive at. Or (b) he lifts by a constitutive declaration on his part his obligation as to counter-performance and seeks compensation, in the calculation of which his release from the counter-performance will now be included, from which, that is, the value of the counter-performance will be subtracted. It is at this solution, wholly or in part (non-exercise of the right of compensation, wholly or in part, is possible; *see also*, however, Article 454 CC), that Article 380, subparagraph 1, compensation according to the difference theory and rescission, arrive. The question of whether release from the obligation as to the counter-performance will act *ex nunc* or *ex tunc* is an issue which obviously did not concern the legislator nor is there any special practical reason for the relevant differentiation, since any retroactive force would have obligational effects, while the question of the fruits of the performance, if this is crucial according to the will of the parties, could be dealt with in the determination of the level of the compensation.

Since, then, the regulation of the CC in essence arrives at the two possibilities above, the complicated legislative road which has been followed was unnecessary. The new – and only – problem which needed to be regulated in reciprocal contracts is the problem of the fate of the counter-performance, that is, the question of whether the obligation for this is lifted, whether, in other words, the creditor also has the second, constitutive, option; and if, as is the rule, the compensation is determined in money and the counter-performance (which it had been agreed to exchange with the impossible performance) is in money, the constitutive act which is needed for the extinction of the obligation for counter-performance may be achieved by the creditor by a declaration of offsetting (Articles 440, 441 CC – *see* paragraphs 243 et seq. *supra*). There is no need for a special provision. If, however, the counter-performance either has already been fulfilled or is non-monetary and, more general, not of the same kind (in which case offsetting is not possible), the only need is for special provision for the possibility of a constitutive act. For the purposes of this instance, Article 382 CC should have provided – and this would have been sufficient – in general terms that the creditor may seek to be released from his obligation, in which case his release would be taken into account in the compensation which he is entitled to receive. There was no reason for the complete extinction of the whole contractual relation, and consequently of the debtor of the impossible performance; nor, anyway, is this stipulated for similar instances in the case of non-reciprocal contracts (Article 335 CC). Moreover, the solution of reduced compensation in conjunction with rescission could have been avoided: first, because in the quantitatively greater compensation which the creditor achieves by the second option, of Article 382 CC, the lesser is included and the creditor can exercise his rights to whatever extent he wishes; and, second, full compensation is more just for both sides here, since their contractual commitment pre-existed and the reason in law for liability is none other than the non-fulfilment of the (original) performance. The question of reduction of compensation for other reasons (see, for example, paragraph 314 *infra*) is a different one.

II. Default of the Debtor: Delay without Fault

A. In the Case of All Obligations

271. The debtor is in default, basically, when, because of his fault, he delays fulfilling the performance. More specifically, the *conditions* for default of the debtor are the following:

(a) A performance must be owed; that is, a *valid* obligational relationship is presupposed.
(b) The performance must be *possible* (otherwise the rules as to impossibility of performance are already applied).
(c) The performance must have matured (*fallen due*). That is, the time of its fulfilment must have arrived without its having yet been fulfilled (*delay* in fulfilment). The

performance must also be *actionable* (e.g., it must not be possible to advance the plea of Article 377 CC for provision of security by reason of the insolvency of the creditor in reciprocal contracts).

(d) The creditor must give *warning* to the debtor, that is, call upon him to fulfil the performance. The warning is a *quasi-juridical act* without prescribed form, since its effects (the debtor falling into default) occur *ex lege* and regardless of the will of the person giving it. Warning is not required if a *fixed date* has been agreed (expressly or tacitly) (Article 341 CC), that is, a specified day for the fulfilment of the performance (e.g., 20 March or Easter Day, etc.), in which case the debtor has certain knowledge as to when he must fulfil the performance and has no need to wait for a warning – the mere elapse of the fixed date renders him in default.

(e) The debtor must be *at fault* for the delay. His fault is, however, *presumed*, as can be seen from Article 342 CC and as is the general rule in the case of contractual liability. This is a rebuttable presumption. The burden of proof (as to the absence of fault) is borne by the debtor.

272. Basically, two *consequences* follow for a debtor who is in default:

(a) He owes compensation (positive interest, which may include *lucrum cessans* or *damnum emergens*) for the prejudice caused to the creditor as a result of the delay. It will be obvious that he also continues to owe the delayed performance (Article 343, paragraph 1). For example, A leases an apartment to B from 1 March 2008. The apartment is not ready on 1 March 2008. A owes compensation to B for the expenses which the latter incurs, for example, by staying in a hotel because of the delay in taking delivery of the apartment. If the expenses are unjustifiably high, the compensation can be reduced by virtue of Article 300 CC (*see* paragraphs 325 et seq. *infra*). The apartment, naturally, continues to be owed.
The creditor may decline acceptance of the performance and seek compensation (positive interest) as if the performance were impossible if he no longer has an interest in the delayed performance (Article 343, paragraph 2).
Compensation in the case of *monetary debts* is limited (Article 345 CC). Thus:

- Default interest (abstract calculation of the prejudice – *see* paragraphs 315 et seq. *infra*) is always owed (without it being necessary for the creditor to prove that he would have earned interest from the money).
- Additionally, *damnum emergens* is owed if the creditor proves that he has suffered such a loss (e.g., the creditor has incurred expenses because of the delay in payment of the monetary debt). Exception: in the case of a loan, this *damnum emergens* is not made good (Article 808 CC).
- Compensation for *lucrum cessans* is never owed. As to the *ratio* of this prohibition, suffice it to say here that the legislator wished to place a limit on liability in order to deprive the creditor of scope for invoking indirect losses which would create a danger of the bounds of the debtor's liability being lost. At the same time his object was to ensure in this way the maximum security of law both for the creditor and for the debtor as to the consequences of default in the case of monetary debts. The legislator has deemed crucial the differentiation

of monetary from non-monetary performance as to its use and exploitation by the creditor. The former provides unbounded possibilities, which must be brought within a reasonable framework (with money almost anything is possible – the creditor can claim that he has lost the opportunity of profitable investments of every kind), while the latter, for example, the provision of a piece of machinery, provides limited possibilities which are determined by the nature of each object of a non-monetary performance. For more on *lucrum cessans*, *see* paragraphs 313 et seq. *infra*.

(b) For as long as his default lasts, the debtor is liable for any negligence (a matter of importance if previously he had reduced liability, for example, only for wilful and grossly negligent conduct), Article 344, subparagraph 1, and even for chance events (whether in the strict sense or force majeure),[170] Article 344, subparagraph 2. Thus, if the thing owed is destroyed by chance, for as long as the debtor is in default, he will be liable for the impossibility of performance (for compensation: Article 335 CC). Exception (Article 344, subparagraph 2): if the debtor proves that the prejudice would have occurred even if the performance had been fulfilled on time. For example: a house which is owed is destroyed by earthquake; it would have been destroyed even if it had been delivered punctually to the creditor.

273. Debtor's default and its consequences are *lifted*:

(a) On the fulfilment of all the obligations (including the new ones) of the debtor.
(b) By agreement between creditor and debtor (e.g., release of debt or the provision of a new time-limit, etc.)
(c) By subsequent default of the creditor (Article 349 CC).
(d) By subsequent impossibility of performance (Article 344, subparagraph 2, in fine CC).

274. If the delay is *not due to fault*, the debtor naturally continues to owe the performance, but he is not, in principle, burdened with other consequences. If the debt was a monetary one and a writ initiating legal action or a payment order is served on the debtor for the debt in arrears, the debtor will owe legal interest (litigation interest, Article 346, subparagraph 1 CC).

B. Particularly in the Case of Reciprocal Contracts

275. In the case of reciprocal contracts also, the general rules (Articles 343 et seq. CC) in principle have force. The new problem is the possible effect of the delay in performance on the fate of the counter-performance. In this connection, Article 383 CC gives to the creditor of the debtor in default (when the former does not wish to confine himself to compensation by reason of default, in accordance with Article 343 CC, and the fulfilment of the counter-performance) two rights which may be exercised alternatively, not cumulatively:

170. *See* AP 769/1958, NoB 1959, 403.

First, to seek compensation (positive interest), having rejected the delayed performance. As to this compensation, what has been said above (paragraph 269) holds good. The creditor will be released from his counter-performance only if he seeks compensation according to the difference theory (see paragraph 269, b, ii supra).

Or, second, to rescind the contract, seeking reasonable (reduced) compensation, in accordance with Article 387 CC (see paragraph 269, c supra).

However, he does not have the above rights immediately upon the occurrence of the debtor's default (as he has them, according to Article 382 CC, immediately after impossibility of performance due to debtor's fault). He must first set for the debtor a reasonable time-limit for performance, declaring at the same time that if this time-limit passes without action being taken, he rejects the performance. He has the two rights above after the time-limit has passed without action being taken. The reasonableness of this time-limit will be judged in the specific case on the basis of good faith. The time-limit must be set when the debtor is already in default, not before his default. If, however, the default begins with warning by the creditor, the latter may serve the warning and set the time-limit in the same declaration.

276. It is not necessary for a time-limit to be set, that is, the creditor may exercise the rights of Article 383, subparagraph 2 immediately after the debtor is in default, in the following instances:

(a) If it can be seen from the whole attitude of the debtor that it would be pointless to set him a time-limit (Article 385, No. 1 CC). For example, the debtor has already stated that he will not observe, or it is obvious that he is unable to observe, any reasonable time-limit.
(b) If the creditor no longer has an interest in the execution of the contract (Article 385, No. 2). For example, the purpose of the contract was to meet seasonal needs of the creditor and the season is over.
(c) If the parties have agreed that there is no need for a time-limit to be set (Article 361 CC). Article 383 CC is a provision of non-mandatory law.

277. The practical significance of the release of the creditor from the obligation of counter-performance (release which he obtains, for example, by rescission) is apparent chiefly when the creditor wants to spend the counter-performance differently. For example, A sells B a motor car for EUR 20,000, but through his fault delays delivering it to him. If B, not being able to wait, buys another car with the EUR 20,000, he would risk having to give another EUR 20,000 for A's car, which is offered with delay. However, by rescinding the contract with A, he liberates the EUR 20,000 owed to him for the purchase of the other car. If the new purchase which B has been forced to make as a result of the unreliability of A (a 'cover contract', since B is covered with this from the non-performance of the first contract) is more costly (e.g., B pays a higher price), the loss to B is due to the delay of A and is included in any compensation which may be owed by A. However, any recklessly expensive purchase by B perhaps entails the implementation of Article 300 CC (*see* paragraphs 325 et seq. *infra*).

III. Performance Not Duly Fulfilled

A. In the Case of All Obligations

278. All instances in which the debtor fails to perform his obligations without there being impossibility of performance or default are covered by the present – third – category of anomalies in the development of the obligation (improper, not duly effected, performance). It consists chiefly of the following inadequacies:

(a) *Infringement of collateral duties.* For example, the debtor (vendor) delivers the thing to the purchaser (principal performance), but he does not give him the instructions for use or he gives him the wrong ones, with the result that the object suffers damage from mishandling.
(b) *Inappropriate fulfilment of the main performance.* For example: the leased object was given to the lessee, but it was defective and thus unsuitable for the use agreed.
(c) *Non-performance of one or some of the principal obligations.* For example: the vendor of an immovable property transfers its ownership to the purchaser, but delays, or is unable to carry out, delivery of it to him (Article 513 CC), thus performing only one of the two principal obligations which are incumbent upon him.
(d) *Infringement of an obligation of omission.* For example: A engages in the act which he has an obligation to omit, for example, he opens a shop in the same street as his counterparty, in spite of his promise to him.
(e) *Repudiation of a contract.* Before the performance falls due (because otherwise it would be a case of default), the debtor declares that he will not fulfil the performance.

279. The CC contains no special regulation for any of these instances. It has regulated only impossibility of performance and default. There is, then, a *lacuna*, which will be filled by *analogy of law*, that is, analogy with the entirety of the provisions which govern impossibility of performance and default of the debtor. The liability in general of the debtor for every instance of failure to perform his obligation is, of course, provided for in Article 330 CC. But on exactly what terms the liability exists and in what it consists will be discovered by analogy of law. Therefore:

(a) If the inadequacy of the performance is due to fault, the debtor continues duly to owe the performance (therefore he owes correction of the inadequacy in the performance), but he is not liable for compensation, etc.
(b) If the inadequacy is due to fault of the debtor, he must – apart from the correction of the defect in the performance – compensate the creditor for any prejudice which he has suffered as a result.
(c) The fault of the debtor is presumed.

B. Particularly in the Case of Reciprocal Contracts

280. The gap in the law as to performance not duly fulfilled in the case of reciprocal contracts is also filled by analogy of law. The additional rights which will be recognized to the creditor of the improper performance are the right of rescission or the right of rejection of the improper performance and of compensation for non-performance if the debtor is at fault for the inappropriate performance (Articles 382, 383 CC). Conditions for the exercise of these rights are:

- That the creditor should set the debtor a reasonable time-limit for the correction of the inadequacy of the performance (Article 383 CC – default is closer to improper performance than total impossibility of performance – Article 382 CC). That the defect is substantive, so that the creditor's ends are not served by the improper performance (cf. Article 386 CC – *see* paragraph 281 *infra* and Article 288 CC).

281. A *special* case of improper performance in reciprocal contracts is covered in Article 386 CC, which deals with contracts which are *to be executed by successive partial performances* (single contracts, but in which, however, the one performance is divided into more than one self-contained instalment, which are fulfilled at successive chronological intervals, for example, supply of goods which are made available once a week or once a month, etc.). If in such a contract of successive performances there is, through the fault of the debtor, impossibility of performance or default as to one performance only, for example, of the thirty performances to be successively executed, the debtor fulfils the first ten normally, but not the eleventh, the rules of impossibility or default may be implemented only as to the eleventh performance. Since, however, the contract is a single one, the non-fulfilment of a part of the whole of the performance means improper performance as to the whole contract. The question is whether there will be an effect on the other performances (first to tenth, twelfth to thirtieth). Article 386 CC gives the answer: the creditor can rescind his contract as to these (in which case, what may have been paid can be sought by virtue of unjust enrichment) or seek compensation, provided that one of the following two conditions is fulfilled:

(a) If delay or impossibility as to one instalment of the performance is so substantive that the creditor no longer has an interest in the rest of the contract (the future part, or, if the circumstances justify this, also that which has already been fulfilled).
(b) If there is an (objectively) well-grounded fear that the remaining performances will not be fulfilled.

IV. Rescission: Restitution

A. Grounds for Rescission

282. One of the contracting parties has a right of rescission of the contract if this is recognized in special cases by the law (*legal rescission*) or when this right has been provided for one or both of the two contracting parties in their contract (*contractual rescission*, Article 389, §1 CC).

Provision is made for legal rescission in the case of all the instances dealt with above where we have failure of the debtor, *through his fault*, to fulfil his duties in a *reciprocal* contract (Articles 382, 383, 386 CC). Rescission in the case of failure not due to fault is also provided for in Article 401 CC, where *fixed-date performance* is concerned (*see* paragraph 268 *supra*).

Articles 389 et seq. CC are implemented directly in the case of contractual rescission and, by virtue of Article 387, §2, *mutatis mutandis* in that of legal rescission.

B. Exercise of the Right of Rescission

283. The right of rescission is constitutive, because by its exercise a new state of affairs in law is constituted (*see* paragraph 284 *infra*) and is exercised by a unilateral declaration of will (juridical act) of the person rescinding the contract. The declaration has to be addressed to his counterparty (Article 390 CC).

C. Effects of Rescission: Restitution

284. If there are grounds for rescission *and* this right is exercised by its holder, the following effects occur (Article 389, §2):

(a) The contractual obligations are extinguished.
(b) If one performance has been fulfilled, restitution follows. More specifically, recovery of the performance which has been fulfilled is sought by virtue of the provisions as to unjust enrichment. That is, the ownership of the performance which has been fulfilled does not revert *ipso jure* to the person who fulfilled it, but the recipient 'is obliged' (= obligation, not an effect in rem of rescission) to re-transfer the ownership. It is chiefly at this point that rescission differs from *annulment* of the contract, which has effects in rem (Articles 184, 180 CC and paragraphs 151, 155 *supra*).

It should be noted, finally, that rescission differs from *termination notice* (which also reverses the contract) in that the former has retroactive (*ex tunc*) effects (e.g., the fruits of the intervening period are returned), while termination notice, which is given only in continuous contracts, such as lease of a thing, a contract for services, partnership, etc. (*see* paragraph 239 *supra*), has force only for the future (*ex nunc*), which means that for the time up to the termination notice the contract remains in force (and the performances which correspond to that period are retained) and is reversed only for the time thereafter.

§4. Default of the Creditor

285. The creditor has a right (the claim) to the performance, not an obligation where it is concerned. Consequently, anomaly in the development of the obligation on his part does not mean failure to fulfil an obligation, but *non-acceptance* of the performance. Non-acceptance of the performance is termed creditor's default (or default of acceptance). What the special conditions are for this (Articles 349–354 CC) and what its effects are (Articles 355–360 CC) are examined below.

I. Conditions

286.

(a) The debtor must *offer* the performance to the creditor (Article 349 CC, § I). *Exception:* Even without the offer of the performance the creditor is in default if he does not *co-operate* in the preparation of its offer and fulfilment (Article 351 CC). For example: I do not go to the tailor (who owes it to me to make me a suit) for a fitting; I do not go to the home of the debtor for the offer and fulfilment to take place, although the place of fulfilment was the home of the debtor; I do not supply the building materials to the contractor who has undertaken to build me a house with my own materials, etc.

(b) The offer must be made *by action*, not simply verbally (Article 349 CC, §2). Thus the offer is not 'in deed' in the case of a plumber who has undertaken to repair the plumbing fittings if he comes to the place of performance without bringing the necessary tools. *Exception:* An offer in deed is not required if the creditor has already declared that he does not accept the performance (Article 350 CC).

(c) The offer must also be *appropriate* (Article 349, §2), that is, it must take place at the appropriate place, at the due time, and must be in the correct quality and quantity – in general, it must be in accordance with the content of the obligation.

(d) The offer must be *possible* (Articles 349, 352 CC), otherwise it will be a case of impossibility of performance.

(e) The creditor *must not have accepted* the performance offered (Article 349, § I). For example, he expressly refuses it or is absent from the place of the performance at the agreed time, etc. Temporary impediment of the creditor, if the time of the performance was not specified or if the debtor offers the performance before the time specified, when he has a right to do this, does not cause him to be in default, unless the creditor had been given notice of the impending fulfilment (Article 354 CC). In one instance non-acceptance is not required, that is, the creditor is in default in spite of the fact that he accepts the performance: if the contract is reciprocal, that is, if the creditor owes a counter-performance, which, however, he does not offer, while he is willing to accept the performance of the counterparty (Article 353 CC). For example: the purchaser wishes to take delivery of the object but does not offer the price. In this instance not only is he a debtor in default as to the price, but he is also a creditor in default as to the thing.

If the above conditions are fulfilled, the creditor is in default, even if he was not at fault for the non-acceptance of the performance offered. Fault is not a condition for creditor's default as it is for debtor's default. For that reason, the former is termed *objective* default and the latter *subjective*.

II. Effects and Lifting of Default

287. Basically, the creditor does not have liability for his default, since, anyway, he had no obligation (i.e., an enforceable engagement) to accept the performance. *The only special duty* which arises for him is that of Article 358 CC: the creditor is obliged to pay the debtor the latter's expenses, if any, for the ineffectual offer of the performance (e.g., the debtor has paid freight charges for the transporting of the performance to the house of the creditor, who was absent), as well as expenses for the safeguarding and maintenance of the performance for as long as the default of the creditor lasts (e.g., warehousing charges for the performance, food for the animals owed, etc.).

The principal consequence of the creditor's default is *reduction of the liability of the debtor.* Thus, for as long as the creditor is in default, the debtor is liable only for wilful and grossly negligent conduct (Article 355 CC). If the performance is destroyed during this period as a result of slight negligence on the part of the debtor, he is released.

In spite of the default of the creditor, the obligation continues to exist – the debtor continues to owe the performance. This, of course, may become onerous for the debtor if the creditor's refusal to accept continues indefinitely. For the protection of the debtor, the law provides for the following possibilities:

- In the case of movable objects owed which are subject to deposit with a public body, the default of the creditor constitutes for the debtor a reason for deposit with the Deposits and Loans Fund (Articles 427 et seq. CC – *see* paragraphs 240 et seq. *supra*). By this, the debtor achieves extinction of his debt.
- In the case of a movable object owed which is not capable of deposit, the debtor may auction it publicly and deposit the sum realized with the Deposits and Loans Fund (Article 428 CC).
- In the case of an immovable property, the debtor may bring about the appointment of a sequestrator by the court, thus achieving the extinction of his debt (Articles 359–360 CC).

288. Default of the creditor is lifted:

(a) By a declaration on the part of the creditor that he is ready to accept the performance. If the debtor refuses performance, he himself is then in default.
(b) By an agreement between debtor and creditor.
(c) By a declaration of the debtor to the effect that he revokes the offer of the performance.

III. Borderline Cases Between Creditor's Default and Impossibility of Performance

289. Examples: A doctor is summoned to treat a patient, but the latter dies or has recovered before the doctor arrives to proffer his services; a breakdown truck is called to remove a damaged car from the site of an accident. It arrives, but in the meantime the car has been moved by other means or has been repaired; an employee attends to offer his services, but the factory where he works is closed because of a strike or because of demonstrations in the city or because of a power cut; a contractor attends to demolish a derelict building, but this has already collapsed or the authorities have refused to issue the demolition permit.

In all these and in other similar instances, the question is whether the cause of the non-performance is impossibility (without fault) on the part of the debtor or refusal to accept the performance on the part of the creditor, that is, the latter's default. The consequences are different in each of the cases.

The issue is disputed. Formerly it was dealt with on the criterion of spheres of influence: if the cause of the anomaly belongs to the sphere of influence and action of the debtor, impossibility of performance was accepted; if it belonged to the sphere of influence of the creditor, his default was accepted.

It would be a proper solution for us to accept in these cases that the debtor is released by reason of frustration of the purpose of the obligation (*see* paragraph 247 *supra*). At the same time, however, since the debtor 'was in a position to fulfil the performance' (*see* Article 352 CC), there is no obstacle to default of the creditor (which does not presuppose his fault and therefore can be due to force majeure). Consequently, this default will be accepted and the creditor (the person who called the doctor, the breakdown truck, the employer, etc. in the examples above) will owe the expenses of the ineffectual offer (Article 358 CC). Whether he will also owe the counter-performance, a problem which arises in the case of reciprocal contracts, has been examined above (paragraph 269).

§5. Unforeseen Change in Circumstances: The Problem of Frustration of Contracts – Termination of Contracts for 'Serious Reason'

I. Introductory Remarks: Pacta Sunt Servanda versus Clausula Rebus Sic Stantibus and Restorative Contractual Justice

290. In the most abstract and general sense, the problem of frustration of contracts concerns, at least in English authorities, the effect of supervening changes in circumstances, unforeseen and unforeseeable at the time of conclusion of the contract, on the obligations stemming from a contractual agreement. It is admitted that the problem principally arises in three cases: (a) when the performance becomes physically or legally impossible (e.g., destruction of the owed car without fault on part of the debtor, death or illness of the employee, etc.); (b) when the performance is still physically (and legally) possible but the *underlying purpose* of the contract is no longer attainable und thus the performance becomes useless or valueless to its recipient (e.g., the expected coronation procession is postponed, whereupon the tenant of an apartment with a view on the procession has no longer interest in receiving the performance of the landlord, that is, the temporary use of his apartment); and (c) when the performance, though physically (and legally) still possible, has become excessively difficult, that is, economically far more onerous or burdensome than anticipated by the parties (e.g., the price of the oil that the supplier is obliged to import rises sharply by 100%). The so-called doctrine of frustration, i.e., the doctrine of discharge of contract by supervening events, encompasses all the above mentioned possible excuses for non-performance – which, in turn, might be viewed as the *main subdivisions* of the doctrine. A contract may, therefore, be brought to an end due to physical (or legal) impossibility of performance, frustration of the underlying purpose of the contract (this subdivision could be also defined as *frustration stricto sensu*; *see also supra* paragraph 247), and 'impracticability' or *supervening hardship of performance*. This rather holistic approach to the problem, however, should not conceal the fact that, but for the first, the last two subsets give rise to significant practical problems, which have to be effectively addressed by the judge in each particular case. To put it bluntly: the only –relatively– 'certain' case of discharge is the one of impossibility, whereas the most 'uncertain' and problematic one appears to be that of supervening hardship. It is not difficult to see that in the latter case the judge is actually faced with a crucial dilemma, namely, with the *value judgment* whether to grant priority to the principle *pacta sunt servanda* (or *stare pactis*) or to the doctrine of *clausula rebus sic stantibus*.

291. At first sight, there can indeed be little doubt that in the case of supervening hardship an antagonism between the sanctity of contracts and the *clausula rebus sic stantibus* –which seeks to 'bend' the former– is reflected. But this is a rather truncated, or epiphenomenal, approach. For one can rather easily suspect that behind these two *'middle-level rules'* there are to be found two more fundamental principles, that is, *the principle of security and stability in transactions* on the one hand and *the principle of equity and restorative contractual justice* on the other.

The first principle demands the unaltered enforcement of contractual obligations despite the supervening change in circumstances, so that the 'security of orientation' (*Orientierungssicherheit*) of the contracting parties might be preserved. The parties must thus start out from the fact that their contract cannot be affected by a possible change in the extra-contractual economic environment (e.g., by drastic socio-political changes, inflation, currency fluctuations, energy crises, etc., which often cause a significant increase in performance costs). The denunciation of a possible claim for discharge or judicial adjustment of a contract relies, in fact, upon the idea of the so-called *moral hazard*: it is submitted that a positive stance on a claim like this ought to reckon with the possible corruption of promisors, who may easily accept obligations as long as they know that they can be released from them in case their performance becomes solely more onerous or burdensome; on the other hand, such a stance would –allegedly– cause a certain hesitation on the part of (would-be) promisees to contract in view of the fact that (would-be) promisors may easily be released from their obligations in case of supervening changes in the extra-contractual environment. This double-founded *'moral hazard'*, which is deemed to expose the security and stability in commercial transactions to great danger, represents the gist and essence of the concerns expressed by those scholars who rigidly insist upon the sacred character, i.e., the inviolability, of the contractual agreement.

On the other hand, equity and restorative contractual justice play a significant role too: Reciprocal contracts –i.e., contracts in which obligations are created *on both sides*– are founded upon the economic balance of performance and counter-performance which was determined by the contracting parties; since this balance rests upon the will of the parties it might be called *subjective* balance. In case supervening events significantly distort this 'synallagmatic' balance and thus render the fulfilment of a contractual obligation excessively difficult, it could be argued that it would be unjust, inequitable or contrary to good faith to continue to demand performance from the debtor and, furthermore, to let the creditor profit from the other party's emergency. And in such a case the above mentioned principles may require either (a) the restoration of the distorted equilibrium between performance and counter-performance –*within, however, the bounds of the possible and necessary* –, usually by means of reducing the performance owed by the debtor (e.g., supply of half the owed goods) or by increasing the counter-performance of the creditor (e.g., increasing the supplier's or contractor's fee); or (b) the partial or total dissolution of the contract, a solution that must undoubtedly have an extraordinary character (*ultima ratio*). It is undeniable that this *equitable* approach squares better with the *social* orientation of German and Greek law than with the liberal foundations of Anglo-American law. In any event, it must be borne in mind that particularly the endeavour to restore the initial equivalence between performance and counter-performance (*aequalitas*) by virtue of contractual adjustment corresponds to the requirements of *contractual justice*, as first conceived by *Aristotle* and later further developed by *Grotius*: *ne plus exigatur quam par est*.

Against the equitable perspective, however, it may well be argued that if the parties wish to guard themselves against future contingencies, they can do so by inserting express stipulations and conditions into their contract; in other words, the freedom of contract affords them the capacity to effectively deal with possible (future) changes in circumstances. Yet this argument is flawed, above all, because it neglects the fact that the parties cannot always provide for every contingency, that is, *express contractual clauses often cannot cover every unforeseeable event.*[171]

II. Greek Law

A. General Remarks on the Statutory Provision on Supervening Hardship

292. Although the Greek Civil Code of 1946 has to a great extent been influenced by the German BGB of 1900, on this particular issue, i.e., the issue of supervening hardship and its impact upon undertaken contractual obligations, it went far beyond the paradigm of BGB by including a truly innovative provision – with regard to the time of its being put into effect–, namely Article 388 CC. The Article is properly situated in the general provisions of the Code on reciprocal contracts (Articles 374–388 CC), and runs as follows:

If, in view of the requirements of good faith and common usages, the circumstances upon which the parties mainly founded the conclusion of a reciprocal contract have subsequently changed for extraordinary reasons which could not have been foreseen,

171. For the above *see* Karampatzos, *Supervening Hardship as Subdivision of the General Frustration Rule: A Comparative Analysis with Reference to Anglo-American, German, French and Greek Law*, 2 Eur. Rev. Priv. L. 105 et seq. (2005).

and the performance of the debtor, taking also into consideration the counter-performance, has as a result of the change become excessively onerous, the court may, at the request of the debtor and according to its appreciation, adjust the debtor's performance to the appropriate extent or decide upon the dissolution of the contract, wholly or to the extent of its non-performed part. If the dissolution of the contract has been decided upon, the obligations to perform arising therefrom shall be extinguished and the contracting parties shall be reciprocally obliged to return the performances they received according to the provisions on unjust enrichment.

This provision is one of the most basic and most forward-looking of those contained in the Greek Civil Code. Starting out from the principle of the inviolability of contracts, Article 388 CC provides, on strict conditions, for the concession of this principle in recognizing the possibility of a judicial dissolution or revision of the content of a reciprocal contract in the event of an unforeseen change in circumstances and upsetting of the balance between performance and counter-performance. The provision of Article 388 CC is none other than a special expression of the principle of good faith which is formulated generally as to the law of obligations in Article 288 CC (obligation to perform according to the principle of good faith and to common usages – a provision corresponding to §242 BGB; *see supra* paragraphs 53 et seq.). Without the introduction of Article 388 CC, Article 288 CC could basically lead to similar solutions. Nevertheless, in practical terms, the adoption in the CC of the special provision is useful, because it gives clearer and more particular expression to the will of the legislator in this connection. However, it has been accepted that whenever the conditions of Article 388 CC are not met, the possibility of resorting to Article 288 CC remains as an 'ultimum refugium'.[172] In Article 388 CC we ascertain a combination of views and criteria drawn both from classic theories on the need for an equilibrium between performance and counter-performance (here of course in order to deal with the ex post facto upsetting of any initial balance) or on *the clausula rebus sic stantibus* (but on strict terms today), and more modern doctrines that have been developed internationally in the twentieth century, particularly the German doctrine of the collapse of the underlying basis of the transaction (*Wegfall der Geschäftsgrundlage*) and the French theory of the unforeseen (*théorie de l'imprévision*). The basic idea, however, which permeates the institution is that of bona fides.

B. Conditions

293. It can hardly be doubted that the wording of Article 388 CC lays down strict conditions, thus allowing an inroad into the principle *pacta sunt servanda* only in extraordinary cases. Its basic conditions may be analysed as follows:

(1) The contract must be a *reciprocal* one. In the case of unilaterally charging contracts and other obligations (e.g., from bequest), revision is possible, by virtue of the general clause of Article 288 CC.

---

172. *See* AP (in Plenary Session) 927/1982, NoB 1983, 214; AP 474/1976, NoB 1976, 1051; AP 627/1987, NoB 1988, 1420; AP 1537/1991, HellD 1993, 318; AP 671/1994, HellD 1995, 1130. *See also* para. 296 *infra* .

(2) There must have occurred *a change in the circumstances* upon which, in view of good faith and common usages, the parties based the conclusion of their contract. This condition is reminiscent of the theory of the underlying basis of the transaction, but in an objectivized form, since its crucial nature must emerge not only from the will of the parties (motivation of their will, which as a rule is irrelevant – *see* Article 143 CC and paragraphs 113 et seq. *supra*), but also from the objective criteria of good faith and common usages. Hence, the circumstances forming the foundation of the contract (at the time of contracting) are to be identified on the basis of *subjective* (the will of the parties) as well as *objective* (good faith and common usage) criteria – which in any event are bound to be specified, in each particular case, through the court's sovereign judgment.

(3) The change should have occurred *subsequently*, that is, after the conclusion of the contract. If the change already existed at the time of the conclusion of the contract (and, for example, the contracting parties, or one of them, were unaware of it), recourse to Article 288 CC is possible, or, if their conditions are met, to Article 142 CC (error as to qualities) or 179 CC (exploitative contract).

(4) The causes that have brought about the change should be *exceptional and unforeseen*. Such causes are unusual events of a natural, political, social, economic, etc. nature (e.g., a significant – and not normal – devaluation of the currency, a sudden increase in import tariffs resulting in price rises and in an increased cost of performance, an unexpected change in legislation, etc.), occurrences, that is, which lie outside the normal course of events.

(5) As a consequence, the performance of one of the contracting parties must have become *excessively onerous*. This actually means that the economic balance between performance and counter-performance must have been either completely subverted or disturbed to such an extent that the resulting burden for one of the contracting parties is 'unconscionable'. In regard to this condition, it is further accepted that on the one hand the mere fact that the disadvantaged party suffers a loss or that she has difficulties in performing her contractual obligation is not sufficient, but on the other hand nor is her (complete) economic ruin required. This starting-point helps us perhaps to understand in general the rather opaque and mesomorphic nature of the cases of supervening hardship that give rise to judicial litigation, a nature which might be stated with the following paraphrase: *it's neither a 'horse' –i.e., mere difficulties in performance– nor a 'mule'– i.e., economic impossibility or economic ruin of the debtor– but 'something in-between'*. And this is the very difficulty the courts have to deal with.[173]

C. *Effects*

294. If the above mentioned conditions are fulfilled, the *effects* of the provision occur, that is, the contracting party for whom the contract has become excessively burdensome acquires the *formative* (*constitutive*) right to seek judicial adjustment or (total or partial) dissolution of the contract. But the latter can only be *ultima ratio*;

173. For the above *see* Karampatzos, *Supervening Hardship as Subdivision of the General Frustration Rule: A Comparative Analysis with Reference to Anglo-American, German, French and Greek Law*, 2 Eur. Rev. Priv. L. 105 et seq. (2005).

hence the judge must first try to find a just solution within the framework of the various forms of contractual adjustment. On the possibility of awarding compensation, *see infra* paragraph 295 in fine.

The right that leads to dissolution or adjustment of the contract is exercised before the courts. That is, for the formative act (dissolution or adjustment of the contract) a formative court decision is needed. It is only with a formative act that the debtor is protected according to Article 388 CC. Without this act, she continues to be bound by the original terms of the contract; invocation of the fulfilment of the conditions of Article 388 CC without a formative judicial act does not lead to the dismissal of the action of her counterparty. It is rather obvious that a contracting party may also seek as defendant such a judicial decision.

In exercising his formative power, the judge, basing himself mainly upon good faith, shall take into account all the specific circumstances surrounding the conclusion and performance of the contract as well as the specific purpose of the transaction at hand. Departure from the initial agreement must be ordered only to the extent to which this is dictated by good faith. The fulfilment of the conditions of the provision does not justify just any –even that most destructive for the contract– solution. *Whatever can be salvaged from the contract must be preserved.* The judge who establishes that there is, for example, excessive prejudice to the debtor as a result of the change in circumstances is not obliged to adjust the performances in such a way that the prejudice is fully covered. An action lodged by virtue of Article 388 CC is not an *action for compensation.* The crucial criterion is the restoration of the disturbed economic between performance and counter-performance to the extent that it will correspond to the requirements of good faith, and not the making good of a prejudice.

295. Dissolution of the contract and restitution: The judge may decide upon the *total* or *partial* (e.g., only as to its still unfulfilled part) dissolution of the contract. Consequences of the dissolution are the extinction of the contractual obligations and the return of any performances that may have been received. Such return does not take place *ipso jure* upon the dissolution of the contract. By this, obligations for the restitution of the performances (i.e., the 'enrichment') are generated in accordance with the provisions on unjust enrichment (Articles 904 et seq. CC; the cause of the enrichment was not non-existent *ab initio*, but expired *ex post facto*). In the event of *partial* dissolution, the judge shall determine the level of each performance which corresponds to that part of the other which has been preserved. Over and above this level (as to which the contractual obligations are retained), the performances are returned, in accordance with Articles 904 et seq. CC, had they been fulfilled.

In the judge's formative (constitutive) power to dissolve or adjust the contract should be included, in accordance with the purpose of the provision, his power to *combine* these two measures, for example, to dissolve the contract and at the same time to take some measure (e.g., to impose an obligation upon the released debtor to pay a certain sum by way of compensation to the creditor), in order to avoid an outcome of the dispute that would be disproportionate for the parties.

Adjustment of the contract: The court, instead of reaching the point of taking the extreme step of dissolving the contract, may decide only upon the 'tailoring' of the performance of the debtor (who invokes the implementation of Article 388 CC) to the appropriate extent, i.e., he may reduce it so that it ceases to be excessively onerous for the debtor. In spite of the strict wording of the provision, it is in accordance with its purpose for us to accept that the judge also has the power, instead of reducing this performance, to increase the counter-performance or to proceed both to the reduction of the former and the increase of the latter. Moreover, it should be concluded from the purpose of the provision that the judge has broader powers of adjustment, that is, he may take other measures which in the specific case restore the equilibrium of the contract, for example, by setting a new time-limit for fulfilment for the debtor, so that the latter avoids the consequences of default ('suspension' of the force of the contract), by abolishing a term of the contract that is burdensome for the debtor, etc., provided, of course, that such solutions may be deemed just and reasonable in view of the creditor's interests as well, as the principle of good faith clearly demands (i.e., taking both parties' interests into account).

D. Practical Application of the Provision

296. After the First World War and before Article 388 CC came into force, Areios Pagos, the supreme civil court in Greece, facing cases of –even extreme– devaluation of currency disturbing gravely the equivalence between performance and counter-performance, was plainly reluctant to accept a departure from the principle of sanctity of contracts and thus dismissed any solution resulting from the doctrine of *clausula rebus sic stantibus*. The dominant policy consideration was evidently the need for preserving the stability in transactions. After the Second World War, however, the Greek courts have adopted a different, namely equitable, approach on the matter. The social character of many provisions of the 'new' CC, like Article 388 or 288 CC, made the courts more capable of intervening in the contractual programme. Sometimes though, this is done in a way that circumvents the strict conditions of Article 388 CC. This is, for instance, the case where the change in circumstances has been foreseen or where the fact that it has not been foreseen is due to fault of the disadvantaged party; here, the courts may still grant contractual adjustment by invoking the general clause of Article 288 CC, which is deemed to empower the judge not only to 'supplement' but also to *'correct'* the will of the contracting parties. The lenient stance of Areios Pagos may be illustrated by a characteristic case concerning the oil crisis of 1973 that followed the war between Egypt and Israel (Areios Pagos 1733/1986): In this case, the plaintiff had agreed to supply the defendant with a certain quantity of cast-iron to be delivered by instalments during the two-year period between October 1972 and October 1974. When the oil crisis broke out, the production and, in general, performance costs of the plaintiff started to increase drastically; in the latter's estimation, the pertinent increase for the period between January and October 1974 amounted to 50%. In view of this, the supplier turned to the courts claiming a proportional adjustment of the contract price on the grounds of Article 388 CC. In last instance, Areios Pagos ruled in his favour. Its judgment was founded upon the thought that the relative stability during 1972 in the prices of goods, in wages, in the cost of living, and more specifically in the production costs of the supplier, had become *the foundation of the contract* in question; and the subsequent crisis in the Middle East brought about an abrupt and significant increase in all goods' prices and in the cost of living, which in turn upset the aforesaid foundation and rendered the remaining performance of the debtor 'excessively onerous'.

Greek courts have also accepted the application of Article 388 CC in cases, for example, of a sharp increase in the value of an immovable property by reason of revaluation of the drachma (the currency in circulation before the introduction of the euro), major devaluation of the currency to a degree that upsets the calculations of the parties, a change in the legislation in force, etc.[174] On the other hand, court decisions have not accepted the application of the provision in cases of a 35% increase in the value of the performance, ordinary increases and reductions in the purchasing power of drachma by reason of devaluation of foreign currencies, non-renewal of the operating permit for a hotel, etc.[175]

Further, according to relevant Greek as well as German case law, *changes in the legislation* relating to the nature, purpose, or execution of a specific contract are capable of upsetting the economic balance of the contract and, thus, may pave the way for a contractual re-adjustment (or even the dissolution of a contract) by virtue of the doctrine of supervening change in circumstances. In such a case there is no room left for application of the old Roman law rule '*casum sentit dominus*' (the loss lies where it falls).[176] Greek case law offers characteristic instances relating to the alteration of a sector-specific statutory framework, which may end up in activating the protective mechanisms of Articles 388 and/or 288 CC.[177] Similar instances may also be found in German case law; so, for instance, the case where a drugstore concession, which had been sold shortly after the introduction of the unrestricted freedom of establishment,

174. See, *inter alia*, AP 766/1954, NoB 1955, 361; AP 62/1957, NoB 1957, 534; AP 672/1963, NoB 1964, 398; AP 34/1965, NoB 1965, 736; AP 1733/1986, NoB 1987, 1057; AP 598/1992, HellD 1993, 1286; Thessaloniki Court of Appeals 534/1955, EEN 1956,192.

175. See, *inter alia*, AP 399/1961, NoB 1962, 83; AP 509/1962, NoB 1963, 159; AP 1138/1990, HellD 1991, 808; Aegean Court of Appeals 68/1975, NoB 1976, 810; Athens Court of First Instance 5036/1976, EEN 1977, 88. For most recent case law in view of the deep economic crisis that Greece suffers from 2009 *see* in detail Karampatzos, *Financial Crisis and Re-adjustment of Contractual Performances – Especially in View of the Recent Case Law of Instance Courts on Commercial Lease*, ChrID 2013 (in Greek), pp. 92 et seq.

176. Cf. Finkenauer, in: Münchener Kommentar zum BGB (Commentary to German CC, 7th ed. 2016; in German), § 313 no. 231, 233, 234 and 255; *Grüneberg*, in: Palandt Kommentar zum BGB (Commentary to German CC, 72th ed. 2013; in German), § 313 no. 34.

177. In detail *see* Karampatzos, Unforeseen Change of Circumstances in a Bilateral Contract, no. 67, 515 et seq. See, for instance, Athens Court of Appeals 2213/1994, EDPol 1995, 112: The enactment of the statutory measure of withdrawal of used cars acted as a very powerful incentive for people to buy new environmentally friendly cars and thus led to the sheer boost of the profits of car dealers; this unexpected change in the relevant market could justify the increase of the rent in a lease contract between a car dealer-tenant and the landowner, pursuant to Art. 388 CC. *See also* Decision of First Instance Court of Katerini 1/2012, Legal Database of Athens Bar Association: In this case, the lease contract was influenced by the enactment of Law 3730/2008 on 'the protection of minors against smoke and alcohol consumption', by virtue of which, inter alia, smoking in bars-cafés, such as the lease in question, was banned: 'As direct result of this statutory provision, the financial activity of the café and the consumption of its goods/services fell rapidly, since smoking in the main place of the café is henceforth banned. Before the aforesaid development, the business of the claimant was characterized by great activity and consumption. When said Law was enacted the circumstances changed.'

practically lost afterwards its entire financial value due to a subsequent and unexpected statutory provision, was considered as a case of legally crucial upset of the economic balance of the contract and, therefore, the purchase price was subjected to a significant reduction.[178] With respect to expectations related to the tax law framework that was in force at the time when entering into the contract, once more according to German case law such expectations, i.e., that the then existing tax law framework would not alter, may lead to an overturn of the foundation of the contract, if it may be indeed inferred that the parties based their agreement, *inter alia*, upon such an expectation.[179]

Apart from the above, according to the prevailing view in Greek literature and case law, the principle entrenched in Article 388 CC (as well as Article 288 CC) also applies in case of a public law contract.[180] In such a case, if the supervening event is related to a subsequent interference with the contractual content deriving from the legislature or the public administration, the state bears in essence a double identity, that is, it is not only contracting party to the public law contract but also the regulator that causes, through its own actions, the supervening change (*fait du Prince*).[181] And in this vein, even if a subsequent statute or administrative act that interferes with the contractual content is deemed to be compatible with the Greek Constitution, this does not mean that the upset of the foundation of the contract, caused by the aforesaid State interference, will not have legal repercussions: For in such a case it is accepted that[182] the principle entrenched in Article 388 CC (as well as Article 288 CC), when applied to public law contracts, does not cover only supervening changes that are not attributable to the conduct of the parties to the public law contract but also supervening changes that relate to State's actions, which in case of a public law contract constitute actions of one of the contracting parties (e.g., the amendment to a statutory framework that has as a result the preclusion of a certain contractual right of the counter-party of the State). Therefore, the application of the principle entrenched in Article 388 CC (as well as Article 288 CC) is, in public law contracts, possible in both categories of supervening change in circumstances, i.e., even if it is attributable to the State bearing the capacity not only of the regulator but also of a contracting party.[183]

In all events, it is to be noted that the Greek courts often rely solely on Article 288 CC, rather than Article 388 CC, to find that a change in circumstances has occurred,

178. *See* Finkenauer, *supra* , § 313 no. 234, whereby further references to pertinent German case law.
179. *See* Finkenauer, *supra* , § 313 no. 233, whereby further references to pertinent German case law.
180. *See* Dagtoglou, General Administrative Law (7th ed. 2015; in Greek), no. 786 et seq.; Spiliotopoulos, Handbook of Administrative Law (14th ed. 2011; in Greek), no. 206 et seq.; Flogaitis, The Public Law Contract – Notion and Nature (1991; in Greek), no. 145 et seq.; Decision of the Council of State (i.e., the Supreme Administrative Court of Greece) 1093/2005, Legal Database of Athens Bar Association. On the three main characteristics of a public law contract according to Greek case law see, indicatively, Decision of the Council of State 1213/2015, Nomos Legal Database, as well as paras 9–10 *supra* .
181. *See* Dagtoglou, General Administrative Law, no. 787 (p. 365); also *Flogaitis*, The Public Law Contract – Notion and Nature, no. 146.
182. Dagtoglou, *supra* , no. 787 (p. 365); also *Flogaitis*, *supra* , no. 146 (esp. p. 208); cf. further Spiliotopoulos, Handbook of Administrative Law, no. 209.
183. *See* once more Dagtoglou, *supra* , no. 787 (p. 365); Flogaitis, *supra* , no. 146 (p. 208).

as the relevant case law accepts that Article 288 CC, unlike Article 388 CC, applies even where (a) the change was foreseen by the claimant, (b) the latter, through its own fault, did not foresee the change in circumstances, and (c) the claimant's performance has not become extremely onerous but *merely burdensome*. Some scholars suggest that in this manner the Greek courts often circumvent the strict preconditions of Article 388 CC (by relying on Article 288 CC).[184] So, if the change in circumstances has been foreseen by the debtor, or the fact that it has not been foreseen is due to his or her own fault, or further the change has rendered the debtor's performance *merely burdensome*, the Greek Courts may still decide on a contractual re-adjustment by invoking the general clause of Article 288 CC, which is deemed to empower the judge not only to 'supplement' but also to 'correct' the will of the contracting parties.[185]

E. Waiver

297. Whether Article 388 CC contains a rule of non-mandatory or mandatory law, i.e., whether it is permissible or not for the contracting parties to waive its protection, is a subject of dispute. It is more justifiable to accept, in principle, the mandatory character (*jus cogens*) of the provision, since it constitutes an expression of good faith. This, however, does not mean that the parties cannot contractually undertake a certain, specifically stipulated risk or risks. The specification of the risk undertaken is not crucial (the parties could easily list a series of probable risks in order to circumvent the rule of mandatory law); what is crucial is mostly the serving of the purpose of the contract in question by means of shifting the risk on to one of the contracting parties. A significant indication towards this direction might be the type of the specific contract in question. In this vein, such undertaking of risk by the contracting parties will be justified in aleatory contracts (*see* paragraph 31 *supra*), but it will be without justification when it constitutes not realization of the purpose of the contract, but the submission of the weaker party to the contractual content imposed upon her by her counterparty. It is precisely the latter which is prohibited in a mandatory manner by the principle of good faith that governs Article 388 CC as well. As it might be obvious, the above holds good for the advance waiver from the protection of Article 388 CC; on the other hand, *ex post facto* waiver (after occurrence of the unforeseen change in circumstances) is valid, as is the case with every acquired alienable right. In more general terms, the problem encountered in cases of supervening hardship might be essentially treated as one of *proper risk allocation* between the contracting parties. This point has been a common topos in German literature for years; it also becomes more and more discernible in recent German case law as well as in English literature. The proper risk allocation is usually meant to follow from the *type* to which the contract in question belongs (*vertragstypische Risikoverteilung*). It is important to note here that the perspective of risk allocation paves the way to an 'economic' analysis of the cases of supervening hardship. Within the 'economic' framework, namely, the fundamental consideration

184. *See* Karampatzos, Unforeseen Change of Circumstances in a Bilateral Contract, esp. no. 478–514 and *the same,* Financial Crisis and Re-adjustment of Contractual Performances – Especially in View of the Recent Case Law of Instance Courts on Commercial Lease, ChrID 2013 (in Greek), pp. 92 et seq., passim, whereby further references to pertinent literature.

185. *See* Stathopoulos, Law of Obligations – General Part, § 5 no. 55.

is to identify which contracting party represents the '*superior (i.e., more efficient) risk bearer*', having regard to the ability of each party to estimate ex ante the probability of a materialization of the risk in question as well as the extent of the possible loss, and further to obtain insurance against the risk by way either of 'self-insurance' (e.g., the supplier increases the prices of her products) or 'market insurance' (i.e., through the purchase of insurance policy). Such considerations might sometimes prove useful and persuasive when the courts seek to address relevant disputes; yet they may often make things worse by involving the judge in subtle and complicated assessments, which certainly demand more time than the judge usually has at his disposal.

At any rate, the widespread use of *force majeure* or adjustment clauses in French Law and in Common law (especially in international trade contracts) alike shows the way in which the parties (and their lawyers) are well advised to cope with the problem of risk allocation in view of an eventual change in circumstances; by including an express allocation of risks in their contract, the parties may construct a (relatively) safe contractual environment and thus reduce the uncertainties arising out of possible litigation. Nonetheless, it will be recalled that, as especially the experience in common law shows, even if the parties agree to such clauses and hence rely upon 'self-help', they cannot exclude the danger of these clauses being 'narrowly construed' by the courts – a construction that often amounts to their practical '*frustration*'. This aspect alone strongly indicates that the 'self-help' solution is a far cry from being a panacea.[186]

III. German Law and the Recent Legislative Intervention

298. On occasion of a fundamental reform of the statutory provisions of the BGB (: German CC) on the law of obligations, which came into effect in Germany on 1 January 2002, the German legislator decided to introduce into the BGB a special provision concerning the problem of 'collapse of the foundation of the contract', namely §313, which reads as follows:

(1) If the circumstances which became foundation of the contract have considerably changed after the conclusion of the contract, and if the parties would not have concluded the contract or would have concluded it under a different content had they foreseen the change, then adjustment of the contract may be claimed as long as adherence to the unaltered contract cannot be demanded from the one party, taking into consideration all the circumstances of the particular case, especially the contractual or statutory risk distribution.
(2) Equivalent to a change in circumstances is the case in which fundamental assumptions that became foundation of the contract prove to be false.
(3) If an adjustment of the contract is not possible or cannot be demanded from one party, then the disadvantaged party may rescind the contract. In continuing contractual relationships the right of termination takes the place of the right of rescission.

---

186. For the above *see* Karampatzos, *Supervening Hardship as Subdivision of the General Frustration Rule: A Comparative Analysis with Reference to Anglo-American, German, French and Greek Law*, 2 Eur. Rev. Priv. L. 105 et seq. (2005).

By introducing the provision of §313 I BGB, the express aim of the German legislator was solely to offer a statutory cover to a doctrine that had already attained the status of 'customary law' through its widespread recognition in German case law and academic literature; any thought of constructing at statutory level *typical cases* of 'collapse of the foundation of the contract' was consciously dismissed. The *'restatement-character'* of this provision –as well as of several other 'new' provisions of the reformed German law of obligations (e.g., §241 II, §311 III BGB)– conveys the legislator's will not to bring about any change in the case law. In light of the above observations, it is no coincidence that the scope of §313 I BGB is narrowly constructed so as to allow contractual adjustment or discharge –and thus an incursion into the principle *pacta sunt servanda* – only in extraordinary cases. The *strict* character of the provision is indicated by its following fundamental conditions: (a) the change in circumstances must have been *considerable* (*schwerwiegend*); (b) the contracting parties should not have concluded the contract at all or should have concluded it under a different content had they foreseen the change; (c) the change must go beyond the limits of the risk that the disadvantaged party has to bear according to the contract in question or to statutory law; and (d) the adherence to the contract on the terms originally agreed upon must place an 'unconscionable' (*unzumutbar*) burden on the disadvantaged party. It is certainly clear that within the statutory framework the critical factors turn out to be the 'unconscionability-test' and the aspect of risk allocation. The latter also underlines the *subsidiary* character of the provision, that is, first comes the contractual will of the parties as regards the risk allocation and, only if the parties did not provide, explicitly or implicitly, for the change in circumstances, might a judicial interference with the contractual content take place.

299. The 'unconscionability-test' again becomes crucial at the level of legal remedies (§313 III BGB) – a position long accepted in German case law. For rescission (*Rücktritt*) or termination (*Kündigung*) of the contract are designed as *ultimae rationes*, i.e., rights granted only when the contractual adjustment places an 'unconscionable' burden on one of the contracting parties – or, further, when the adjustment is (objectively) impossible. Equally important is the observation that the adjustment, since it is constructed as a *claim* ('adjustment of the contract may be *claimed* ...'), only comes into operation following a *formative* (*constitutive*) judicial decision. This is a contrast to the former view that the adjustment comes about by 'force of law' (*kraft Gesetzes*) and that the subsequent judicial judgment can thus only have the effect of *recognizing* it. This amendment evidently meets the requirements of the principle of legal certainty (*Rechtssicherheit*), since it presupposes a judicial decision upon the need of contractual adjustment or dissolution. But, furthermore, it entails that the parties are *first* obliged to enter into negotiation for a possible adjustment, and only if this proves fruitless are they entitled to ask for judicial intervention. Under this *'formule de collaboration'* the sanctity of contracts seems to gain an additional protection bar; for the parties are initially forced to search for a solution that corresponds to their real will and interests, and, in this way, to make an attempt to avoid a contractual modification *imposed* by the 'reasonable third party', i.e., the judge, at his almost free discretion. This is also the reason why this formula has been adopted by the French *Conseil d'État* at the beginning of the twentieth century and, moreover, why it is presently being endorsed by several significant French scholars.[187]

IV. Termination of a Contract for 'Serious Reason' by Virtue of Article 288 CC

300. Apart from the above mentioned protective mechanism of Article 388 CC, a contract may also be terminated *for 'serious reason' by virtue of Article 288 CC (in conjunction with Article 281 CC as well as Articles 672, 725, 766 CC)*, even if such termination is not provided for in the contract.[188] 'Serious reason' for termination of a *continuous* (standing) contract exists if, taking into account all the circumstances of the particular case and weighing the interests of both parties, the terminating party cannot reasonably and according to the principle of good faith be demanded to continue the contractual relationship until the agreed termination date; in essence, in such a case the continuation of the contract must have become unbearable/unconscionable (in German: *unzumutbar*) for the party wishing to terminate the contract and this may be due, amongst other things, to an unforeseen change in circumstances as well.[189] The existence of a serious reason to terminate the contract is to be accepted especially in case where the person bound by its promise could not have weighed all relevant future factors at the time she/he undertook the contractual commitment.[190] In this context, fault on the part of the other contracting party is not required.[191] Furthermore, the existence of a serious reason for the termination might also be accepted even when

187. For the above *see* once more Karampatzos, *Supervening Hardship as Subdivision of the General Frustration Rule: A Comparative Analysis with Reference to Anglo-American, German, French and Greek Law*, Eur. Rev. Pri. L. 105 et seq. (2005).

188. *See* AP 1836/2007, Legal Database of Athens Bar Association; AP 21/2004 (in Plenary Session), HellD 2004, 1337; AP 10/1995 (in Plenary Session), NoB 1996, 181; AP 856/1989, EEN 1990, 264; Stathopoulos, Law of Obligations – General Part (4th ed. 2004; in Greek), § 5 no. 37, 85, § 21 no. 74, 135; Karampatzos, Unforeseen Change of Circumstances in a Bilateral Contract, no. 47, 122, 654. Cf. also § 314 I of the German Civil Code (BGB): Gaier, in: Münchener Kommentar zum BGB (Commentary to German CC, 7th ed. 2016; in German), § 314 no. 1 et seq.

189. *See* AP 1836/2007, Legal Database of Athens Bar Association; 856/1989, EEN 1990, 264; Thessaloniki Court of Appeals 2955/1988, DEN 1989, 797; Zerdelis, The Law of Termination of the Contract for Dependent Employment (2nd ed. 2002; in Greek) no. 57, 156 et seq. Cf. further *Gaier, supra* , § 314 no. 10 et seq.

190. *See* Kitsaras, Contractual Constraints to the Power of Disposal (1999; in Greek), p. 57.

191. *See* AP 1836/2007, Legal Database of Athens Bar Association; AP 21/2004 (in Plenary Session), HellD 2004, 1337; AP 10/1995 (in Plenary Session), NoB 1996, 181; *see also* Thessaloniki Court of Appeals 2408/2006, Arm 2007, 1312; Stathopoulos, Law of Obligations – General Part, § 5 no. 85, § 21 no. 74, 135; Gaier, *supra* , § 314 no. 10; German Supreme Civil Court (Bundesgerichtshof, BGH), NJW 1991, 1828, at 1829.

the events that give rise to it fall –objectively– within the *sphere of interest* or control of the party that proceeds to the termination declaration.[192]

Said termination may be declared even *extra-judicially* and without giving notice beforehand. It terminates the contractual relationship with an immediate *ex nunc* effect, that is, only for the future, which means that there are no claims for return of past performances pursuant to the provisions on unjust enrichment.[193] In any event, though, the existence (or not) of a serious reason for termination will be definitely assessed by the Courts, which must rely on an overall assessment of all relevant factors of each particular case.[194]

In essence, the right to exceptional termination of a contract is to be viewed as an offset to a significant risk couching in any long-lasting contractual relationship, that is, the risk that the extend of the performance owed by a party as well as the circumstances under which the performance will be, throughout the contract's entire life, fulfilled are not clear and easily foreseeable at the time of the conclusion of the contract (in German: '*Prognoserisiko*').[195] And this is the very reason why said right also covers the cases of supervening change in circumstances, especially when the latter upsets the economic balance between performance and counter-performance.[196]

301. In principle, *only continuous contracts* are subject to termination for serious reason. According to the prevailing view, a contract is considered to be *continuous* if the performance of at least one of the parties is defined by the duration of the contract and/or if the debtor's performance consists of a continuous act or omission. Such contracts may be concluded for a definite or indefinite period of time (e.g., lease or labour contracts, partnership contracts, etc.). Continuous contracts are subject to termination for reasons expressly provided for by law (e.g., Articles 585, 588, 594, 597, 672–674, 766 CC). Moreover, continuous contracts are, according to the unanimous opinion in legal theory and case law, subject to termination for serious reason, precisely because of their permanent character and the trust relationship that is inevitably generated in the course of this kind of contracts. On the other hand, a contract is, in principle, considered to be fixed or non-continuous if performance and counter-performance are firm and fixed and if performances consist of coherent acts or omissions, even though such acts or omissions may be divided into more than one instalment extended over a certain time period (e.g., in contracts with successive partial performances). Fixed contracts are subject to termination only for the reasons expressly and restrictively provided for by law, i.e., in case of faulty impossibility of performance (Article 382 CC) or debtor's default (Article 383 CC). Disturbances of fixed contracts with successive partial performances are governed by Article 386 CC. No general right of termination for serious grounds is provided for such contracts.

---

192. *See* Kapodistrias, in: ErmAK, Commentary to CC (in Greek), Introduction to Arts 416–454 no. 22; *Georgiadis*, Law of Obligations – General part (2nd ed. 2015; in Greek), § 53 no. 9; Eleftheriadis, in: I.Rokas (ed.), Insurance Contract – Commentary to Law no. 2496/1997 (Insurance Law), Art. 8 no. 35; cf. also *Gaier*, *supra* , § 314 no. 10.
193. *See* indicatively, once again, Gaier, *supra* , § 314 no. 23.
194. *See also* Gaier, *supra* , § 314 no. 10.
195. *See* Gaier, *supra* , § 314 no. 5, 14; also German Supreme Civil Court (BGH), NJW 2010, 1874, at 1875.
196. *See* Gaier, *supra* , § 314 no. 14.

302. However, with respect to the above a significant *caveat* must be entered here: *As a general rule*, prevailing in Greece as well as abroad, *contracts for indefinite period* –i.e., contracts that either do not contain any specific duration or explicitly state that they are for an indefinite period– can be terminated unilaterally by just giving reasonable notice – therefore, no 'good or serious reason' at all is required for terminating such a relationship.[197] For contractual obligations *ad infinitum* are not accepted in our legal system, first and foremost because they amount to an excessive binding of the parties' private autonomy and contractual freedom; in this vein, under Greek Civil law they might be already null and void pursuant to Articles 178 and 179 case a 'CC, *since in general the legal order does not favor commitments for long or indefinite duration (cf. Articles 610, 768, 1923 § 3 CC)'.*[198] Nonetheless, the latter assumption is dependent upon the specific nature and purpose of the contract in question as well as upon the precise length of the contractual commitment. For it is rather self-evident that there are some *continuous* contracts whose very nature justifies their indefinite duration, such as, for instance, the contracts for life insurance[199] – the latter, though, could also be viewed as contracts for definite duration since they last as long as the policyholder lives.[200]

On the other hand, a *contract for definite duration* can, in principle, be early terminated only by virtue of the above mentioned right to exceptional termination for serious reason.

303. Last but not least, with respect to the relation between the right to exceptional termination of a contract and the doctrine of supervening change in circumstances pursuant to Articles 388/288 CC, it is rightly submitted that in case of long-lasting contracts the former prevails over the latter, unless (a) the change in circumstances may be dealt with by means of a contractual re-adjustment and (b) the continuation of the contract is bearable for both contracting parties.[201]

---

197. See, for instance, *Principles, Definitions and Model Rules of European Private Law – Draft Common Frame of Reference (DCFR) – Full Edition* (von Bar & Clive ed., 2009), vol. 3, Comments on Art. IV.E.–2:302, pp. 2303 et seq., and Intr. p. 74.
198. *See* Georgiadis, General Principles of Civil Law (4th ed. 2012; in Greek), § 36 no. 13; *see also* Karampatzos, Private Autonomy and Consumer Protection – A Contribution to Behavioral Economic Analysis of Law (2016; in Greek), no. 9–10, 64 et seq. (esp. 65 fn. 163).
199. In general, for the *continuous* character of insurance contracts *see* Al.Rokas, in: I.Rokas (ed.), Insurance Contract – Commentary to Law no. 2496/1997 (Insurance Law) (2014; in Greek), Art. 1 no. 22; I. Rokas, Insurance Law (3rd ed. 2014; in Greek), no. 21; Sinanioti-Maroudi, Insurance Law (2014; in Greek), p. 42; Hatzinikolaou-Aggelidou, Private Insurance Law (4th ed. 2014; in Greek), § 8 no. 95.
200. Cf. further Al.Rokas, *supra* , Art. 1 no. 22.
201. *See* Grüneberg, in: Palandt Kommentar zum BGB (Commentary to German CC; in German), § 313 no. 14, § 314 no. 9; Gaier, in: Münchener Kommentar zum BGB (Commentary to German CC), § 314 no. 14; German Supreme Civil Court (BGH), in: Zeitschrift für Wirtschaftsrecht (ZIP) 1997, 257, at 259, and Neue Juristische Wochenschrift 1958, 785.

V. The 'Adjusting/Amending' (tropopoiitiki) Termination of a Contract

304. A somehow *mesomorphic* Civil law instrument, standing between contractual re-adjustment and termination of a contract, is the so-called adjusting/amending termination of a contract, which actually comes from the field of Labour law and refers to the individual employment contract, but may effectively also lead to the termination of a contract – by means of an *extra-judicial* declaration. More specifically:[202]

The adjusting termination of an employment contract is a termination combined with a proposal for the amendment of certain employment contract's terms. It is submitted that the adjusting termination declared by an employer may basically take the following two forms: (a) the form of a termination under the *suspensive* condition (Article 201 CC) that the employee will not accept the proposed change, which actually means that the termination will take effect as of the time the employee will reject the change in her/his working terms; and (b) the form of a termination under the *resolutive* condition (Article 202 CC) that the employee will accept the proposed change, which actually means that the termination takes effect immediately upon its declaration; however, the termination will be reversed if the employee accepts the change.

In essence, whereas the common (definite) termination –as per above– aims at immediately ending the contractual relationship, the adjusting termination seeks to change specific contractual terms (in the case of the employment contract, the working terms of the employee); in other words, primary goal of the adjusting termination is not the termination of the contract, but its amendment and continuation under new terms.[203] This is also the reason why in Germany the adjusting termination (*'Änderungskündigung'*) is, actually, viewed as a means *to consensually re-adjust the contractual content.*[204]

In this context, the employee has the right to accept or reject the adjusting termination. The above mentioned condition is a *potestative* condition –that is, its

202. In detail: Leventis & Papadimitriou, Individual Labor Law (2011; in Greek), pp. 718 et seq.; Leventis, Adjusting Termination, DEN 2015 (in Greek), pp. 239–240; Koukiadis, Labor Law – Individual Labor Relationships and the Law of Employment Flexibility (7th ed. 2014; in Greek), pp. 1024 et seq.; Bakopoulos, The Termination of the Employment Contract (2012; in Greek), pp. 181 et seq., esp. 183; Zerdelis, Labor Law – Individual Employment Relationships (3rd ed. 2015; in Greek), no. 1293 et seq.; *the same*, Applications of Labor Law – Individual and Collective Employment Relationships (2015; in Greek), pp. 303 et seq.; Pazas, The Amending Termination of Employment Contract, available at http://www.kremalis.gr/index.php/en/firmprofile/our-people/partners/720-h. In German literature *see* in more detail Schneider, Vertragsanpassung im bipolaren Dauerschuldverhältnis (2016; in German), pp. 117, 126, 137–138, 218–219, 226–227, esp. 296 et seq., 420 et seq.

203. *See* Leventis, DEN 2015, p. 240; Leventis & Papadimitriou, Individual Labor Law, pp. 719, 730–731; Schneider, Vertragsanpassung im bipolaren Dauerschuldverhältnis, p. 296.

204. *See* Schneider, Vertragsanpassung im bipolaren Dauerschuldverhältnis, pp. 117, 126, 137–138, 296 et seq., 420 et seq.

fulfilment (or not) is dependent upon the employee's will–, which is also the reason why the termination upon condition is considered here as valid.[205]

The employee's acceptance might be explicit or tacit; in the latter case, it is inferred from certain actions without being openly expressed. If the employee continues to –unreservedly– provide his/her services under the new working conditions, then there is a tacit acceptance of the new contractual terms.[206]

The reasons justifying the adjusting termination are usually related to the financial-technical needs of the company-employer or to a significant change in circumstances (introduction of new technology, new production methods, production of new goods, reduction of the financial turnover, closure of certain departments, restructuring, and so forth).[207]

305. In general, the judicial treatment of the adjusting termination is more lenient in relation to the common (definite) termination. Therefore, in case the common termination is held abusive, the adjusting termination may be considered as valid.[208] More particularly, the legality of the adjusting termination –especially with respect to the question whether its exercise is *abusive or not under Article 281 CC*– is primarily dependent upon the fairness of the new terms proposed by the employer, which must correspond to the requirements of good faith, meaning that their acceptance can reasonably be demanded by the employee.[209] In any event, the relevant judgment presupposes, according to the requirements of good faith, *an overall assessment of both parties' conflicting interests as well as other critical surrounding circumstances* (e.g., on the one hand, the financial situation of the employee, on the other, the serious character of the reasons that necessitate, for the employer, the amendment of the initial contractual terms).[210]

306. The adjusting termination is not provided for explicitly in Greek law, i.e., there is no relevant specific statutory provision. However, it may well be argued that, in general, it corresponds to the demands of good faith and fair dealing, as entrenched in Article 288 CC. In particular, the adjusting termination is in harmony with the more specific *duty –stemming from the principle of good faith as well– to co-operate and re-negotiate the initial contractual terms in case a contracting party faces hardship*

---

205. *See* Leventis & Papadimitriou, *supra* , no. 1788–1789; Koukiadis, Labor Law – Individual Labor Relationships and the Law of Employment Flexibility, p. 1025; also Stathopoulos, Law of Obligations – General Part, § 21 no. 132 fn. 149.

206. *See* Leventis & Papadimitriou, *supra* , pp. 721–722; cf. further Gaier, *supra* , § 314 no. 18.

207. *See* Leventis & Papadimitriou, *supra* , pp. 731–732; *Zerdelis*, Labor Law – Individual Employment Relationships, no. 2034 et seq.; Zerdelis, Applications of Labor Law – Individual and Collective Employment Relationships, pp. 307 et seq.; Schneider, Vertragsanpassung im bipolaren Dauerschuldverhältnis, pp. 308 et seq.

208. *See* Pazas, The Amending Termination of Employment Contract, available at http://www.kremalis.gr/index.php/en/firmprofile/our-people/partners/720-h; in more detail Leventis & Papadimitriou, *supra* , pp. 728 et seq., esp. 731.

209. *See* Leventis & Papadimitriou, *supra* , pp. 731 et seq.

210. *See* Leventis & Papadimitriou, *supra* , p. 732.

or difficulty to keep on performing under the initial contractual terms.[211] Above all, it does not lead to an abrupt and 'without further ado' end of the contractual relationship but on the contrary it gives the other side a chance to come to term. It actually constitutes an *ultimum refugium* with a view to avoiding breaking the relationship definitely apart and paving the way for an *heteronomous* judicial ruling; and it is certainly a milder means in comparison to the common (definite) termination, compatible with the constitutionally entrenched principle of proportionality at that (*see* Article 25 §1 sent. d' of the Greek Constitution).[212]

For all the above reasons, the adjusting termination of the contract as per above is nowadays an institution in principle accepted in Greek legal literature and case law.[213] And since that is the case for the sensitive field of employment relationships, it rather goes without saying that the adjusting termination might, in principle, be applicable to other (continuous) contractual relationships as well (e.g., bank loan contracts, lease contracts, etc.).[214]

§6. Damages

I. General

307. We have seen above in §3 in which cases a right to compensation for breach of contract is given to the contracting party. Basically, these are cases of impossibility of performance, default or improper performance of the contract due to fault by the other contracting party – cases of so-called contractual liability to compensation. Other

211. On this ancillary/incidental duty within the general framework of a 'relational contractual theory', in detail Karampatzos, Unforeseen Change of Circumstances in a Bilateral Contract, passim, esp. no. 623 et seq., whereby further references to relevant literature and case law; *the same*, The Provision on Unexpected Change of Circumstances of the Draft Common Frame of Reference and the Duty to Contractual Re-Negotiation, NoB 2010 (in Greek), pp. 623 et seq.; *see also* Stathopoulos, in: Georgiadis & Stathopoulos' Commentary to CC (in Greek), Art. 288 no. 2 and 4; *Principles, Definitions and Model Rules of European Private Law – Draft Common Frame of Reference (DCFR) – Full Edition* (ed. von Bar & Clive, 2009), Intr. pp. 72, 77, as well as Art. III.1–1:104 DCFR ('*The debtor and creditor are obliged to co-operate with each other when and to the extent that this can reasonably be expected for the performance of the debtor's obligation*').
212. *See also* Leventis & Papadimitriou, *supra* , pp. 719, 730, 739 et seq.; Leventis, DEN 2015, p. 240; Zerdelis, Labor Law – Individual Employment Relationships, no. 2032 et seq. Especially as regards the fact that the adjusting termination is a *milder means* in comparison to the common (definite) termination *see* AP 1124/2007, DEN 2007, 1555; AP 573/2007, DEN 2007, 677; AP 351/2004, EErgD 2004, 1477; AP 397/2004, EErgD 2004, 1279; AP 902/1998, DEN 1998, 1580; AP 279/1996, DEN 1996, 581.
213. See, indicatively, Koukiadis, Labor Law – Individual Labor Relationships and the Law of Employment Flexibility, pp. 1025–1026; Leventis & Papadimitriou, *supra* , pp. 720, 726, 741–742; Leventis, DEN 2015, p. 240; Bakopoulos, The Termination of the Employment Contract, p. 183.
214. See, indicatively, Schneider, Vertragsanpassung im bipolaren Dauerschuldverhältnis, pp. 296, 311 et seq., whereby further references to relevant German case law.

legal grounds for compensation are precontractual liability (*see* Articles 197–198 CC, paragraphs 88 et seq. *supra*), delictual liability (*see* Articles 914 et seq. CC, paragraphs 39 et seq. *supra*), etc. In each case where the law stipulates that compensation is owed, certain general rules hold good (concept, nature and extent of the damage which must be restituted, a causal relation between the damage and the legal grounds for liability, etc.). Basic, but not the only, rules of this general law of compensation are contained in Articles 297–300 CC, which we shall examine below; these apply to compensation also in the case of contractual liability. The particular question of the distinction between *positive and negative* interest has been discussed above (paragraphs 92 et seq.).

308. In imposing the obligation of compensation, the legislator had as his aim basically the *furnishing of reparation* for the prejudice which the injured party has suffered. The purpose is his protection, which is pursued by providing him with a counterweight, capable of balancing out the prejudice which has been caused.[215] It is only when the evaluation of this and, consequently, the finding of an exact counterweight is not possible, that 'compensation', with the purpose not of reparation, but of some *satisfaction* of the injured party for the injury which he has suffered, that is, relief of the feelings and alleviation (by material means) of the consequences of the damage, is provided for (*see* paragraph 309*infra*). However, in either case, the person of the injured party and his protection are central.

On the other hand, as is often pointed out, the imposition of a *sanction* on the injuring party is not a purpose of the liability to compensation; the fate of his person is secondary. This is the explanation of the fact that while normally liability to compensation presupposes fault in the injuring party, as a rule the degree of fault is irrelevant for this (for an exception, see, for example, paragraph 327 *infra*). The level of the prejudice which must be compensated does not alter depending upon the seriousness of the fault. The person responsible as a rule owes the same compensation whether the fault is wilful conduct or gross or slight negligence. This is because the purpose is the protection of the injured party and not the punishment of the culprit.[216]

---

215. The restitution of damage also constitutes the upper limit of the protection of the injured party, so as to avoid his enrichment (*see* AP 1006/1977, EEN 1978, 281).

216. By way of contrast, in criminal law, the penalty provided for criminal offences is none other than a sanction imposed upon the culprit. For that reason, his culpability is always necessary and its degree crucial for the criminal nature of the act or the magnitude of the penalty. The injured party is marginal. As a rule, his collaboration is not even required in a prosecution which is initiated ex officio.

II. Damage and Its Varieties

A. Damage as a Difference in the Status of Property: In Natura and Monetary Compensation

309. For the discovery particularly of damage to property in a broad sense (i.e., pecuniary damage),[217] a comparison is made, according to the prevailing – and correct – view, known as the *difference theory*,[218] between the present (after the event causing the damage) status of property and that which would have existed without this event. The difference between the two magnitudes is the damage. The first of the two magnitudes being compared refers to the actual property status of the injured party and the second to a hypothetical property status (that which the injured party would have had without the event causing the damage). The whole property status is crucial, that is, the effect of the event causing damage on all the items of property of the injured party and not only the harm to the specific asset directly affected. In practical terms, of course, we will start out from the latter for purposes of the determination of the damage. This is precisely because the asset which has been affected is of primary interest to the injured party. Frequently the examination of other items of property is superfluous. This explains up to a point the criticism which has been levelled at the difference theory. If, however, there are effects of the damage to the specific item on other areas of the injured party's property, these must also be taken into account, which this theory succeeds in doing. At this point, criticism of it is unjustified.[219] Naturally, a limitation in this connection will also arise from the condition of the causal relation and the other factors which are crucial for liability (*see* particularly paragraphs 317 et seq. *infra*). Consequently, in the end, any change in property status, even the most distantly related, which happens to be due to the same injurious event will not be (or not fully) included in the calculation.

310. The Greek Civil Code, unlike, for example, the Swiss Code of Obligations,[220] contains no provision to the effect that the extent of the damage is to be determined by the judge according to the circumstances (and particularly the seriousness of the fault of the debtor) and that it is not required that all of the damage should be covered. Thus in Greek law, provided that the conditions for compensation are fulfilled, all the damage must be in principle covered by the compensation (without flexibility). If one condition is lacking, no compensation is due. Nevertheless, the inflexibility of 'all or nothing' can be overcome by the recourse of the judge to Article 288 CC, which to

217. In contractual liability, only the restitution of the damage to property is owed. Non-material (so-called *moral*) prejudice is satisfied only in the instances stipulated by the law (thus Art. 299 CC), as well as in cases of delictual liability (Art. 932 CC) or in those of prejudice to rights attaching to personality (Arts 57, 59 CC).

218. This theory was first developed by Mommsen, Zur Lehre von dem Interesse, 1855. Greek court decisions have followed in essence the difference theory. *See* AP 172/1969, NoB 1969, 836; AP 45/1973, NoB 1973, 742; AP 807/1973 (in Plenary Session), NoB 1974, 321; AP 1286/1976, NoB 1977,906; AP 89/1978, EEN 1978, 463; AP 394/1997, NoB 1998, 1425.

219. Even in the case of restitution *in natura* (*see* para. 312 *infra*), it is only in principle that there will be otiose recourse to this theory. If further items of damage arise, e.g., loss of profit, they will be determined on the basis of this theory.

220. *See* Arts 43, 44, 99, para. 3 of the Swiss Code of Obligations.

the same degree that it justifies reduction of the original (contractual) performance, also justifies the reduction of the secondary performance as to compensation. For the fact that this is of particular importance in a case of damage which consists of lost profit, *see* paragraphs 313–314 *infra*.

311. The law introduces a special instance of limitation of the extent of compensation when it uses the expression 'reasonable' compensation. We are speaking here of cases where normally compensation would not be owed (because, for example, a condition for it is lacking), but out of equity towards the injured party the law provides for the payment of reasonable, that is, limited (as the court may judge) compensation. We saw such an instance above (paragraph 269), in connection with cases of rescission (Article 387 CC). Another instance of reasonable compensation is stipulated in Article 918 CC (which also has force as to contractual liability: Article 331 CC), which lays down that a person who has caused prejudice may, where he is not held responsible because of lack of capacity for tortious liability, be ordered by the court to pay a reasonable compensation if the prejudice cannot be compensated in some other way.

312. Compensation, in principle, is paid in money (Article 297, subparagraph 1 CC). Provision, however, is made, by way of exception, for the possibility of its payment *in natura*. Thus, subparagraph 2 of Article 297 CC lays down that the court may, taking into consideration any special circumstances, order, in lieu of compensation in money the restoration of the former state of affairs (*status quo ante*) if this is not contrary to the interests of the creditor.

B. Positive Damage (Damnum Emergens) and Loss of Profit (Lucrum Cessans)

313. The reduction of the existing estate of the injured party (usually a reduction of the assets, but also an increase in the liabilities, for example, the incurring of new debts) is termed *positive damage* (*damnum emergens*). Damage also exists, however, when the estate is not reduced, but an increase is prevented which would have taken place if the event causing the damage had not occurred – that is to say, without this, the assets would have increased (e.g., commercial profits or income from work, etc. would have been realized) or the liabilities would have been reduced (e.g., debts would have been paid off, etc.). In this case we speak of *loss of profit* or *lost profits* (*lucrum cessans*).

In order to obviate any dispute as to whether loss of profit also constitutes damage which must be made good, this is expressly stipulated in Article 298, subparagraph 1 CC. We have seen above a basic exception to this, where only positive damage is the object of restitution, in the case of default of a debtor of a monetary performance (Article 345, subparagraph 2 CC – *see* paragraph 272 *supra*).

In Article 298 CC, subparagraph 2, the legislator has set certain limits as to the level of the legally relevant loss of profit. The need for such limits arises from the fact that while positive damage is as a rule a fact which exists already and, consequently, can normally be easily proven, loss of profit is a magnitude which is determined only hypothetically. It is the profit which would have been realized if the event causing the damage had not occurred. A supposition must necessarily be made as to the hypothetical course of events, and certainty is not a feature of hypotheses, which, moreover, are proven only with difficulty. Thus, in order to facilitate proof, since certainty is impossible, but also to impose a check upon unbridled hypotheses, the law provides in Article 298, subparagraph 2 CC, that 'that which can be expected as probable profit in the usual course of events or by reference to the special circumstances and particularly to the preparatory measures taken' shall be reckoned as loss of profit. It is necessary, that is, for the profit to be able to be expected by an average, reasonable man on the basis of *objective* criteria ('in the usual course of events'), and, moreover, to be anticipated *in advance*, that is, at the time of the event causing the damage. The special circumstances at that time, any preparatory measures which the parties may have taken, etc. will be taken into consideration.

314. The division of damage into positive damage and loss of profit is also crucial, *inter alia*, for the scope of the determination of their extent. Positive damage can as a rule be established with exactitude. It is chiefly here that the principle of Greek law that all the damage is restituted finds application. Loss of profit, on the other hand, is not, as we have seen, a certain damage, but a magnitude which is determined hypothetically and which is therefore difficult to prove with certainty. It is principally in this case that the principle of good faith (Article 288 CC) and the criterion of adequate damages find implementation for the reduction of damage which is to be restituted. Here too the Greek judge can – or should – provide compromise solutions more easily. However, over and above this character of loss of profit, which facilitates restrictions on the compensation, there is another feature of loss of profit which functions along the same lines: loss of profit is a smaller and basically less palpable sacrifice than positive damage. The mandate of commutative justice (*justitia commutativa*) for the restitution of the damage is as a rule stronger and more morally imperative in the case of positive damage, that is, where items of property once existed and have been lost, and less stringent in the case of loss of profit, that is, where it concerns items of property which the 'injured party' never had but which he would simply have acquired (when, especially, the loss of profit of the one person would involve positive damage for the other).

C. Actual and Abstract Damage

315. The division of damage into *actual* (or *concrete*) and *abstract* is related to the manner and criteria of its calculation. The same injury to an item of property may have economic effects of varying extent, depending on who is the owner of this item and what are the conditions prevailing. In some cases, because of the specific circumstances in which the injured party finds himself, the same injury can have more or less unfavourable economic consequences than in another case. If what is taken into account is the damage which occurs in a normal, average case and in the usual course of events (general, abstract calculation of the damage), we speak of abstract damage. If, on the other hand, there is a specific calculation, that is, if account is taken of the damage which the injured party has sustained in the circumstances of his individual case, which will either coincide in its extent with the abstract damage or will diverge from it, then we speak of actual damage.

The answer to the question 'what is made good, the actual or the abstract damage' emerges from what has already been said. It can be concluded both from the concept of damage and from the spirit and purpose of the law of compensation that all the *actual* damage which the injured party has sustained must be made good, regardless of what may be the damage to another person – and so to the hypothetical average member of society. Consequently, a specific calculation of the damage is made. Included in this are whatever further items of damage the specific injured party has suffered, whether or not another person would have suffered them.

316. The legislator has established certain exceptions to the rule of specific calculation of the damage in certain cases, in which he stipulates the damage to be made good or its upper limit on general criteria, regardless of its actual extent in the individual case. Thus, Article 345, subparagraph 1 provides that default in the payment of a monetary debt (which constitutes grounds for liability to compensation, Article 343 CC) has as a consequence a claim on the part of the creditor on default interest for the delay, even if he does not prove damage; Article 345 subparagraph 2 provides in the same instance, as we have already pointed out, for a claim on the part of the creditor that other damage (over and above default interest) should be made good, but only positive damage, thus precluding the possibility of a claim for loss of profit; Article 808 CC, by way of exception to the provision quoted above (Article 345, subparagraph 2 CC), precludes even the possibility of a claim for positive damage over and above interest in the corresponding instance in the case of a loan; Law 2112/1920 lays down in Article 3 on general criteria the sum of compensation owed by an employer to an employee in the event of the termination of a contract for service, etc.

III. Causal Relation

317. A basic condition of liability for compensation is the existence of a causal relation between the legal grounds for liability (here breach of contract) and the damage. Only the damage which has occurred as an effect of the breach as cause is made good.

Difficulties arise not in connection with the necessity (in law) of this condition, which is beyond doubt, but as to its exact meaning. A basic question is whether the concept of causal relation is governed only by the rules of causation, as these are determined by reason, or it is a legal concept whose meaning is in the last analysis determined by the will of the legislator. The practical importance of this becomes an issue chiefly in connection with the further damage brought about by the act after its immediate damage. The need for some limitation so that liability is not extended to these more distant consequences but remains within an acceptable framework has led internationally to a quest for criteria for such a limitation.

318. For the purposes of the resolution of this problem, the older *theory of a conditio sine qua non*, which constitutes the implementation of causation as that is conceived by the natural sciences and reason, is not now regarded as satisfactory. This theory accepts that there is a causal relation between an act and an effect when the former is a necessary condition (*conditio sine qua non*) for the occurrence of the effect, when, that is, it is inconceivable that the former should be absent without the specific effect also being absent. Any effect which would not have occurred (in the manner in which it did in fact occur at the specific time and place) if a condition had not previously been fulfilled is precisely an effect of that condition, that is, it is causally related to it (relation of cause and effect). *Vice versa*, any term will be regarded as a cause of a certain effect – it will be accepted that there is a causal relation between them – if the effect would not have occurred had this condition been absent. There can be a large number of such conditions whose absence would, logically, preclude the occurrence. All are of equal force from the point of view of causation, since the absence of even one of them is sufficient for the frustration of the effect. Perhaps each of these on its own would not have brought about the effect (which they have all caused jointly), but, since it was necessary for the occurrence of the effect, it will be regarded even on its own, in accordance with the *conditio sine qua non* theory, as a cause of the effect.

It will be obvious that this theory does not place a sufficient limitation on the extent of liability, since it accepts as given the condition of a causal relation also for the most distant and fortuitous consequences. It is difficult to establish a cut-off point in the series of causally linked events either in the past in the search for the cause – even the most remote – or in the future in tracing the direct and indirect effects occurring by the use of the logical concept of causation. This critique is justified to the extent that it denies the *sufficiency* of causation in its logical meaning for the affirmation of liability. It does not, however, affect its *necessity* for the existence of liability. In this regard, the *conditio sine qua non* theory is a useful one. If there is no causal connection between damage and act (in a logical sense), there can be no question of liability. The existence of causation, as that is meant by the theory under review, is, from the legal point of view, required but not sufficient.[221] Other additional limitations must be found.

319. The theory of the *adequate cause* (*causa adaequata*), which was developed chiefly in Germany (its foundations having been laid by von Kries), but which also prevails in Greece,[222] selects as crucial that condition of the damage which can be deemed to be its 'adequate cause' (*causa adaequata*). That cause is regarded as adequate which has not simply brought about the damage in terms of logical causation (in the sense of a conditio sine qua non), but which had the tendency, the capability, of leading to it in accordance with the normal course of events. Damage which has been caused by an unforeseen, chance or extraordinary circumstance or which is due to the peculiarity of the specific case and not to the general trend of the condition is not regarded as being linked in an adequate way with it.[223] Thus causation is given a normative, legal meaning. It is argued that support in the law for such a meaning of causal relation can be derived from the spirit of the whole complex of rules on compensation, and, more particularly, from Article 298, subparagraph 2 CC, dealing with loss of profit (*see* paragraph 313 *supra*). This theory succeeds in setting a limitation to liability, since it does not accept this for forms of damage brought about by an inadequate cause.

---

221. AP, for instance, by its Decision 302/1979, NoB 1979, 1293 invoked the *conditio sine qua non* precisely as being a necessary but not sufficient condition for liability.
222. See, *inter alia,* AP (in Plenary Session) 54/1990, NoB 1991, 380; AP 23/1994, NoB 1996, 41; AP 510/1959, NoB 1960,251; AP 273/1970, NoB 1970, 1046; AP 854/1974, NoB 1975, 479; AP 1286/1976, NoB 1977, 906; AP 1261/1985, NoB 1986, 860; AP 579/1993, HellD 1994, 1099; AP 568/1996, HellD 1997, AP 65; 869/2000, HellD 2001, 74.
223. Cf. the criterion applied in this connection in England of reasonable contemplation or reasonable foresight or the relatively broad discretion of French court decisions.

The concept of adequacy does not lend itself to strict delimitation such that we can always have solutions which are beyond dispute. There are, anyway, a number of variations in views held on this. In particular, there is disagreement as to *who* must decide – and *when* – whether there was a general tendency of an act to bring about a result. Furthermore, to the extent that the statistical frequency of the occurrence of an item of damage is taken into account, there is a danger that adequacy will end up as a mechanistic criterion which leaves no room for the assessments which are essential here.

320. In recent years, chiefly in Germany and Austria, but with reverberations in Greece, the *theory of the purpose of the rule of law* has been developed. This theory regards as crucial the purpose of the rule of law (or of the contract) in which the liability is grounded. It examines, that is, what interests and to what extent this rule seeks to protect ('protective purpose') in order to determine the extent of the protection. This examination will discover whether the interests which have been prejudiced directly or indirectly fall within those which it was the law's purpose to protect and whether, consequently, its infringement gives rise to liability for damage caused by this injury. In the last analysis the problem is how far the range of the rule of law which has been infringed extends. The example which is usually quoted is that of a bank which has given erroneous information to a client as a consequence of which the latter has sustained, on the one hand, economic damage in his business and, on the other, a breakdown in his health which has incurred further expenses (hospital fees, etc.). The former damage is covered by the purpose of the contract, but the protection of his health is not.

These two theories (of adequacy and of the purpose of the rule) are not mutually exclusive. Adequacy provides a simple and integrated criterion for the limitation of liability in all cases, while the criterion of the purpose of the rule of law performs the function of the reasonable restriction of liability following a special examination of the purpose of every rule of law (or contract) which has been violated.

IV. Compensation of Damage and Profit (compensatio lucri cum damno)

321. In parallel with the damage, it is possible for the same event which has caused it also to result in certain benefits for the injured party. Examples:

(a) A completely writes off the motor car which he has rented from B. B sells what remains of the car as parts.
(b) A, the lessee of an apartment which belongs to B, leaves the apartment, when the lease expires, with serious damage (resulting from improper use, etc.). C, a rich friend of B, makes him a gift of a sum of money for the repair of the premises.
(c) A destroys goods belonging to B which he has undertaken to have in his safekeeping. These goods were insured with the C insurance company, which pays the injured party B the insurance compensation, in accordance with the insurance policy between B and C.

(d) A murders B, father of the minor C. C has lost the maintenance provided by his father, but at the same time has inherited a part of his estate.

Provided that all the conditions for liability of the injuring party (A in all the examples quoted) to compensate the injured party (B) have been fulfilled, the question arises as to whether the damage which must be restituted will be reduced to the extent of the benefit which the latter has enjoyed. An affirmative answer would mean, naturally, that where the benefit is equal to or greater than the damage, the injuring party is released. The fact that the purpose of the law of compensation was to help the injured party to neutralize the injurious consequences and to restore his property to the state it would have been in if the event causing the damage had not occurred, and not to make him richer or to punish the party at fault leads in principle to the thought that the profits of the injured party arising from the injurious event will always be included in the calculation, that is, they will be subtracted from his damage (*compensation of damage and profit*). Nevertheless, a more careful examination of the various instances of profits derived by the injured party shows that it is frequently unjust that these should operate to the benefit (and perhaps bring about the release) of the injuring party. If, for example, fate has decreed that the injured party should enjoy some profit or, even more so, if third parties have shown sympathy towards him and have provided him with financial assistance with a view to supporting him in his efforts to overcome the unfavourable consequences of the act of the party responsible – and not in order to release the latter from his liability, it would not seem reasonable for the injuring and not the injured party finally to benefit. Some exceptions, at least, must be accepted.

322. A general criterion which is accepted in achieving this limitation in the compensation of the profits is that of the adequacy of causation. That is to say, only those benefits which can be foreseen as occurring in the normal course of events should be included in the calculation.[224] The statistical criterion of normality is, however, inflexible and sometimes difficult to apply to the needs of the particular case.

This problem with adequacy for the compensation of damage and profit of the injured party can be dealt with if we take into consideration the criterion of whether the performance from which the profit is derived (which is grounded either in the contract or in law) serves an independent aim. In this case, the compensation of damage and profit would not be the proper solution.

Such will not normally be the case where the profit to the injured party is a direct consequence of the event causing the damage as to which no activity of the injured party or a third party has occurred, but, at the most, further action on the part of the injuring party himself. A self-contained aim is not being pursued by this profit, independent of that of the law of compensation. Thus it is here a case of profits which simply constitute items included in the calculation of the damage, that is, subtracted from it (*see* paragraph 321 *supra* – example a.).

224. *See* AP 447/1962, NoB 1963, 24. The courts usually invoke causal connection, without any reference to adequacy; *see* AP (in Plenary Session) 807/1973, NoB 1974, 321; AP 127/1971, NoB 1971, 616; AP 560/1972, NoB 1972, 1421; AP 45/1973, NoB 1973, 742; AP 1025/1977, EEN 1978, 288; AP 89/1978, EEN 1978, 463; AP 642/1982, NoB 1983, 499; AP 1833/1987, NoB 1988, 1643; AP 394/1997, NoB 1998, 1425.

If, on the other hand, the benefit is based upon a self-contained performance by which an independent aim is pursued, the solution will not be found only in the law of compensation; this aim will also be taken into consideration and the grounds, in accordance with the relevant contract or provision of law, for the acquisition of the benefit will be examined. Thus, this will not be included in the calculation of the damage when (first) it is based on a self-contained ground for acquisition and, at the same time (second), when this ground is stipulated in favour of the injured party. Such grounds for acquisition are basically:

(a) the activity of the injured party himself which is an autonomous activity and not that which is a consequence of his obligation to limit the extent of the damage (e.g., the injured party undertakes overtime in order to deal with the damage suffered);
(b) the performance, voluntary or obligatory (by virtue of a law or a contract, etc.) of a third party which has as its purpose support for the injured party (*see* paragraph 321 *supra*, example b., and paragraph 323 *infra*);
(c) a direct provision of law which recognizes the benefit to the injured party independently and in parallel, and therefore cumulatively with the damage.

323. It is to the second exception above that cases – of great practical importance – where the occurrence of damage creates an obligation on third parties to effect a performance in favour of the injured party belong. Included in these are chiefly cases of sums of insurance compensation which are paid to the victim of an instance of damage by insurance companies or insurance funds. The purpose of these performances is care for the victim and not for the injuring party. Consequently, any inclusion of these in the calculation of the damage and corresponding reduction of the liability of the culprit would be contrary to this purpose. The same applies to the maintenance owed by a third party to the injured party (e.g., a father to a child who has been injured or even another relative), which, naturally, includes medical expenses; to a pension awarded by reason of death or disablement which is owed respectively to the family of the victim or to the party himself by his employers; to remuneration owed by an employer to an employee who is not working, for example, because he has been injured, etc. The fact that such compensation of damage and profit is precluded in these cases can also be seen from the provision of Article 930, §3 CC, which provides that 'a claim for damage shall not be precluded on the grounds that another person is liable to indemnify or to maintain the victim'. This provision, admittedly, mentions only indemnification or maintenance which are owed to the injured party and reference is made only to the instances of Articles 928 and 929 CC (i.e., only to future damage for harm to a person's life, body or health). Nevertheless, it should be accepted that the provision expresses a more general spirit. Performances by virtue of the law or of the contract to the injured party are effected as a rule in his favour, not in favour of the injuring party. The ratio of Article 930, §3 CC consequently has force as to any other performance, apart from 'indemnification' or 'maintenance', to the injured party and, moreover, regardless of whether or not he has effected a counter-performance (e.g., contributions for the pension awarded to him by an insurance fund by reason of the damage). The crucial, and sufficient, criterion is that the performance should be effected in his favour and not in favour of the culprit. Furthermore, and for the same reason, it is irrelevant whether the life, health or some other interest of the victim (e.g., ownership, as in the case of theft, where its victim was insured against it) has been harmed, or whether the third party is simply liable to effect the performance or whether he has already effected it.

324. The question still remains open as to whether the injured party should retain cumulatively both the indemnity which he receives from the injuring party and the performance which he receives from the third party, or whether he should let the latter have the indemnity. The answer to this question is not to be derived only from the law of compensation but basically from the rules which govern the relations between the injured party and the third party (e.g., in the case of insurance benefits, from the insurance policy or the rules of insurance law, the law of social security, etc.).

As a rule, it will emerge from the contract or the provisions of law which govern these relations that the third party has a right to claim from the injured party the indemnity which the latter has received or (if this has not yet been paid) the assignment of the relevant claim of the injured against the injuring party. Thus such assignment of the claim for indemnity is normally stipulated in insurance policies. More particularly, in the case of the insurance of things, the provision of Article 14 of Law 2496/1997 provides for assignment 'by law' (*cessio legis*) to the insurer. However, the insurance policy may also stipulate cumulative collection of both performances by the injured party, that is, his enrichment. In case of doubt, however, we should accept in the interpretation of the contract and in accordance with the demands of good faith (Article 200 CC) that the parties willed such assignment, since basically the purpose of insurance compensation is to cover the victim directly for damage to him and not to give rise to his enrichment. If it cannot be deduced by means of interpretation what the parties wished, the obligation of the injured party to give up the indemnity which he has received or to assign the claim for it to the insurance company will be deductible as a rule from Article 288 CC. On the other hand, the solution of the cumulative collection of both performances should be accepted when it is a case of the insurance of a *person*, since in these cases the purpose is as a rule not to cover the damage but the payment of a certain sum ('the sum insured') which the insured relies upon in the event of the risk insured materializing. However, the opposite may be concluded from the contract.

What has been said about insurance policies also applies accordingly to the other performances dealt with here. If these do not arise from a contract but from the law, they must be discovered by means of interpretation whether included in its purpose is only the (direct) restitution of the actual damage or whether cumulative collection is accepted. The examination of the relevant provisions of law is the work of the appropriate branches of law.

V. Contributory (Concurrent) Fault

325. If the injured party has contributed by his own conduct to the causing or the extent of the damage he has sustained, it would be unjust for this fact to be ignored and for the injuring party to bear the full liability for compensation because all the conditions for liability are fulfilled in his person. In Roman law, the injuring party would have been released completely when the injured party 'by his own fault' (*ex culpa sua*) had contributed to the damage to himself or to its extent, unless the former had acted deliberately (with *dolus*). This regulation was, however, inflexible, since it provided only for the complete liability or the complete release of the person responsible.

The Greek Civil Code provides (Article 300) in this instance for the possibility of the court either not awarding compensation or reducing its sum. Naturally, the option of its finally awarding full compensation remains.

326. There are two *conditions* for the implementation of Article 300 CC. *First*, there must be a liability to compensation. The ground, however, on which the liability of the injuring party is based is irrelevant – whether, that is, this is failure to perform a pre-existing obligation or a tort, etc., subjective or objective liability,[225] or even liability to reasonable compensation imposed by reasons of equity (e.g., Article 918 CC – paragraph 311 *supra*). In the latter case, of course, it is within the judge's discretion to determine the sum of the compensation in such a way that without any other legislative support he is able to take into account as a criterion for the sum of the reasonable compensation the contributory fault of the injured party. *Vice versa*, the reason for the absence of liability to compensation – absence which has as a consequence the non-implementation of Article 300 CC – is irrelevant. Thus, this provision will not be implemented if, for example, the injuring party was not at fault or was not accountable for his actions (in cases of subjective liability) or if there are grounds for the lifting of the illegal nature (crucial, for example, for the implementation of Article 914 CC) of the act of the injuring party, etc. As a *second* condition, the law requires the injured party to have contributed to the damage or to its extent 'by his own fault'. By interpreting the provision in a broad sense, we can accept that, apart from fault, any other act or omission on the part of the injured party which in itself is capable according to the law of giving rise to his liability (cases of objective joint liability) is sufficient.

327. The *consequences* if the conditions of Article 300 CC are fulfilled are that the judge is able either to release the injuring party or to reduce his liability or, finally, to determine that, in spite of the *contributory* fault, he must bear full liability. The last possibility can be seen from the formulation of the provision, which leaves the reduction or release to the discretion of the judge. Nevertheless, the judge is not allowed to exercise his discretion arbitrarily, but on the basis of certain criteria which are, in accordance with the spirit of the law, deemed crucial. Such criteria are: the gravity of the fault of the injured party by comparison with the gravity of the fault of the injuring party (it is not, however, necessary that there should be a 'mathematical balancing of the equation' between the reduction of the compensation and the 'ratio' of the share of the parties in the fault);[226] the objective (in accordance with the rules of causation) contribution of the parties to the generation and extent of the damage; the prevailing social ideas[227] and, more generally, the principles of good faith, and consequently the economic standing of the parties; good morals (e.g., it is contrary to these for a person who has stolen an object to invoke the inadequate safeguarding of it by the victim of the theft or for an employee who has abused his employer's trust to invoke the inadequate

225. *See also* AP 190/1960, NoB 8, 916.
226. *See* Athens Court of Appeals 3291/1971, NoB 1972, 89.
227. *See* AP 521/1968, NoB 1969, 36; AP 1005/1972, NoB 1973, 501; AP 1237/1975, NoB 1976, 530; AP 289/1997, NoB 1998, 629.

supervision of his employer). It should be noted that Article 300 CC is one of the few instances (*see also* Article 927 CC) in which the degree of fault is crucial. Thus, if one of the two parties has acted wilfully, it is possible that he should bear the liability in full, etc.

§7. LIMITATION OF ACTIONS (PRESCRIPTION)

328. With the passage of time, if the holder of a right takes no action, rights lose their force. The time-limitation of rights is regulated basically by the institution of *prescription* (Articles 247 et seq. CC), which does not directly concern the rights themselves, but the claims which stem from them. This means that when the prescribed period for the limitation of actions has elapsed, the right and the corresponding obligation continue to exist, but the claim which stems from them has been subjected to 'prescription', that is, it is no longer enforceable. What remains is a natural obligation (*see* paragraph 15 *supra*). The debtor is no longer bound to perform his obligation. He can successfully defend himself from any attack of the creditor by opposing the plea of prescription. If, however, he voluntarily effects the performance, he cannot seek its return (Article 272, §2 CC). The claim has been subjected to prescription, but the right remains as a just cause of the retention of the enrichment of the recipient. Moreover, the claim is not subject to prescription when it is to be put forward as a plea, that is, for the defence of its holder against a right of the other party (Article 273 CC).

By way of contrast with the above 'extinctive' prescription, in other cases, the passage of time may bring about the acquisition of rights (cf. the Roman institution of 'acquisitive' prescription). In Greek law currently in force such an effect of the passage of time exists chiefly through the institution of *usucapio*, that is, acquisition of ownership over a movable or immovable thing by means of a certain period of time[228] of possession as owner (Articles 1041 et seq. CC).

Extinction of rights themselves – and not simply prescription of claims – is brought about by the so-called *term of extinction*, which may be stipulated for a right either by the law or by agreement of the parties (*see* Articles 279–280 CC). Here, with the elapse of the period of time specified the right itself is extinguished. An example of a term of extinction is that stipulated for the constitutive right of the contracting party to annul the contract for defect of will (error, fraud, duress – *see* paragraph 155 *supra*).

329. In principle, all claims are subject to prescription, unless, by way of exception, the law provides otherwise. For example, family law claims aimed at restoring the status of family law relationships which are 'appropriate' to this relationship are not subject to prescription. The term of prescription is as a rule twenty years. Exceptionally (e.g., in the case of commercial claims or claims for salary or fees or interest or rent, etc. – *see also* paragraph 352 *infra*), it is five years or, when special provision is made for this, different, that is, even shorter. On the prescription of delictual claims, *see* paragraph 43 (e) *supra*.

228. Three years in the case of movable and ten in the case of immovable things, if the possessor is in good faith and has a legal title. Otherwise a twenty-year period is required for both movable and immovable things.

Prescription is *suspended* (i.e., the period during which the reason for suspension holds good is not counted and continues when this reason ceases to apply from the point at which it was when suspension began, but for at least a further six months) in those cases stipulated by the law (Articles 255 et seq. CC). For example, cessation of administration of justice or force majeure within the last six months of the period of prescription, etc. Special protection is provided at this point for claims of minors or against spouses or parents or children (during the minority of the latter). Furthermore, prescription is *interrupted* (in which case, immediately after the interruption, a new full period of prescription begins, without the time which has passed up to the interruption being counted) if the obligor acknowledges the claim or the holder of the right institutes legal action or other legal proceedings (Articles 260 et seq. CC).

The provisions on prescription are basically imperative law and may not be precluded or modified by a private agreement. However, the renunciation of the rights of the obligor resulting from the prescription is valid if it is declared after the elapse of the prescription period. Prescription must be proposed to the court by the interested party, since the court does not take it into account ex officio.

330. Although this is not specially stipulated by the law, *forfeiture*, i.e., *deactivation of a right* by reason of the failure of its holder to take action for a long period is accepted even before the elapse of the prescription period or regardless of whether such a period is stipulated. Legal grounds for accepting such forfeiture are the general provision on abuse of a right (Article 281 CC). Thus forfeiture of the right will be accepted not simply because the holder of the right fails to take action for a relatively long time, not exercising his right, but when at the same time he has created in the obligor the justifiable impression that he is no longer going to exercise it; or when a change of course on the part of the inactive holder of the right would contradict his conduct up to the present (*venire contra factum proprium*) and would conflict with the principle of good faith or the other criteria of Article 281 CC (cf. the English doctrine of laches or equitable estoppel). A consequence of the application of the provision will be that the obligor rebuts by his plea the exercise of the right as being abusive. The institution of forfeiture has also been accepted by the Greek courts.[229]

229. As early as 1948. See, for instance, AP 408/1948, EEN 1949, 90; AP 442/1971, NoB 1971, 1239; AP 1014/1975, NoB 1976, 299.

Part II. Specific Obligations

331. The Greek Civil Code, in its second book on the law of obligations and following the general rules which apply to all obligations – and therefore to all contractual obligations – also contains special regulations for special categories of obligations, particularly of contracts (nominate contracts, *see* paragraph 28 *supra*). We shall give below (Chapter 1) in summary form the most important of these regulations of contracts, which, however, are of secondary importance when compared with the general law of contracts, of universal application, which we examined in Part I. It should be noted that most of these special (mainly supplementary) rules are dispositive law, adapted to the type of contract being regulated, in the event that the parties do not provide otherwise, which they are at liberty to do. Contracts not regulated in the CC (innominate contracts, *see* paragraph 28 *supra*) can be concluded by virtue of freedom of contract. Business practice has given rise to new forms of contracts which have as their purpose first and foremost the satisfaction of needs of enterprises, forms which have arisen from today's advanced and many-faceted economic life and the galloping development of technology and of international commercial transactions. Needs of new means of financing and new methods of exploiting material and intangible goods have shaped, by virtue of contractual freedom, types of contract which are not expressly provided for in the CC.

Such forms of contracts which have developed in today's transactions are, for example, leasing, factoring, forfaiting, franchising, time-sharing, sponsoring, consulting, management contracts, etc. Naturally, the general law of contracts in force (general law of obligation of the CC) is applied to these new forms of contracts. But a large part of the regulation of these contractual types is drawn from the specific (usually standardized) contract itself. Private autonomy (here: freedom of contract), as expressed in the content of the contract determined by the parties, has a wide range of regulatory applicability. It is a well-known fact that, particularly in international commerce, the so-called *lex mercatoria* has developed: the will of the parties is their 'law', which is shaped in international practice and provides solutions to many problems. Furthermore, the new forms of contract have given rise to a *trend towards special legislative regulations* for each of these (*see*, for example, Laws 1652/1986 on the time-sharing contract, 1665/1986 on the leasing contract, 1905/1990 on the factoring contract, etc.). However, over and above the special regulations, these contracts are governed, as we have said, by general law. These new forms of contract are not examined in the present monograph, which is concerned chiefly with the interpretation of the provisions of the CC. See, however, paragraph 375 *infra* on leasing, which has affinities with the lease contract of the CC.

Administrative *contracts* have been discussed above, paragraphs 9–10. After special contracts, the rules of certain non-contractual obligations will be examined (Chapter 2). These are contained in the same special section of the CC since in other systems of law they are considered as related to contractual obligations and are known by the name of 'quasi-contracts' (*see* in this connection paragraph 45 *supra*).

In the law of obligations (Special Part), the CC also regulates contracts for services (labour contracts) – particularly in Articles 648–680. The interpretation, however, of these basic articles, as they have been supplemented by the special labour laws, is the work of the special branch of labour law.

Finally, three articles of the special law of obligations (Articles 873–875 CC) deal with the institution, of general importance, of the abstract promise of debt, of which we have spoken already (paragraphs 140 et seq. *supra*).

Chapter 1. Special Contracts

§1. Agency (Mandate: Representation)

I. General

332. The CC provides, in Articles 713–729, for the contract of *mandate*, which is similar (without being identical) to the English institution of *agency*. The latter also covers to a considerable extent the institution of *representation*, which is regulated by the Greek Civil Code in its first book 'On General Principles' (more specifically, in Articles 211–235 CC), since it is of a more general application which goes beyond the bounds of obligatory contracts. The Greek 'representative', as well as the mandatary, corresponds to a great extent to the agent in English law.

Although a mandate and a representation are frequently linked and co-exist, in Greek law they must be clearly distinguished from one another. The former is a promissory contract (and not a unilateral juridical act) whose effects, in accordance with the theory of privity of contracts, are developed between the two contracting parties: one of these, the mandatary, undertakes by the contract to the other, the mandator (who has the corresponding claim) the obligation to conduct an affair entrusted to him by the mandator. The mandatary does not acquire any powers as to third parties by the mandate contract. The power which the mandatary normally needs when the affair of the mandator is the undertaking of a juridical act with a third party in the interest of the mandator, that is, the power to bind the mandator by this juridical act, is acquired by the mandatary through the institution of representation. For this purpose, the mandatary must also be a representative of the mandator, that is, have precisely this power to undertake the juridical act 'in the name' of the mandator. The carrying out of a juridical act by a person (representative) in the name of another person (the person represented, the principal) means that the effects of the juridical act occur immediately in the person of the latter. Thus, after the undertaking of, for example, a contract by the representative (with a third party), provided, of course, that this contract is within the limits of the power of the representative, the principal immediately has any contractual rights and obligations without it being necessary for any other act to follow (e.g., transfer from the representative to the principal). A person may have the power of representation by law (legal or statutory representative – *see* paragraph 197 *supra*). Usually, however, he acquires it by the will of the principal, that is, by a juridical act effected by the latter, which is termed the granting of a 'power of attorney' (Article 216 CC). This juridical act, unlike a mandate, which is a contract, is a unilateral act of the principal. By the mandate the mandatary acquires as to the mandator only the obligation to conduct the latter's affair: by a power of attorney he acquires the power as against third parties to bind him through juridical acts. The contract which the attorney concludes with the third party in the name of the principal is the third juridical act in the series (after the mandate and the power of attorney).

333. Frequently both juridical acts (mandate and power of attorney) are concluded together. They may be united in a single act, though the distinction between them from the legal point of view remains. The power of attorney usually presupposes the mandate. The mandate, as its subjacent contract, is the *causa* of the power of attorney. However, a mandate without a power of attorney can be envisaged, either because the latter is not necessary (e.g., the affair which the mandatary is to handle is material and not legal), or, for example, because the mandator does not wish it. In this case, the mandatary who lacks the power of representation will carry out the juridical act in his own name, but, of course, in the interest of the principal (*indirect representation*). The effects of the juridical act occur in the person of the mandatary (indirect representative) and in all probability a new juridical act will be required between the latter and the principal for any right which he has acquired to be transferred to him. A power of attorney without a mandate may also be envisaged, either because the cause of the power of attorney is another subjacent contract (e.g., a contract for services, a contract for work, partnership, etc.),[230] or because the cause is completely absent (which is extremely improbable) or because it is void. In the latter instances the validity of the power of attorney is not affected, since it is a juridical act which is *abstract* (not dependent on its cause).[231]

II. Mandate

334. A mandate is a *unilaterally obliging contract.* The sole necessary and basic contractual obligation which is generated is that of the mandatary, to conduct the affair of the mandator. Collateral obligations of the mandatary are, particularly, to furnish information to the mandator about the affairs entrusted to him; to render account to the mandator upon termination of the mandate; and to restore to the mandator everything he has received for or acquired from the performance of the mandate. He is responsible to the mandator for any fault in the course of the performance of his obligation.

The fact that the mandate is not a reciprocal contract (*see* paragraph 32 *supra*) does not mean that obligations cannot be created upon the mandator, though these do not constitute the contractual quid pro quo of the performance of the mandatary (as is the case with the counter-performance in reciprocal contracts). In these cases the term '*imperfectly reciprocal contracts*' is often used. Thus, the mandator is obliged to reimburse the mandatary for everything which the latter has spent in performing the mandate (he is obliged to make payment in advance). He is liable to compensate any damage which the mandatary has suffered, without his fault, in the performance of the mandate.

335. The mandatary must perform the mandate in person. Only if the contract permits him or if substitution is usual or if he is forced by circumstances may he *substitute* another for himself in the performance of the mandate. In these exceptional cases of permissible substitution, the mandatary is only liable for fault as to the choice

230. Cf. AP 887/1974, NoB 1975, 492; AP 593/1992, HellD 1995, 607.
231. The law has given to the power of attorney the shape of an abstract juridical act in the interests of the protection of third parties, e.g., the counterparty of the attorney, who has no need to interest himself in the internal relations between the representative and the person represented.

of the substitute or as to the instructions he has given him. Otherwise, he is liable for the fault of the substitute as for his own fault. The fact that the mandator may, by way of exception to the principle of the privity of contracts, take action directly against the substitute with the actions which the mandatary has against him has already been pointed out (paragraph 193 *supra*).

336. The mandate contract has as its aim basically the serving of the interests of the mandator. Thus, he may *revoke* the mandate at any time, without there being any need for him to justify such revocation. Agreement which precludes or limits this right of the mandator is null and void, except if the mandate also concerns the interest of the mandatary or of a third party. In this exceptional instance, revocation in spite of a valid agreement to the contrary is without effect. The mandatary may also in principle *terminate* his mandate at any time, provided that such termination does not occur at an inappropriate time, but he may waive this right, in which case he may terminate the mandate only if serious grounds manifest themselves. If there are such grounds, the question of whether the time of termination was appropriate or not is not examined.

The decease of the mandator or of the mandatary is as a rule a ground for dissolution of the mandate, by reason of its personal nature. The contrary may, however, be agreed, in which case the mandate continues in favour of the heirs of the mandator or is continued by the heirs of the mandatary (if they have not repudiated inheritance).

On the contract – related to the mandate – of brokerage, *see* paragraph 396 *infra.*

III. Representation

337. Representation, as has already been explained, creates the power for a person (the representative) to bind by his own juridical act (obligational, real or otherwise) another person (the party represented – the principal). This is an institution which has broader significance and application. In the internal relations between the party representing and the party represented, the subjacent contract, usually a mandate (*see* paragraph 333 *supra*) has force. Representation operates externally, since the representative carries out acts with third parties *in the name of the principal.* After the undertaking by the representative, for example, of a contract with a third party, the effects occur in the person of the principal and the latter and the third party now exist as contracting parties (holders of the contractual rights and obligations). However, the involvement of third parties creates certain problems: these are dealt with in Articles 211 et seq. CC.

A. Direct or Indirect Representation

338. When a juridical act is concluded, it must be clear whether the contracting parties are acting in their own name (as is usually the case) or in the name of some other person, that is, as his representative. In the latter case, the effects of the juridical act occur in the person of this other person. However, the fact that a juridical act also (or only) serves the interests of a third party does not mean that it is concluded in his name also. The CC establishes the rule (Article 211, paragraph I and Article 212) that for it to be deemed that one of the contracting parties has not acted in his own name but in the name of someone else (i.e., as his representative), this must be expressly stated or be clearly deducible from the circumstances (the principle that representation must be apparent). Otherwise (and in cases of doubt), each of the contracting parties will be deemed to have acted in his own name and acquires rights and obligations from the contract. If, in spite of this, a contracting party who concludes a juridical act formally in his own name has as his purpose to serve the interests of another person by it, this is termed indirect representation (*see* paragraph 333 *supra*) – which is not, literally, representation.

When we speak simply of representation in the sense of a technical term (*terminus technicus*), we mean direct representation, that is, the undertaking of a juridical act in the name of another person. Indirect representation is not regulated specially by the law. Here what is being concluded is a normal juridical act which produces effects for the contracting parties. Its special characteristic is that since the interests of a person indirectly represented are being served, the indirect representative must, for example, subsequently (by virtue of his contractual or other legal relationship to the person indirectly represented) transfer to him what he has acquired by a *new act* or be covered by him as to the obligations undertaken. From this point on, when we speak of representation, direct representation is meant.

B. The Person of the Representative

339. Although the (direct) representative is finally not regarded as the contracting party who has acquired the contractual rights and obligations (this is the person represented, the principal), he remains the person who has concluded the juridical act. He declares his own will 'in the name' of the principal. This is how he differs from a mere 'messenger' who only conveys the will of the person concluding the act. A representative himself, *and by his own will*, concludes the contract, while a messenger conveys the will of the contracting party. This means that the representative cannot be (as perhaps a messenger could) incapable of entering into a juridical act. It is, however, sufficient that he should have limited capacity (Article 213 CC), that is, that he should have completed his tenth year. Furthermore, defects of will (error, fraud, duress) or other subjective factors are judged by reference to the person of the representative. The will of the principal can be of significance only if the representative acted in accordance with certain instructions of the principal, in which case the latter may not invoke ignorance on the part of the representative of facts which he (the principal) knew or ought to know (Articles 214–215 CC).

C. The Granting of Power of Attorney

340. The representative can acquire, as we have seen, the power of representation from the law or – more commonly – by a unilateral juridical act of the principal. This juridical act of the principal is addressed either to the representative (here called an attorney) or to the third party with whom the juridical act of the attorney is to be concluded. If this juridical act with the third party is subject to a form, for example, a notarial document, the granting of the power of attorney should also be subject to the same form. Otherwise, the latter is informal, and therefore can be effected orally or can be assumed indirectly. A power of attorney is in principle freely revocable. A waiver of the right of revocation is possible, unless it concerns exclusively the interest of the principal. A power of attorney, provided that it cannot be concluded that there is a will to the contrary, expires on the decease of the principal or of the attorney or on the termination of the subjacent legal relationship (such as the mandate contract on which it is based).

D. *Lack of Power of Attorney*

341. If someone has concluded a contract as the representative of another person without in fact having the power of his representation or having exceeded this power (*falsus procurator*), the validity of the contract for the person thus falsely represented depends upon his approval. If he approves it, the contract has force and binds him. If not, then, on the one hand the party falsely represented is not bound and the pseudo-representative is obliged, at the choice of the other contracting party, either to perform the contract (which is again valid, with the pseudo-representative as contracting party instead of the principal) or to pay damages (positive interest), that is, to put the other contracting party in the position he would have been in, had the contract been performed. If, however, the pseudo-representative was ignorant of the lack of power of representation, he owes only negative interest (if this does not exceed the positive interest), that is, he has to put the other party in the position in which he would have been, had the contract not been concluded at all. For more on the distinction between positive and negative interest, *see* paragraphs 92 et seq. *supra*. The pseudo-representative is released from any obligation if the other contracting party knew or ought to have known of the lack of power to represent.[232]

E. *Self-Contracting*

342. If a representative concludes a contract in the name of his principal with himself in his own name as the other contracting party or with himself as representative

232. The problem is a different one if there is no exceeding of the power of representation, but rather an abuse of it. This exists when the act which the representative has engaged in, though falling within the limits of his power of representation, is nevertheless contrary to the interests of the principal or to the aim of the power of the representative in such a way that it is apparent that the principal would never have carried out this act (*see* AP 213/1965, NoB 1965, 1149; AP 1797/1985, NoB 1986, 1074; AP 1150/1997, EEN 1999, 145; AP 267/2000, HellD 2000, 1371). In this case, Art. 281 CC (which prohibits the abuse of a right) could probably be implemented, but only if the specific circumstances are particularly grave, such as to justify, for example, the acceptance of obvious bad faith. This is because the need for protection of the third party in good faith involved in the transaction, for whose benefit the power of attorney has been given the form of an abstract juridical act, that is, independent of the internal relations between the representative and the principal, should not be forgotten. Perhaps in the last analysis good faith according to Art. 281 CC imposes consequences for abusive exercise of the power of representation only in the relations of these two parties (e.g., provision of compensation by the former to the latter in conjunction with Art. 914 CC) and the retention of the validity of the contract of the representative with the third party, which binds the principal.

of a third contracting party (i.e., in this latter case the same representative represents both contracting parties), we speak of a self-contract. It will be obvious that such an act is risky for the principal or principals since the representative represents the interests of more than one person – and, indeed, conflicting interests. For this reason, the provision of Article 235 CC prohibits self-contract, unless this contract has been specially permitted by the principal or principals or the self-contract is nothing more than a fulfilment of an obligation which has already been validly undertaken (e.g., by a promise to contract which has been concluded without self-contracting). In these exceptional cases, the self-contract must be effected with the form of a notarial document.

A self-contract which is concluded without being permitted or without a notarial document, where it is permitted, is null and void. It is argued that such nullity is relative in favour of the principal, since the prohibition has been established in his favour (on relative nullity, *see* paragraph 153 *supra*).

§2. Sale of Goods: Exchange

I. Meaning: Conditions for Sale – Exchange

343. Sale is a contract whereby one of the contracting parties (the vendor) undertakes the obligation to transfer to the other contracting party the ownership of a thing and to deliver it to him or to transfer to him another right, while the other contracting party (the purchaser) undertakes the obligation to pay the vendor as a quid pro quo the agreed purchase price (Article 513 CC).

This contract, which is regulated in Articles 513–572 CC, is the commonest and most important in transactions. It is by this means chiefly that the circulation of goods is achieved. It is this, more than any other contract, which the CC had in mind in establishing the provisions of the general law of obligations, and it is in this that these provisions chiefly find scope for implementation (e.g., the provisions on liability in the event of non-performance of Articles 380 et seq. CC), to the extent that they are not modified by the more particular provisions of Articles 513 et seq.

344. Sale is an *obligational* and, moreover, a *promissory* contract (*see* paragraphs 12 and 19 et seq. *supra*). Therefore, for the transfer of the right sold in fulfilment of the obligation which has been undertaken by the sale contract, a new contract, of disposition this time, which, however, may be concluded simultaneously with the sale, is required. The sale is valid even if the vendor does not have, on its conclusion, the right being sold (e.g., the ownership of the thing). If he does not acquire it by the time of the fulfilment of his obligation, there will be (legal) impossibility of performance. On the other hand, for the validity of the transfer of the right it is as a rule required that the transferor should be the holder of the right (*see* paragraphs 48 et seq., 210 *supra*). Furthermore, sale is a *reciprocal* contract, a fact which does not mean, of course, that the two performances exchanged must be objectively of the same value: it suffices that the parties should regard the one as a quid pro quo for the other (*see* paragraphs 32 and 150 *supra* – also on the limits to any disproportion in value between the right sold and the purchase price).

Sale is often combined with other contracts: for example, sale and lease or sale and a contract for work; this will then be a *mixed contract*. On the provisions applicable to mixed contracts, *see* paragraph 29 *supra*.

345. As can be seen from the definition of sale contained in Article 513 CC, the object of the obligation of the vendor may be: (a) *A thing*, that is, a corporeal object or part of a thing or even incorporeal objects, such as 'natural forces or energies, particularly electric current and heat, to the extent that such forces, being concentrated within a delimited space are subject to control' (Article 947, paragraph 2 CC). In these cases, the right sold is ownership over the thing; (b) *Another right*, such as rights in personam (e.g., a contractual right), limited rights in rem (e.g., usufruct on a thing), intangible property rights (e.g., copyright, know-how of an enterprise, right on software), etc. Furthermore, the object of the obligation of the purchaser is the *purchase price*, which consists exclusively or chiefly in money. A monetary performance must be defined or definable. If the right transferred is exchanged for a non-monetary performance, that is, the 'purchaser' owes, for example, another thing also, we no longer speak of a sale contract but of an *exchange contract*, as to which the CC (Article 573 CC) stipulates that provisions relating to sale are also applicable, *mutatis mutandis*, to exchange. The provision adds that each contracting party to the exchange shall be deemed a vendor as to the performance which he owes to the other party and a purchaser as to the performance to which he is entitled.

346. Sale as a rule does not need to be subject to a form. It may even be concluded orally. It is only in the special cases provided for by the law that a form must be observed, for example, in the sale of the *whole* of an existing estate or a percentage of it (Article 367 CC),[233] in the sale of immovables (Article 369 CC), etc. A real contract as to immovables is subject to transcription into the transcription registers, that is, here the transfer contract of the immovable sold (Articles 1033, 1192 CC) and not the promissory contract of the sale of the immovable. The real contract transcribed, however, must mention its cause, which is the promissory contract. Anyway, in practice, sale and transfer of ownership of an immovable usually occur together and are formulated in a single notarial document. (On the introduction of the land register in Greece, instead of the system of transcriptions, see *supra* paragraph 50.)

II. Obligations of the Vendor: His Liability for Defects

A. Primary and Collateral Obligations: Defects in Title

347. The two primary obligations of the vendor can already be derived from the definition of sale. The first and most basic is the obligation of transferring the ownership or any other right which is being sold. The second, which concerns only things transferred, is the obligation of delivering the thing sold. Collateral obligations may be provided for in the contract (e.g., those which are appropriate to the special

233. If the whole of the future estate or a percentage of it is sold, the sale will be void, even though a form has been observed (Art. 366 CC).

case) or are stipulated in the CC (e.g., Article 519 CC, obligation of information on the legal relations of the object and delivery of the documents proving the right) or may be derivable from good faith (*see* paragraphs 53, 158 *supra*).

If the vendor does not fulfil one of his obligations, the purchaser has, first of all, the claim for performance and, on the conditions of Articles 380 et seq. CC, the rights stipulated there, such as the right of rescission, compensation, etc. (*see* Part I, Chapter 6 *supra* for the remedies in the event of non-performance). Furthermore, he may oppose to the vendor if the latter demands the purchase price the suspensive plea of '*non adimpleti contractus'* (paragraph 229 *supra*).

348. The same rights are basically held by the purchaser in the event of the right being sold having a *defect in title* (in Greek terminology: legal defect). Here too we have an instance of non-performance, wholly or in part, of the obligations of the vendor, who was obliged to transfer the right with full title, and therefore without legal defects. A legal defect is considered to be any right of a third party over the thing or right being sold, where the right of the third party in rem or in personam may be opposed to the purchaser and impede the full transfer of the right being sold or the exercise of the right being sold or the exercise of the powers which stem from the right being sold (*see* the summary formulation of Article 514 CC). Thus there is a legal defect when, for example, the purchaser has not acquired – in spite of the transfer contract which followed the promissory contract of sale – the ownership since this was not held by the vendor but by a third party,[234] or when the thing was encumbered with a pledge or mortgage, or is leased and the lessee can oppose his right in personam against the purchaser (*see* Articles 614, 1095 and paragraph 194 *supra*), or is seized in execution or distressed or sequestrated or confiscated or encumbered with taxes or duties which can be collected from the purchaser also, etc. On the other hand, legal limitations of ownership (e.g., restrictions on building or restrictions stemming from the law of neighbours, that is, for the benefit of neighbours – *see* Articles 1003 et seq. CC, etc.) are not considered to be legal defects.

According to the prevailing opinion as to the legal defects which existed before the conclusion of the sale, the liability of the vendor (and the corresponding remedies of the purchaser given to him by the general law of obligations) does not presuppose fault on the part of the vendor (even presumed fault, as in the case of legal defects which occurred after the conclusion), that is, it is independent of whether the vendor was aware or not, through his fault or otherwise, of the existence of the legal defect (cf. the formulation of Article 516 CC, which speaks only of non-performance of the obligations of the vendor and not of non-performance through fault). This constitutes a deviation in favour of the purchaser from the fault principle of the general law.

If the purchaser knew of the legal defects, the vendor is not liable, unless it is a case of mortgage, pledge or seizure (Article 515 CC).

234. It is here supposed that the provision of Art. 1036 CC on acquisition *in good faith* of ownership of a *movable* from a person not the owner (para. 52 *supra*) is not implemented.

B. Defects of the Thing and Lack of Agreed Qualities

349. In accordance with the Roman law tradition, the CC distinguished defects in title from *defects of the thing*, which are *material* defects or, more generally, defects of *quality* (*lato sensu*) of the thing sold.

In the case of defects of the thing, the CC provided for liability on the part of the vendor, which, however, was different from his liability for legal defects. The CC, that is, started out from the thought that the vendor ought to deliver the thing, provided that this was already specifically determined (*see* paragraphs 143, 266 *supra*) in whatever (qualitative) state it was.[235] He thus did not have an obligation to rid it of any defects, that is, to deliver it without defects (here he has, as we have seen, an obligation to deliver it without legal defects). The purchaser did not have a claim for performance in the sense of a claim for the correction of defects of the thing itself (unless, of course, something of this kind has been agreed, or if, under specific circumstances, it is demanded by good faith). However, there was a secondary liability of the vendor for these defects, which was normally called 'warranty liability for defects'. The liability consisted in the assignment of the following rights to the purchaser, which he may exercise as alternatives (Articles 534 et seq., 540 et seq. CC):

350. A right of *reversal* (*cancellation*) *of sale* (an institution which comes from the Roman *actio redhibitoria*, similar to rescission of the contract – the differentiation has come about for historical reasons), which has the consequence that the purchaser must return the thing and the vendor the purchase price (Article 547 CC). The right of *reduction of the purchase price* (cf. the Roman *actio quanti minoris*), depending, of course, upon the extent of the reduction in value or usefulness of the thing. In cases of doubt, this will be decided by the court. Or, if there is fault of the vendor here, a right of *compensation* for non-performance of the contract (Articles 543–544 CC). This compensation has as its purpose to put the purchaser in the position in which he would have been if the defect had not existed. Or, finally, in the case of sale of a thing determined in kind, a right of *replacement* of the defective thing by another without defect. The CC provided for the same rights of the purchaser and, accordingly, the same liability of the vendor in cases of lack of agreed qualities of the thing sold.

351. By Law 3043/2002 on 'liability of the vendor for defects of the thing and lack of agreed qualities, etc.', which is an expanded adaptation of Greek legislation to Community Directive 1999/44/EC, the old provisions on defects of the thing and lack of agreed qualities were replaced by new regulations.

The first basic reform of Law 3043/2002 concerns the conversion of what was up till then the 'warranty liability' of the vendor for defects of the thing or lack of agreed qualities into *full contractual liability*, like liability for non-performance because of impossibility of performance, or default of the debtor or legal defect, etc.

Thus in the new Article 534 there is provision now that the vendor has, apart from the obligations of Articles 513, 514 CC (on the transfer of the ownership of the thing free of legal defects, and on the delivery of the thing), the obligation to 'deliver

---

235. If, on the other hand, performance determined in kind (unidentified goods) is owed, the vendor must supply a thing of average quality (Art. 289 § 2: 'The debtor shall not be bound to furnish things from among the best of the kind nor shall he be entitled to furnish things from among the worst.').

the thing with the agreed qualities and without defects of it'. The lack of the agreed qualities and the existence of defects of the thing are identical with lack of conformity with the contract in accordance with the terminology of the Community Directive (see an indicative citation of instances of non-compliance with the contract in the new Articles 535 and 536 CC). The CC uses both terminologies as synonymous. Consistently with this obligation of the vendor, there is a provision in the new Article 540 for the right of the purchaser to seek the *repair* of the thing (i.e., the fulfilment of the obligation that there should not be a defect of the thing, etc., that is, by bringing the thing into conformity with the contract) in parallel with the earlier rights of replacement, reduction of the purchase price, and reversal (today, rescission – *see* immediately *infra*). The existence of a defect of the thing or the lack of an agreed quality now constitutes *breach of a contractual obligation* of the vendor, like impossibility of performance, default of the debtor, etc., and, consequently, gives rise to full contractual liability, and therefore for performance.

The right of *reversal* in the earlier law has been hereafter *named a right of rescission*, as has the right of rescission of the contract in other cases of breach of contractual obligations according to the general law of contracts. The terminological differentiations of what are in essence the same institutions can give rise only to problems, without serving real needs. These too are remnants of casuistic Roman law, in which there was no developed general law of obligations and which usually supplied solutions separately for each type of contract and for each reason for its rescission (reversal), and, therefore, without a terminological (and often without a substantive) harmonization and systematization of these solutions.

Terminological unification serves better understanding, economy, consistency, and (in the present instance) harmonization with most foreign legislations. Thus to rescission according to the new law for defects of the thing or lack of agreed qualities will the general rules of the law of rescission apply, and only where there is provision to the contrary in Articles 540 et seq. CC will the special provisions hold good.

There is also provision for the accumulation of the rights of rescission and compensation, which is a just solution, because it corresponds to the will of the party rescinding the contract, but also because, objectively, it satisfies practical needs and legitimate interests (new Article 543 – but see on the general law of obligations *supra* paragraph 269 (c)).

352. The liability of the vendor for defects of the thing and lack of agreed qualities was and remains objective (i.e., it does not presuppose fault on the part of the vendor) where the rights of repair or replacement or reduction of the purchase price or rescission are to be exercised. In addition, as to the right to compensation, if this is case of lack of an agreed quality, the liability to compensation is objective (Article 543, subparagraph 1, CC). On the other hand, in a case of defect of the thing, the liability to compensation is subjective, that is, fault is required (Article 543, subparagraph 2), and this is presumed, as is the case in principle in contractual liability.

For the exercise of the right of rescission, but not for the other rights of the purchaser, the prerequisite of the existence of an essential (not 'minor') defect of the thing (this is also in accordance with the Directive) is stipulated (Article 540, §1, No. 3, which by its wording imposes on the vendor the burden of proof that the defect was not minor). The explanation is obvious: rescission is the most drastic of the rights of the purchaser, since by its exercise the contract is overthrown. It would be inequitable for the vendor if the purchaser also exercised this right for a slight defect which could, for example, easily be corrected or even lead to a reasonable reduction of the purchase price or some small compensation.

Reinforcement of the protection of the purchaser is also provided for in the new Article 559 CC, which is in accordance with the corresponding provision of the Community Directive. If by a statement of the vendor or a third party or by the relevant advertisement a 'guarantee' is provided by the vendor or a third party as to the thing sold, this 'guarantee' gives rise to full contractual liability of the vendor. Thus, any doubt as to whether these statements are legally binding are removed – in favour of an affirmative reply.

A problem of prescription also arises in the case of successive sales which intervene before the thing arrives at the final purchaser. In this case, if the defect makes its appearance in the hands of the final purchaser, as will be the case as a rule, since this is the person who will use the thing, this purchaser may in due time exercise his rights. But until such time as the matter is settled, particularly if judicial pursuit of his rights is needed, so much time will pass that it may be to the detriment of any rights of the preceding vendors. If, for example, it is held that the last vendor is liable for the defect or lack of qualities, he will be able to sue (now as a purchaser) his own vendor, but there is a danger that the period of prescription will have elapsed, since the starting-point for the prescription is the time of delivery of the thing to the purchaser in each case. This danger increases the further we advance in the liability of preceding vendors as far as the initial vendor. In order to deal with this danger, the new Articles 560, 561 CC provide that the prescription of the rights of redress of a purchaser, when there is such a chain of sales, against the previous vendor starts from the point where the purchaser who bought the thing from the person exercising the right of redress was satisfied, or from when the judicial decision in favour of the purchaser in question (the next) becomes final and non-appealable.

353. The *crucial time* at which it will be judged whether or not there is an essential defect of the thing or whether or not there is a lack of an agreed quality is the time when the risk passes to the purchaser, that is, as a rule the time of delivery of the thing to the purchaser (*see* paragraph 356 *infra*).

Liability of the vendor is also precluded here if the *purchaser knew* upon the conclusion of the contract of the non-conformity with the contract, or if the non-conformity is due to materials which the purchaser supplied (Article 537 CC).

The *disputed* issue of whether the above rights of the purchaser *are concurrent with* the rights which he has in the event of *defects of consent*, for example, if he had been in error as to the defect of the thing (*see* paragraphs 107 et seq. *supra*) should be resolved in the affirmative. Each of these institutions serves its own ends, which are not fully covered by the ends of the others. The purchaser, then, will be able to choose those remedies which he believes best serve his purposes and to have recourse either to the provisions on error or to those on defects of the thing or lack of agreed quality. This is of practical importance, since the latter provisions provide for *a short prescription* (as a rule, as we have already said, five years for immovables and two years for movables from the delivery of the thing – Articles 554 et seq. CC: this short period does not apply in certain instances, chiefly if there is wilful conduct on the part of the vendor, or is extended if a time-limit for liability has been agreed).[236] If this brief prescription expires without action being taken,[237] there is no obstacle to the purchaser, as has been explained, having recourse to the provisions on error. However, this latter question too is among those in dispute.

C. *Exoneration Clauses*

354. The regulation of liability of the vendor as to legal defects (and more generally as to failure to fulfil his obligations), and as to defects of the thing is in principle non-mandatory law. The parties are free to regulate the consequences of their contract differently. We have seen, however, in the general section (paragraphs 160 et seq.) that exoneration clauses[238] (here: non-warranty clauses) are void when they preclude liability for intentional (wilful) conduct or gross negligence or, in certain cases, also for slight negligence (Article 332 CC).

III. Obligations of the Purchaser: Time of Undertaking of the Risk by the Purchaser

355. The principal *obligation* of the purchaser is to pay the purchase price (in money, as has been pointed out *supra* – paragraph 345). If no agreement to the contrary has been made, the rule of simultaneous fulfilment of performance and counter-performance applies (*see* Article 374 CC). If the purchaser does not conform with this obligation, he has the liability stipulated in the general provisions (*see* Part I, Chapter 6 *supra*). Secondary obligations of the purchaser may arise from the contract, from special provisions (see, for example, Article 529 CC on the obligation of payment of interest on a purchase price which has not been credited), or from good faith whose infringement in the majority of cases will constitute defective fulfilment of the obligation (*see* Part I, Chapter 6, §3 III).

356. The *risk* in the case of any chance destruction or deterioration of the thing (i.e., that not due to the fault of any party) is basically that of the owner (*casum sentit dominus*). In the law of sale, while this rule applies without any problem prior to the conclusion of the contract (the owner is the vendor) and after the performance of the vendor's obligations (the owner is the purchaser), a problem arises as to how far this rule should apply during the period when the thing is owed (is the object of an obligation), that is, after the conclusion of the contract and before its performance. The CC resolves this problem in Articles 522–524. The basic provision (Article 522 §1 CC) is that the purchaser undertakes this risk not from the moment when he becomes owner, but from the moment when the thing is *delivered* to him (what is meant is a specified thing – cf. paragraph 349 *supra*). This means that even if the vendor has

236. On the other hand, claims of the purchaser for legal defects are subject to the general twenty-year prescription (Art. 249 CC). *See* AP 525/1986, NoB 1987, 193.

237. This prescription is, of course, suspended and interrupted according to the general provisions (para. 329 *supra*). *See* on suspension AP 608/1988, NoB 1989, 1421.

238. *Mutatis mutandis,* what has been said about exoneration clauses also holds good for clauses whereby the liability is only limited.

temporarily reserved the ownership but has delivered the thing to the purchaser, the later bears the risk. The *ratio* of the regulation is that by delivery the thing has now entered into the sphere of influence of the purchaser, who is in a position to look after it, as he thinks fit, but also to use and enjoy it. If, on the other hand, the vendor has performed the obligation to transfer the ownership to the purchaser but not the obligation to deliver it (which is somewhat difficult, particularly in the case of movables, where the transfer of ownership occurs basically on delivery – Article 1034 CC, but *see also* Article 1035 CC), the risk remains, for the same reason, that of the vendor.[239]

357. In the more particular case of immovables whose ownership is transferred by transcription and not by delivery (paragraphs 49 et seq. *supra*), if transcription precedes delivery, the purchaser already bears the risk from transcription onwards (Article 522 §2 CC). This solution is in accord with the rule '*casum sentit dominus*', since on transcription (and without delivery) the purchaser becomes the owner, but it is not fully consistent with the *ratio* of Article 522 §1 CC. This is perhaps to be explained by the fact that in the case of immovables, delivery has, from the legal point of view, a somewhat secondary significance, while transcription plays the part which delivery basically does with movables, that is, to bring about transfer of ownership. But although delivery is not required for the transfer of ownership of an immovable (Article 1033 CC), it is needed for the completion of the fulfilment of the obligations of the vendor (Article 513 CC). In this sense, it is reasonable to regard delivery of immovables as crucial in the law of sale. The rule of Article 522 §1 CC that if delivery has taken place, the purchaser has thus already acquired the risk is in fact also retained in the case of immovables. The transfer of the risk on to him thus occurs with whichever of the two acts, delivery or transcription, comes first. It would be difficult to justify this favour shown towards the vendor *de lege ferenda*.

358. A consequence of the transfer of the risk to the purchaser is that if the thing is destroyed or deteriorates as a result of chance events after the time of the transfer of the risk, the purchaser owes the price in full. The vendor does not owe compensation or another thing. At the most, he owes the 'substitute' which he may have gained (*see* paragraph 264 *supra*). From the moment that the purchaser bears the risk, he also receives the benefits and bears the burdens of the thing (Article 525 CC). If the thing is transferred at the request of the purchaser to a place different from the place of performance, the risk is transferred to the purchaser from the point when the thing is handed over for dispatch (Article 524 CC).[240] The above regulations are dispositive law: the parties may agree differently.

---

239. *In the event of the delivery of the possession of a movable thing to the purchaser through constitutum possessorium (constructive possession) in such a way that the purchaser acquires the* ownership while the vendor retains physical power and control over the thing by virtue of a special contractual or similar relationship (Arts 977, 1034 CC), it could be accepted as consonant with the *ratio* of Art. 522 CC that the risk still remains with the vendor. In the end, however, the opposite view has come to be accepted. We could indeed take the view that in this case the vendor has completed the fulfilment of his obligations arising from the sale and there is no reason why the rule '*casum sentit dominus*' should not apply. Any different distribution of the risk which arises (if it arises) from the special contract which permits possession for the vendor naturally will prevail.

240. A special provision is contained in Art. 523 CC on the risk in conditional sale.

IV. Particular Kinds of Sale

359. Frequently in transactions the vendor retains or reserves the title, that is, he agrees not to fulfil immediately the first of his two principal obligations, that is, to transfer the title, but delivers the thing to the purchaser, thus fulfilling the second of his obligations. Retention of the title occurs until the purchaser pays the purchase price in full, that is, for the security of the claim of the vendor (e.g., in cases of sale by 'instalments'). This is the so-called pact of retention of title (*pactum reservati dominii*). In Article 532, the CC provides an interpretative rule in connection with this pact: that 'in doubt' it is reckoned that the transfer of ownership has been agreed on the suspensive condition of the payment of the purchase price and that the vendor, in the event of default of the purchaser, is entitled either to demand the purchase price or to rescind the contract, exercising his rights of ownership. If the purchase price is paid, the condition is fulfilled and the purchaser, already the possessor of the thing, acquires *ipso jure* the title. The parties are basically free to make a different agreement as to the consequences.

360. Another form of sale is '*sale on approval*' (or upon trial) (Articles 563 et seq. CC), in which it is deemed, again in the event of doubt, that is, provided that the parties have not determined otherwise, that the thing is sold on the (potestative) suspensive condition of the approval of the purchaser. The latter has the right to give his decision (approving or repudiating the sale) within the time-limit which has been set for him by the contract, or, otherwise, within a reasonable time-limit, set by the vendor. Also a particular kind of sale is '*repurchase*' (Articles 565 et seq. CC), in which the vendor has the right within a certain time-limit to take back the thing against a purchase price which has been agreed. The obligations of the purchaser as to the return of the thing and of the vendor as to the payment of the purchase price are generated when the vendor exercises his right of repurchase by his unilateral declaration to the purchaser.

Exchange has been dealt with above (paragraph 345).

On the strict liability of the producer for *defective products*, by way of exception from the principle of privity, *see* paragraphs 164, 196 *supra.*

§3. Contract for Work

I. Meaning: Kinds – Distinction from Related Contracts

361. In Articles 681–702, the CC regulates the *contract for work.* This is a *reciprocal* (*promissory*) contract by which the contractor undertakes the obligation to carry out a work and the other contracting party (master of the work, person ordering the work) is obliged to pay the agreed fee (Article 681 CC). The object of the performance of the contractor is the production of the agreed work. What is important in the performance is the result. It is chiefly in this that the contract for work differs from the *contract for service*, in which what is important is the performance of the services of the employee as such, regardless, basically, of the result. If, moreover, the contract for service is a contract for dependent service, as is usually the case (and in which case the rules of labour law are applied), there is the additional difference of the factor of dependence of the person who provides his services (dependence chiefly on the instructions of the recipient of the services), a factor which is basically absent in the contract for work. Furthermore, while the contract for service has as a rule a term, the contract for work is provisional: its term lasts until the completion of the work. In practical terms, however, it is often difficult to distinguish between the two contracts in view of the basic element which they have in common: their connection with the supply of work against a fee. The Greek courts have accepted on a number of occasions that contracts which have been described by the contracting parties as contracts for work were in reality contracts for dependent service (on the basis of their purpose and the actual will of the parties), in which case the rules governing that contract (e.g., regulations on social security of the employee), rules which the parties obviously wanted to avoid, should be implemented.

The difference between the contract for work and *sale* is clearer (*cf.* paragraph 343 *supra*). It becomes fluid if the contractor himself provides the materials which are required for the carrying out of the work (in which case we have, in the end, a transfer of the ownership of the materials by the contractor to the master of the work, as in the case of the performance of a sale contract). To cover this instance, the CC, in Article 683, has included an interpretative rule to the effect that in cases of doubt the provisions on sale are implemented, while, if the materials have been supplied by the master of the work, in cases of doubt, the provisions on the contract for work are applied. The issue, however, will be judged *in concreto* on the basis of the will of the parties and the purpose of the contract. It is possible that it will be decided that the contract is compound (*see* paragraphs 28 et seq. *supra*). The problem of the correlation of a contract for work and *lease of a thing* will be approached similarly (on the latter, *see* the next paragraph).

362. Cases of contracts for work, quoted indicatively: a contract of a client with a civil engineer or architect or construction company and, more generally, a building contract, a contract for the carrying out of public works, a contract for (sea, land or air) transport of things or persons, a contract for presentations (with a theatre, cinema, etc.), a publisher's contract,[241] etc. It should be noted that a contract for work is one of those contracts which is often combined with others in the form of a *compound contract* with the features of the contract for work predominating (something which in the last analysis will be distinguished *in concreto*).

II. Obligations of the Parties

A. The Contractor

363. A principal obligation of the contractor is to provide (as a result) the work which he has undertaken. He must, however, keep the master of the work informed, render accounts, use any materials which he may have been given by the master of

241. On this *see* the special law 2121/1993, as amended by Laws 2557/1997, 2819/2000, 3057/2002, and 3524/2007.

the work with care, return to him any materials left over, begin the work on time and continue with care the execution of the job, etc. If he delays the beginning of the work or its execution in such a way that timely completion of the work becomes impossible, the master of the work can rescind the contract (Article 686 CC). If the work manifests minor defects, the master may demand their correction or a reduction of the fee, while, if the defects are so substantive as to render the work useless or if qualities which have been agreed upon are lacking, the master may seek reversal of the contract (*see* paragraph 350 *supra* – Articles 688–689 CC). If there is fault on the part of the contractor for the defects, the master of the work may seek compensation for non-performance of the contract or a reduction in the fee (Article 690 CC). Provision is also made for a prescription of his claims shorter than the general one (six months for movables, ten years for immovables) and loss of the claims if the master of the work is himself at fault for deficiencies or if he approved it. Approval of the work is not, however, a ground for release of the contractor if the deficiencies could not have been discovered by a normal inspection when the work was delivered or if the contractor intentionally concealed them (Articles 690–693 CC). A differing regulation of the liability of the contractor by the contract is possible, since the above provisions are dispositive law.

B. The Master of the Work: Transfer of Risks to Him

364. A principal obligation of the master of the work is to pay the agreed fee to the contractor. If a fee has not been agreed, but the work is such as is usually carried out only for a fee, it is deemed that a fee has been tacitly agreed (Article 682 CC). Unless there is a different agreement (e.g., prepayment, payment by instalments, etc.), the fee is paid on delivery of the work. The contractor cannot demand an increase in the fee if he has guaranteed the accuracy of the budget for the work. Otherwise, an increase in the fee is possible, but in that case the master of the work has the right of rescission (Articles 696–697 CC).

As long as the work is in progress, the risk of chance destruction or deterioration is borne by the contractor (except for the materials which the master supplies). This risk is transferred to the master from delivery of the work or from the point where the master is in default as to acceptance of the work (*see* paragraphs 285 et seq. *supra* – Article 698 CC). This too is basically a case of dispositive law and thus the liability of the master of the work may be agreed differently. His liability stemming from the general provisions for breach through his fault of his main or collateral obligations (e.g., arising from good faith) and the corresponding rights of the contractor remain, as long as no agreement to the contrary has been made (*see also* Article 699 CC).

It should be noted also that it is possible for any workman whom the contractor employs to exercise the rights which the latter has against the master of the work directly against the master for the satisfaction of the claims for their wages (Article 702 CC – *see also* paragraph 193 *supra*).

III. Premature Dissolution of the Contract

365. The CC (Article 700) gives the master of the work the right of free termination by notice of the contract at any time up to the completion of the work, provided that he pays all the fee. He has, however, the right to subtract from the fee the expense which the contractor has saved by reason of the cancellation of the work or of a part of it or which he has intentionally omitted to benefit from. The contractor may rescind the contract only in the event of non-performance *by fault* of the obligations of the master of the work (e.g., his default as to payment by instalments if a time-limit for performance has been set), in accordance with the general provisions.

In the event of the decease of the contractor, the contract is dissolved if the parties had relied chiefly upon his person. Article 701 CC provides for partial payment of the fee in this case.

§4. Contracts of Lease

I. Meaning: Principal Obligations of the Parties

366. Unlike contracts which have as their aim the transfer of a right, and therefore the definitive alienation of the transferor from the right over the object of the contract and its definitive acquisition by the transferee (such as sale and exchange), contracts for *the ceding of the use* of a thing aim at a non-definitive movement of the object. For this reason, they provide for its return. The person ceding the use remains the owner of the thing, while the counterparty acquires power simply to use it or, possibly, to exploit it. Here we must include the giving of capital with an obligation to return it, since in this case what is happening in essence is the ceding of the use and enjoyment of capital. However, for technical and practical reasons, and chiefly because capital normally consists of money or other fungible things which do not have individuality, the ceding party does not retain ownership of the money or the other fungible things, but will receive on return other things in the same quantity and of the same quality. For this reason, here the ownership is transferred to the recipient, who has, however, the obligation to return it. It is to this category, finally, that the ceding of the use of non-material benefits belongs.

The most important contract in the category which we will examine in this paragraph is the *lease of a thing* (Articles 574–618), by which one of the contracting parties, the lessor, undertakes the obligation to cede to the other, the lessee, the use of a thing, the leased object (movable, or, more usually, immovable) and the lessee undertakes the obligation to pay the lessor the rent. Another contract in this category, which we shall review in summary form in §7 *infra*, is the *loan for use.*

Lease of a thing is a *promissory*, *reciprocal* contract and is a *continuous* one, since the ceding of the use of the thing occurs for one, specified or indefinite, period, to which the rent paid, usually periodically, corresponds. The lease is not in principle subject to a form, but is usually in writing. If, however, it is agreed for a period greater than nine years, it must be concluded with a notarial document and be transcribed in order to have force against any new owner of the thing leased (Article 618 CC).

367. The CC regulates in a general and abstract manner the leasing of anything, movable or immovable, for whatever purpose it is carried out. For this reason, this general regulation cannot answer to special social needs which are frequently served by leases, particularly of immovables (e.g., for their use as residences or as professional premises). This gap is filled by special laws, of which a brief account will be given at the end of the paragraph (III). Unlike these laws, which contain to a great extent jus cogens with a protective purpose, the general law of leases is to a greater degree dispositive law, which leaves the parties scope for the free shaping of their contractual relation.

368. The main *obligation of the lessor* is to cede the use of the leased thing and, moreover, the appropriate use – for the purpose agreed, as well as to see that the thing leased remains suitable throughout the term of the lease. In addition, the lessor bears all the public and private charges and taxes on the leased thing which relate to the title of ownership and are not incurred by its use. He also is chargeable with a part of the expenses, particularly with the necessary expenditure for the maintenance and security of the thing leased, and with wear and tear due to the passage of time and not the agreed use (Articles 590–592 CC). The provisions in this connection, however, constitute dispositive law. Collateral obligations of the lessor, which stem chiefly from good faith, are, for example, that of supplying instructions for use of the thing leased (e.g., a piece of machinery), of informing the lessee of any dangerous properties which it may have, etc. The chief *obligation of the lessee* is the payment of the rent, as a rule in instalments, by the agreed or customary time-limits. In case of doubt, the rent is paid in arrears for the period to which it applies (Article 595 CC). As a rule it consists of a monetary performance. However, rent in kind may also be agreed upon. In this latter case this will probably be a compound contract, in which the performance of the lessee will be judged in accordance with the provisions of the type of contract which it resembles (sale, lease of service, etc., depending upon what the lessee is supplying). Collateral obligations of the lessee, which, even if they have not been agreed upon, stem from good faith, are to treat the thing leased with care, to permit when necessary (e.g., for the carrying out of repair work) visits by the lessor to the thing leased, to inform the latter of defects or other problems in connection with the thing leased which have presented themselves (*see also* Article 589 CC), etc.

There is no obligation on the lessee not to sub-lease the thing leased as a rule. That is to say, as a rule, the lessee has a right to *sub-lease* (Article 593 CC). However, the opposite may be agreed upon, but, if the lessee does exercise his right to sub-lease, he is liable to the lessor for any fault of the sub-lessee.

II. Means of Protection of the Contracting Parties

369. A basic right of the lessee if the use of the leased thing or suitable use is not ceded is that of terminating the lease by notice, usually after a reasonable time-limit has first been set for the lessor to conform. Termination has an effect, unlike rescission, only for the future (*see* paragraph 239 *supra*). A right of termination is also given to the lessee by Article 588 CC if the use of the thing leased involves serious danger for his health or his household living with him on the leased premises. For legal defects and defects of the thing or lack of the agreed qualities,[242] the lessee has as alternatives the rights of reduction or non-payment of the rent, or of compensation, in accordance with the definitions of Articles 576 et seq. CC. It will be obvious that, if he prefers, he can exercise the claim for performance of the main obligation of the lessor.

A special regulation is provided for the instance of disposition of the thing leased by the lessor. The question is whether the new owner of the thing leased is obliged to respect the lease concluded by his predecessor in title or can evict the lessee, exercising the rights of ownership which he has over the leased thing. The principle of privity which governs promissory contracts would tend to support the latter view. Article 614 CC, however, basically introduces an exception to this principle, as has already been explained above (paragraph 194).

370. The lessor, in the event of breach of contract by the lessee, also has, apart from the remedies of general law, the right to terminate the lease in certain cases (e.g., in the event of improper use of the thing leased,[243] Article 594 CC, in that of arrears in the rent, Article 597,[244] etc.), in parallel with the right of compensation for any damage which has already occurred. Furthermore, for as long as the lessee retains the thing leased after the expiry of the lease, the lessor may demand as compensation the agreed rent,[245] as well as any further proven damage. For rents in arrears, the lessor has a *legal pledge* on those movables of the lessee and members of his family who are on the premises which are not subject to seizure. When the lease expires (either by the elapse of the agreed period or by termination by one of the contracting parties),[246] the lessor can require the return of the thing leased, either by virtue of his contractual rights (*see also* Article 599 CC) or by exercising his rights of ownership, to which the lessee can no longer oppose a plea of his own right of possession (Article 1095 CC). However, if the time of expiry of the lease elapses and the lessee continues to use the thing leased, while the lessor is aware of this and does not oppose it, the lease is deemed to have been renewed for an indefinite period (*tacit renewal* – Article 611 CC).

---

242. On these concepts, *see* paras 348 et seq. *supra* .

243. Following prior protest on the part of the lessor, or even without prior protest, if it has been so agreed. *See* AP 718/1989, EEN 1990, 186; AP 834/1984, NoB 1985, 764; AP 635/1984, NoB 1985, 605; AP 1254/2001, HellD 2002, 141; AP 1041/2006, HellD 2006, 1421.

244. The prevailing view requires delay *through fault.* Termination for *temporary* economic embarrassment of the lessee may be abusive (*see* Art. 281 CC, but also Art. 288 CC – *see also* AP 133/1999, HellD 1999,1080; Corfu Court of Appeals 91/1985, HellD 1985, 916).

245. This is the minimum compensation which, by way of exception, is determined in an abstract way by the law, regardless of the specific circumstances of actual damage, fault, etc. (*see* AP 629/1989, EEN 1990, 163 and paras 315 et seq. *supra. See also* AP 1221/2001, HellD 2002, 143; AP 1512/2000, Hell 2001, 1327).

246. This termination does not presuppose a special ground. It occurs when the contract has been agreed to be of indefinite term. However, notice must be given within a minimum time-limit before the date of termination. This time-limit is set in Art. 609 CC, depending on the term of the individual periods for which each instalment of rent must be paid. For example, if the rent on an immovable is paid each month, notice must be given at least 15 days in advance and has force for the end of the calendar month.

III. Particular Lease Relationships and Similar Contracts

A. Family Home

371. If the thing leased is used as premises for the principal residence of a family, if, that is, it is a 'family home', the CC, following the latest (1983) reform of family law, makes special provision. Thus, in Article 612 A it stipulates in this case, provided that the lessor has been informed of the use of the thing leased as a family home, that any termination on the part of the lessor is void if notice of this is not also given to the spouse of the lessee; in Article 612 §2 CC it is stipulated that if the lessee dies, the surviving spouse is entitled to continue the lease relationship on the premises which have served as a family home; in Article 1393 provision is made basically for the court to have the power, in the event of discontinuation of marital cohabitation, to grant to one of the spouses the use of the family home, regardless of who has the right of ownership or the right from the lease contract.[247]

B. Lease of a Residence

372. When the thing leased is used as the *main residence* of the lessee (and of his family), special legislation (the law in force up to the present is Law 1703/1987, which has been repeatedly amended on a number of matters – *see* paragraph 67 *supra*) provides for increased protection of the lessee. This protection consists chiefly in the provision of a minimum term for the lease (three years). In favour of the lessor, special grounds for termination of the lease are stipulated, in which case the above protection of the lessee is lifted (e.g., when the lessor intends to rebuild the property, to live in it himself, etc.).

C. Business and Professional Premises

373. A special law (PrD 34/1995, as amended mainly by Law 2741/1999) protects lessees who use the leased movable for the carrying on in it of occupational activity (trade, a clinic, doctor's surgery, lawyer's office, school, engineer's office, etc.). Protection of occupational leases consists in the provision that the lease has force for twelve years, even if a shorter or an indefinite term has been agreed upon, unless it is terminated by a later agreement, which is proven by a written form with a certain date; in provision for a contractual method of adjustment of the rent; in a provision that in the event of there being no agreement on the adjustment of the rent or of this agreement having been made dependent upon an invalid clause, the adjustment is made two years after the beginning of the contract and is set at a percentage per annum not lower than 6% of the objective value of the property, and 4% for its unimproved areas, and where this does not exist, of the market value of the property. Further adjustment is possible each year at 75% of the Consumer Price Index. The lessor is

247. The court has a similar power as to the right of ownership over the family home which is an item of inherited property when the inheritance is divided among the heirs and the surviving spouse is among these (Art. 1889 CC).

given the right to terminate the lease for him to use the premises himself or for rebuilding of the property, for the creation of parkland, etc.

D. Usufructuary Lease (Lease of Agricultural Land or Other Fruit-Bearing Thing and Lease of Land in Consideration of a Share in the Produce)

374. The CC, in Articles 619 et seq. provides for a special lease contract by which the lessor cedes the use *and the enjoyment of the 'fruits'* (*proceeds*) of the leased thing, particularly of agricultural land, under the rules of ordinary management. The rules provided are adjusted to the needs of such a lease – for example, a minimum term of the lease for agricultural land is set as four years; special obligations on the part of the lessee are stipulated of keeping the thing productive; sub-leasing is in principle prohibited; as a rule, payment of the rent at the end of the annual period of lease and the possibility of reduction of the rent in the event of a significant drop in income as a result of force majeure, etc. are provided for. In every other respect, the rules governing the normal lease of a thing hold good.

Finally, the CC also provides, in Article 641, for a contract for agricultural land in which it is agreed that the rent should be a percentage of the produce.

E. Leasing

375. The familiar trilateral relation of leasing is a compound contract, but what is predominant in the relation of the leasing company and the user of the goods with which that company supplies him are the characteristics of the lease. The latter, usually an enterprise which needs business equipment, prefers not to lay out capital for its purchase and 'leases' it from the leasing company, which ensures for it the use of the equipment for a long period by the leasing agreement. The capital for its purchase is made available by the leasing company, which itself buys in its own name from the supplier the equipment which the counterparty wants (indirect financing of the 'lessee'; it is for this reason that this form of leasing is termed 'financial leasing'). As a quid pro quo, the leasing company collects rent from the lessee which throughout the long-term of the leasing contract normally covers (together perhaps with any subsequent leasing contracts for the same thing) the capital which the company supplied and its profit. It will be obvious that by virtue of the freedom of contract, differing forms of leasing may be provided for, adjusted to the needs of the parties in each particular case.

In Greek law, financial leasing of a movable object, which is intended for the business or occupation of the lessee, is regulated by Law 1665/1986, as amended (*see* paragraph 67 *supra*); *inter alia*, a right of the lessee to purchase the thing or to renew the lease is stipulated. The leasing company must be a '*société anonyme*' specializing in this form of business and permission from the Bank of Greece is required for its setting up. The leasing contract is concluded in writing, is entered in a special register kept at the Athens Court of First Instance and must have a term of at least three years. Its registration entails a consequence which constitutes an exception to the principle of privity of promissory contracts: the rights of the lessee deriving from the contract 'are opposed against any third party'. Third parties cannot before the expiry of the financial leasing in any way acquire ownership or any other right in rem over the thing, even if they are in good faith.

This special law has left many issues without regulation; here general law or the special agreements of the parties will have force.

§5. Guarantee Contract (Suretyship, Personal Security) – Real Securities: Pledge – Mortgage

I. General Provisions on Guarantee

376. The accessory contract (i.e., a contract which presupposes another principal obligation and depends on the existence and validity of this principal obligation) by which one of the contracting parties (who is a third party as to the principal obligation) undertakes the obligation towards the other (who is the creditor of the principal obligation) that the performance which is owed to him (by the debtor of the principal debt, the 'principal debtor', who is not a party to the accessory contract) will be effected, is known as *guarantee* (*or suretyship or personal security*) and is regulated in Articles 847 et seq. CC. Its purpose is the reinforcement and securing of the principal obligation. If the principal debtor does not fulfil his obligation, the obligation to make payment is that of the guarantor. A guarantee is a promissory, unilaterally obliging contract. Only the guarantor undertakes an obligation. The contract is concluded in writing between the guarantor and the creditor of the principal obligation, but it suffices for the declaration of the guarantor to be in written form. Here the form is constitutive and not merely evidential; absence of the form thus entails nullity of the guarantee.[248]

377. A basic feature of the guarantee is its *accessory character.* Without a principal obligation (or if the principal obligation is void or is annulled), there is no valid guarantee (*see* Article 850 CC). If the parties wanted the liability of the 'guarantor' to be independent (without, that is, such dependence upon a principal obligation), this is not a case of a guarantee, but perhaps (and this is a matter of the interpretation of the contract) of another contract. A consequence of the accessory nature of the guarantee is that the guarantor is liable only for the extent which the principal obligation has at any time and is released when this obligation is extinguished (Articles 851, 864 CC). Only in one case is an exception accepted: according to subparagraph (b) of Article 850 CC 'a guarantee shall be valid if it is given in respect of a debt contracted by a person lacking legal capacity or enjoying only limited capacity to enter into contracts if the guarantor gave his guarantee for this person in the knowledge of his incapacity'.

378. For the debt of the guarantor to the creditor, another person can give a guarantee by contract to the creditor (*guarantee for a guarantee*). This is a special instance of a guarantee, as to which, naturally, the rules of guarantee are applied. Also, by virtue of the freedom of contract, a person (the '*counter-guarantor*') can guarantee to the guarantor that the principal debtor will fulfil his obligations to the creditor or to

248. The lack of the document is supplied if the guarantor fulfils the obligation (*see* para. 79 *supra*).

the guarantor himself (i.e., cover of the recourse claim of the guarantor), in which case the rules governing guarantees are again, mutatis mutandis, implemented. The letter of guarantee is a familiar feature of banking business. This is granted by banks to creditors of their clients (by concluding, that is, a 'guarantee' contract with them for the benefit of their client – the principal debtor) and by it they usually undertake unreservedly the obligation to pay the creditor on simple notice from him alone, that is, without advancing any plea arising from the relation of the principal debtor and the creditor. This gives some degree of independence to the letter of guarantee from the principal obligation and lessens its accessory character. That is to say, this is a sui generis 'guarantee' (permissible by virtue of the freedom of contract – cf. also abstract promise of a debt, paragraphs 140 et seq. *supra*), in which the provisions on guarantees are implemented, except for those which are not compatible with the unreserved declaration of the bank.[249]

II. The Relations of the Parties to the Guarantee

379. In the relations *between the principal debtor and the creditor* nothing changes. The principal debtor continues to be liable as before, and has the same possible pleas against the creditor, who retains the same rights against the principal debtor, now reinforced by the guarantee.

In *the relations between the guarantor and the creditor*, the rule of Article 853 CC is fundamental. According to this, the guarantor may advance 'as against the creditor pleas in defence which are not personal to the principal debtor, even if the latter has desisted from such pleas subsequent to the issue of the guarantee'. The obligation of the guarantor is, however, *subsidiary*, that is, the guarantor is obliged in the second place, after the debtor. Thus he can refuse to make payment of the debt 'until the creditor has carried out judicial execution on the property of the debtor and this has proven fruitless' (Article 855 CC – 'defence of prior execution' against the principal debtor – *beneficium excussionis*). This rule is dispositive law. It may be agreed that the creditor is not obliged to take action first against the principal debtor. The same applies in certain exceptional instances, for example, if the taking of legal steps against the principal debtor has become particularly difficult because of a change in his address, etc.

380. The *relations between the guarantor and the principal debtor* are governed basically by the internal relationship between them, which contains the *causa*, that is, here, the explanation of why the guarantor is supplying the guarantee. This relationship may be a contract, either gratuitous (liberality of the guarantor towards the principal debtor) or reciprocal, of a provisional or a standing nature. However, the force of the guarantee does not depend upon the existence or the validity of the contract between the principal debtor and the guarantor. It will be decided on the basis of the internal relation between these persons whether the guarantor, having satisfied the creditor, can take action against the principal debtor, seeking to recover what he has paid (right of recourse). If the relationship is a gratuitous one, there will be no right of recourse.

249. *See* AP 653/1973, NoB 1974, 50; AP 635/1988, HellD 1989, 966; AP 467/1992, HellD 1993, 1074; Athens Court of Appeals 2783/1966, EEmbD 1967, 61.

Otherwise, the answer will be affirmative, even if there was no contract between them. In the latter case, the right of recourse will be based on the management of another's affairs, *negotiorum gestio* (Articles 730 et seq. CC) or on the unjust enrichment of the principal debtor (Articles 904 et seq. CC). The existence of relations which justify recourse must be proven by the guarantor. If the latter has a right of recourse, 'he shall be subrogated to the rights of the creditor' (Article 858 CC). This subrogation is equivalent to assignment by operation of law (*cessio legis*) of the rights of the creditor who has been satisfied against the principal debtor to the guarantor, accompanied by any securities for these (*see* Article 458 CC). If, however, the guarantor, in satisfying the creditor, omitted to oppose to him well-grounded pleas of the principal debtor of which he was aware or should have been aware, he loses the right of recourse.

Finally, in the relations between *more than one guarantor*, the rule of dispositive law (Article 854 CC) applies, that the co-guarantors are liable jointly and severally (*see* paragraph 191 *supra in fine*). A co-guarantor who has satisfied the creditor has recourse against the other guarantors to the extent determined by the relations between them. If nothing to the contrary emerges from these relations, distribution among the co-guarantors will be in equal proportions (Articles 860 and 487 CC).

III. Pledge, Mortgage

381. A guarantee is a form of security granted to the creditor to reinforce his claim, that is, to ensure his satisfaction more effectively. It is a personal security, since another person (other than the debtor), the guarantor, undertakes, additionally, the liability for the fulfilment of the performance. The creditor has a right in personam against the guarantor. Apart from the guarantee, there are real securities which give to the creditor a right in rem. These are a *pledge* on movables and a *mortgage* on immovables, which are regulated outside the law of obligations, that is, in the law of real rights of the CC. The pledge (Articles 1209 et seq. CC) is provided by the owner of a movable thing (whether he is the debtor or a third party) by a contract on his part with the creditor (contract in rem), which is subject to a form (a notarial document or private document bearing an officially certified date) and by delivery of the movable thing to the creditor or a third party (the pledge-custodian). A mortgage (Articles 1257 et seq. CC) is provided to the creditor by the owner of an immovable (whether the debtor or a third party) by a unilateral notarial juridical act (in rem), which is entered in the public mortgage registers.[250] Ownership is retained by this person supplying the pledge or mortgage. The pledgee or mortgage creditor has a limited real right over the thing belonging to another (*see* paragraphs 19 et seq. *supra*), which gives him the power of privileged (prior in relation to other creditors) satisfaction from the thing, if need be, by compulsory sale (by public auction, etc.) of the thing on the terms of the law.

A special law, 2844/2000 ('Contracts as to movables or claims subject to publication and other contracts for the provision of security'), answering to the above

250. Apart from a mortgage which is given by the private will of the owner of the mortgaged immovable, a right of registration of a mortgage on immovables of the debtor may be given by the law (e.g., for taxes in arrears) or by a non-appealable court decision.

need for fuller security of creditors (who receive movables, claims, or other rights, etc. as an object of security), and in the interests of expanding the credit rating of debtors (enterprises, professionals), has introduced a system of publication, particularly of contracts providing security on movables, claims, or other rights by their registration in public books to be kept at pledge registries (and provisionally at mortgage registries or land register offices – Articles 3 and 19 of the law).

In the particular case of claims, publication by entry in public registers is provided for (Article 11) where the claims are business claims (of enterprises or professionals against clients, but not against consumers) and concerns both their pledge and their assignment (fiduciary or otherwise). Pledge and assignment must be concluded in writing. In addition, the debtor must be notified by the assignee or pledge-holder creditor of the registration in public books. In every other respect, the provisions of the CC are implemented (Article 14 §2). A basic consequence and advantage of registration of the assignment (or pledge) of a claim (including a future claim or a group of claims – Article 12) in public books is the now certain solution of the problem of priority in the event of a conflict of the rights of more than one creditor. The registration, that is to say, is not a prerequisite for the validity of the assignment or pledge (which will be valid without it), but a criterion for determining priority among many parties entitled.

The above mentioned publicity is not compulsory for business claims. If the parties prefer discretion to transparency, because they consider that their interests are better served in this way, they can avoid registration in public books and follow the system of the CC, that is, of confining themselves to give notice to the debtor.

§6. Contract of Civil Partnership

382. Partnership is a contract by which the (two or more) contracting parties have as their aim the pursuit of a common purpose. More specifically, the contracting parties undertake mutually, as a union of persons, the obligation to pursue a common aim, particularly an economic, but also possibly ideological, public benefit, charitable, etc. aim by common contributions. The CC regulates this contract in Articles 741–784. The main characteristic of the partnership contract, the community of the aim and interests of the partners, distinguishes it from other contracts, in which the contracting parties usually pursue contrary interests, without this meaning that they must be regarded as opponents (*see* paragraph 53 *supra*).

In present-day business life, commercial companies (personal and capital-based) which are established by a founding partnership contract for the pursuit of commercial aims have become very widespread. There are special rules for such companies in commercial law and special laws.[251] The regulation of the CC applies to civil law partnerships, but can be implemented by way of supplementation in the case of commercial companies (at least personal companies) to the extent that the special provisions on these leave gaps.

251. As for the capital-based companies *see* codified Law 2190/1920 (for joint-stock companies), as amended; Law 3190/1955 (for limited-liability companies), as amended and as for the personal companies and the new partnership form, the private capital-based company, *see* Law 4072/2012.

383. A civil law partnership does not have in principle a legal personality. Whatever is acquired for the partnership belongs to all the partners in proportion to the share of each in the partnership (Article 758, §1). This partnership may, however, acquire a legal personality if it pursues an economic aim and provided that the conditions of publication which the law lays down for this purpose in the case of joint and several (personal, commercial) partnerships (Article 784 CC) are observed. In this case, the property of the partnership belongs to the legal person of the partnership and not directly to the partners. The partnership concludes contracts and is itself liable with its property – and not the partners with theirs.

384. The contributions of the partners (which may consist also in the provision of their own services) are not required to be equal. If, however, some other proportion of their participation is not agreed upon, the partners are obliged to make equal contributions. The partnership's agreement determines its manner of management. If a different agreement is not reached, the management of the partnership's affairs belongs to all the partners together (Article 748 CC). Moreover, its agreement also lays down the proportion of participation of the partners in the partnership's profits and losses. If there is no agreement to the contrary, the partners participate in the profits and losses in equal shares, regardless of their contribution. However, an agreement whereby one of the partners is excluded from the profits or released from the losses is void.[252] Only an agreement whereby a partner who contributes only his work will not share in the losses is valid (Articles 763–764 CC).

385. A partnership is dissolved (Articles 765 et seq. CC) if the time for which it was set up has elapsed or before the completion of this period if there are serious grounds and termination notice is given by a partner for this reason. A partnership which has been set up for an indefinite period can be dissolved at any time by termination notice by any of the partners. Limitations exist as to termination at an 'inappropriate' time. The property of a partnership which has been dissolved, at the stage of liquidation and after the payment of debts and rendering of contributions, is distributed among the partners in the proportion of the share which each has in the profits. If the debts of the partnership are in excess of its property, the partners are liable for the difference in the proportion of their participation in the losses (Articles 782–783 CC).

§7. Other Nominate Contracts and Unilateral Acts

I. Loan: Loan for Use

386. The contract for a loan is regulated in Articles 806 et seq. CC. This is a *delivery* contract of loan (*see* paragraph 30 *supra*) in which the obligation which is generated is that of the borrower. This obligation arises on the giving of the loan (which means transfer *as to ownership* of money or other fungible things) and consists in the liability of the borrower to return other things of the same quantity and quality. By

252. The nullity is relative. It may be invoked only by the partner who is precluded or released (Art. 764, para. 1, subpara. 2). By corrective interpretation of this provision the nullity caused by the exoneration from losses may be invoked by the other partners.

virtue of the freedom of contract, an obligation may, of course, be generated before the giving of the loan: more specifically, an obligation of the lender to make the loan. Until the loan is given, however, no obligation on the borrower arises.

If the borrower falls into default as to the return of the loan, the *right to compensation* of the creditor for default (*see* paragraphs 272, 316 *supra*) is determined in an abstract manner and consists only in legal or agreed interest. An agreement on further compensation is void.

If a *time for the return* of the loan has not been agreed, it is returned on the elapse of a month from the termination notice of the lender or the borrower. If it is without interest, the borrower may return it without termination notice. On discount interest, *see* paragraph 225 *supra.* In the case of *monetary debts*, the principal of nominalism applies. On protection in the event of a major devaluation of the currency, *see* paragraph 230 *supra.*

387. An interest-free loan is *a unilaterally obliging contract.* Corresponding to any obligation undertaken on the part of the lender to give the loan is, of course, an obligation of the recipient to return it. The two obligations, however, do not co-exist, in such a way that we would have a reciprocal contract. The second is generated, as we have said, on the giving of the loan, that is, when the first is fulfilled (and therefore extinguished). A *loan at interest* is, however, a *reciprocal contract*, since, over and above the obligations of giving and returning, there is (after the loan is given) the obligation of the lender to allow the borrower the use of the capital for a certain period and, against this, the obligation of the borrower to pay interest, which is the quid pro quo for the use of the capital (in the case of an interest-free loan, the use is free). The interdependence of these two performances which are exchanged (use of capital – interest) explains the application to them of the rules of reciprocal contracts (e.g., Article 383 CC, *see* paragraphs 275 et seq. *supra*).

Interest can be divided into legal interest (fixed by law) and interest by agreement. The most important instance of legal interest is default interest. The upper limit of agreed interest and legal interest are determined by law and today, through delegation of the law, by the Bank of Greece. An agreement on higher interest is void as to the excess (Article 294 CC). The greater is inflation, the greater is the percentage of interest set by the Bank of Greece. Compound interest (interest on interest) is subject to restrictions (*see* Article 296 CC).

388. The contract for a loan for use (*commodatum* – Articles 810 et seq. CC) is also a delivery contract (*see* paragraph 30 *supra*) by which the lender cedes to the borrower the use of a thing (not as to ownership, as in the case of a loan) *without a reward* and the latter is obliged to return it on the expiry of the contract. This is a gratuitous contract, and for this reason the lender is liable only for wilful conduct and gross negligence. If a term has not been set for the contract, the loan for use expires as soon as the use of the thing or the period within which the borrower could make use of it ends. The borrower does not have a right to cede the use of the thing to a third party without the permission of the lender. On the right of the lender to take action directly against the third party in the event of the ceding of use to him, *see* paragraph 193 *supra.*

II. Special Forms of Bailment (Deposit: Sequestration)

389. Greek law does not know bailment as a single concept. In Anglo-Saxon law, where this institution has been developed more, the essence of the obligation which flows from bailment is regarded as being possession. A modern view is that 'a bailment comes into being whenever one person is knowingly and willingly in possession of goods which belong to another'.[253] Normally, the bailor is the owner of the goods which he delivers by virtue of a contract to the bailee for use, custody, carrying, performance of other services, with or without a reward, for security of claims of the bailor, etc. It will be obvious that bailment also covers other contractual obligations – or overlaps with them – (or even with non-contractual ones) which are examined at other points of this monograph. Here we shall deal with two instances which are regulated in the CC and which have not been examined so far: *deposit*, which, when it is for reward, is regarded as 'in many ways the classic form of bailment',[254] and *sequestration*, which is an institution related to deposit, or, when it is based on a contract, with a particular form of deposit. The major practical importance of bailment becomes clear, of course, if we take into account every other contractual, quasi-contractual and tortual obligation, nominate or possible by virtue of the freedom of contract, which falls within the above definition of it. The separate treatment of these other forms of obligations is due to the fact that each of them is subject, depending upon its nature, to different special rules. All the obligations which are included in bailment, and together with them every other contractual obligation, are subject to common legal treatment in the general rules of the law of contracts which we have examined in Part I, many of which, moreover, have force for every (contractual or non-contractual) obligation.

390. The contract for *deposit* takes shape in the CC (Articles 822 et seq.) also as a delivery contract (*see* paragraph 30 *supra*). By the contract, the depositary takes delivery from the depositor of a movable thing for safekeeping, with the obligation to render it when required. A reward may be agreed upon, or this may be a gratuitous contract. In the latter case, the depositary is liable only for *diligentia quam in suis* (*see* paragraph 258 *supra*), in the former, for any fault. The depositary does not have a right, without the permission of the depositor, to deposit the thing with a third party. An exception is if he was compelled by circumstances or further deposit is customary. On the right of the depositor to take action against this third party, *see* paragraph 193 *supra.* The depositor may seek the return of the thing at any time. He must, however, pay to the depositary whatever he has spent on safekeeping. By way of supplementation, the rules of general law of obligations are naturally implemented. If money or other fungible things have been deposited and the depositary has the power to use them, the deposit is deemed to be '*irregular*' (Article 830 CC), that is, it is equivalent to a loan: the depositary acquires ownership and is obliged to return (at whatever time this is required by the depositor) other money or fungible things of the same quantity and quality.

391. Sequestration (Articles 831 et seq. CC) exists when two or more persons deliver to a third, the sequestrator, a movable or immovable for the safeguarding of

253. *See* N. Palmer, Bailment, 1979, p. 2.

254. *See* N. Palmer, *supra* n. 185, at p. 434.

their contested or uncertain rights over it. The sequestrator has the obligation to render it only with the consent of all of them or by a court decision. If the carrying out of acts of administration by the sequestrator is needed, he will function as mandatary (*see* paragraph 334 *supra*). A sequestrator of an immovable is appointed by the court also where an immovable is owed to a person who is in creditor's default (Articles 359 et seq. CC – *see* paragraph 287 *supra*).

III. Donation

392. Donation (Articles 496 et seq. CC) is made by a contract, that is, acceptance by the donee is also required. A unilateral juridical act on the part of the donor does not bind him. A basic conceptual element in donation is that the promise of performance of the donor is without any quid pro quo. The donor is alienated from the performance proferred. It is at this point that it differs from the contract for a loan for use, in which the lender is deprived only temporarily of the use of the object of the contract.

Donation is the chief gratuitous juridical act. Because of his intention that this should be gratuitous, the donor has reduced liability. He is liable, that is, only for wilful conduct and gross negligence, does not owe default interest and has the right to refuse the fulfilment of the donation if this would endanger his own maintenance and that of his close relatives. As far as the donee is concerned, the gratuitous cause is a *causa minor*, on which, *see* paragraph 31 *supra.*

Donation is subject to the form of a notarial document. The form here is constitutive, that is, non-observance of it entails nullity of the donation. However, fulfilment of the donation in spite of this (delivery of the thing to the donee) validates the donation.

A donation may be revoked by the donor particularly if it has been coupled with a charge imposed upon the donee and the latter omits by his fault to comply with this charge or if the donee proves ungrateful. Revocation is a unilateral juridical act of the donor which brings about extinction of his obligation or gives him, if he has already effected it, a claim for recovery of the performance in accordance with the provisions on unjust enrichment. Revocation is precluded if, *inter alia*, the donation was made from a special moral duty or for reasons of propriety.

IV. Aleatory Contracts (Life Annuity: Games, Wagers)

393. On the meaning of aleatory contracts, *see* paragraph 31 *supra.* The insurance contract is an object of a special branch of commercial law. The CC has a special regulation on *life annuities* (Articles 840–843) and on *games and wagers* (Articles 844–846). The former is the contract whereby the obligation is undertaken for a life-long provision of money or other fungible things in periodical instalments. It may also be constituted for the whole of the life of the holder of the right or of the obligor or of a third party. The contract is concluded by a notarial document (constitutive form, absence of which entails nullity of the contract). On the other hand, an agreement from a game or wager does not give rise to an enforceable claim, but if the debt from a game or wager is paid voluntarily and without any fraud or other trickery on the part of the person who won, its recovery cannot be sought. In other words, this is a typical instance of natural obligation (*see* paragraph 15 *supra*). There is, however, apart from the CC, special legislation which forbids some games of chance entirely and permits others (sometimes with the permission of the authorities). The latter give rise to an enforceable obligation (e.g., football pools, called in Greece 'Pro-Po'). An enforceable obligation can also be generated by a lottery, providing its setting up has been approved by law (Article 846 CC).

V. Compromise

394. The *compromise* contract is provided for in Articles 871–872 CC. It presupposes, first of all, the pre-existence of a legal relation between the contracting parties; second, the existence of contestation or uncertainty as to this legal relation or as to certain points of it; and, third, mutual concessions of the parties which are agreed upon (by the compromise contract) in order to resolve the contestation or uncertainty. Compromise is not in principle subject to a form, unless in the particular instance this is established from a special provision (e.g., it concerns the transfer of an immovable, Article 369 CC). Compromise, which is a promissory and reciprocal contract (since the concession of one of the parties – which constitutes his performance – corresponds to the concession of the other), creates a new legal cause for the retention of the performances of the original (contested) legal relation which remain after the concessions, but also a legal cause for the loss of the performances to the extent that they constitute the concessions.

Naturally, the new legal relation which is created by compromise is subject, apart from the general grounds of nullity of every contract (e.g., by reason of the lack of capacity of the parties or because of profiteering within the meaning of Article 179 CC, etc.), to annulment by reason of error, fraud or duress, also in accordance with the general provisions. The possibility of annulment, however, is recognized particularly in the instance of Article 872 CC. This article provides that: 'A compromise may be annulled if the facts which, according to the contents of the contract, had constituted the foundation of the compromise are not true and the contestation or uncertainty would not have arisen if the parties had been aware of the true situation.' This is in essence error on motivation, which as a rule does not justify annulment (*see* Article 143 CC and paragraphs 113 et seq. *supra*), which, however, is common error of both of the contracting parties. In the latter case, and where the error concerns a fundamental point of the contract, the possibility of annulment by virtue of the general clauses is now widely maintained (*see* paragraph 127 *supra*). Here a condition, in reality, for annulment is that the error should concern facts which constituted the basis of the compromise (as to which there was no contestation or uncertainty).[255] Regardless of

255. The Court of Cassation of *Areios Pagos* has also accepted that the 'basis' of compromise mentioned in Art. 872 CC, is a form of the underlying basis of the transaction (*see* Art. 388 CC and AP 411/1973, NoB 1973, 1301; AP 1784/2001, HellD 2002, 1400; Athens Court of Appeals 10357/1988, HellD 1991, 1678). This does not mean, of course, that the two concepts in Arts 388 and 872 CC coincide completely.

the general possibilities, the special provision of Article 872 CC removes any doubt and provides in this instance the right of annulment. The consequences of the annulment of the compromise by virtue of Article 872 CC are those which are also provided for other instances of annulment of a juridical act (*see* paragraphs 148 et seq., 155 *supra*).

Compromise may also be reached before the court (*judicial compromise*) provided that the conditions of substantive law (stipulated in the CC) are fulfilled. A procedural consequence is the *ipso jure* termination of the proceedings (Article 293, paragraph 1 CCPr).

VI. Delegation (Instrument Ordering Payment): Bearer Bonds

395. By '*delegation*', 'an instrument is handed to the delegated payee whereby the latter is authorized to collect in his own name from a delegated payer a payment in money or other fungible things and the delegating party is authorized to effect payment to the payee on the account of the delegating party'. Thus delegation takes the form of a trilateral relationship which has as its purpose to serve the subjacent obligations of the parties (between the delegating party and the payee and between the delegating party and the delegated payer) by direct payment by the delegated payer to the payee, without, that is, it being necessary for performances to be effected between the parties of the subjacent relationships. Delegation, which is a descendant of the simpler Roman *delegatio*, is of little practical importance, since special forms of securities (which have been given shape by international conventions and special laws), more specifically, the bill of exchange and the cheque (which constitute an object of a special branch of commercial law), have more or less replaced delegation in business transactions today.

The CC also includes provisions (Articles 888 et seq.) on *bearer bonds* (anonymous bonds). By a bearer bond is meant a document by which the person which signs it promises a performance to the bearer of the document. This is a security which has similarities with the 'bill to order' – which is of greater practical application. For that reason, its treatment belongs more to the field of commercial law, where the various theories as to the legal nature of the bearer bond as a contract or as a unilateral juridical act are examined.

VII. Brokerage

396. The brokerage contract, related to the mandate contract, but with a reward, is regulated in a self-contained fashion in the CC (Articles 703–708). By this contract, the broker (who corresponds to the mandatary), promises to the other contracting party (the 'mandator') mediation or the notification of an opportunity for the conclusion of a contract which is of interest to the latter, who, on his part promises a fee to the broker. The payment of the fee is compulsory only if the contract is actually concluded as a consequence of the mediation or notification of the broker. If only a promise to contract has been concluded, half the fee is owed. The rules of the CC on brokerage are basically dispositive law. It is, however, stipulated as mandatory law, *inter alia*, that if the agreed fee of the broker is 'disproportionately large', it is reduced by the court on the petition of the debtor to the appropriate extent (Article 707 CC). On certain categories of brokerage there are special laws.

VIII. Public Announcement of Reward

397. The *announcement of reward* is not, precisely speaking, a contract, but one of the few instances of a unilateral juridical act which are recognized by the CC as sources of the creation of obligations. It is regulated in Articles 709–712 CC. This is the (unilateral) juridical act by which a person announces publicly a reward for the carrying out of an act, particularly for the achievement of a result. By this juridical act, the person offering the reward undertakes the obligation to make a payment to the person who carries out the act or achieves the result, even if the latter acted without reference to the announcement. Until the act is carried out or the result achieved, the offerer may revoke his promise by the same (or a similar) method which he used for the announcement. If the act is carried out independently by more than one person, the reward belongs to the first to carry it out, or, in the event of it being carried out simultaneously by more than one person, to all of them in equal share. If more than one person has contributed to the achievement of the result, each is entitled to a part of the reward, in proportion to their contribution.

Here too the provisions of the CC are basically dispositive law.

IX. Responsibility of Innkeepers

398. To conclude, the CC has special provisions (Articles 834–839) on the responsibility of 'innkeepers' (and of those who engage in occupations of an equivalent nature and provide accommodation to persons or things in any form, such as hostels, clinics, passenger vessels, etc.) from the contract with their clients. The following are basic rules: (a) that the innkeeper is liable for any damage, destruction or removal of things which the clients have brought to the 'inn', unless the damage is due to the client himself (or a person visiting or escorting him or in his employment) or to the peculiar nature of the thing or to force majeure; (b) that any unilateral notice on the part of the innkeeper which precludes or limits his liability is void. Furthermore, the innkeeper has a legal pledge on the things which the client has brought to the inn for his claims arising from the client's stay there and from related performances.

Chapter 2. The So-Called 'Quasi-Contracts'

399. It has been explained above (paragraph 45) that the so-called quasi-contracts (*negotiorum gestio* – unjust enrichment – money paid but not due) do not constitute a special single category of obligations. These are non-contractual obligations which stem from the law. In its special law of obligation, the CC provides for and specially regulates the following non-contractual obligations (in the order in which it sets them out): negotiorum gestio (Articles 730–740); joint rights (community of rights) (Articles 785–805); exhibition of a thing (Articles 901–903); unjust enrichment (Articles 904–913); delicts (Articles 914–938); and creditors' defrauding (Articles 939–946).

These *obligations do n*ot belong to the subject-matter of the law of contracts. It is only incidentally and in relation to other issues that reference has been made to the meaning and basic features of some of these (torts, paragraphs 39 et seq. *supra;* creditors' defrauding, paragraphs 220 et seq. *supra*; exhibition of a thing, paragraph 82 *supra*). On joint rights, we shall confine ourselves to noting that the law regulates, on the one hand, obligations which stem from the law between persons to whom a right belongs jointly (obligations concerning the use of the thing, its management, the participation in the proceeds and expenses, etc.), and, on the other, the possibility of the dissolution of the community of rights and its division amongst the participants. In this chapter we shall examine unjust enrichment and negotiorum gestio, which are more closely related to the law of contracts and which in other legal systems are termed 'quasi-contracts'. The CC does not contain a special regulation of the obligation from payments which were not due (*condictio indebiti*), since it includes this case within the institution of unjust enrichment.

§1. Unjust Enrichment

I. Basic Characteristics of the Obligation

A. General

400. After contractual obligations and delictual obligations, third in importance as a source of obligations is unjust[256] enrichment. These are obligations which are produced, as are delictual ones, directly by the law; they are not based, that is to say, on private autonomy. The reason for their creation is the fact that a person has been enriched at the expense of another and his enrichment is not regarded by the law as justified. The consequence is that the law imposes on the recipient (and possessor) of the enrichment (the debtor from unjust enrichment) the obligation to return it to the party thus impoverished (the creditor from unjust enrichment). More specifically, Article 904, paragraph 1, subparagraph 1 lays down that: 'A person enriched without a lawful cause from the patrimonium or to the detriment of another person is obliged

256. The exact translation of the Greek would be 'unjustified'. In the English language, the term 'unjust enrichment' has prevailed.

to restitute the benefit.' By the concept of 'lawful cause' (legal cause, just cause), the CC is rendering terminologically the Roman 'justa causa', but conceptually something more substantive (*see* paragraphs 406 et seq. *infra*).

Such enrichment which must be returned is brought about, for example, in cases of payment of a non-existent debt, payment in error of another person's debt, frustration of the receipt of a quid pro quo for a performance which has been effected, receipt of a performance by virtue of a contract which has been annulled or overturned in some other way, disposal or use or consumption of a thing or right belonging to another, expenses for the benefit of a thing belonging to another, benefits from an illegal or immoral contract or from a tort (where the conditions for delictual liability may not be met, for example, fault), etc. The institution of unjust enrichment, which is regulated in Articles 904–913 CC, presupposes a shifting of property (even more generally, an increase in the property of one person at the expense of somebody else) which public policy regards as unjustified, and it has as its purpose the correction of this unjustified change in property and the setting aside of the injustice which this involves, in accordance with the mandate of commutative justice (*justitia commutativa*).

The shifting of property, though unjustified, normally means that the recipient has already acquired a right over the object which has been transferred, for example, since the transfer occurred *by virtue of an abstract contract*, so that the acquisition of the right is valid, as being independent of its (non-existent or defective) cause (see, for example, paragraphs 51, 141, etc. *supra*). The recipient has the obligational liability to return the right as being unjust. The institution, however, is not exhausted in the correction or, even, the alleviation of the consequences of the abstract nature of a contract. The existence of these contracts simply broadens the field of implementation of the institution, by which also cases with no connection with abstraction are governed (e.g., enrichment by material acts, such as by encroachment into the lawful sphere of another, from expenses in favour of the estate of another, cases of '*causa data, causa non secuta*' (*see* paragraph 403 *infra*), enrichment which consists in simple possession, etc.).

B. *Independence of the Obligation*

401. The claim arising from unjust enrichment stems directly from the law and is *self-contained as regards contractual obligations* (which stem from private autonomy), even though the enrichment was brought about by a contract and became unjust and returnable afterwards because the contract, for example, was overturned. The function of the claim from unjust enrichment and the ultimate objective are, according to the law in force, *the removal of the enrichment* (from the person enriched in favour of the person at whose expense it occurred) and not simply *reverse settlement* of a contractual obligation by the restitution of a performance received to the giver in the framework of the contract between them whose normal fulfilment has been frustrated. For this reason, when the starting-point of the unjust enrichment was a contract, the return of the enrichment will usually occur, but not necessarily between the contracting parties themselves. The relation of obligation from unjust enrichment is not a contractual one. It links the party enriched and the injured party. The subjects of this new obligational relationship (based on the law – Article 904 CC – and not on the contract), on the one hand, and the contracting parties, on the other, do not always coincide (*see* on trilateral relations, paragraphs 408 et seq. *infra*).

Furthermore, the mention of the damage of the plaintiff in Article 904, paragraph 1, subparagraph 1 should not mislead us into thinking that what we have here is an action for compensation, as, for example, in the case of *delictual liability* (Article 914 CC). The liability of the party enriched consists in the return of his enrichment and not the making good of the damage of the plaintiff. The person enriched must return his enrichment, but not become poorer than he was before the enrichment. The plaintiff will seek not the restitution of all the damage, but the enrichment of the defendant to the extent that it was acquired to his detriment. The obligations arising from Article 904 CC, on the one hand, and Article 914 CC, on the other, have a different object, even if they stem from the same event or if in the specific instance enrichment and compensation have to coincide. If the plaintiff can ground his claim on both provisions, there will be concurrence of rules (*see also*, however, paragraph 404 *infra*).

C. Nature of the Claim

402. The relationship from unjust enrichment is an obligation in personam (i.e., it creates obligations, not real rights), but less personal than contractual obligation. This is because the person of the debtor in Article 904 CC, which is determined on the criterion of the possession of the enrichment, may change. Loss of the enrichment in principle releases the debtor (Article 909 CC) and the appearance of the enrichment in the hands of another makes the latter now the debtor from unjust enrichment, whether he acquires the enrichment from a gratuitous cause (Article 913 CC) or not (provided, of course, that in acquisition from an onerous cause, by coincidence the new possessor of the enrichment cannot show *justa causa* for retaining it which is, of course, not usual – Article 904 CC). Thus the person of the debtor is not determined from the start, as is the case with contracts. His connection with the possession of the enrichment is similar to the connection of the person of the debtor in certain other cases with the possession of a certain thing (*actiones* in rem *scriptae*). The possibility of a change in the person of the debtor of the claim of Article 904 CC and the manifestations of such change, provided for in Articles 909, 913 CC, give ground and the person of the debtor is finalized and becomes stable basically from the moment that there is bad faith on the part of the person enriched in accordance with the definitions of Articles 910–912 CC. In spite of the reduced personal character of the claim from unjust enrichment, this does not cease to be one of obligation. The property of the claim as in rem *scripta* does not mean, naturally, that it is a real right.

D. A General Unitary Claim

403. The question of whether recognition is given to a single, unitary claim from unjust enrichment with common conditions for all cases or to many special claims, each with separate conditions is clearly answered by Article 904, paragraph 1, subparagraph 1. This provision (which basically more closely resembles the formulation of paragraph 62 of the Swiss Code of Obligations than the corresponding paragraph 812 of the German Code), in setting the seal on the historical development from the casuistry of Byzantine-Roman law towards a single claim, provides a claim directly ('A person enriched...is obliged...'); it contains, that is, a directly applicable general *rule* of law and not only a general *principle* which would be implemented only through a special claim. The general clause is the legislative source of the claim and not simply an explanation of special claims which follow. As in the case of the two other fundamental sources of obligational relations (Article 361 CC on contracts and Article 914 CC on torts), the CC here too gives a general provision, which in principle includes all cases of unjust enrichment. Consequently, this provision binds the interpreter as to the identification of general, common conditions for one, unitary claim from unjust enrichment. From the introduction of the CC, the Court of Cassation of *Areios Pagos* and the courts of substance, as well as theory, with very few exceptions, have understood Article 904, paragraph 1, subparagraph 1 as a directly applicable rule which provides a general claim.[257] Any casuistic treatment of the institution by the interpreter (specifically, either the traditional distinction of *condictiones*, derived from Roman law, or contemporary German distinctions – *see infra*), even though necessary or useful, cannot set aside the general clause and rob it of its character as a directly applicable rule of law.

It should be noted that a danger of excessive implementation of the institution as a result of the recognition of the general claim, which the supporters of a casuistic enrichment action system call attention to is avoided by the clear demarcation of the condition of lack of '*justa causa*' (*cf.* also paragraph 406 *infra in fine*) and of other conditions for the claim.

In Roman law, provision was made for various special claims from unjust enrichment, under the name of *condictiones*. The legislation of Justinian distinguished between the claim for a cause which did not follow (*condictio causa data causa non secuta:* D 12.4), the claim for an immoral or illegal cause (*condictio ob turpem vel injustam causam:* D 12.5) and the claim for payment made without being due (*condictio indebiti:* D 12.6). Last, it made provision for the *condictio sine causa* (D 12.7), in which were included the claim for a cause which has expired (*condictio ob causam finitam*), the claim of liberation (*condictio liberationis*), etc. All these claims are today covered by the general provision of Article 904, paragraph 1, subparagraph 1. They are, nevertheless, mentioned in the subsequent subparagraph of the article ('Such obligation shall particularly arise by reason of a payment made which was not due or of a payment made for a cause which does not follow or ceases to exist or is illegal or immoral' – on immoral cause, *see* paragraph 149 *supra*). This mention of the special instances often leads to their being put forward as independent special claims with their own conditions. Such an endeavour is, however, superfluous. The listing of the special instances of the implementation of the institution in Article 904, paragraph 1, subparagraph 2 is indicative: it is a legislative clarification as to when 'this obligation', that is, that stipulated by the preceding subparagraph (the general clause), exists. Its significance is, at the most, positive. That is to say, the very establishment of the fact that there is a payment made without being owed, an expired or unlawful cause, etc. is sufficient in principle for the acceptance of unjust enrichment, since then the lack of a lawful cause is presupposed. This lack, however, which constitutes the real reason

257. See, for example, AP 562/1957, EEN 1958, 293; AP 343/1970, NoB 1970, 1093; AP 379/1975, NoB 1975, 1154; AP 321/1982, EEN 1983, 166; AP 1027/1987, EEN 1988, 503; AP 1002/1992, EEN 1993, 695; AP 673/1999, HellD 2000, 436.

for the provision of the claim (a reason which will give the right solution in every disputed case) would be also concluded from the general clause. The casuistic formulation of the second subparagraph is not of negative significance, in the sense that any failure to fall within one of the special instances precludes unjust enrichment. What is crucial then is whether the conditions of the general claim are met.

It should be noted that in Germany today, the casuistic system has prevailed (recognition of special *condictiones* – *'Leistungskondiktion'*, *'Eingriffskondiktion'*, *'Verwendungskondiktion'*, *'Rückgriffskondiktion'*, etc., with the abandonment of the unitary claim, which could be based on paragraph 812, I, 1 of the BGB as indeed was the approach of the first interpreters of the Code). In France, on the other hand, in spite of the lack of an express legislative provision, a general clause on *'enrichissement sans cause'* has been created by court decisions, while in England, the home of case law, there is an increasing tendency towards generalization in the field of unjust enrichment.[258]

Over and above the clear legislative will in favour of the unitary character of the claim from unjust enrichment, the abandonment of common conditions for all instances of implementation and the search for separate conditions for each type of enrichment has also led to practical disadvantages. Thus, (unnecessary) problems of demarcation between the various types of claims from unjust enrichment are created. Typical here is the example which has led to divisions of opinion in Germany: A uses a means of transport belonging to someone else (he was a passenger on an aeroplane) without having a right (a ticket) to this use. For whatever solution here it is irrelevant whether the journey by air was a 'performance' to A by the airline or whether A obtained the enrichment by his 'encroachment' or whether both are the case. The question is whether A benefited without legal cause at the expense of the airline. What is important for the provision of the claim is, in the end, the existence and not the manner of acquisition of the unjust enrichment. Furthermore, it is often not a person who has been enriched who is looked for by the casuistic theory, but the addressee of a performance. (It should be noted that in the case of multilateral relations, a number of people may be considered to be the addressees when by one payment two or more creditors are, directly or indirectly, satisfied). Thus we are getting away from the ultimate purpose of the institution – the removal of the unjust enrichment.

None of the above means that the formulation of different types of implementation of the general clause is not useful in making practice easier and in understanding better the specific content of the provision. The most basic types are in fact enrichment through a performance to the enriched person (*'Leistungskondiktion'*), through an encroachment on a foreign property (*'Eingriffskondiktion'*), or by reason of expenses

258. The chief contributions to the prevalence of the casuistic approach in Germany were made by the works of *von Caemmerer*, dating from 1953 (for a collection of these works, *see* in the *Gesammelte Schriften* of von Caemmerer, 1968, Vol. I, pp. 207 et seq.). He was also influenced by the monograph of the Austrian Wilburg, Die Lehre von der ungerechtfertigten Bereicherung, 1934. On the contemporary shaping of the institution in France, *see* Carbonnier, Droit Civil, Vol. IV, 22ème éd., Nos 307 et seq., Mazeaud, Leçons de Droit Civil, *Vol. II 1, 6ème éd.*, Nos 693 et seq. On the corresponding theory of restitution in England and the trend towards the recognition of a generalized right to restitution, *see* Goff-Jones, The Law of Restitution, 3rd ed., 1986, pp. 12 et seq., *Birks*, Introduction to the Law of Restitution, 1985 (2001).

of the impoverished person (*'Verwendungskondiktion'*), which have developed in Germany as separate claims. However, this typology does not render unnecessary the drawing of the boundaries of the implementation of the general clause by exact determination of its conditions.

E. The Subsidiarity of the Claim

404. In Greece the view prevails (though it is not grounded in the letter of the law) that the claim from unjust enrichment is subsidiary, which means that it is granted to the claimant by the law only if he does not have any other claim for his satisfaction. There is, however, also support for the view that, if the conditions of other provisions are fulfilled, there will be concurrence of these provisions with that on unjust enrichment. The matter is not one of great practical importance, mainly for two reasons. On the one hand, frequently, if there is another claim, the substantive conditions of unjust enrichment will not be fulfilled: for example, if there is a claim from a valid contract, we shall have as a rule a just cause of enrichment, in other words, the element of unjustifiability will be lacking. On the other, since the plaintiff cannot cover all the damage to him through the institution of unjust enrichment, but only to the extent that there is enrichment (and, in principle only, enrichment which still survives – Article 909 CC), he usually has recourse to this action, by his own will, only as a last remedy, that is, in a subsidiary manner from a procedural point of view.

II. Conditions for the Claim

A. Enrichment of the Defendant: Impoverishment of the Plaintiff – Causal Relation

405. According to the general clause of Article 904 (paragraph I, subparagraph I), there are three conditions for the generation of unjust enrichment: that there should be *enrichment* of a person, that is, of the debtor (who is obliged to return the enrichment); that the enrichment should have come about 'from the *patrimonium* or to the detriment' of the creditor (who has a claim from unjust enrichment), and that the enrichment should be unjustified ('without just cause'). Moreover, the need that there should be a causal relation between the enrichment of the one and the impoverishment of the other emerges indirectly from the wording of the general clause.

Enrichment is any actual, concrete property benefit of the defendant (debtor), whether this consists in a *positive* increase in his estate (increase of his assets or reduction of his liabilities) or in a negative increase (avoidance of reduction of his property, for example, *saving of expenditure* which he actually would have incurred or ought to have incurred).

The enrichment must be *actual* and have current economic value. Unexploitable enrichment, which provides a purely theoretical potential for reaping benefits does not suffice. This is important when, for example, the enrichment was 'imposed' on the beneficiary (e.g., luxury expenditure on the house of another) and cannot be returned as such, but only in terms of its money value, while the beneficiary would not have proceeded (nor had he a duty to proceed) to this monetary expenditure. If the beneficiary returns money, perhaps in this specific instance we would not have a return of enrichment, but impoverishment of this person. Perhaps, then, in the case of imposed enrichment, the element of actual, exploitable enrichment is missing. Preclusion of the return of such enrichment may in other cases be deduced also from Article 905 CC (enrichment with the will of the impoverished person).

The condition of impoverishment should be understood more widely. This is the purpose of the giving of alternatives in the formulation of the law. The plaintiff is a person at whose expense the enrichment has been caused, whether this expense, this 'detriment' of the plaintiff consists in actual, concrete damage to him or consists on some other contribution on his part, for example, in removal from him, temporarily or otherwise, of means which provide their holder with scope for economic beneficial use.

The causal relation between enrichment and impoverishment may be direct or indirect, that is, the shifting of the enrichment to the defendant may have occurred through third parties (or it may have passed through the property of third parties). The law does not require directness as a condition.[259] The institution of unjust enrichment serves substantive ends. For this reason the law does not recognize the right to the defendant where he has not in fact a lawful cause for retaining this enrichment and this is actually derived from the plaintiff, to invoke the technique through which the unjust enrichment arrived in his hands.

B. Lack of Lawful Cause

406. The general clause of Article 904 CC requires that the enrichment of the defendant should be unjustified, more specifically, that it should have occurred without lawful (just) cause. What is important in the last analysis is not the cause of acquisition, but the cause of the retention of the enrichment, and this is broader and more substantive than the *causa* of Roman law, although in many cases it will coincide with it. The cause of enrichment cannot be explained only by the technical distinction between a promissory and a dispositive juridical act nor by the due formal conditions for the acquisition of the enrichment, but by substantive principles and criteria. This is also shown by comparative investigation. These principles find expression under the most widely differing legal systems (e.g., continental European and Anglo-Saxon legal systems), in spite of their differing technique, and lead to the obligation of returning the enrichment to a very great extent in the same cases.

The general clause does not on its own solve the question of when there is and when there is not a lawful cause, but nor should it be accepted that the existence or otherwise of a lawful cause emerges exclusively from other, special provisions to which (tacitly) Article 904, paragraph 1, subparagraph 1 refers. This provision can be understood as making reference to the whole system of law and to the more general

259. On the contrary, the prevailing view in case law demands a direct causal relation between enrichment and impoverishment; see, for instance, Athens Court of First Instance 3592/2004 NoB 2005, 112 (with comment by *Christakakou*); AP 1548/2007 HellD 2009, 770 (with critical comment by *Katras*). Cf., however, the opposite stance adopted in AP 1773/2007 HellD 2008, 191.

spirit which finds expression, it could be argued, in many special provisions. What is crucial in parallel is also the purpose and meaning of this institution of unjust enrichment, as manifested in all its provisions and particularly in the general clause.

A first, usual, perhaps the most usual, justification of enrichment, and consequently a lawful cause of its retention, is the *will of the injured party*, which, in the majority of cases, is included in the promissory *contract* between him and the person enriched (the former had undertaken an obligation to give the enrichment to the latter; consequently, he must recognize and accept the retention of it by him). Its force in justifying the enrichment stems from the autonomy of private will, which imbues the whole of the law of patrimony (chiefly as freedom of contract). He who has by his free and legally valid will benefited someone else binds himself and cannot, overlooking his voluntary act and the trust which the person enriched has shown in this, seek the return of the benefit. It will be obvious that if, for example, the contract (which contains this will) loses its force by reason of annulment, rescission, etc., the lawful cause also ceases to exist ('expired cause'). If, moreover, the declaration of will is on a condition or other term, it will be obvious that it justifies the enrichment only as long as the condition or term is fulfilled (or is going to be fulfilled). In the event of their frustration the lawful cause is forfeit.

In other cases, there can be another, second, justification. That is, the *law directly* can justify the retention of enrichments in certain instances (*causa ex lege*). The lawful cause may emerge either from a special provision of law (e.g., payment with the knowledge of the payer of a debt not owed, Article 905, paragraph 1 CC, payment by the payer from a special moral duty or for reasons of propriety, Article 906 CC, acquisition of ownership by long use – usucaption – Articles 1041 et seq., which not only ratify formally the transfer of ownership to the possessor, but justify it substantively, etc.) or from the more general spirit of legislation (e.g., profits from permissible business activity).

Thus, in fact, the court rulings often accept that, basically, the lawful cause, according to Article 904 CC, has as its source *the law or the contract*.[260] The fact that the *justa causa* is not required to be a specific contractual or legal reason, but may, naturally, lie in the more general approval by a legal system of an activity, to the extent that this does not exceed legal restrictions and prohibitions is ignored by the view which *de lege ferenda* is opposed to the general enrichment action.

407. The will of the injured party and the law directly do not exhaust, as is normally believed, all the cases of lawful cause of enrichment. Retention of the enrichment which is not based on one of the two lawful causes above is not necessarily unjustified. It may have another, third, *justa causa*. It may, that is, find its justification (within the meaning of lawful cause of Article 904 CC) also in any *counterbalance* of the benefit, that is, any 'price' (in the broadest sense of the term) the beneficiary has paid in consideration of his benefit to the impoverished or a third person. It is the sacrifice he has undergone for the acquisition of his benefit. If the acquisition of the enrichment is accompanied by some loss of property which the person enriched has incurred, there is no enrichment which is unjust and which must be rendered to the injured party, since the loss covers the acquisition, or exists only to the extent of any surplus, that is, as to the difference between benefit and damage. The recipient does

260. See, for example, AP 201/1959, NoB 1959, 715.

not have to become poorer than he was before his enrichment. The institution of unjust enrichment has as its purpose only the removal of the enrichment.[261] It will be obvious that this quid pro quo takes on significance in practice as a reason justifying the enrichment when it has not been given within the framework of a contract with the injured party, since then this contract would already justify the enrichment. Examples:

(1) A sells B a thing and delivers it to him, collecting the purchase price. The thing is destroyed (or lost) in the hands of B (without his fault). The sale was void; consequently the retention of the purchase price by A is not justified by the contractual will of B. It is justified, however, by the countervalue which A paid. Otherwise, A would have to return the purchase price, without, however, being able to take back the thing, since this (i.e., the enrichment of B) is lost (Article 909 CC – *see* paragraph 412 *infra*).
(2) A thinks, as a result of error, that he has a debt to B. On the suggestion of the latter, he pays the relevant sum of money direct to C, creditor of B from a valid sale. C has not been unjustly enriched. If he is sued by A, he will oppose as a lawful cause not the sale contract with B, which for A is *res inter alios acta* (principle of privity of obligational contracts), but the countervalue as a *factum* (against all) which he gave or owes to B. (On the question of who is the unjustly enriched party here against whom the injured party can take action, *see* paragraph 408 *infra*).

It cannot be said that the recipient who, in order to acquire his enrichment, has undergone some sacrifice comes into conflict with the purpose of the institution of unjust enrichment.

The usefulness and necessity of the countervalue as a lawful cause of enrichment can be seen, on the one hand, in cases of void reciprocal contracts and, on the other, in cases of de facto contractual relations. In the former, when the performances have already been fulfilled, but one of these cannot be returned, because, for example, it has not survived, the recipient of the surviving performance (and giver of the non-surviving one) has not been enriched unjustly, although he does not base his enrichment on a valid contract. The lawful cause is to be found in the giving of the (non-surviving) countervalue (*see* Example I above). If we deny its justificatory force, we should have to compel the recipient of the surviving performance to return it, without there being any possibility of seeking the return of the performance which he has provided, since the latter does not survive (Article 909 CC). We should be led, in other words, to damage to him contrary to the purpose of the institution.[262] If, of course, the value of the surviving performance is greater than the value of that which has been lost, the former is justified only to the extent that it is covered by the latter. Consequently, the recovery of the difference may be sought by the claim of unjust enrichment, since, outside the framework of a valid contract (where the will, as long as the contract remains valid, basically justifies the exchange of unequal performances), the counterbalance

261. This view (recognition of the counterbalance of the enrichment as its *justa causa*) has now been accepted by court rulings (*see* especially AP 379/1975, NoB 1975, 1154; Piraeus Court of Appeals 136/1998, PirN 1998, 77; Athens Court of Appeals 1665/2001, EEmbD 2001, 535).
262. This solution is also accepted by the 'balance theory' (of German origin – *Saldotheorie*), though with a different foundation.

develops its justificatory force by virtue of its objective value: performances of unequal value justify one another in principle only to the extent that they cover one another.

Furthermore, in de facto contracts there is no valid will to justify the performances which are effected within the framework of these relations. However, the performances can find their justification in the countervalue paid. Thus, if, in spite of the nullity of a continuous contract, for example, lease of a thing or contract for service, the thing leased is de facto used and the rent is paid, or the services are provided and the remuneration is paid, respectively, the rent and the remuneration cannot be recovered, since their retention by their recipient is justified by the giving of the countervalue, that is, the use of the thing leased or of the services. A claim from unjust enrichment will only be recognized for any difference between the (objective, market) value of the two benefits which have been exchanged.

However, the principal area in which the practical worth of the countervalue as a lawful cause of enrichment is provided by trilateral relations (*see* Example 2 *supra* and paragraph 408 *infra*).

It is not necessary that the countervalue should without fail be given to the plaintiff (injured party). It is sufficient that the enrichment should be justified, not the damage. The recipient of enrichment who for its acquisition gave, even to a *third party*, a countervalue does not himself put forward the equalizing mandate of commutative justice, does not reap net enrichment, is not unjustly enriched. If he were obliged to make a return, we should have not the removal of enrichment, but damage to the recipient.

The countervalue can cover the enrichment only *in part*. This will be judged on the basis of objective criteria (ideas about business transactions, but also specific special conditions). Then the part of the enrichment not covered remains unjustified and returnable.

By way of exception, although a countervalue was given for the enrichment, this *will not be capable of justifying the enrichment:*

(1) if its giving and, more particularly, its connection with the enrichment is unlawful or immoral or conflicts with the principle of good faith, in which case its invocation is contrary to prohibitive rules of laws;
(2) if in the end the reverse effects prevail, that is, return of the countervalue and the enrichment to their source. On the latter, *see* paragraph 410 *infra*.

Thus, the condition of lack of *justa causa* is fulfilled, if any of the three above causes is absent (will – countervalue – law), which may co-exist, but of which each alone is also sufficient for the justification of the enrichment.

III. Implementation of the Institution in Trilateral Relations and Reciprocal Contracts

A. Trilateral Relations

408. Particular difficulty in the functioning of the institution of unjust enrichment arises in trilateral relations. For example, payment to a third party (cf. Article 417 CC) or from a third party (Articles 317 et seq. CC), contract in favour of a third party, assumption of debt or novation with a new debtor, assignment or novation with a new creditor, guarantee, joint and several obligation, disposition of a right by one who is not the holder, etc. Here the main problem is identification of the two persons (of the three in the trilateral relation) between whom there is the relation of unjust enrichment. The claimant or the obligor for restitution of the enrichment is not necessarily the person who gave it or its recipient, but may possibly be the intermediary person in the trilateral relation who has actually suffered damage or has actually been enriched. In order to find the correct solutions, the following simple case, which can be applied accordingly to all the above legal relations, will be taken as a basis.

A has a debt to B and B to C; A pays C directly. What is crucial here is not the capacities of the giver or the recipient of the performance, but the capacities of the injured and the enriched parties. Therefore, it should be accepted that if the relation between A and B is valid and the B – C relation is non-existent or invalid (*ab initio* or as a consequence of a subsequent reversal of it for any reason), the person unjustly enriched and liable to render the enrichment is the recipient C, but the claimant is not A, who effected the performance, since he was in fact the debtor by virtue of the valid relation A – B, but the intermediary B, that is, the 'debtor' of the non-existent or defective relation B – C. If, on the other hand, the relation B – C is valid and the relation A – B non-existent or defective, A, who paid C actually suffered damage (he is not covered by his relation with B) and can seek to recover the enrichment; the person liable to return it is the person who has actually been enriched, the intermediary B, that is, the 'creditor' of the defective or non-existent relation A – B, and not the recipient of the performance, C, who had a right (and a lawful cause) to receive the performance by virtue of the valid relation B – C. Finally, if both relations (A – B and B – C) are absent or are void or are reversed, etc. (problem of the so-called *double defect*), there will be a direct claim on the part of A (injured party) against C, who was unjustly enriched, since he cannot derive a lawful cause from his relation with B. B has neither suffered damage nor benefited. Examples:

(1) A, who believes that he has inherited from X, pays the debts of the inheritance to the creditor C, bringing about their extinction. The party unjustly enriched is the actual heir (and therefore the real debtor) B, who has been released from his debt, and not C, who has collected a claim which he actually had.

(2) B (who is not entitled) sells and transfers a thing belonging to A to C. The sale B – C is void, but C becomes owner by reason, let us suppose, of the validity of the juridical act of disposition. The claim from unjust enrichment against C will be held in principle by the injured party A, and not B who disposed of the thing. The latter will perhaps have the claim of possession (*condictio possessionis*) if

he had and continues after the disposition to have the right of possession over the thing by virtue of his legal relation with the owner, who will retain the claim for return of the ownership by virtue of Article 904 CC (*condictio rei*).

It is frequently argued that the return of unjust enrichment in the case of trilateral relations must take place between the parties themselves of the void or reversed contract, and more generally between the persons who are already linked by a contractual bond (even if invalid), that is, always either between A and B or between B and C, even if both relations are defective. Nevertheless, the obligation from unjust enrichment stems from the law (Article 904 CC) and not from a contract; and the law defines, in accordance, anyway, with the mandate of the prohibition of unjust enrichment at the expense of another, as subjects of the obligation from unjust enrichment the party enriched and the injured party and not the subjects of, for example, the invalid contract. Any desire of the parties to abide by the settlement with their own counterparty is probably satisfied by direct recourse to contractual liability (e.g., Articles 713, 721 et seq. CC). If, for instance, in the above examples, B delegates A to pay C directly, he is in some way guaranteeing to A that A will not be damaged by this payment, that is, B gives A a promise which means that he provides him with contractual protection, that A and B have a contractual relation. It is thus consistent that A has a claim against B. This claim is not grounded in unjust enrichment (as the opposing opinion maintains), but in the contractual relation (e.g., from a mandate). A is in effect invoking contractual liability of B. Unjust enrichment has different objectives.

409. More particularly in cases of gratuitous movement of property, there is the provision of Article 913 CC. This provision deals with the case in which the recipient of the unjust enrichment further transfers it to a third party by a gratuitous act. The provision stipulates liability of the third party to return the enrichment to the giver (injured party). Article 913 CC finds its justification in the fact that the law does not regard acquisition from a gratuitous cause as a sufficient ground for retention (lawful cause) of the enrichment when the person to whom the thing donated actually belongs, that is, the person at whose expense the enrichment has occurred, has not given his consent to the acquisition. A donation made with items of property of a third party, and not of the donor, even if it is valid as a contract, is not tolerated, that is, it does not constitute justified enrichment. The gratuitous cause is here equivalent to the non-existent or invalid cause; it is, that is, reasonably, treated less favourably by the law. The purpose of Article 913 CC is to make it clear that a donation contract with the non-injured (first) recipient of the enrichment does not constitute a lawful cause for retention of it for the third party. The gratuitous cause in itself is not a sufficient cause for enrichment. If, on the other hand, the third party received the enrichment by an onerous cause, he will not be liable, since he will have a lawful cause also against the injured party (the payment or debt of a countervalue) and not because he will have indirectly received the enrichment.

B. Reciprocal Contracts

410. If a reciprocal contract is *ab initio* void or is reversed *ex post facto*, the recovery of the performance which has been effected will be sought as unjust enrichment.

No particular problem arises if only one performance of the reciprocal contract has been fulfilled or if both performances have been fulfilled, but one of them no longer survives (*see* paragraph 407 *supra*). An issue does arise, however, if both performances have been fulfilled and survive, in which case two intersecting claims from unjust enrichment for their recovery arise. Their retention (over and above the possible instance of set-off of the two performances, where the conditions of Articles 440 et seq. CC are fulfilled) is not possible here, in the sense, for example, that the effecting of the one performance justifies, as a countervalue, the retention of the other, to the extent that they overlap. This is because the provision which stipulates the nullity of the contract imposes an effect, where this is possible, which lies beyond the institution of unjust enrichment: the restoration of the *status quo ante*, that is, the return of the performances. It imposes, in other words, a reverse settlement. Thus the provision which stipulates the nullity of the contract affects not only an unfulfilled contract (extinction of contractual obligations), it also affects a contract which has been fulfilled in requiring the above restoration, provided that this is possible, and creating an additional ground for the impermissibility of the linkage of enrichment with countervalue (*see* paragraph 407 *supra* in fine). The same holds good for other grounds of invalidity or reversal of the contract (see, for example, on rescission, Article 389 §2 CC, which provides for extinction of unfulfilled obligations and an obligation of return in the case of those which have been fulfilled). On the technique of return, these provisions refer us (expressly or tacitly) to the institution of unjust enrichment. In this instance, that is to say, the reverse effects prevail by virtue of the special provisions on invalidity, since, anyway, the purpose of Articles 904 et seq. CC (avoidance of unjust enrichment) is not affected. Insofar, however, as the full restoration of the previous state of affairs is not possible, since, for example, the performance which the plaintiff has received does not survive, the purely reverse settlement has given way. It no longer corresponds to the restitutive purpose of the provisions concerning invalidity. Thus the settlement of the case is left entirely to the law of unjust enrichment, which has as its purpose the removal of enrichment, and only the balance will now be sought.

IV. Effects

411. The consequence of the existence of unjust enrichment at the expense of another is the obligation of the person enriched to return it (Article 904 CC). The facts which substantiate the conditions for the claim are basically to be proven by the plaintiff.[263] A more exact definition of the object of the obligation and of the extent of the liability of the recipient are contained in Article 908 CC. This provision imposes the return of the 'thing received'. Its meaning is that it is sufficient and obligatory, when this is possible in the specific case, for the enrichment to be returned *in natura*. The ultimate justification, however, is that the return of the enrichment as an economic value (the 'benefit'), the evaluation of which in money, which may be particularly difficult anyway, is avoided, is thus achieved in the best way. When the enrichment cannot be returned *in natura* (e.g., enrichment from the use of a thing or right belonging

263. *See* AP (in Plenary Session) 2/1987, NoB 1988, 69; AP 209/1977, NoB 1977,1170; AP 355/1999, HellD 1999, 1535; AP 673/1999, HellD 2000, 436.

to another, from the provision of the services of another – as well as any other case of enrichment which consists in the saving of expenditure), the recipient will owe the value of the enrichment *in money.*

When the original enrichment has been lost for the recipient, but its place has been taken by a surrogate (e.g., insurance compensation which the enriched person has collected by reason of destruction of the original enrichment, a claim for compensation against third parties by reason of theft, loss, destruction, etc., a price from the disposition of the original enrichment with an onerous cause, such as the purchase price from its sale, etc.), this surrogate is owed.

A question arises as to whether, where the countervalue which the recipient has realized from the sale of the original enrichment is greater than the value of the object which was sold, the whole of the (greater) countervalue will be returned or whether it will be returned to a limited extent, for example as the sum of the value of the object or of the damage to the plaintiff, etc. In line with what has been said about the purpose of the institution, only the actual enrichment is returnable and only to the extent to which this was acquired at the expense of the person entitled. Where the purchase price which the defendant (the person enriched) has realized is regarded as having been achieved in its entirety by means belonging to the plaintiff and, consequently, at his expense, the whole of it must be returned. However, in the event of a part of the sum of the purchase price being due to a contribution (e.g., of a business nature) of the defendant, to the extent of this part the enrichment did not occur to the detriment of the plaintiff and will not be returned. Anyway, the defendant may, to the extent that his enrichment is due to his own contribution, regard it as justified, as being based on a countervalue which he provided. The extent of the contribution of each of the parties to the achievement of the purchase price will be decided *in concreto* by the judge. The starting-point, however, must be the fact that the purchase price is due to the object which was sold itself, that is, to the contribution of the plaintiff. This position, however, will be subject to differentiation, to the extent that some contribution of the defendant is proven.

The person enriched must also return 'fruits collected, as well as anything else which he has derived from the thing' (Article 908, subparagraph 2 CC).

412. A basic rule as to the extent of the liability of the party enriched is contained in Article 909 CC. This provision stipulates the extinction of the obligation of the recipient where he is no longer richer at the time of the serving of the action, that is, insofar as *the enrichment does not survive or to the extent that it does not survive* (e.g., it has been destroyed, stolen, given to a third party or has disappeared in some other way from the estate of the recipient, wholly or in part). According to Article 904 CC, what is of importance is that the defendant should have become richer and, as Article 909 CC now adds, should continue to be richer. It is not of importance that the recipient should continue in possession of the specific thing which he received. The disappearance of this from the estate of the recipient does not entail extinction of his liability if the recipient collected a surrogate in place of it, since he thus continues to be richer. If, however, the enrichment has not survived either in its original form or in the form of any surrogate for it (even in the form of expenditure saved which the recipient would otherwise have incurred), matters are different. The legislator has determined (and his thinking here is derived from the corresponding regulation of the BGB and the Swiss

Code of Obligations, but also goes back to the Byzantine jurists) that the *equity* which imposes the return of the unjust enrichment requires equally that the obligation of restitution should not last longer than the possession (retention) of any form of enrichment. However, he (the legislator) regards this equity towards the person enriched as justified only to the degree that the latter is *in good faith* and for as long as he is in good faith (he was unaware or could not have known that the enrichment was unjustified and would have to be returned). Thus, Article 909 CC provides for the extinction of the obligation of restitution of the enrichment by reason of its loss only as a rule. Where bad faith on the part of the person enriched is proven (subject to the more particular distinctions of Articles 910–912 CC, which introduce exceptions to Article 909 CC),[264] the liability of the person enriched continues, in spite of the loss of the enrichment. A person who loses the enrichment and is in bad faith is not released. Consequently, what is frequently asserted – that the limitation of the liability to the surviving enrichment necessarily attaches to the nature of the liability from unjust enrichment – is not accurate.

Loss or reduction of the enrichment must also be accepted when by reason of the unjustified acquisition, the remaining property of the person enriched is adversely affected; it suffices that this effect should be in a causal relation with the unjustified acquisition (e.g., expenditure for the repair of the enrichment acquired).

The fact that the enrichment survives does not constitute an element in an action for unjust enrichment to be proven by the plaintiff. It is the defendant who, in putting forward the plea of Article 909 CC, must invoke and prove the loss or reduction of the enrichment and the extent of the reduction. The burden of proof of the facts from which any bad faith of the defendant (Articles 910–912 CC) is established is, however, borne by the plaintiff.

§2. Management of Another's Affairs (*Negotiorum Gestio*)

I. Concept: Kinds

413. Management of another's affairs (*negotiorum gestio*) exists when a person, the *manager*, handles an affair of another without relying for this purpose on the actual will of the *principal of the affair*. The CC regulates the consequences which follow from such a relationship in Articles 730–740. In Article 730, it speaks of the management of an affair of another 'without mandate'. The formulation, however, is narrower than the spirit of the law. A mandate is simply the usual legal cause for the management of another's affairs. Other legal causes may be either another contractual relation between the manager and the principal (e.g., a partnership contract, a contract for service, for work, etc.) or a provision of law which permits management (enforced management,

264. These provisions provide basically for the retention of the liability of the recipient when the loss or reduction of the enrichment occurred after the serving of the action on the party enriched; when there was knowledge or – in accordance with certain more particular distinctions – culpable ignorance of the enriched person as to the lack of lawful cause of his enrichment; and when the lack of lawful cause is due to the fact that the cause of the enrichment was illegal or immoral.

liquidation, etc.) of another's property. The provisions on the management of another's affairs are implemented in every case in which there is no legal ground for the management of the affair of another. The affair managed may consist in the exercise of a right or the fulfilment of an obligation of the principal or the execution of any other act which concerns the circle of interests of the principal. It may concern the *patrimonium* of the principal (e.g., repair of someone else's house, cultivation of the land of a neighbour, putting out of a fire, provision of maintenance which is the obligation of another, etc.) or his personality (e.g., conveying of a sick person to hospital, saving a person in danger, etc.).

Negotiorum gestio may be due to the arbitrary action of the manager, in which case it meets with the disapprobation of law. It may, however, be from a willingness to provide assistance to the principal (who, for example, is absent or cannot himself manage his affair), and, further, it can objectively benefit the principal.

The affair managed may also be that of a legal person, just as the manager may itself be a legal person (acting through its organs).

414. From *genuine negotiorum gestio* (in which the manager knows that the affair which he is managing is that of another and manages it as such)[265] we must distinguish the so-called *non-genuine negotiorum gestio*, in which the manager, though aware that the affair is that of another, manages it as if it were his own, with the will, that is, that it should be his own and should serve his own interests. This instance will be discussed under section IV *infra.* Genuine *negotiorum gestio* is sub-divided into *licit*, that is, that which the manager carries out (as he should) in the interests of the principal and in accordance with his (actual or presumptive) will, and *illicit*, that is, that which the manager carries out as another's affair, but in a manner which objectively does not correspond to the interests or the (actual or presumptive) will of the principal. The CC regulates chiefly genuine (licit and illicit) *negotiorum gestio.* Finally, there is also the instance of *negotiorum gestio in error*, in which the manager handles the affair of another as his own since, in error, he believes that it is his. This too will be dealt with under IV *infra.*

II. Obligations and Liability of the Manager in Genuine Negotiorum Gestio

415. The principal obligation of the manager in genuine *negotiorum gestio* is 'to conduct the affair in the interests and according to the actual or presumptive will of the principal' (Article 730, §1 CC). By the actual will of the principal is meant his psychological will, since any contractual will would mean that the management is an act of contractual performance (*see* Articles 713 et seq. CC) and not *negotiorum gestio.* It is reasonable to suppose that the (actual or presumptive) will of the principal also expresses his interests. The management must be consonant with the interests of the principal, as a separate criterion, when his actual will cannot be proven and his

265. The fact that by the management of another's affair the interests of the manager also are, even partially, served (e.g., provision of maintenance to parents which is the obligation of the person providing it and of his siblings) does not cancel the character of an act of *negotiorum gestio* to the extent that it concerns the interests of others (others' rights, obligations).

presumptive will cannot be arrived at by means of interpretation. In one case we judge directly on the basis of the interests of the principal: when the will (as opposed to the management) of the principal is contrary to the law or morality (*contra bonos mores*) (Article 730, §2 CC – for example, an attempt to save a potential suicide who insists on killing himself).

More particular obligations of the manager are those of keeping the principal informed, of seeking his instructions as far as possible, of rendering account to him, and of restituting what he has acquired for his management (with interest, if the case requires this), in accordance with the provisions of the mandate (Articles 733–734, in conjunction with Article 719 CC).[266] Only if the manager has no capacity or has limited capacity to carry out juridical acts is he liable not in accordance with the provisions on mandates, but in accordance with those on unjust enrichment, and, if the necessary conditions are met, those on tort (Article 735 CC).

416. If the manager does not conform with his above obligations, he is liable to the principal, for example, to compensate him. However, here too the fault principle applies. That is to say, he is liable only if he is at fault, but for every degree of fault (wilful conduct, gross or slight negligence). There are two exceptions from the fault principle, in the opposite direction: reduction of the liability of the manager only for wilful conduct and gross negligence if he undertook the management to avert a danger which was threatening the principal; the augmentation of his liability to include chance events if he undertook the management against the actual or presumptive will of the principal (*illicit negotiorum gestio*) and he should have been aware of this or the damage would not have occurred without his involvement (Articles 731–732 CC). The latter is presumed, that is, the manager bears the burden of proof that the damage would have occurred even without his involvement. It has been accepted that chance events are to be understood here in the strict sense. In other words, they do not include events of force majeure, as to which in this instance the manager is released (*see* paragraphs 259–260 *supra*).

III. Rights of the Manager in Genuine Negotiorum Gestio

417. As to the rights of the manager from *negotiorum gestio* (and the corresponding obligations of the principal), we must make the following distinctions:

If the manager observes his principal obligation of Article 730 CC, that is, he manages the affair of the principal in accordance with the actual or presumptive will and the interests of the latter (licit negotiorum gestio), he has those rights which a mandatary has from the fulfilment of the mandate. That is, he can seek the expenses which he has incurred and the restitution of any damage which he may have suffered without his own fault in the management of the other's affair (Art 736, in conjunction with Articles 722, 723 CC). These claims of the manager are independent of whether his management was effective or otherwise. A condition, of course, is that the expenses and the damages should have arisen during the normal performance of the management.

266. If the manager has contributed with his particular personal skills to the extent of the things acquired, what has been said above (para. 411) will be implemented *mutatis mutandis*.

A fee will be owed to the manager if the affair in question is one for which a fee is usually paid (e.g., operation performed by a doctor, cf. Articles 649 and 682 CC).

If the manager did not act in accordance with the actual or presumptive will and the interests of the principal (i.e., in a case of so-called illicit negotiorum gestio), he may seek only the payment of the expenses which he incurred (not compensation), in accordance with the provisions on unjust enrichment (Article 737 CC) and provided that the conditions for this are fulfilled (e.g., the enrichment survives).

Finally, if the manager in carrying out the management intended not to seek expenses or compensation, he has no claim. This intention, in case of doubt, is deemed to exist if the *negotiorum gestio* consists in the provision, without, let us suppose, an obligation arising from the law, of maintenance to a close relative (as Article 738 CC lays down in detail).

In the exercise of claims between the manager and the principal, the suspensive plea of retention may be opposed by the defendant (manager or principal) (*see* paragraph 228 *supra*).

IV. Special Cases

418. In the case of *non-genuine negotiorum gestio* (*see* paragraph 414 *supra*), the manager has, in accordance with Article 739 CC, all the obligations and the liability of a manager of the affairs of another (and for chance events – *see* Article 731, subparagraph 2 CC),[267] as well as, if the necessary conditions are met, delictual liability. However, his rights are confined to a claim for expenses in accordance with the provisions on unjust enrichment.

In the case of *negotiorum gestio in error* (paragraph 414 *supra*), Article 740 CC lays down that the provisions on *negotiorum gestio* are not applied. Possible rights of the manager or the principal could at the most be grounded directly in the provisions on unjust enrichment or torts, if the conditions for these are fulfilled.

267. However, the limitation as to the level of the claim of the principal in the instance noted in the preceding note also applies here.

Selected Bibliography

Prepared with the help of Mrs Klamari-Papadopoulou, Professor of Civil Law (University of Athens) and Marina Chatzikyriakou (LL.M. Civil Law). Greek titles have been translated into English.

Commentaries on the Civil Code

ErmAK (Interpretation of the Civil Code – collective work), under the general supervision of A. Ligeropoulos. *Law of Obligations*. 1949–1987.
Georgiadis, Ap. *Brief Commentary on the Greek Civil Code* (collective work). Vol. I (SEAK I, Articles 1-946), 2010 and Vol. II (SEAK II, Articles 947-2035), 2013.
Georgiadis & Stathopoulos. *Civil Code* (collective work). Vols I–X (1st and partially 2nd edn), 1978–2007.
Karakostas. *Civil Code* (collective work). Vols I–V and Vol. IX, Interpretation – Commentary – Court Decisions, 2005–2008.
Spyridakis & Perakis. *Civil Code*. A, B1, B2, 1976–1978.
Vathrakokoilis. *Analytical Interpretation and Court Rulings on the Civil Code*. 1989.

Systematic Works

Agallopoulou. *Basic Concepts of Greek Civil Law*. 2005 (in English).
Asprogerakas-Grivas. *General Principles of Civil Law*. 1981.
Balis. *General Principles*. 1955; *Law of Obligations*. 1954.
Deligiannis & Kornilakis. *Law of Obligations*. Special Part Vols I–III. 1992 and Vol. IV. 1998.
Filios. *General Principles of Civil Law*. 4th edn. 2011; *Law of Obligations*. General Part, 6th edn. 2011, Special Part, 10th edn. 2011.
Fourkiotis. *Greek Law of Obligations*. General Part, 1964.
Gasis. *General Principles of Civil Law*. 1971–1974.
Georgiades, Ap. *Law of Obligations*. General Part, 1999, and Special Part, Vols I and II. 2004, 2007.
Georgiades, Ast. *Law of Obligations*. General Part, 5th edn. 2007.
Kafkas. *Law of Obligations*. Special Part, 1993.
Karassis. *General Principles of Civil Law*. 1993–1996.
Kerameus-Kozyris (ed.). *Introduction to Greek Law*. 3rd. revised edn. 2008 (in English).
Kornilakis. *Law of Obligation*. Special Part, Vol. I. 2012 and Vol. II. 2005.
Ladas. *General Principles of Civil Law*. Vol. I. 2007 and Vol. II. 2009.
Litzeropoulos. *Law of Obligations*. 1960–1968.
Mantzoufas. *Law of Obligations*. 1971.
Michailidis-Nouaros. *Law of Obligations*. 1959.

Papachristou. *General Principles of Civil Law*. 1987; *Law of Obligations*. 1986.
Papantoniou. *General Principles of Civil Law*. 3rd edn. 1983.
Papasteriou-Klavanidou. *Law of the Juridical Act*. 2008.
Simantiras. *General Principles of Civil Law*. 4th edn. 1988.
Spyridakis. *General Principles of Civil Law*. 1987.
Spyridakis. *Law of Obligations*. General Part, 2004.
Stathopoulos. *Law of Obligations*. General Part, 4th edn. 2004.
Toussis. *General Principles of Civil Law*. 1979; *Law of Obligations*. General Part 1973, Special Part, 1975.
Zepos. *Law of Obligations*. General Part, 1955, Special Part, 1965.

Books or Self-Contained Publications on Special Subjects

General on Obligations: Good Faith

Androulidaki-Dimitriadou. *The Obligations from Business Good Faith*. 1972.
Christodoulou, K. *The Monetary Obligation – Even in View of the Regulation on the Euro*. 1999.
Doris. *The Specification of Good Faith in Article 2 of Law 2251/1994 on Consumer Protection*. NoB 2000, 737 et seq.
Flogaitis. *The Administrative Contract*. 1991.
Fourkiotis. *The Action on Forbearance*. 1952.
Gasis. *The Conflict of Rights*. 1959.
Georgakopoulos. *The Law of Continuous Obligations*. 1979.
Kallimopoulos. *The Law of Money*. 1993.
Koumantos. *Subjective Good Faith*. 1958.
Litzeropoulos. *Natural Obligations and Related Legal Forms*. 1971.
Papantoniou. *Good Faith in Civil Law*. 1957.
Papachristou, A. *The Quasi Juridical Act*. 1989.
Schinas, G. *Mixed Contracts*. 1962.
Stathopoulos. *The Application of the Civil Code in the First Fifty Years of Its Force*. KritE 1996, 1 et seq.
Stathopoulos. 'Equality in the Law of Contract'. In *Law in Motion (International Encyclopaedia of Laws)*, edited by R. Blanpain, 1997, 365 et seq.
Tsolakidis. *Contractual and Delictual Liability for Assistants*. 2008.

Formation of Contracts: Precontractual Liability

Filios, C. *The Causa Contrahendi*. 2007.
Georgiades, Ap. *Option Contracts and Option Right*. 1970.
Kabitsis. *On Precontractual Liability*. 1960.
Karakatsanis, J. *The Legal Nature of Lawful Form of Declaration of Will*. 1980.
Karakatsanis, J. *The Signing of a Private Document by Representative*. 1982.
Karybali-Tsiptsiou. *Approval of Juridical Acts – A Contribution to the Interpretation of Articles 236 and 238 CC*. 1990.
Kritikos. *The Promise to Contract*. 1980.

Selected Bibliography

Liappis. *Drafting of Contracts*. 2003.
Livanis. *Causal Acknowledgement of Debt*. 1984.
Mentis. *Tacit Granting of Power of Attorney*. 2005.
Pantelidou. *Irrevocable Power of Attorney*. 1987.
Papadopoulou-Klamari. *Self-Dealing Transaction According to the Greek Civil Code*. 2000.
Pitsirikos. *New Ways of Communication (Telefax, Telex, Electronic Document) for the Constitution of a Formal Legal Act as a Subject of the Relationship of Written Form and Legal Act*. 2002.
Pournaras. *Abuse of Power of Attorney*. 2006.
Stabelou. *Validity of Contract Concluded Per Telefax*. KritE 1994, 142 et seq.
Xypolias. *The Mandatory Contract*. 1971.
Zorba-Psouni. *Declaration of Will through Computer*. 1988.

Conditions of Validity and Contents of Contract: Performance and Termination of Contracts

Aravantinos, J. *Error as to the Object of the Performance*. 1954.
Aravantinos, J. *Nullity, Partial Nullity, Conversion*. 1957.
Deloukas. *General Terms of Business*. 1952.
Doris. *Limitations of Contractual Freedom in Clauses of Exclusive International Jurisdiction*. 1988.
Karagiannis. *The Problem of Simulation (Sham Agreement) in Private Law*. 2002.
Karakatsanes, J. *The Set Off by Unilateral Act*. 1980.
Karassis. *General Terms of Business*. 1992.
Karybali-Tsiptsiou. *Nullity by Reason of Simulation, a Contribution to the Interpretation of Articles 138 §1 and 139 CC*. 1998.
Kitsaras. *Obligational Engagement of the Power of Disposing*. 1999.
Klavanidou. *Error as to the Qualities of a Thing in Sale*. 1991.
Kotzabassi. *Exoneration Clauses in General Terms of Business*. 2001.
Ladas. *Nullity of a Juridical Act as contra Bonos Mores*. 1979.
Mentis. *General Terms of Transactions in Consumer and Commercial Contracts*. 2000.
Papadopoulou-Klamari. *Contract with Prohibited Performance*. 1992.
Papanikolaou. *Improperly Exploitative ('Katapleonektikes') Juridical Acts*. 1984.
Papanikolaou. *Abuse of Contractual Freedom*. 1986.
Papanikolaou. *On the Limits of the Protective Intervention of the Judge in the Contract*. 1991.
Spyridakis. *Nullity of Juridical Acts of Persons Incapable*. 1974.
Spyridakis. *Lack of Capacity for Juridical Acts*. 2000.

Contracts and Third Parties: Plurality of Parties – Assignment

Archaniotakis. *Transfer of Patrimonium or Enterprise*. 1997.
Filios, C. *Fiduciary Transfers*. 2002.
Georgiades, G. *The Assignment of Future Receivables*. 2006.
Karassis. *The Concept of the Joint and Several Debt*. 2nd edn. 1990.

Kefalas. *The Effect of Obligational Relationships on Third Parties*. 1986.
Kornilakis. *The Fiduciary Assignment of Claims*. 1978.
Ladogiannis. *Security over Trade Receivables*. 2005.
Lekkas. *Charge for Securing Debentures and Securitisation*. 2005.
Livanis. *Disposal of Future Rights*. 1990.
Mantzoulas. *Trilateral Obligational Relations*. 1967.
Papantoniou. *Assignment of a Contractual Relationship*. 1962.
Papazissi. *The Contract in Favour of Third Parties Causa Mortis*. 1982.

Breach of Contract: Damages – Remedies

Chelidonis. *Termination and Damages*. 2007.
Christodoulou, Ph. *Inappropriateness of Contractual Pelformance*. 1973.
Gasis. *Non-performance of Obligational Contract*. 1940 (reprint 1987).
Georgiades, Ap. *Problems of Civil Liability*. 1972.
Karakostas. *Liability of the Producer for Defective Products*. 2008.
Karampatzos. *Unforeseeable Change of Circumstances in the Bilateral Contract*. 2006.
Kontogianni. *Contributory Negligence in Civil Law*. 2006.
Kornilakis. *Liability from Exposure to Danger (Strict Liability)*. 1982.
Koumanis. *Non-performance of Obligational Contracts according to the Civil Code*. 2002.
Kounougeri-Manoledaki. *The Problem of Hypothetical (Intervening) Causation in the Law of Compensation*. 1981.
Liossi. *The Claim from Penalty Clauses and its Relation to Claims for Performance and for Damages*. 1993.
Livanis. *Application of Article 300 CC to the Field of Strict Liability*. 1970.
Paterakis. *Compensation in Money for Moral Damage*. 2nd edn. 2001.
Pouliades. *Collective Action and Consumers' Protection*. 1990.
Pouliades. *Concurrence of Norms of Special and General Law of Obligations in Seller's Civil Responsibility*. Vol. 1. 1997.
Pouliades. *The Seller's Responsibility in the System of Breach of Contract*. 2005.
Rokas, I. *Product Liability*. 1997.
Stamoulis, J. *The Problem of Causal Cohesion in Law*. 1961.
Theodoropoulos. *The Rescission of the Contract by the Creditor in the Debtor's Default*. 1967.
Valtoudis. *Liability for Defective Products*. 1999.
Zervogianni. *The Restoration of the Status Quo as a Form of Damage Compensation*. 2006.

Specific Contracts and Other Specific Obligations

Avgoustianakis. *The Contest of Fraudulent Alienation*. 1991.
Alexandridou (collective work). *Law of Consumer's Protection*. 2008.
Androulidaki-Dimitriadou. *The Obligation of Informing the Patient*. 1993.
Christakakou-Fotiadi. *Creditor's Protection Through Personal Legal Security*. 2002.
Christodoulou, K. *Digest of Electronic Civil Law*. 2nd revised edn. 2013.

Selected Bibliography

Christodoulou, K. *Electronic Documents and the Electronic Contract*. 2004.
Dakoronia. *Sub-Lease of a Thing*. 1994.
Dellios. *Consumer's Protection and System of Private Law*. Vol. I, II, 2005.
Deliyannis. *The Power of Attorney*. 1954.
Farmakidis. *The Brokerage Contract*. 1989.
Filios. *Lease of a Thing*. 1981.
Filios. *Professional Leasing*. 10th edn. 2000.
Filios. *Leasing of a Residence*. 4th edn. 1991.
Flabouras. *The Allocation and Transfer of Risk in the Contract of Sale of Goods*. 2007.
Fountedaki. *Human Reproduction and Medical Practioner's Civil Liability*. 2007.
Georgiades, Ap. *New Forms of Contract in the Modern Economy (Leasing Factoring – Franchising, etc.)*. 5th edn. 2008.
Kallimopoulos. *Non-genuine Negotiorum Gestio (Article 739 CC)*. 1978.
Kannelopoulou-Boti. *Informed Consent Medical Liability in Greek and Community Law*. 1999.
Karakostas. *Consumer Protection Law*. 2nd edn. 2008.
Karakostas. *Consumer Protection Law*. 2012 (in English).
Klavanidou. *Consumer's Loan Contracts*. 1997.
Kotsiris. *Enquiry into the Law of Unjust Enrichment*. 1972.
Linaritis. *The Access to Financial Services through the Internet*. 2005.
Mazis. *The Leasing Contract*. 2nd edn. 1999.
Nikolaidis. *The Scope of Applicability of the Vienna Sales Convention*. 2001.
Nikolopoulos. *Rescission in Sales Law*. 2007.
Pantelidou. *Notice of Termination of Contracts for Work*. 1991.
Papanikolaou et al. *The New Law of Seller's Liability*. 2003.
Paparseniou. *The Leasing Contract*. 1994.
Paparseniou. *Community Directives and Rights of Individuals. An Example: The Time-Sharing Contract*. 2002.
Stathopoulos. *The Claim to Unjust Enrichment*. 1972.
Stathopoulos, Chiotellis & Avgoustianakis. *Community Civil Law*. I, 1995.
Theodoropoulos. *The Guarantee According to the Civil Code in Force*. 1953.
Valtoudis. *Sale of an Enterprise*. 2005.
Vathis. *The Factoring Contract*. 1995.
Vouzikas. *The Claim of Unjust Enrichment and Usucapio According to the Roman Law Previously in Force and the Civil Code*. 1948.

Articles, notes and comments on court decisions on special items are to be found in the works listed above.

Selected Bibliography

Index

The numbers here refer to paragraph numbers.

Index

Index

Index

Made in the USA
Monee, IL
18 October 2026

66037599R10168